RADICALS ON THE ROAD

A volume in the series

The United States in the World

edited by Mark Philip Bradley, David C. Engerman, and Paul A. Kramer

A list of titles in this series is available at www.cornellpress.cornell.edu.

RADICALS ON THE ROAD

Internationalism, Orientalism, and Feminism during the Vietnam Era

Judy Tzu-Chun Wu

Cornell University Press
Ithaca and London

First published 2013 by Cornell University Press
First printing, Cornell Paperbacks, 2013

Printed in the United States of America

Library of Congress Cataloging-in-Publication Data

Wu, Judy Tzu-Chun.
    Radicals on the road : internationalism, orientalism, and feminism during the Vietnam Era / by Judy Tzu-Chun Wu.
        p.   cm.
        Includes bibliographical references and index.
        ISBN 978-0-8014-4675-7 (cloth : alk. paper)—
ISBN 978-0-8014-7890-1 (pbk. : alk. paper)
        1. Political activists—Travel—United States—History—20th century.   2. International travel—Social aspects—United States—History—20th century.   3. Social movements—United States—History—20th century.   4. Internationalism—United States—History—20th century.   5. Orientalism—United States—History—20th century.   6. Feminism—United States—History—20th century.   7. Vietnam War, 1961–1975—Social aspects—United States.   8. Vietnam War, 1961–1975—Protest movements.   9. United States—Social conditions—1960–1980.   I. Title.
        E839.5.W8   2013
        973.92—dc23
        2012043980

Cornell University Press strives to use environmentally responsible suppliers and materials to the fullest extent possible in the publishing of its books. Such materials include vegetable-based, low-VOC inks and acid-free papers that are recycled, totally chlorine-free, or partly composed of nonwood fibers. For further information, visit our website at www.cornellpress.cornell.edu.

Cloth printing   10   9   8   7   6   5   4   3   2   1
Paperback printing   10   9   8   7   6   5   4   3   2

Contents

Introduction

Traveling to Hanoi during the U.S. war in Vietnam was a long and dangerous undertaking. Cora Weiss—a Jewish middle-class housewife, a mother
of three young children, and a peace activist—recalled that in 1969, when
she embarked on her first journey to North Vietnam, "you couldn't pick
up your telephone and call the travel agent and say, 'Book me to Hanoi.'"[1]
To arrive in the Democratic Republic of Vietnam, she first departed New
York City for Copenhagen, Denmark, then boarded another flight to
Bangkok, Thailand, where she then waited for a third plane to take her to
Hanoi. There were no guarantees of how long the delay would last. Only
three flights per week were scheduled between Thailand and North Vietnam, and the planes were small: "We're talking about nine, twelve, or eigh-
teen seats."[2] So the travelers from the West, which included United Nations
personnel as well as international diplomats, passed the time trying to adjust
to the time, climate, and cultural differences between North America or
Europe and Southeast Asia.

Those lucky enough to obtain a seat to Hanoi embarked on an even
more perilous stage in their journey. Weiss described the planes as "tiny
old pieces of equipment which took off by the grace of God."[3] The International Control Commission, a neutral body that observed the war, operated these flights. Consequently, "when the plane went in, it was a signal

to the fighters on the ground [as well as those in the air] to stop their fire and create a corridor, a safe corridor."[4] Even so, the possibility of being shot down was very real. On the plane, Weiss thought of her "three little babies at home" and wondered whether she would see them again.[5] Other travelers recalled landing in blackout conditions, without lights even for the runway.

After surviving the harrowing ride, there was still the risk of being injured or killed by American bombers. On another of her five trips to North Vietnam, Weiss and her fellow travelers immediately sought refuge in a shelter. These bomb shelters were located at the airport, throughout Hanoi, and in other parts of North Vietnam because of the likelihood and frequency of attacks. Over the course of the war, American pilots dropped more than three times the amount of bombs on Vietnam than all the bombs used during World War II. Weiss recalled:

> There could be days when there were none; when there were no sirens and then there could be days when it lasted for, I don't know, an hour. . . . I just remember jumping into a hole in the sidewalk and the water is up to your hips and there are undoubtedly lots of leeches in the water and then you pull a concrete manhole cover over your head and you suffer from claustrophobia. You don't give a . . . about the bomb because you can't . . . you can't bear suffocating in this hole.[6]

This book tells the story of international journeys made by significant yet underrecognized historical figures. These men and women of varying ages, races, sexual identities, class backgrounds, and religious faiths held diverse political views. Nevertheless, they all believed that the U.S. war in Vietnam, one of the longest wars in American history and the first one that the country "lost," was immoral and unjustified. In times of military conflict, heightened nationalism is the norm. Powerful institutions, like the government and the media, work together to promote a culture of hyperpatriotism. The subjects of my study questioned their expected obligations and instead imagined themselves as "internationalists," as members of communities that transcended national boundaries. They felt compelled to travel to a land at war with their own country. And they believed that their personal journeys could change the political imaginaries of other members of the American citizenry and even alter U.S. policies in Southeast Asia.

Benedict Anderson famously proposed that the nation is an "imagined community." It is imagined, because "all communities larger than primordial villages of face-to-face contact . . . will never know most of their fellow-members . . . yet in the minds of each lives the image of their communion."[7] The intensity of nationalist communion was particularly acute during the U.S. war in Vietnam. Most Americans could not even locate the Southeast Asian country on a map, and few had any personal connections to Vietnamese people and culture. It was a foreign, faraway land, populated by people whose Asianness marked them as racial inferiors.

Furthermore, the decision to fight a "hot" war in Vietnam occurred in the context of the Cold War. Following World War II, the United States and its allies engaged in a protracted series of military, political, economic, and ideological conflicts with the Soviet Union, the People's Republic of China, and other socialist powers. The Cold War took place on the global stage, with each side seeking to develop alliances to contain its opponent. The United States regarded itself as a proponent of individualism, democracy, and capitalism. Its Cold War enemies, in contrast, represented godless totalitarianism. Perceiving Vietnamese opponents of the United States as part of an international communist conspiracy further intensified the divide that most Americans drew between deserving insiders and inhuman outsiders.

The travelers in this story were not all ready-made critics of their own government and society. Living in the midst of war, both hot and cold, these individuals evolved in their political beliefs and came to perceive themselves as members of international communities that collectively challenged American policies in Southeast Asia. This book posits that the physical journeys that these individuals made, the face-to-face contacts that they established with people outside of the United States, inspired their political imagination and expanded their sense of communion beyond the confines of the nation and its allies. Government-issued reports and the mainstream media encouraged racial, cultural, and political distance between most Americans and their Cold War enemies. Increasingly suspicious of these sources, skeptics of U.S. policies sought alternative information. Traveling abroad allowed American activists to engage in dialogue, to acknowledge the humanity of their country's foes, and to witness the conditions of war. These journeys were often physically and psychologically arduous but almost always intellectually and emotionally transformative.

Furthermore, the fruits of these encounters were circulated within activist circles and mainstream society. Travelers shared their experiences through articles, books, reports, letters, interviews, speeches, short stories, poetry, photographs, film, and artwork. Travelers' reflections appeared in the mainstream media and the underground press. The latter publications, many of them fly-by-night, were created, produced, and disseminated by activists. These newspapers and journals included local, regional, national, and international news. In fact, an "underground press syndicate" was formed to facilitate the circulation of knowledge among these publications, which were based in the United States and abroad.[8] Consequently, activist newspapers tended to print and reprint similar reports, essays, images, fiction, and poetry. Through repetition, the underground media fostered a common political language and a sense of simultaneity for their readers. Cumulatively, the accounts of activist travelers fostered a global public sphere of civic debate about the morality of the U.S. war in Vietnam. They encouraged their readers to regard themselves as members of a shared international community who owed humanitarian responsibility to one another.

In forming an internationalist consciousness, American activists both challenged and reinscribed Western perceptions of Asia. The political travelers who journeyed abroad earnestly wanted to learn and expose the "truth" about the U.S. war in Vietnam. At the same time, their perceptions of Asian people and places were refracted through idealized projections of the decolonizing Third World. I propose the concept of *radical orientalism* to capture how some American activists romanticized and identified with revolutionary Asian nations and political figures.

Cultural theorist Edward Said conceptualized orientalism as a system of knowledge that the West developed about the East.[9] This way of seeing and understanding the "Orient" emerged as Occidental imperial powers engaged in colonization. Within this framework, the East historically serves as a contrasting and not coincidentally inferior image to the West. While the Occident is associated with modernity, science, and masculinity, the Orient is perceived as tradition-bound, fanatical, and feminine. This polarization not only constructed an image of the East in the Western imagination but also served to define the West. The Occident became the opposite of the Orient.

American Studies scholar Christina Klein has revised Said's thesis in her study of a specifically American form of orientalism during the early Cold War era.[10] She argues that during this time period, middlebrow culture in the United States, examples of which include Rodgers and Hammerstein musicals or the *Reader's Digest*, actually emphasized the similarities between the East and the West. This tendency to minimize duality was part of a broader geopolitical project. The United States became the foremost economic, political, and military power following World War II. However, the country sought to distance itself from European imperialism. Instead, Americans claimed their mission as one of democratizing and saving the world from communist tyranny. To enlist domestic support in this global project and to encourage mainstream Americans to feel a sense of connection with Asian countries and peoples as potential Cold War allies of the United States, the mass media emphasized bridging East-West divides. This sense of commonality, however, did not imply an absence of hierarchy. With greater access to material resources and technology, as well as a claim to democratic exceptionalism, Americans presumed the responsibility of saving worthwhile Asian charges. The imperialist intent persisted but was masked by benevolence. Furthermore, even as some Asian people and lands became objects of rescue and uplift through modernization policies, Asian countries became the site of both covert and overt warfare. As Jodi Kim and others point out, in the midst of such destructive conflict, it was difficult for most Americans to distinguish between their Asian friends and their Asian foes.[11]

The activists who questioned the United States' global policies wanted to name American imperialism. These critics distanced themselves from what they perceived as the militaristic, materialistic, and racist values of mainstream society. Instead, they wanted to identify with Asian people and societies resisting colonialism (or formal control by another country) and neocolonialism (or indirect control). Consequently, these individuals ironically followed an orientalist tradition of perceiving a dichotomy between the East and the West, specifically between decolonizing Asia and imperial America. The radicalness of their orientalism stemmed from how they inverted and subverted previous hierarchies: American travelers idealized the East and denigrated the West. They turned to Asian countries and peoples for political, personal, and, at times, religious inspiration. Radical critics therefore replicated an orientalist logic that cultural theorist Edward Said identified, whereby the decolonizing East helped to define the identities and goals of activists in the West.

In addition to the hierarchical inversion, radical orientalism differed from dominant forms of orientalism in that Asian individuals actively shaped Western understandings of Asia. In Said's critique of Occidental representations of the Orient, the East is inert and silent; instead, the West speaks for the East. The perceptions of Western antiwar travelers, however, were not just projected onto Asia. Asian individuals and political organizations cultivated connections with U.S. activists of diverse backgrounds and interpreted decolonizing Asia for these visitors. In other words, the East and the West worked together to foster a radical orientalist sensibility. These idealized portrayals of decolonizing Asia were not necessarily accurate or complete depictions of these dynamic societies undergoing complex political, military, and social changes. However, by serving as a source for alternative values, revolutionary Asia assisted American activists in imagining new political possibilities.

In addition to foregrounding the relationship between travel and internationalism as well as introducing the concept of radical orientalism, I also explore how men and women of varying racial and ethnic backgrounds worked together and separately to critique American foreign policies in Asia. The U.S. antiwar movement against the Vietnam War is commonly understood as dominated by men, particularly white men. Historically, military service constituted a culturally authorized avenue for fulfilling masculine obligations of citizenship to the nation.[12] Consequently, male antiwar protesters of varying racial backgrounds played a significant symbolic role in criticizing their own country by refusing to join or support the armed forces. However, rejecting the military did not necessarily mean renouncing masculine privilege. In fact, feminist scholars trace the emergence of the women's liberation movement in the late 1960s in part as a reaction to the chauvinism of male antiwar activists.[13] Even so, American women of diverse backgrounds did not abandon peace activism. They also traveled internationally and engaged in political dialogue, particularly with their female counterparts in decolonizing Asian countries. Together, these women attempted to create an international peace movement based on a global sense of sisterhood.

The belief that women everywhere might share similar experiences and hence might embrace common political goals is a powerful yet also heavily criticized idea. Female activists, particularly white, middle-to-upper-class women from the West, have historically used the call for international sisterhood to promote their own political engagement across social, cultural, and geopolitical boundaries.[14] Examples include worldwide campaigns to abolish slavery, eliminate prostitution, and advocate for peace. Critics of the concept of global sisterhood have countered that it also represents a form of "women's orientalism" and feminist colonialism.[15] That is, elite Western women tended to conceive of marginalized women in their own societies as well as non-Western women as victims of patriarchy in need of rescue by their more enlightened sisters. This emphasis on the degradation of non-white, working-class, and non-Western women depicts these women's communities and cultural practices as inherently and irredeemably backward. In contrast, middle-class and elite Western society becomes the source of gender enlightenment. This dichotomization leaves little room for the agency of marginalized women. The condemnation of allegedly less en-lightened societies also does not account for Western collusion in global female oppression. In sum, critics of the "politics of rescue" approach charge that the call of international sisterhood masks cultural, class, and racial hierarchies in the name of female universalism.

During the U.S. war in Vietnam, the politics of rescue persisted to some degree. However, women of varying racial backgrounds from the West also exhibited a deep sense of admiration for their Asian "sisters." Through travel and correspondence, they learned to regard Third World female lib-eration fighters as models of revolutionary womanhood. These idealized depictions exemplified a radical orientalist sensibility. The emphasis on Viet-namese female warriors countered classical orientalist depictions of exotic, sexualized, and victimized Asian women. Nevertheless, these radical por-trayals served an orientalist purpose. The dichotomy between the revolu-tionary hope of the East and the entrenched sexism of the West helped American women of varying backgrounds to redefine their own identities and political goals.

This exploration of internationalism, orientalism, and feminism contrib-utes to our understanding of social activism during the "long 1960s" in three ways. First, the political journeys of U.S. activists provide an opportunity to frame the antiwar movement of the 1960s and 1970s in an international context. Scholars, most notably Mary Hershberger, have examined the journeys of peace activists to North Vietnam and other parts of the world.[16] This book builds on her study in order to highlight the travels of U.S. pro-testers not only to Hanoi but also to South Vietnam, Cambodia, North Korea, the People's Republic of China, Canada, and Europe. This global circulation of people and ideas shaped the American political imaginary during the era of the Cold War and decolonization.

Within this expanded geopolitical framework, I also examine the initia-tive of Asian representatives in establishing contacts with American activ-ists. Asian opponents of the U.S. government cultivated relationships with members of the U.S. citizenry as part of their strategy to end the war. In *Guerrilla Diplomacy*, historian Robert K. Brigham analyzes the foreign rela-tion efforts of the National Liberation Front in South Vietnam as an over-looked yet integral component of their overall plans to win the war.[17] Similarly, William J. Duiker argues that the international diplomacy of the Democratic Republic of Vietnam contributed to the success of the North Vietnamese.[18] My book elaborates on these insights by examining how Vietnamese individuals seriously engaged in political dialogue with *nonstate* actors from the United States. These Americans, for the most part, did not have the formal authority of government officials. However, they represented significant social, political, and/or religious organizations and movements, or they had the ability to mobilize these sectors of American civil society. In other words, Vietnamese antiwar activists regarded American travelers as "citizen diplomats" who had the potential to significantly shape the political discourse in the United States and the decisions of American policymakers.[19]

Second, I offer insight into how individuals of diverse racial and ethnic backgrounds developed political partnerships with one another. My reexamination of the historical record challenges the predominant image of the antiwar cause as a "white" movement, and I go beyond the usual black-white paradigm for understanding American race relations. The decades of the 1950s, 1960s, and 1970s witnessed the emergence of a variety of racial liberation movements, including Asian American, Chicano/a, Latino/a, and indigenous peoples. In addition, the racial category of "white" encompassed a variety of ethnic and religious backgrounds. The antiwar movement fostered multiracial and multiethnic coalitions between these groups and individuals.

Looking at the heterogeneity of the antiwar movement offers the opportunity to reinterpret the long 1960s. Early scholarship tends to celebrate the civil rights and the predominantly white student movements through the middle of the decade as the "good sixties." These same works portray the end of the decade as the "bad sixties," a period characterized by violence, fragmentation, and decline as racial, gender, and sexual separatist movements emerged.[20] By utilizing a case study approach that focuses on previously understudied individuals, events, and political relationships, I highlight a broader range of historical actors who engaged in the antiwar movement. For the early period of the U.S. involvement in Vietnam, I foreground African American and Vietnamese Buddhist advocates who shaped the broader American peace movement. These international, interracial, and interfaith partnerships provide an opportunity to consider the racial triangulation of black, white, and Asian political activism.[21]

For the latter part of the 1960s and early 1970s, I focus on the rise of identity-based liberation movements and illuminate how political fragmentation coexisted with fermentation. Recent studies by Max Elbaum, Daryl Maeda, Lorena Oropeza, Laura Pulido, and Cynthia Young point to the rich coalition-building efforts as a "Third World Left" emerged.[22] This formation developed mainly among people of color in the United States who built alliances with one another and turned to socialist movements in the Third World for political role models. The process of forming coalitions across various boundaries was a difficult one. Nevertheless, the global Third World played a significant role in inspiring the political imagination of American activists who connected domestic aspirations for social justice with global critiques of imperialism.

Finally, in this book I contribute to the growing understanding of how gender shapes the conduct of war, the performance of international diplomacy, and engagement in political activism.[23] As historian Joan Scott argues, "gender is a primary way of signifying relationships of power."[24] Gender, the socially constructed roles associated with biological sex, is almost always linked to differential access to political, economic, cultural, and social resources. Furthermore, conceptions of ideal versus deficient forms of manhood and womanhood, normative versus deviant sexuality, and recognized versus illegitimate forms of family mark certain people, desires, behaviors, and relationships as acceptable while designating others as outside the pale.

In order to understand how gender was significant for the political journeys of U.S. antiwar activists, I explore the ways in which men and women had differential access to travel and also experienced their trips differently. I examine how intimate interactions, including romantic and sexual encounters, affected relationships among American activists and with their Asian hosts. Moreover, concepts of gender served as powerful metaphors to understand the relationship between nations and between people from diverse backgrounds. Discussions concerning gender roles, sexuality, and family at times facilitated and at other times obstructed the imagining of international political communities. In other words, the personal and the intimate held global political significance.

To illuminate how travel shaped politics, how decolonizing Asia inspired activists in the West, and how men and women of varying backgrounds and convictions engaged in the antiwar movement, I tell the story of three different sets of journeys. Rather than providing a comprehensive overview, I utilize a case study approach to emphasize the experiential nature of political encounters and personal transformation. Each topic illuminates important yet largely overlooked historical actors and events, which in turn shed light on broader dynamics within the social movements of the 1960s and 1970s.

In the first three chapters I introduce Robert S. Browne. An African American economist who was stationed in Southeast Asia from 1955 to 1961 as a U.S. aid adviser, Browne subsequently became one of the earliest critics of American foreign policy in that region of the world. Despite his visibility in and important contributions to the early phase of the American peace movement, Browne has received little historical attention. Examining his life and activism sheds light on African American engagement in international affairs in the context of the Cold War, the civil rights movement, and the era of global decolonization. Furthermore, Browne played a central role in facilitating political alliances among peace activists of varying generations, races, and religions. In particular, he emphasized the need to include and respect Vietnamese voices in U.S. policy debates. To do so, Browne utilized his personal life, particularly his Afro-Vietnamese family, to frame his political message. In addition, he partnered with Buddhist monk Thich Nhat Hanh to advocate for a "third solution," a peaceful resolution that would allow South Vietnam to make decisions independent of Washington, DC, and Hanoi. As an expression of their commitment to pacifism, Browne and Hanh made journeys for peace.

In the second three chapters I examine the U.S. People's Anti-Imperialist Delegation. Led by Black Panther Party leader Eldridge Cleaver, this eleven-person group toured North Korea, North Vietnam, and socialist China in the summer of 1970. The delegation had representatives from a cross-section of political movements that emerged by the end of the 1960s, including the black power, antiwar, women's liberation, alternative media, and, very significantly, the Asian American movements. In contrast to Robert Browne, who advocated radical views but did so within the existing political system, members of the Anti-Imperialist Delegation embraced the goal of revolution. Invested in anticolonial and socialist politics, they embarked on a journey for liberation.

In the final three chapters I analyze the Indochinese Women's Conferences, which were held in Vancouver and Toronto, Canada, in the spring of 1971. Some Americans had previously traveled to Hanoi and other parts of the world to meet with Vietnamese revolutionaries. In fact, female activists were among the earliest travelers and played significant roles in organizing the peace movement. However, the conferences provided an unprecedented opportunity for large numbers of North American women to encounter female leaders from Southeast Asia. Conference participants came from diverse backgrounds and held different political beliefs and goals. Their collective gathering offers insight into the difficult yet empowering process of creating an international women's peace movement. Together, they made journeys for global sisterhood.

These journeys for peace, liberation, and sisterhood facilitated inspirational and contentious dialogues. Traveling internationally fostered the expansion of political communion but also reinforced essentialist under-standings of racial, national, and gender difference. There is a tension between radical orientalism, which posits a binary sense of opposition between the Orient and the Occident, and internationalism, which empha-sizes the possibility of genuine dialogue and collective identification among people across various borders. However, I believe this tension was a produc-tive and generative one that allowed American activists to develop a sense of social responsibility and mutuality with those from the East. Understand-ing these rich and complex relationships illuminates the difficult work of crossing borders and reimagining political possibilities.

Part I

Journeys for Peace

Chapter 1

An African American Abroad

There is a wonderful picture of Bob Browne, taken when he was perhaps five years old. It must have been close to 1929, when the United States was on the verge of the worst economic depression in the country's history. You would not know it, though, from this sepia-toned image. Browne is dressed to the nines, clearly marking him as the child of a comfortable, even well-to-do, family. Almost everyone who lived in "Bronzeville," the segregated black neighborhood on the South Side of Chicago, went to Mr. Jones to have their picture taken.[1] Most children found their nicest outfits to be uncomfortable. Furthermore, Mr. Jones brooked no nonsense. Browne's half sister Wendelle, who was nine years older and in her early teens, recalled her sense of intimidation before the photographer's commanding presence.[2] In contrast, her brother did not want to be posed. Out of sheer spunk, he asked if he could show Mr. Jones how he wanted to stand. So the final image shows the young boy as he wanted to express himself. In addition to his dapper clothes, he wears a huge, confident smile as he looks directly into the camera. Looking at this picture, one thinks, "Look out world, here he comes!"

Robert Span Browne, whose life bridged nearly eight decades from the 1920s to the early years of the twenty-first century, circumnavigated

Figure 1. Bob Browne as a young boy. Personal collection of the Browne family.

the globe several times as he traveled and lived in Europe, Africa, Asia, and Latin America.[3] Growing up during the Great Depression, he reached adulthood during World War II and spent the middle decades of his life in the midst of the Cold War, the black liberation struggles in the United States, and the decolonization movements of the so-called Third World.

Browne was on the front lines of these dramatic social changes. During the crucial years of 1955–1961, when the United States escalated its military, political, and economic commitment to containing communism in Southeast Asia, Browne worked as an American aid adviser, first in Cambodia and then in South Vietnam.[4] Upon his return to the United States, he became a leading and not yet fully recognized figure in two of the major movements of the 1960s and 1970s: the protests against the U.S. war in Southeast Asia and the black power movement that sought economic, political, and cultural autonomy for people of African descent, both in the United States and in the broader black diaspora.[5]

Despite Browne's political accomplishments, he is not acknowledged among the pantheon of antiwar or black liberation leaders.[6] His omission is rather striking, because he was a key and visible figure in the antiwar movement. As he reflected, "I was the one Black who had been connected with that movement before prominent Blacks like Martin Luther King, Julian Bond, and Dick Gregory eventually spoke out."[7] In fact, Browne's absence from the historical record renders the peace movement even more "white" than it actually was. Not only are Browne's contributions as an African American activist slighted, but his personal and political partnerships with Vietnamese individuals also receive little historical attention. Examining Browne's political contributions sheds light on African American and Asian peace activism that shaped the broader U.S. antiwar movement.

African Americans have long had internationalist aspirations. Their marginalized status in the United States fostered not only desires for full citizenship but also an interest in linking their struggles for equality with those of racialized and colonized others on the global stage. Yet as various scholars remind us, African American internationalism waxed and waned based on historical context. Also, like all complex political ideas and movements, various individuals and organizations espoused different analyses and goals. Bob Browne's early life, then, provides a window into how a member of the black middle class developed an internationalist outlook as he came of age during the Great Depression, World War II, and the early Cold War.

Historian James Meriwether, in his study of African American relationships with Africa, identifies three main explanations for African American internationalism. The "bad times" thesis suggests that "African Americans promote stronger ties with Africa when they feel more alienated in the United States."[8] In contrast, what might be characterized as the "good times" argument posits that "as blacks in America increase their confidence in their status as Americans, they feel greater comfort in looking to Africa."[9]

Meriwether critiques these two arguments for focusing exclusively on the U.S. context. In contrast, he suggests that historical developments in Africa during the 1930s through the 1960s, particularly the efforts to resist colonization and obtain independence, changed the perspectives of African Americans toward their ancestral continent.

Browne's early life in the United States and abroad indicates that all three explanations help to explain his internationalist outlook. As a member of the black middle class coming of age during World War II, Browne had aspirations for and some access to educational and professional achievement. At the same time, the persistence of Jim Crow, in both the North and the South, eventually led Browne to leave the United States out of frustrated hopes. As an African American overseas, he faced constraints and also gained access to unique opportunities in the context of the early Cold War. Furthermore, Browne's gender facilitated his ability to embark on world travels. And, through his experiences while traveling in Europe, Africa, and the Middle East in the early 1950s, Browne developed a deeper appreciation of American race relations, international politics, and the possibilities for his life and career.

In many ways, Browne's early life qualified him as a member of the "talented tenth." This term, coined by scholar and activist W. E. B. DuBois, describes the educated elite among African Americans who provide leadership and service to their people. Browne grew up in a segregated but vibrant community, the South Side of Chicago, where he absorbed a love of politics and people.[10] Coming of age in the Great Depression, he also developed a fascination for economics, a social conscience, and a sense of social responsibility.

Bob Browne's father, Will Browne, was born in Buffalo, New York, but had become a longtime resident of Chicago by the time his children were born.[11] Bob described Will Browne as "a modest functionary of the municipal government."[12] His half sister Wendelle explained that their father was a "civil service employee. . . . In those days, if you paid your water bill personally, you had to meet him. He was in room 101, City Hall."[13] Will's position was secured through the widespread practice of political patronage in Chicago, which operated primarily among the city's white residents but extended, to a much smaller degree, to African Americans.[14] Like many African Americans at the time, the Brownes were Republicans because that was the party of Lincoln. The Democrats, on the other hand, represented "the Southerner . . . the oppressive lynchers of black people."[15] Although black voters began shifting their support toward President Franklin Delano

Roosevelt during the Great Depression, Republicans tended to dominate the Illinois elections and hence patronage networks. Even so, Will Browne was among a small black elite to benefit from these political connections. He seemed to have a deep interest in politics, though, beyond the financial remuneration of a civil service position. Will Browne did not attend college, but his daughter described him as "a political analyst" with "a very excellent mind. . . . Every time when I saw him, which was about two or three times a month, he would tell me about what was happening in the nation."[16]

Browne seemed to have absorbed this love of politics from his father. In high school, Browne "became an avid reader of *The Chicago Defender*," a premier black newspaper in the country.[17] Through the paper, Browne "soaked up" news about "the indiscriminate lynching of blacks, especially in the South"; he also learned of the "non-life-threatening injustices inflicted upon blacks, both in the South and the North."[18] In addition, the *Defender* introduced him to black literature. When Richard Wright's novel *Native Son* was released in 1940, Browne read it "within months of its publication"; the novel "held a special attraction . . . because its locale was just a few blocks from [his] home in Chicago."[19] The *Defender* also exposed Browne to the leading African American political figures of that time: Mary McLeod Bethune, a member of the so-called Black Cabinet who advised President Roosevelt on issues related to race; the executive secretary of the National Association for the Advancement of Colored People (NAACP), Walter White; the renowned scholar and NAACP founder W. E. B. DuBois; and the Renaissance man—athlete, actor, singer, and activist—Paul Robeson.[20]

While Will Browne shared his passion for politics with his children, Julia Browne, Bob's mother, made sure that her children learned manners, "a strict, inflexible code of moral conduct," as well as a love of people.[21] Remembered as "a very attractive and highly stylish woman" by her son, she not only focused on the appearance of her children but also wanted to shape their character and behavior.[22] Julia was from the South. Born in Atlanta, Georgia, and raised in South Carolina, she came to Chicago as part of the great migration of over a million and a half African Americans who moved to northern urban centers between 1910 and 1930.[23] They came seeking better economic opportunities and hoping for better lives, away from Jim Crow laws, lynchings, and sharecropping. Julia Browne did not come from the poorest family. Wendelle believes that "they were better off than the average," because Julia "was able to go to boarding school."[24] Even so, "her memories of the South were very, very bitter. . . . She had seen things . . . that made [her never] want to . . . go back."[25]

In Chicago, both longtime residents and newer migrants continued to be shaped by racial discrimination, as evidenced by the pattern of residential segregation. Bronzeville, swelling with the influx of new migrants, became the "second largest Negro city in the world" in the 1940s, second only to Harlem.[26] With limited housing options beyond the South Side, Bronzeville became home not only to working-class African Americans but also to the middle- and upper-middle classes, who collectively constituted approximately one-third of the population.[27]

Class was tangible in ways that Bob Browne recognized. Although he described himself as being "born into a lower middle class black family," Browne recalled that his family "had a telephone, which many people in the neighborhood did not. In fact, a couple of our neighbors would regularly come over and ask if they could use our telephone."[28] In addition, they had a car, which his mother drove, a "somewhat . . . daring practice for a woman in the mid 1920s."[29] Wendelle described her father and half siblings as living in the Woodlawn section of Bronzeville, close to Washington Park, where families tended to own their own homes and "the cutest kids came from."[30] Bronzeville residents used to think, "Well, if you lived in Woodlawn—nice, nice."[31]

In Bronzeville, Julia was known as a gracious hostess, and Bob Browne inherited his mother's affinity for cultivating positive social relationships. As his stepsister recalled, he was "interested in people. . . . He just liked to know people."[32] In Browne's youth, his social network mainly included other members of the black middle class in South Side Chicago. Although he worked a variety of odd jobs to earn pocket money and even to help support his family after his father's death, Browne described himself as leading an "appallingly bourgeois" life: "My teen age crowd was used to throwing and attending lavish formal dances several times a year, for which we rented tuxedos and/or tails, bought our dates corsages, and behaved pretty much as we felt middle class white folks did, except that our music was infinitely better."[33] His cohort of black middle-class teenagers included individuals who would become prominent intellectuals and artists. Jewel Plummer Cobb became "the first black woman to be named president of a major white university," namely California State University, Fullerton. Browne also socialized with the family of "Lorraine Hansberry, author of *A Raisin in the Sun*."[34] Hansberry's parents were known for throwing "fabulous New Years Eve" parties. Browne recalled Lorraine criticizing "the glamorous displays of conspicuous consumption such as these super-parties exhibited"; he, in contrast, reveled in these occasions, particularly for the opportunities to mingle with celebrities like Paul Robeson, "who usually stayed with the Hansberry family" during visits to Chicago.[35]

Despite his relatively privileged background, Bob Browne recalled that coming of age during the Depression years made economics particularly fascinating to him. In his memoir, he describes in great detail:

> One recollection from this period which has never dimmed over the past seven decades. It inflicted a scar on my brain which shaped my every economic decision and stalked my every expenditure, at least until the time of my retirement. The precipitating event must have taken place about 1932 or 1933, during the early years of the great depression, when I was perhaps 8 or 9 years old. I was aware that times were very hard, that there were many people who did not have enough to eat, and even that people were being put out of their homes because they had no money to pay the rent. One heard about such happenings on the radio and they were spread across the newspapers and the movie house newsreels. But walking home from school one day, passing a small apartment building which I had passed dozens of times before, I found four generations of a family sitting forlornly in their front yard on their living room furniture, with dressers, beds, mattresses, mirrors, tables, kitchen furniture and utensils, clothing, luggage, bulging boxes of goods, in fact, the family's entire belongings, all spread along the sidewalk. I instantly realized that this was a family which had been evicted and which had nowhere to go. It would soon be getting chilly, and dark, and I sensed they would still be sitting there. I couldn't fully comprehend why they were there, what they would do at nightfall, or why no one seemed to be helping them. . . . That evicted family was a specter which never left my subconsciousness.[36]

This personal encounter with the deprivations of poverty raised troubling questions for Browne about the causes and solutions for such suffering. He recalled receiving little helpful information to help him make sense of the Great Depression:

> One evening I saw a newsreel at the local movie house which showed the government dying a massive mountain of raw potatoes a deep blue color. Widespread poverty was at that moment subjecting millions of Americans

to severe hunger and undernourishment and the streets were filled with beggars, so it made no sense to me that the government would be deliberately rendering vast tonnages of food inedible. The reporter described the action as a means to support higher potato prices so as to aid ailing farmers. I could not grasp this reasoning and when I asked my mother for an explanation she could only reply that it had something to do with "economics." . . . I think it was at that moment that I decided that I would probably major in economics in college.[37]

Browne pursued the subject when he enrolled at the University of Illinois, Urbana–Champaign, in 1941.

Economics was a vibrant field during the Great Depression and World War II. In college, Browne studied "the social security program, the agricultural program, fair labor legislation, and the newly approved National Labor Relations Act."[38] In a 1970s interview, he explained that the periods of the Great Depression and World War II were eras of economic experimentation: "These were issues of great concern at that time. . . . The whole idea of setting prices and rationing became the issues people were wrestling with and that was what we studied in school."[39] Despite the compelling nature of the topics studied, out of the over one hundred African American students enrolled at the University of Illinois, Urbana–Champaign, Browne was the only one majoring in economics. When he graduated in 1944 with honors, it was a noteworthy accomplishment. At the time, few in his home community of Bronzeville had gone beyond the sixth grade, and the number of college graduates constituted "about two in every 100 individuals."[40]

During his college years, Browne also joined the black fraternity Alpha Phi Alpha, an organization whose membership included such luminaries as W. E. B. DuBois and Martin Luther King Jr.[41] His decision to become a member of the fraternity was partly motivated by practical reasons, though. The dormitories were for whites and this policy did not change until a year after Browne graduated, when a popular black football player enrolled at the school. In addition, "the University's host towns of Urbana and Champaign were strictly Jim Crow communities."[42] The Alpha Phi Alpha House, "a run down frame structure . . . [that was] sparsely furnished" and poorly heated, was one of the few places where black male students could live, since they were not allowed to reside in the dormitories.[43] Furthermore, "virtually all the fellows at the Alpha House worked as waiters in the many elegant fraternity and sorority houses which lined the major campuses [*sic*] roadways."[44] Browne was among this crew, who tended to receive their payment in meals. He worked as a waiter because so few economic opportunities were available for African American students. According to a 1940 report, "The University of Illinois Negro Students," they "seldom found employment in University offices, libraries, laboratories, shops and Physical Plant."[45] With these professional, clerical, or skilled positions closed to them, members of the black elite were forced to turn to positions of servitude. This lesson was repeatedly taught to Browne as he searched for additional educational and professional opportunities in both the Jim Crow South and the Jim Crow North.

Browne's rise through the academic ranks was initially interrupted in 1944 when he was drafted into the U.S. Army.[46] World War II had started just three months after Browne matriculated at the University of Illinois, and he recalled hearing Roosevelt's famous speech on the radio after Japan's attack on Pearl Harbor. In response, "a couple of [his] upper classmen buddies rushed home the next day to enlist in the armed services."[47] Even before the start of World War II, African American leaders launched the Double V Campaign to draw attention to the need for victory, not only against the Axis powers but also over racial prejudice in the United States. African Americans who served their nation, either through the military or on the home front, generally had raised expectations of what a land of democracy might offer its citizens. The eager young men who enlisted were among the over 2.5 million African American men and women who served in the military. This was their opportunity for recognized national public service, which could bring symbolic recognition as well as material rewards.[48]

In contrast to his classmates who readily enlisted, Browne initially had a more measured and mixed response to the prospect of serving in the war. He possessed a strong streak of independence and "just hated the thought of entering the army, where [he] would be entirely under the control of others."[49] He also expressed skepticism about the fight against fascism when people of color in the United States received so little respect and so few rights. Year later, he recalled that during the war "the bitter cynicism of America's blacks had been stretched to within a whisker of the breaking point."[50] African Americans throughout the country were well aware of the 1943 three-day race riot in Detroit that resulted in thirty-four deaths. They discussed reports circulating about how "Nazi prisoners" in the South were accorded "eating and recreational facilities which southern Jim Crow practices denied to blacks, even to blacks wearing the US uniform."[51] Browne also recognized the discrimination directed against other racial minorities. In his memoir, which was written much later, he recalled the "unforgivable humiliation and racism" experienced by Japanese Americans who were interned en masse in camps by the U.S. government during World War II.[52] Because of their Japanese heritage, these individuals were suspected and treated as enemies of the United States, regardless of their individual beliefs or behavior. Browne initially tried to delay military service but eventually served for two years in segregated units that stayed stateside.

After two relatively uneventful years in the military, Browne's honorable discharge in 1946 allowed him to utilize the G.I. Bill to obtain additional educational training. His ability to access the benefits of this federal legislation was somewhat unusual, considering the ways in which the allocation of the G.I. Bill, like other social service programs, tended to privilege white male recipients.[53] Browne's residency in the North as well as his educational background granted him certain advantages. In 1947, he graduated with an MBA from the University of Chicago, the elite private institution on the South Side, located close to his family's home. His class included an unprecedented number of five African American students.[54] In his opinion, "this surpassed the cumulative number who had been so honored since the University's founding and set a precedent that would not be repeated for another four decades."[55] The same year that Browne received his MBA, Jackie Robinson broke the color line in major-league baseball.

Browne's academic successes could not surmount the racial barriers against African Americans in the early post–World War II era. He later recounted the "traumatic experience" of searching for a position: "Because of my race the University was unable to obtain an interview for me with a single prospective employer amongst the numerous banks and brokerage houses which were interviewing the graduating class."[56] Forced to seek his livelihood elsewhere, Browne initially relocated to the South, where he both worked as an accountant for Dillard University in New Orleans and taught economics as an instructor there from 1947 to 1949. Browne recalled that of his four African American classmates, two others also found employment at black colleges and a third worked for a black bank. He had no information about the fourth graduate. In other words, their education at an elite and predominantly white school simply paved the way for their return to their racial communities.

Given his mother's background and the coverage of Jim Crow conditions in northern black newspapers, Browne found "the mere prospect of going to Dixie . . . paralyzing."[57] He discovered, though, that Dillard was more gracious than he expected. He enjoyed the society of the students and other faculty members on the idyllic campus and after some initial hesitation also explored the segregated city of New Orleans in his recently purchased 1946 Ford convertible. Browne even became involved with an interracial political campaign to support Henry Wallace's Democratic bid for president in 1948 but encountered "some difficulty with the [university] administration" when he participated in an effort to form a labor union on campus.[58] Browne recalled that the president of Dillard University "did not fire me, but instead informed me that a dear friend of his . . . , the president of a local black life insurance company in Houston, Texas, was desperately in need of someone with my skills to fill a vacant executive position. . . . I realized that I was being eased out of my job."[59]

Browne "lasted there less than a year. Living outside the cocoon of a college campus [he] found the daily battle with racism to be oppressive and inescapable."[60] A routine traffic stop led to "an altercation with the white police [and] resulted in [Browne] being briefly imprisoned."[61] The officer had addressed Browne as "boy," a common racial practice in the South. In response, Browne, who was in the company of a woman, requested the officer's "name and badge number, informing him, when he asked 'why?', that I planned to report him for disrespecting me."[62] In jail, Browne was taunted and threatened with violence. Luckily, he was able to secure his release through his employer's connections and to leave Houston before suffering any physical harm. Other African Americans had been mutilated and lynched for similar and even lesser offenses. Browne was tired of the routine humiliations required by the racial status quo. Soon after his release, he decided to leave the South. He was relieved and happy to be driving back north in the spring of 1950, he said, "whistling and singing aloud to myself as I sped along US 61 with my top down."[63]

Chicago offered little reprieve. While Browne could easily reimmerse himself in the rich social world of Bronzeville, he still faced limited prospects for obtaining a job commensurate with his training and aspirations. He eventually found a position with the Chicago Urban League as an industrial field secretary. Incorporated in 1917, just as the United States entered World War I, the Chicago chapter of the National Urban League espoused the "mission of promoting the social and economic advancement of Chicago's African American citizens."[64] Robert E. Park, the University of

Chicago sociologist who became renowned for his studies of urban race relations, had served as the league's first board president.

Browne embraced the opportunity to challenge racial wrongs. He decided to organize, in his words, "a campaign to get Blacks employed in the banks. Obviously, this was a personal vendetta from my days at the University of Chicago."[65] Despite his planning and persistence, he ran into a thick and impenetrable glass ceiling. After much effort, he obtained "an interview with the chairman of the board of the First National Bank of Chicago, one of the leading and most powerful banks in the country."[66] The chairman not only flatly refused Browne's request but also patronizingly explained that he financially supported the Urban League. Browne recalled the banker saying: "Don't think that I have any ill will toward your people. I contribute to the Urban League. I'm prepared to make contributions to pay your salary so you can come here and ask me to do this, but I have no intentions of doing it. And incidentally, just to show you where my heart is, you know that green carpet that's on the floor of your director's office? That carpet used to be right here in my office and when I redecorated my office I sent my old carpet over."[67] Fifty years after the fact, Browne recalled the conversation "vividly," particularly since he remembered "biting hard on my lip so as to hide my emotion"; he went "home nearly in tears" and feeling totally "demeaned."[68]

Shortly afterward, Browne decided to go abroad. He had reached his breaking point; he had had it with Jim Crow America. Even with the advantages of his class status within the black community, his educational accomplishments, his personal social skills, and his increasing interest in political change, he could see few prospects for racial improvement in his home country. Certainly there were glimmers of hope, but Browne felt frustrated and depressed by the glacial pace of change. He could not foresee the massive rise and impact of the civil rights movement just a few years later. Perhaps Browne felt akin to a laboratory test subject, finally freed to explore the world around him, only to discover a maze of dead ends. Tired of the obstacles, he chose to leave the American racial labyrinth.

Browne recounts that he always had a desire to travel internationally. His wanderlust stemmed partly from his early interest in racial politics on the global stage. In his 1961 publication *Race Relations in International Affairs*, Browne recalled, "My most vivid recollections of adolescent reading [were] not the exciting adventure stories of Mark Twain, Jack London, and Zane Grey, but news accounts in the Negro press [most notably the

Chicago Defender] of atrocities, insults, and injustices being inflicted by white men on colored persons everywhere."[69] To experience life abroad, Brown liquidated his assets in April 1952 and traveled for a year on his own throughout Europe and North Africa. As he recalled: "I thought, why not do it now. I was still single. My family and friends thought that I was nuts. I had a good job, a fairly nice car, all the things people were after in those days, and I guess they still are. It wasn't certain that I would have my job when I got back, but I was willing to get rid of the car, turn all the little assets I had into cash, and take all the risks. . . . It was the greatest thing I ever did in my life."[70]

Browne's desire for global exploration reveals the influence of a variety of factors. His repeated run-ins with Jim Crow America fueled a sense of alienation from and frustration with his home country, thereby fostering a desire to engage with other societies and cultures. In interpreting his life experiences, Browne refers consistently to the black press as an institution that fostered a broad sense of racial and anticolonial consciousness.[71] In addition, the global events of the middle decades of the twentieth century, particularly World War II, and the anticolonial critiques of racial domination encouraged Browne's interest in overseas affairs. Furthermore, his status as a member of the talented tenth instilled in Browne a desire for professional and social advancement as well as a sense of social responsibility—or, in the words of historian James Meriwether, a belief that "integration and rising cultural nationalism are not mutually exclusive developments."[72] In fact, it was Browne's assets as a member of the black middle class that financed his explorations abroad. Finally, Browne's gender facilitated his mobility as well. He was a single man, without familial responsibilities and also not in need of supervision. As a bachelor, Browne could roam the world on his own. However, being African American abroad raised the stakes in era of the Cold War, decolonization, and civil rights.

In the years after World War II, Americans had unprecedented access to travel. Their ability to do so was intimately connected to war, both hot and cold. The U.S. economy bounced back from the Great Depression because of the production, expenditures, and markets necessitated by World War II. The national recovery continued as the United States engaged in the Cold War against the Soviet Union, the People's Republic of China, and other socialist powers. In order to stem the tide of communism globally, the U.S. government invested in what President Eisenhower described as "the military-industrial complex." In the post–World War II period, the

United States committed a significant portion of the national budget to the military as the size of the armed forces increased to prepare for potential conflicts almost anywhere around the world. In addition, the government prioritized the improvement and construction of the national transportation infrastructure, committing twenty-six billion public dollars to create the interstate highway system. These roads, deemed a national security priority, prepared the country for defense. To make the United States more competitive in the arms and space race, the government also invested nearly nine hundred million dollars in higher education as well as the science and technology industries.

The national growth in the overall economy meant that average citizens, particularly those of the white middle class, had more savings or access to credit for personal consumption.[73] They not only purchased houses, appliances, and cars but also financed trips. The postwar period witnessed the proliferation of roadside motels and diners as families and individuals took to the expanding highway system to explore America. Jack Kerouac's famous novel, *On the Road*, captures the spirit of that era. Kerouac wrote this semiautobiographical work in 1951, the year after Browne drove back to Chicago in his Ford convertible and the year before he decided to walk away from the perks of his black middle-class lifestyle to go abroad. Finally published in 1957, *On the Road* offers a glimpse into a subculture of people, eventually dubbed the Beat generation, constantly on the move. For those attracted to experimentation, the road, even if it was financed by the U.S. government for strategic security interests, could still represent freedom and rejection of conventionality.

Americans took not only to the road but also to the air and the seas. The millions of U.S. soldiers stationed abroad during World War II and the Cold War came back with colorful stories of their exploits in foreign countries. Browne, who never had the opportunity to travel overseas with the military, recalled hearing these "tales of fabulous adventures, real and imagined. Most envied were those chaps who had been fortunate enough to have participated in the liberation of Italy. . . . Even after we had made allowance for the blatant exaggeration which we secretly hoped characterized their narratives . . . we [still] lapped it all up."[74] Stories like these inspired Browne and many others to venture beyond U.S. borders.

In addition to the personal thrill of travel, civilians going abroad also could perform patriotic service for their country.[75] To stem the worldwide spread of communism, the United States formed international alliances with countries, people, and movements more inclined to support American policies. These relationships, though, came with a hefty price tag. When Browne decided to travel abroad in 1952, the United States was just completing the Marshall Plan or European Recovery Plan. Instituted from 1948 to 1952, this package alone siphoned thirteen billion U.S. dollars from the national budget. Concurrent with this economic aid, the United States committed its troops to the Korean War, the first conflict in which integrated military units were deployed. After fighting over a period of three years, 1950–1953, the war ended with a stalemate, the loss of over fifty-four thousand American lives, and fifty-four billion dollars in expenditures.

In this tense political context, international travel fulfilled multiple goals. By physically moving beyond the borders of their country, Americans could meet new people, experience unfamiliar cultures, perhaps even learn foreign languages, and hopefully gain a greater awareness of the world. The U.S. government promoted this international sensibility, even among those who did not travel abroad, by investing in foreign language training and so-called area studies, academic fields that analyzed the history, culture, society, and politics of mostly non-Western regions of the world.[76] To encourage Americans to go beyond armchair travel, the U.S. government invested in what historian Christopher Endy has characterized as the "military-tourism complex."[77] Public funds, including a portion of the Marshall Plan, were allocated to strengthen the international transportation infrastructure and subsidize the tourism industry. The U.S. government and its global partners hoped that this new knowledge that Americans gained through travel and study would help them to develop a deeper understanding and commitment to the rather costly international policies necessitated by the Cold War. In addition, Americans when abroad could serve as informal diplomats by personally speaking about the advantages of the U.S. way of life. Upon return, they could help educate their neighbors, friends, and family as well. In other words, American travelers had the potential to bring the United States to the world and the world back home.

Being an African American traveler, in many ways, raised the stakes. Racism was America's Achilles heel during the Cold War. The United States represented itself in the international arena as a land of democracy and equal opportunity. However, America's Cold War enemies focused on the inequalities, the segregation, and the denial of citizenship rights experienced by African Americans as examples of the hypocrisy of U.S. political rhetoric.[78] This debate about race was particularly significant in the scramble for international alliances. From 1945 through 1960, forty nations in Africa, Asia, and Latin America, representing a quarter of the world's population, threw off the yoke of colonialism and achieved independence. As formerly colonized subjects, these newly formed nations were attuned to issues of racial inequality and hence were "susceptible" to communist-inspired critiques of the U.S. racial order. To win the "hearts and minds" of these potential allies, America had to present a better impression abroad. President Eisenhower created the United States Information Agency in 1953 essentially to enhance America's public image and promote U.S. interests to the world community.[79] At times, international considerations forced the federal government to place pressure on certain segments of U.S. society, particularly those in the South but even in the nation's capital, to actually make changes in racial policies and practices. Presenting a cleaner appearance overseas also required monitoring who traveled abroad and how they represented their country.

Bob Browne almost never had the chance to leave the United States. Uncertain of his itinerary, he filled out in his passport application that he intended to visit countries around the world, including "virtually all the nations of Europe as well as a dozen or so countries in Africa and the Middle East."[80] Browne had studied several European languages, including French, Spanish, and German. He also had read about Africa and the broader struggles against colonialism in newspapers like the *Chicago Defender*. His request to visit Africa, however, immediately sent "a red flag . . . up in the State Dept"; at the time "all of Africa except for Liberia, Ethiopia, Libya and Egypt, was still in colonial status. Visitors from other than the colonizing power were not generally admitted to the Africa colonies. . . . To the leadership class, the very concept of an unattached roving, black American visiting the French, British, Belgian or Portuguese colonies was preposterous."[81]

Expecting his passport, Browne received instead a letter requesting his attendance for an appointment: "I of course complied with this instruction and when I arrived I was ushered into a small, drab, room painted a sickly green and sparsely furnished with a metal, government issue desk surmounted by a lamp, and flanked by two grey steel chairs. After a brief delay, a solemn-faced white man with a middle-age paunch entered the room carrying two or three file folders." After explaining the necessity of obtaining additional information before Browne's passport application could be processed, the interviewer "settled comfortably into an inquisitorial mode. . . . He began, slowly and solemnly, to read off organizational names, peering accusingly at me over his iron-rimmed glasses after intoning each name, asking if I had ever been a member thereof."[82] Browne's interrogation exemplified the tactics advocated by Senator Joseph McCarthy during the early Cold War. Seeking to expose and denounce "reds" in American society, McCarthy demanded formal investigations of people in positions of political, cultural, and educational leadership. His accusations of communist subversion also fomented a broader culture of suspicion and paranoia. At the end of this McCarthy-style interview, Browne was still uncertain of his prospects of obtaining a passport. Only after he traveled to Washington, DC, to enlist the support of his congressional representatives did he finally receive authorization to go abroad. Notably, his passport was valid for only four countries in western and northern Europe.

Browne was fortunate to receive permission to travel at all. The State Department had revoked the passports of Paul Robeson and W. E. B. DuBois in 1950 under the McCarran or Internal Security Act, accusing both black leaders of being communist agents and denying them the ability to leave the country. Their passports were only reinstituted in 1958, when the U.S. Supreme Court ruled that political beliefs or associations could not constitute the basis for denying U.S. citizens the right to travel.[83]

Various scholars have argued that this era of Cold War repression led liberal African American leaders and organizations to shift their call for human rights to civil rights. While previous events, like Italy's invasion of Ethiopia, inspired passionate anticolonial politics among African Americans, McCarthyism narrowed the range of black political expression in the United States. While African American leftists tended to be marginalized, liberals adopted anticommunism in order to advocate for equality within the U.S. nation-state.[84] Even as Browne was subjected to political intimidation, he was not a recognizable civil rights leader. Consequently, he did not face the same degree of pressure as Robeson, DuBois, or Walter White of the NAACP. Browne's middle-class background and family involvement with Chicago politics no doubt assisted his efforts to obtain permission to leave the United States. Traveling as an independent citizen, he embarked on an effort to experientially understand the Cold War and the era of decolonization by traversing highly charged geopolitical boundaries.

In the spring of 1952, Browne boarded a luxury ocean liner with a third-class ticket. It offered the "cheapest means for making a transatlantic crossing," for "in the 1950s, only the very rich crossed the Atlantic by air."[85] Even in third class, Browne found his accommodations and means of travel exciting and exotic. He seemed to appreciate the slower pace in transportation. He had enrolled in a summer term at the London School of Economics, but other than this commitment, there were no specific places he needed to be. He intended to travel at his leisure until his savings of twenty-five hundred dollars were exhausted. As Browne journeyed throughout Europe, North Africa, and the Middle East, he eagerly sought opportunities to learn new languages, meet new people, and gain fresh perspectives about race relations. He came from a country that prided itself for being innovative and modern, but as an African American he experienced the United States as deeply entrenched in social conservatism. Ironically, Browne traveled to regions characterized as "the Old World," "tradition bound," or even "primitive" to gain insights about the possibility of social transformation.

Browne used Paris as his base in Europe. France was the premier destination for tourists during the post–World War II era, and it maintains that status even today.[86] He visited famous sites, which he preferred to do "unhurriedly and in some cases repeatedly."[87] He also spent weeks attempting to converse in French and reading French newspapers in Parisian cafés. He tried as much as possible to meet the locals and use whatever language skills he had in their native tongue. This took some effort, since it was usually much easier to stay among other Americans or other English-speaking people. He recalled, "whenever the opportunity presented itself, I would insinuate myself into the company of any native French speakers whom I could find (and who were not aspiring to learn English!), and inflict upon them whatever my verbal skill level was at the time, while clinging attentively to their every syllable and laboriously attempting to decipher what they were saying."[88] Over time, Browne developed a comfortable fluency in French. He also spent a significant amount of time in Madrid, attempting without as much success to improve his Spanish.

Over the course of the year, Browne mainly drifted from place to place with no fixed itinerary. Although his initial passport was valid only for certain countries, he eventually succeeded in removing the restrictions and was able to travel widely. On Browne's application for foreign service in 1955, he stated: "I traveled at my own expense in each country of Western Europe with the exception of Ireland, Finland, and Portugal. I also visited French North Africa, Libya, Egypt, Jordan, Lebanon, Israel, and Turkey."[89] In his travels, Browne discovered that "most of Europe was still largely in ruins."[90] After all, World War II had ended just six years before. He also was curious to visit socialist countries, despite or perhaps because of the red scare tactics that he had been subjected to before he was allowed to leave the United States. He crossed the "iron curtain" for brief trips to East Berlin and Yugoslavia.

What excited Browne most about his travels, though, was the opportunities to meet and talk with people. He recalled that the "real joys came from the random interpersonal contacts which bounced into one's life virtually every day . . . new people from new places with new (to me) ideas. It was chaotic and bewildering and wonderful. Most of the people whom I came into close contact were between 20 and 40 years of age, were bumming around Europe on tight budgets, were people-oriented, and were sharing and supportive of one another."[91] It was not just Europeans or other Americans that Browne encountered: "The Asian, Arab, African and Latin American floaters were not inconsiderable also."[92]

One of the highlights of Browne's journey was meeting and conversing with writer Richard Wright in a sidewalk café in Paris. Browne had long admired the author. He recalled: "Wright would have been about 44 years old when we met in Paris. He was robust, witty and relaxed. He welcomed extended discussion on whatever topics his fans wished to introduce and although his interlocutors tended to be younger and far less informed than he, he was at pains not to be overbearing in his interactions with them."[93] Wright was part of a "small colony of African-American expatriates who were discovering the joys of Paris." Browne describes Wright as "being seduced by the relatively greater freedom which he had found in France."[94] Browne discovered this as well in his travels.

Europe was certainly not devoid of racism. When Browne traveled to Germany, he described "the German ambiance [as being] far closer to the American . . . particularly with regard to orderliness, respect for authority, and something so intangible that I can only think to call it 'whiteness.' "[95] In addition, European powers were still heavily invested in maintaining their colonial possessions in Africa, Asia, and Latin America. The French, in fact, were waging ruthless and ultimately unsuccessful wars in Vietnam and Algeria to protect their empire. Even so, Browne discovered, "for the first time in my life I found my brown skin to be a help rather than a hindrance. In Europe it brought me special favors."[96] As American leaders feared, being "a member of America's most famous oppressed minority, I seemed to be received with particular warmth by most of the European vagabonds and my words seem to carry disproportionate weight when America was under discussion."[97]

When Browne ventured outside of the so-called Western world, his brownness served as an asset for a different reason. "In Africa and the Middle East it enabled me to blend into the peoples and to share their lives a bit more than could white visitors."[98] In future years, Browne would repeat this statement about racial commonality to describe his relationship with the Vietnamese. During this trip, though, Browne expressed a particular affinity for Africans. When he traveled by boat from Spain to Morocco during the early weeks of 1953, he recalled "pausing briefly at the Rock of Gibraltar to enjoy the exciting vista of looking to my right to see the Europe which I was leaving and then turning my head to the left to see the Africa which awaited me. A palpable tension began to build up within me over the next hour as the boat transported me south from the Rock, and it exploded in an emotional burst when the boat reached Africa and I finally planted my foot on the homeland."[99]

Not only did Browne claim Africa as his homeland, he was misrecognized as an African or Middle Easterner, which sometimes placed him in an awkward position. In some ways, Browne had a greater ability to maneuver and travel in Europe, both because of his language skills and because he was an obvious outsider. In addition, he developed relationships with a community of fellow travelers and expatriates in Europe. In North Africa and the Middle East, regions less frequented by tourists, Browne was assumed to be an insider. However, he did not necessarily have the social knowledge to truly be one. When he was in Tangiers, he became lost in the "Moorish quarter" and

> attempted to disguise my growing panic with an external demeanor of composure and self-confidence. . . . At one point my foot inadvertently brushed against an old lady's slipper, knocking it off her foot, and she accosted me in Arabic. Instantly, every one turned instinctively toward the disturbance and stared at me, curious to see how I would reply. My probable ethnicity was already proving to be an unending source of great curiosity everywhere I went in the region and I could already anticipate that it would be an on-going issue throughout the Arab area because I so resembled many of the local people. . . . I smiled at my victim in a pained manner and grunted several unintelligible sounds which, I hoped, might pass for an apology in the dialect of some Arab tribe. . . . I seized on their puzzlement to quickly turn and stride away.[100]

Other incidents like these led Browne to resolve, "I would make a serious effort to learn spoken Arabic before I ventured again into this part of the world."[101]

Browne's desire to pass as a native, despite his lack of language skills, was reinforced by a chance encounter with U.S. troops stationed in North Africa. Browne had been receiving money and letters throughout his journey, but his mail was inadvertently sent to another American with the same name:

> In the course of trying to retrieve these letters I was obliged to ride a US military bus out to the camp and the conversation which I heard on this bus, and the attitudes expressed by the US soldiers about the local people, were virtually unbearable to me, and the southern drawl of several of the speakers upset me even further. The ignorant observations, atrocious English and foul language were familiar to me from my own military experience, but the arrogance and the feelings of superiority which oozed from these characters raised real concern within me as to the wisdom of having such folks representing the US abroad. My travels of the past several months, throwing me into contact with mainly middle class and better educated Americans, had somewhat expunged from my memory how repulsive many Americans really are. I think I had never before seen Americans in such a bad light. The soldiers had nothing but contempt for the poor people whom they were supposedly assisting.[102]

U.S. leaders shared Browne's concern about arrogant and rude Americans presenting a rather "ugly" image of their nation to the world. The Office of Armed Forces Information and Education issued a booklet, *Pocket Guide to Anywhere*, in 1953 to educate the members of the military, who "find themselves for the first time among alien people, whose ways are not our ways, whose language and customs are different from ours, whose religion maybe different [and] whose skin may be of different color."[103] The diplomatic danger posed by the behavior of Americans abroad would receive widespread public attention when the book *The Ugly American* became a best seller after its publication in 1958.

The racism displayed toward North Africans by U.S. soldiers abroad echoed the practices of Jim Crow in the United States. Even if Browne experienced a cultural and social disconnect with the natives of North Africa and the Middle East, he felt a racial affinity and a political connection to their struggles against Western imperialism. In his travels in this region, he had the "opportunity to see colonialism in action [which] strengthened [his] urge to participate in its burial."[104] Browne also visited nations that were newly formed, such as Libya, Egypt, and Israel. He gained new insights into the complexities of nationalism, most powerfully demonstrated by the conflicts between Palestinians and Israelis over the same land. Browne was particularly interested in the Middle East because African American leader Ralph Bunche, as the key United Nations (UN) representative, negotiated a truce between the Israelis and Palestinians in 1948. To the degree that Browne was able to communicate in English and French, he attempted to enter into dialogue with local residents about these volatile issues.

Browne encountered other African Americans who were engaged in international initiatives during his travels in North Africa and the Middle East. During a stop in Derna, Libya, he met by chance another African American, "a Mr. Jones, [who was] an agricultural specialist working for the US Point Four program (a predecessor of the American aid program)."[105] This individual, like the U.S. troops, was in North Africa as part of America's Cold War mandate. Instead of supplying military aid, Jones was offering technical expertise to assist economic development in Libya. Perhaps his racial background also helped him to view the people he was seeking to help in a more sympathetic light than the soldiers that Browne encountered. This meeting may have planted the seed of Browne's subsequent career as a U.S. aid adviser in Southeast Asia. He spent the night with the Jones family: "[Jones] and his wife had a comfortable six room house and they extended me the royal treatment, including such long missed delicacies as hot corn muffins, strawberry preserves, applesauce, mayonnaise, and hot water to bathe in. It was heaven."[106]

After a year abroad, Browne was ready to return home. In the spring of 1952, he boarded another ocean liner and came back, he said, "a vastly richer person than I had been a year earlier. Unquestionably, this had been the most rewarding year of my life, the most pleasant and the most defining."[107] The opportunity to see new sights, meet new people, observe different societies "broadened my perspective considerably and also made me quite eager to see other parts of the world which I had not yet seen. The visit also enabled me to question the way in which many things were done in the United States."[108]

When Browne finally returned to Chicago, the Windy City with its provincial racial hierarchies was too limiting for him. Inspired by his year abroad, Browne wanted to offer his professional and intellectual skills for international

purposes. He quickly relocated to New York City, where he hoped to secure employment through the United Nations. Established in 1945 as World
War II was ending, the UN sought to promote "international peace and
security" by advancing "the principle of equal rights and self-determination"
and "human rights . . . for all without distinction as to race, sex, language, or
religion."[109] Browne frequented the UN and found the "headquarters . . . a
very welcoming place"; because security was not as much a concern in the
1950s, he had ready access to "the delegates' lounge," where he "passed
many an afternoon . . . sipping tea or coffee and engaging in fascinating
discussion with statesmen and diplomats whose pictures were appearing in
the daily press."[110] Browne was not alone in his attraction to the "bustling
international atmosphere which permeated the UN's premises."[111] Other
African Americans, most notably civil rights leaders and organizations, also
had approached the UN, lobbying for the platform of human rights to
advocate for protection and equality for black Americans.[112]

Despite Browne's persistence, no work prospects appeared to be forthcoming from the UN.[113] Due to the racially discriminatory job market, he
only succeeded in obtaining a "dull administrative job" as an accountant
for New York City's Housing Authority.[114] In his hours away from work,
Browne volunteered his time to support the decolonization efforts of Africans. He worked with the newly formed American Committee on Africa,
an organization founded in the early 1950s to support "the African colonial
peoples who were petitioning the U.S. for independence."[115] One of the
people whom Browne assisted was Julius Nyerere, eventually the first president of Tanzania. At the time, Nyerere was a "completely unknown school
teacher from the British colony of Tanganyika, who had been sent to . . .
present a petition imploring the UN to compel Britain to present a plan for
granting independence to Tanganyika within 25 years. He had arrived in
NYC without the slightest idea of how to tackle his task, and someone
brought him to our attention. We promptly scurried around to find him the
specialized legal and other support which he so desperately needed for pre-
paring the petition."[116]

Browne's relationships with the founders of the American Committee for Africa and his familiarity with the UN would become valuable
assets for his future involvement with the antiwar movement. Cora Weiss
and her husband, Peter Weiss, a lawyer and cofounder of the committee,
both worked with Browne to support African decolonization.[117] During
the U.S. war in Vietnam, all three expanded their efforts to Southeast
Asia.

Beyond Browne's political commitments in the early to mid-1950s, he still faced the challenge of finding meaningful work. His time spent around the UN eventually bore fruit when a chance encounter with a Chicago African American leader gave Browne an opportunity to go abroad again. Given the international attention focused on U.S. race relations, "President Eisenhower had continued President Truman's practice of routinely including a black person in the US delegation to the UN General Assembly each year. In 1954 that person happened to be Rev. Archibald Carey, a minister from a prominent Chicago church whom I knew slightly."[118] When Browne ran into Carey at the delegates' lounge, their conversation led to Browne expressing his interest in working in international affairs, preferably abroad. Upon hearing this, Carey's "face brightened. He had that very morning flown into town seated beside Harold Stassen, the head of the US foreign economic aid program, and had learned that that agency was actively seeking personnel to go to Indo-China to work in a US aid program. . . . French speakers were particularly being sought."[119] Following his father's footsteps, Browne applied for a U.S. Civil Service position. In his application, dated 30 May 1955, he indicated that he would be willing to accept an appointment anywhere outside of the United States but left the query about positions inside the United States unchecked.[120] Soon thereafter, Browne "was high above the Pacific" and traveling to what was then a little-known part of the world: Phnom Penh, Cambodia.[121]

Browne's year abroad in the midst of the Cold War, decolonization movements, and the beginnings of the civil rights movement solidified his aspirations for a career in international relations. In many ways, he was pushed out of the United States by its entrenched racism. At the same time, as the American government and various international institutions slowly shifted their racial practices to respond to internal as well as external pressures, Browne also found an opportunity to serve as an authorized representative of his country. As a male member of the black middle class, he had the contacts, the training, and the mobility to assume this internationalist role. Browne's entry into the U.S. government was part of a larger group of African American political leaders, civil servants, and military personnel who gained greater opportunities during the post–World War II era. In the context of the Cold War, the era of decolonization, and the emerging civil rights movement, Ralph Bunche, Archibald Carey, Mr. Jones in Libya, and Bob Browne created niches for themselves as agents of the U.S. nation-state. Historian Michael L. Krenn's study of African Americans and the State Department points out that government accommodations to demands for racial access and equality were made reluctantly and at a glacial pace.[122] Nevertheless, the slight openings allowed African Americans to anchor themselves to the American Cold War mandate in exchange for positions that provided possibilities for professional advancement. At the same time, having the opportunity to spend an extended period of time abroad gave individuals like Browne the experiential basis to develop critical perspectives of U.S. global policies.

Chapter 2

Afro-Asian Alliances

When Browne first arrived in Cambodia in 1955, he was single and in his early thirties. By the time he left South Vietnam in 1961, he was approaching his late thirties and a member of a multiracial family with four children. He initially had little idea of what was in store for him personally or for the entire world politically. Browne recalled, "Like most Americans of my generation, I had learned little about Indo-China in my schooling. To me, it was a vaguely recalled blob of purple on the map of Asia, clinging to the southeastern border of China."[1] Even the State Department, which sent Browne as a member of the International Cooperation Administration (ICA) to administer U.S. economic aid, had little to offer in terms of guidance. During his briefing in Washington, DC, they were "unable to locate a single American in Washington who had ever lived in Cambodia."[2] Within a decade, though, Southeast Asia would become the focus of the world's attention. In Vietnam and its bordering countries, the United States fought and lost a war that was then the longest in U.S. history.[3] The bloody conflicts there aroused passionate antiwar movements both in the United States and internationally. Browne's years of living and working in Southeast Asia would place him at the epicenter of these political developments in the 1960s.

Browne's engagement with Asian people and politics provides an opportunity to examine Afro-Asian connections during the crucial period of the Cold War, decolonization, and civil rights. Various scholars have traced a history of African American interest in Asia. As Bill Mullen and Cathryn Watson argue, W. E. B. DuBois "consistently saw Asia as the fraternal twin to African—and African American—struggle for political freedom."[4] Also, as Marc Gallicchio, Gerald Horne, Reginald Kearney, Yuichiro Onishi, and Nico Slate demonstrate, a variety of black leaders and the black press followed political developments in Asia with great interest throughout the first half of the twentieth century.[5] Japan, in particular, received African American attention. As Japan challenged European dominance on the global stage, the country became perceived as a model for other racialized and colonized people for independence. This interpretation of Japan, however, overlooks that nation's campaigns to colonize other Asian countries and peoples. Bill Mullen describes this tendency among African American thinkers to idealize and romanticize Asia in the name of anticolonial and anticapitalist solidarity as a form of Afro-orientalism.[6] He raises the possibility that this particular form of orientalism could "do the work of both colonizing and decolonizing the mind."[7]

These studies on African American internationalism in relation to Asia have tended to focus on Japan, India, and China and how their status on the global stage has shaped thinking about black liberation struggles. In addition, these studies have analyzed African American leaders and cultural figures who traveled and lived abroad. These individuals tended to either make brief visits or live abroad for an extended period of time due to their status as political exiles. In contrast, Browne resided and worked in Southeast Asia for six years as an agent of the American government. Furthermore, he developed an intimate relationship that mirrored the possibilities of Afro-Asian political unity.

Browne's status as a racial outsider but a national insider provides an opportunity to consider how racial triangulation operated in the global arena during the Cold War. Political scientist Claire Jean Kim proposed the concept of racial triangulation to analyze the relational ways in which African Americans and Asian Americans are racialized in the United States.[8] She posits the importance of understanding social hierarchy beyond a linear or one-dimensional analysis. Instead, she argues for the need to recognize at least two axes by which Asian and African Americans have been conceptualized in relation to each other and to the dominant white group. On the one hand, Asian people in the United States have tended to be "valorized" above African Americans as "model" minorities. On the other hand, African Americans are deemed civically superior, since people of Asian ancestry tend to be regarded as perpetual foreigners. Kim's idea of racial triangulation is intriguing to consider in the context of the Cold War. As a member of a racially marginalized group who could nevertheless become a spokesperson for the U.S. state, Browne served as a unique asset for American Cold War efforts to win the hearts and minds of the decolonizing Third World. However, his potential alliance with Asian people and their interests could upset the racial logic of mainstream America. A personal and political partnership between African Americans and Asian foreign others could potentially invert the power dynamics of the racial triangle, not just in the United States but also globally.

Bob Browne left the United States in 1955, a momentous year in which the Cold War, decolonization, and the civil rights movement converged to generate a world-changing political storm. Browne arrived in Phnom Penh, the capital of Cambodia, when, in his words, "the signatures of the 1954 Geneva Agreement . . . were hardly dry."[9] Under the Geneva Accords, Cambodia, Laos, and Vietnam, colonies of France since the mid-to-late nineteenth century, finally achieved nominal independence. Vietnam, which had engaged in a nine-year war against the French since the end of World War II, was divided into two sections at the seventeenth parallel with the promise of a national election in 1956. Cambodia, which had negotiated its sovereignty previously, remained intact.

Like other decolonizing nations during the postwar era, these liberation struggles were profoundly shaped by the Cold War. In Vietnam, the Viet Minh, or the League of Independence for Vietnam, was the most organized force fighting against French colonialism. Its members held a range of political beliefs, but the league was led by Ho Chi Minh, who also cofounded the Indochinese Communist Party in 1930.[10] Ho was not necessarily anti-American. He had previously traveled to the United States in the 1910s and even lived in Harlem. During World War II, he also cooperated with the U.S. Office of Strategic Services. When Ho pronounced Vietnamese independence in 1945, he quoted from the American Declaration of Independence, proclaiming, "All men are created qual. They are endowed by their Creator with certain inalienable rights; among these are life, liberty and the pursuit of happiness."[11] Ho also petitioned President Truman for his endorsement and cited the Atlantic Charter. Signed by the United States and Great Britain in 1941, the charter pledged "the right of all peoples to choose the form of government under which they will live."[12] Truman never responded to Ho's letter. Instead, the United States, with its own history of racial domination and its fear of the spread of communism, began supporting the French, supplying them with economic and military aid to fight against Vietnamese independence. By the time the French lost the final battle at Dien Bien Phu in 1954, the United States had spent one billion dollars and was paying for 80 percent of the French costs of the war.[13] To counteract this level of support, the Viet Minh had turned to the Soviet Union and to the People's Republic of China for economic and military aid.

The end of the First Indochina War against the French did not bring peace to the region. In 1955, the same year that Bob Browne arrived in Southeast Asia, the United States installed the presidency of Ngo Dinh Diem in South Vietnam. Diem refused to hold the national elections promised by the Geneva Accords. He also resisted instituting domestic political and economic reforms to build support for his rule.[14] Nevertheless, the United States continued to escalate its financial, political, and military commitment to South Vietnam, thereby laying the foundations for the Second Indochina War. More commonly known in the United States as the Vietnam War, the military conflict actually took place throughout the entire Southeast Asian region, including Cambodia.

Because of the high political stakes involved in the Cold War, decolonizing nations sought to neutralize the pressures to choose between the capitalist West and the socialist East. The same year that Bob Browne arrived in Phnom Penh, twenty-nine Asian and African nations, including Cambodia, North Vietnam, and South Vietnam, met at the historic Afro-Asian Conference held in Bandung, Indonesia. Challenging the bipolar perspective of the Cold War, these emerging nations affirmed their alliance with one another as members of a third "nonaligned" force, self-designated as the "Third World."[15] Although it proved almost impossible to remain neutral, the declaration of an independent Third World bloc was a powerful statement that created a degree of political leverage for these nations.

In this context, Browne's desire for professional and life opportunities overseas coincided with American strategic efforts to obtain the allegiance of the emerging Third World. Browne's racial identity constituted a crucial political asset, especially as the civil rights movement blossomed in the United States and gained international attention. The year before Browne went abroad, the U.S. Supreme Court ruled in *Brown v. Board of Education* that segregation was unconstitutional. The year that Browne left for Cambodia, Rosa Parks in Montgomery, Alabama, refused to give her bus seat to a white man and sparked a year-long boycott of segregated public transportation. It was during this campaign that Martin Luther King Jr. became an internationally recognized spokesperson for nonviolence and civil rights. At the time, he was just a young minister leading his first congregation. The Montgomery Bus Boycott, the desegregation of Little Rock High School in Arkansas, and the other dramatic struggles for civil rights throughout the late 1950s and early 1960s brought to light the entrenched inhumanity of American race relations.

Projecting a more positive racial image abroad, then, was crucial to the U.S. position as a global leader. The 1958 best-selling novel *The Ugly American*, published the year that Browne was transferred from Cambodia to South Vietnam, warned of the damage to international relations that resulted from the arrogance and cultural insensitivity of American foreign service personnel in Southeast Asia. One method to promote a more positive representation of the United States was to encourage certain African Americans to travel abroad. While leftists or suspected leftists like Paul Robeson and W. E. B. DuBois had their passports revoked, the State Department enlisted African American jazz musicians to serve as cultural ambassadors for the United States.[16] The presence and music of Duke Ellington and Dizzy Gillespie projected a national image of racial equality and democracy, a particularly necessary propagandistic goal, given the target audience of Third World nations. As Browne pointed out himself, "the State Department [was] becoming aware of the Negro's direct usefulness in international relations [as] evidenced by the . . . growing numbers of Negroes in diplomatic and semi-diplomatic positions."[17] Once almost denied a passport by the U.S. government, Browne now served as a valuable representative of his country.

Instead of taking an ocean liner, Browne flew to Asia on a "pre-jet jumbo carrier . . . a four engine-pot-bellied aircraft which included a few sleeper berths."[18] He stopped in Seattle, Anchorage, and Tokyo before finally landing in Phnom Penh. Never having traveled to Asia before and with little time to prepare linguistically or culturally for his journey, Browne was initially overwhelmed and even somewhat regretful about his decision to spend two years of his life there. His immediate impressions of Cambodia focused on the agrarian and underdeveloped nature of the society there:

> Although the scene at the airport had been one of considerable animation and crowding . . . the road from the airport proved to be sparsely utilized, primarily by slow-moving carts pulled by oxen or small horses, transporting

farm produce of various sorts. There was a sprinkling of cars. . . . Scenically, one faced vast tracts of rice paddies of an unbelievably powerful green coloration, sparkling in the sun because their roots were submerged under a very thin sheet of water. The paddies were periodically interrupted by stretches of lightly forested acreage interspersed with leafy banana plants and stately coconut palm trees. Wooden houses were spotted throughout the area, many of them on stilts, most of them with thatched roofs made from local grasses.[19]

Even though Phnom Penh was the country's capital, it was quite a contrast from the Big Apple. Browne pondered why he was "voluntarily giving up [his] life in New York City to come and dwell in a sleepy tropical town which apparently had little to recommend it."[20] Browne's impressions mirrored the classical orientalist outlook of other people from the West. As scholar Edward Said observes, those from the Occident tend to emphasize the contrast between the First and Third Worlds, between what they regard as the "primitiveness" and "backwardness" of Oriental countries in comparison to the "modern" and technologically advanced West.[21]

Browne's fellow Americans tended to exhibit this orientalist outlook as well. During his two-year stay in Cambodia, he became a member of a U.S. country team, which consisted of four units: the American Embassy, the U.S. Information Services (USIS), the Military Assistance Advisory Group, and the United States Operations Mission (USOM), otherwise known as the ICA. Overall, the country team employed approximately 160 Americans and 260 Asians.[22] All of the Americans stationed in Cambodia were relative newcomers. During the First Indochina War, the United States had provided economic and military aid to Cambodia through the French. Communication and money were channeled through a regional office in Saigon, which was accessible from Phnom Penh by a one-hour plane ride or a six-hour car ride. Following the Geneva Accords, the United States established an office in Cambodia to, in Browne's words, "fill the vacuum which was being created by the departure of the French."[23]

The United States considered Cambodia significant enough to warrant a country team for political, military, and economic reasons. Bordered by Vietnam to the east, Laos to the north, and Thailand to the west and northwest, Cambodia constituted a crucial domino in America's Cold War calculations. U.S. officials feared that "the fall of Cambodia into Communist hands would lay open the flanks" of Southeast Asia. Cambodia, with an estimated population of four million and land size equivalent to the state of Missouri, had relatively few desirable raw materials or exports, aside from rice or rubber; however, "because of its interrelation with the defense of SE Asia," the "loss of Cambodia . . . would endanger sources of raw materials needed by the U.S. in order to prosecute a major war."[24]

To maintain Cambodia's independence from the communists, the United States first and foremost provided significant military aid. Aside from supplying equipment and advisers, the United States also directly financed the budget of the Cambodian military, paying the salary of its personnel. A 1956 report indicated, "the total cost of the Cambodian armed forces is approximately $37 million, of which the Cambodians are contributing some $8 million and the United States some $29 million."[25] The funding was deemed necessary, given the incursions into Cambodia by Vietnamese forces. In addition, the United States at times covered a portion of the deficit spending of the Cambodian government, which was struggling to stabilize itself given the limited revenue stream from its antiquated taxation system.

In addition to these pressing military and fiscal concerns, the United States, through USOM, provided technical and financial assistance with an eye toward modernizing the economy and society of Cambodia. The ICA sought to demonstrate the benefits of capitalism by investing in the transportation infrastructure, encouraging private enterprise, developing the export and industrial capacity of the nation, and generally raising the living standard of Cambodians. As a member of this economic aid team, Browne was inspired sincerely by "the prospect of rendering real service to an area of the world that needed help"; he wanted "to help rebuild the shattered economies of this war torn area and to bring it the benefits of western medicine, technology and education."[26] Years later, Browne recognized the missionary-like approach of this modernization project. He recalled, "Much like a dedicated corpsman of the Salvation Army, I arrived in Cambodia convinced of the rightness of my cause."[27]

The desire to transform Cambodia so that it might serve as an American Cold War ally led members of the U.S. country team to express frustration and at times contempt for the people whom they were seeking to assist. The reports from American personnel frequently contained complaints about what they perceived as the ineptitude and noncooperation of the Cambodian government. The conflicts resulted from a variety of complex factors. At the basic level of communication, there were linguistic and cultural gaps between Americans and Cambodians. Most members of the U.S. country team did not speak French, the language most commonly used within elite Cambodian political and economic circles. The inability to communicate without translation proved frustrating to American personnel, which is why Browne's facility in French was so highly desired. However, hardly any Americans, including Browne, spoke Cambodian, the language actually used by the overwhelming majority of the people in the country. Beyond this linguistic disconnect, cultural differences also fueled misunderstanding. Prince Norodom Sihanouk, the central political leader in Cambodia during this period, was a charismatic and cosmopolitan figure. In contrast, according to historian David Chandler, Sihanouk perceived "the first U.S. ambassador to Cambodia, Robert McClintock, . . . as dogmatic, imperious, and gauche. McClintock attended at least one official reception accompanied by a dog; he moved around the capital in shorts and occasionally affected a baton."[28]

There were also distinct political differences between Americans and Cambodians for historical and contemporary reasons. It is perhaps not surprising that relatively few officials had experience or knowledge about Western forms of governance, a complaint that U.S. personnel frequently raised. After all, as McClintock observed rather dismissively, "under almost a century of French rule, important administrative posts were staffed by French personnel and the Cambodians were relegated to the positions of office boys."[29] The limited pool of potential officials became further reduced as the Cambodian government, led by the somewhat mercurial Prince Sihanouk, experimented with various political structures and leaders in the early years of the nation's founding. Browne arrived just as the country held its first elections. The government was subsequently constituted and reconstituted with varying prime ministers and different degrees of influence from an elected assembly that was ultimately dissolved. In addition to this instability, there were also distinct differences between Americans and Cambodians in terms of political priorities. While U.S. Ambassador McClintock was prone to lecture "Sihanouk about the dangers of Communism," Sihanouk declared his country as a neutral state and sought aid not only from the capitalist West but also the socialist East.[30]

Despite these complex factors that shaped relationships between American and Cambodian leaders, McClintock, as the highest-ranking representative of the United States, boiled down these differences to a fundamental racial distinction between the West and the East, the white and the nonwhite. In a report to Washington, DC, McClintock posited:

In my judgment—and these observations apply generally throughout Southeast Asia as well as to Cambodia—the inherent difficulty of ICA is

its attempt to super-impose on primitive, unsophisticated, highly national-
istic and poorly staffed newly-independent countries a mechanism for aid
which as the Marshall Plan was originally applied to the long-established,
economically sophisticated, financially experienced and ancient countries
of Europe. The attempt is comparable to giving one of Einstein's more
simple equations to an Australian bushman who, on receiving the priceless
formula, promptly goes out and does what he knows best—throw a boo-
merang.[31]

This polarized sense of difference between Westerners and "natives" was
deeply ingrained in the way that the country team functioned. American
and Asian staff members were paid according to different pay scales. In addition, U.S. personnel lived in quarters deemed suitable for Westerners to
occupy. Aside from official functions, Americans tended to socialize exclusively with one another at the few sports and social clubs established for
Westerners.

This practice of social segregation between Americans and Asians ironically situated Browne in a relatively privileged position. Although black, he
was American.[32] He joined and played tennis at the country club for foreigners. His regular career promotions and pay raises in USOM suggest that
his supervisors recognized and rewarded his contributions. He first arrived in
Cambodia as a program accountant auditor in August 1955, became an economic analyst in July 1956, and then served as an assistant program officer of
operations in November 1957 before he succeeded in obtaining a promotion
and transfer to the much larger country team in South Vietnam in February
1958.[33] Milton Esman, the chief program officer for USOM in Saigon from
March 1957 through July 1959, recalled that Browne was a "personable individual" who was "well liked."[34] When asked if Browne's racial background
played a role in the way in which he was treated or regarded, Esman emphasized that "race did not enter into relationships abroad." Although there were
clear hierarchies based on rank within the country team staff, Esman recalled
that he and Browne "socialized frequently in the evenings."

The lack of racial prejudice among foreign service staff seems somewhat exaggerated.[35] After all, *The Ugly American*, which depicted the racism and cultural ignorance of American diplomats and aid workers, was
based on actual incidents and people who were in the foreign service in
Southeast Asia.[36] In fact, the popularity of the book led the director of
the USOM mission in Vietnam, Arthur Z. Gardiner, to speculate who
among them inspired the characters in the book. In addition, the Ameri-

can ambassador to Vietnam, Elbridge Durbrow, even corresponded with his superiors in Washington, DC, to supply ammunition to discredit both the book and the authors.[37]

Yet in the midst of this defensive reaction to charges of racism, Browne discovered a more welcoming environment for him while abroad:

> Despite my rather severe criticisms regarding the general behavior of white people toward colored people, my references are to be interpreted as generalizations, with all the exceptions which that term implies. Not only are several white persons included among my most cherished friends, but my prolonged foreign residence has resulted in my circle of American acquaintances becoming almost exclusively white in recent years. One of the most surprising aspects of my overseas experience has been to witness and enjoy a social intercourse with my white fellow countrymen which is both natural and easy—free of the artificiality which so frequently plagues interracial relationships in the U.S.[38]

Browne's closest friends during his years in Cambodia and Vietnam included Ed Smith, a white Southerner, who worked as an English-language instructor for the Military Assistance Advisory Group. Smith recalled that he and Browne "just had a good time" together.[39] They enjoyed each other's company so much that when they both went on home leave, they traveled together through Europe and sub-Saharan Africa.

Other African Americans, such as the Black Panther Party leader Kathleen Cleaver, also recalled that living abroad as a member of the foreign service mitigated some of the domestic experiences of American racism.[40] Born in 1945, Cleaver spent roughly six years of her formative childhood in Asia. Her father, Ernest E. Neal, was a professor who specialized in rural sociology at Tuskegee University, a historically black college whose first president was Booker T. Washington. Neal first went to India in 1953 as a Ford Foundation Fellow and then to the Philippines in 1956 as a member of ICA, the same organization that employed Bob Browne. Neal attempted to apply the theories that he developed in the American South to the decolonizing nations of Asia to promote rural community development and help eradicate poverty.[41] In essence, his position in Asia was comparable to Mr. Jones's in North Africa and Browne's in Southeast Asia. Growing up in Asia, Kathleen Cleaver recalled the lack of racial segregation among foreign service personnel and the integrated educational opportunities for American children abroad. Her experiences in Asia contrasted sharply with Jim Crow conditions in Alabama, which she experienced firsthand when she returned to the United States.[42]

Despite the greater opportunities available for African Americans abroad, Browne's racial identity still held significance. He was acutely aware of how his race benefited the U.S. government as well as himself. In several interviews and writings, he stated his belief that it was not only "my fluency in French" but also "my dark skin" that resulted in his employment by USOM.[43] His country team sought to capitalize on his presence to address concerns about racism among Asians. For example, Browne recalled:

> While working for the foreign aid program in Cambodia I was once requested by USIS (the U.S. Information Service) to deliver a short orientation talk to a group of Cambodian young men who were going to America to study. The topic designated for my talk was "The United States, a Melting Pot." Inasmuch as Cambodians are brown-skinned like myself I surmised that USIS was attempting to prepare these students for the color antagonisms which they might encounter upon arrival in the United States. My inference was confirmed a day or two later when one of the USIS officials informally mentioned to me that he hoped that I would describe things just as I saw them, keeping in mind that my audience would actually be in the U.S. within a couple of months' time. I assumed that he meant that I should tell the truth. . . . I did not hesitate, therefore, to point out the ugly aspects of race relations in America but at the same time explained the historical reasons for the situations which exist and the progress being made to correct them. During a question period which followed my talk I discovered that one or two of the students had come armed with perceptive and incisive questions about race discrimination in the U.S. which they had culled from a variety of sources. Fortunately, my talk had anticipated and answered most of them and as a result of this initial frankness the group left with complete confidence in what I told them. Admittedly, they left feeling that although America might be a melting pot it was one under which the flame had not yet been turned high enough. They were, however, better fortified to face the realities of American life without being shocked into anti-Americanism.[44]

Browne recognized that the American government sought to use his brownness to further their political goals with Asians. Being in this "middleman" position benefited Browne as well. It gave him a platform to talk about race.

Browne developed a closer rapport with Cambodia and Cambodians than many of his white colleagues. Despite his initial hesitancy about coming to Phnom Penh, Browne came to enjoy "the rhythm of the country."[45] He also felt "great to be earning a decent salary for the first time in [his] life," particularly since his position allowed him to more fully utilize the knowledge and skills that he had acquired through his education. Most significantly, Browne found it "exhilarating to be in a country where colored peoples were in charge of themselves."[46] In contrast to the negative reaction to Sihanouk that many of his colleagues expressed, Browne emphasized the prince's "imaginative and independent" thinking as well as his popularity and accessibility to "his people. . . . Prince Sihanouk regularly made himself available to listen to individual complaints about his government, to settle domestic and marital disputes, to hear public suggestions and to engage in whatever type of verbal exchange his supplicants requested."[47] During Browne's stay in Southeast Asia, he took the opportunity to travel widely throughout the entire continent, where he observed the emerging nations of Thailand, India, Malaysia, Japan, and Taiwan.

Browne's growing connection with Asian people appeared to be recognized and reciprocated by Cambodians. As part of his responsibilities with USOM, Browne advised government officials and business leaders about how to apply for and allocate American funds. He "was the junior member of a two person American team designated to assist the Cambodian government officials in managing the commercial import program which the US was providing."[48] The Commercial Import Program (CIP) served a crucial purpose, because it was the primary mechanism by which the United States contributed aid to Cambodia. Through the CIP, Americans paid for "the purchase of foreign products which were needed or desired by the Cambodian economy and whose purchase required the use of a hard currency."[49] Asian importers then applied to the Cambodian government to purchase these goods, depositing local currency into a "counterparts" fund. The fund was then used to pay for military aid and government expenses as well as technical assistance and economic programs. The CIP basically converted U.S. aid into local currency and did so at an exchange rate, usually half the market rate, that was extremely favorable to Cambodians. This system was utilized to protect the Cambodian economy from "highly dangerous inflationary pressures" that would have resulted had the United States simply given grants of American dollars.[50] In Browne's future speeches and writings about South Vietnam, which also utilized the CIP mechanism to distribute aid, he would critique many aspects of this program. Given the sums involved, there were "fascinating opportunities for local profiteering."[51] More disturbingly, because of the large amounts necessary to fund the military, the CIP did not necessarily prioritize the importation of products that could further the long-term economic development of either Cambodia or Vietnam. Instead, the CIP facilitated the importation of luxury commodities that could quickly generate currency for the counterfunds. Finally, the availability of U.S. goods, along with the low exchange rate, encouraged Asian leaders and entrepreneurs not to invest in the industrial development and economic infrastructure of their own country. Greater and faster gain could be obtained more easily through the CIP instead.[52]

Because the CIP represented the nexus of U.S.-Cambodian relations, Browne, even with his junior status, occupied an influential position. His advice appeared to be appreciated by Cambodian officials. Browne recalled that when they began negotiating with the Soviet Union for economic aid, "a team of Cambodian officials approached me for suggestions as to what kinds of assistance I felt they should request from the Soviets. I was never certain why the Cambodians had chosen to direct this request to me. One possibility was that the Cambodians had decided that I might handle this inquiry more discreetly than some of my colleagues."[53] The Cambodians appeared to perceive Browne as more approachable, trustworthy, and more likely to consider their interests compared to other Americans. The Cambodians also invited Browne to accompany "a delegation . . . to some neighboring countries to see how they were addressing common problems. They asked me . . . as a technical assistant and also to trouble shoot any language problems. . . . The delegation was received at cabinet level in each of the countries, and in Japan and the Philippines I had a major role to play."[54] Although a representative of the United States, Browne was considered a valuable adviser to the Cambodians.

Due to Browne's brownness, he developed the ability to "switch-hit" for both the United States and Cambodia. His very presence in the ICA exemplified some degree of progress in American race relations, and he could serve as a spokesperson about race to interested audiences. With his economic training and work experience, Browne also could advise Cambodians about possible paths toward modernization and national economic development. Browne's intermediary position between the Americans and the Cambodians is reflected by the references on his résumé. Following his departure from USOM, he listed both Milton Esman, who was his ICA supervisor, and the governor of the National Bank of Cambodia.[55] As a racial outsider in the United States, Browne could more easily become a cosmopolitan insider in decolonizing Asia.

In South Vietnam, Browne also claimed a sense of affinity with Asian nationals. In contrast to Phnom Penh, "central Saigon was a sophisticated, bustling city of heavy automobile traffic and diesel buses, of night clubs and classy French restaurants."[56] The differences between the two capitals reflected broader divergences in the two countries. The southern half of Vietnam was approximately the same land size as Cambodia, but it was home to roughly twelve million people, or three times the population of its neighbor.[57] The U.S. country team was exponentially bigger and better financed. The USOM staff alone in Saigon was greater than the entire country team in Cambodia.[58] Furthermore, the ICA budget for Vietnam was roughly ten times the allocation for Cambodia and the second biggest overall among all the USOM units in the world.[59] The U.S. government deemed Cambodia significant because of its geographical location in Southeast Asia, but Vietnam was the primary focus of American strategic interests in this region.[60]

The United States began supplying aid directly to South Vietnam in 1955 in order to help stabilize the Diem government that Americans helped to install. One of the key concerns during this early era was the care and adjustment of political refugees. The temporary division of Vietnam, mandated by the Geneva Accords in 1954, was followed by a resettlement period, during which approximately eight hundred thousand Vietnamese from the north migrated south and approximately one hundred thousand from the south relocated north. Not surprisingly, the refugees to the south tended to be anticommunist and Catholic. Although the overwhelming majority of Vietnamese were Buddhists, President Diem and his family subscribed to and promoted Catholicism. In his new post in Saigon, Browne no longer had "oversight of a commercial import program" but instead "became linked to the programs which American technicians were being brought in to mount and implement in public works, education, agriculture, health or other sectors"; his "contacts were now more frequently with other Americans and less often with local officials."[61]

Browne compensated for his "reduced contact with local officials by greatly enlarging the scope of [his] non-official contacts with the local population."[62] He volunteered to teach English at a nearby school. However, his Vietnamese was rather poor. Browne admitted in his memoir,

> I had ambitions to learn Vietnamese when I moved to Saigon, but I found that to be a hard nut to crack. Vietnamese is a tonal language, which

means that to speak and understand it requires an ability to distinguish the tone in which each word is being uttered, because the tone determines the meaning of the word. Tone is used in speaking English also, but as a means for showing emphasis, not to change the basic meaning of the word. In any case, I found myself making such slow progress in Vietnamese that I devoted ever-diminishing amounts of time to it, and consequently never mastered it.[63]

Despite Browne's limited language skills, his relationship with a woman of Vietnamese ancestry likely facilitated an easier rapport with the locals.

Browne met his future wife soon after his arrival in Cambodia. Two years younger than Browne, Huoi was of Vietnamese and Chinese ancestry and consequently an ethnic minority on two counts. Her great-grandmother had migrated to Cambodia from Vietnam, while her father was born in China. Huoi grew up in an impoverished family and received little formal schooling. Her educational background could be considered typical. According to U.S. reports, the literacy rate in Cambodia was 45 percent among men but only 20 percent among women.[64] When she met Browne, Huoi was working as a cook in a French household to support herself and her daughter from a previous marriage.[65] They encountered each other by chance when Huoi accompanied a friend to make laundry deliveries at the hotel where Browne lived at the time.[66] According to Huoi, Browne pursued her. When he subsequently moved into his own apartment, which was allocated by USOM, he invited Huoi to help decorate his new home. She did not accept. As a single mother, she was leery of courtship. When asked if race was a consideration in her decision to develop a romantic relationship with Browne, she stated that it was not a factor.[67] In her own family, there was intermarriage among Cambodians, Vietnamese, and Chinese. Although these groups may appear racially similar to Western eyes, they had distinct historical, cultural, and social differences. What mattered to her was the quality of the person, which is why she ultimately reciprocated Browne's advances. Huoi and her young daughter, Hoa, described him as a warm and compassionate person. Because Browne persisted in his attentions to Huoi, they eventually moved in together.

Browne and Huoi were in many ways an unlikely couple. Although he had romantic and sexual relationships with other women in his travels around the world, he had qualms about marriage in general and particularly about a union between people of such different backgrounds. He recalled, "My relationship with Huoi was slow in starting and bounced around in an undefined status for quite some time, as much a reflection of my uncertainty about the institution of marriage as of uncertainty about the person in question. . . . Huoi's obvious positives (starting with her disarming smile), and our excellent personal chemistry, were countered by negatives of monumental proportions, with the most important being the drastic difference in our cultural backgrounds."[68]

Despite his vacillations, Browne felt "smitten by" Huoi and decided that he "would never find happiness without her at my side."[69] He adopted Hoa, who was eleven by the time the family left for the United States. In addition, Browne and Huoi had three children in quick succession, each of them with Vietnamese as well as Western names. Mai Julia was born in Cambodia in 1956, while Alexi Ngo and Marshall Xuan were both born in South Vietnam, in 1958 and 1960 respectively. The parental nicknames of Browne and Huoi also reflected the cultural mixture of their family: Bob became "Ba," the Vietnamese term for father, and Huoi became "Mommy."

Browne kept his family life a secret from the foreign service. His supervisor, Milton Esman, regarded himself as a good friend of Browne's but recalled that he simply disappeared on the weekends.[70] When one of Browne's work colleagues unexpectedly visited him at home, his eldest daughter, Hoa, remembered that the entire family had to hide. The secrecy surrounding Browne's personal life stemmed from complex reasons.

It was very difficult to have a private life away from the gaze of the U.S. country team. Marital and family status were the basis for housing allocations and hence were public knowledge. Single personnel lived either in hotel rooms or small apartments. Married individuals and those with children received larger residences, like a house or villa. In addition, personal relationships could be scrutinized if they had the potential to damage the reputation of the U.S. mission.[71] One staff member in Vietnam was investigated because of allegations of drunkenness and domestic abuse.[72] The case came to the attention of the ICA personnel division because of reports circulated by this person's Asian servants as well as his American acquaintances. Private behaviors had the potential to publicly damage the United States. In a memo about reckless driving, L. Metcalfe Walling, the director of USOM in Cambodia, explained, "We are guests of Cambodia and we should conduct ourselves accordingly; there is nothing which can cause more criticism of us than stories circulating, based on fact unfortunately, that we are driving recklessly and with no concern for others."[73]

In the case of interracial personal relationships, the U.S. government turned a blind eye on informal and casual relationships but focused its full

Figure 2. A holiday greeting card from the Browne family. Left to right, back: Bob and Huoi; front: Huo and Mai. Personal collection of the Browne family.

scrutiny when it came to marriage.[74] USOM authored country books and post reports to introduce new staff to their host countries. These writings anticipated that recruits might be curious about entertainment opportunities. The post reports described respectable events like dinner parties, sports functions, and nightclubs. In addition, more risqué information intended for heterosexual males was included. One such publication explained "the dearth of single French girls here" and also warned that "Cambodian girls do not go out without their families. . . . However, lest the single men totally despair, there are many pretty Chinese 'taxi' girls that can be hired by the hour for dancing."[75] Another report compared these Chinese "taxi" girls to Japanese geishas. While these women were not necessarily prostitutes, their company, whether on the dance floor or elsewhere, was explicitly described as being available for purchase. This government advertisement of casual and commercialized relationships between American men and Asian women reflected a broader practice among U.S. overseas missions. The American government and military, as well as the tourist industry, collaborated with one another and their Asian counterparts to develop and promote prostitution.[76] Sociologist Joane Nagel has described this partnership as the "military sexual complex."[77] After all, part of the allure of being stationed abroad for many American men included the prospect of meeting and having sexual relationships with "native" women.[78]

Not all interracial relationships could be characterized as financial and casual transactions. Ed Smith, one of the few people who knew of Browne's relationship with Huoi, also had a Cambodian "girlfriend" during his stay in Southeast Asia. His partner worked as a member of the U.S. country team. Smith did not believe that the type of relationship he had with her was a common practice among other Americans: "There [were] some that just had prostitutes, but not many . . . had a girlfriend who wasn't a prostitute."[79]

An American dating an Asian, although rare, did not receive the same scrutiny as individuals seeking to marry across racial and national lines. In one source, Browne claims that he and Huoi were married in 1956, and they may have done so according to local custom.[80] His personnel file indicates that an official marriage, that is, one recognized by the U.S. government, did not occur until April 3, 1961.[81] The time lag between the two dates reflects the fact that a marriage between a U.S. foreign service member and an Asian national could occur only with the approval of the American's superiors. Taboos against interracial marriage very likely served as a subtext for this regulation. After all, antimiscegenation laws in the United States were not deemed unconstitutional until 1967. In addition, Asian wives of American personnel faced difficulties gaining entry into the United States due to racially discriminatory immigration laws. Although the U.S. Congress enacted special legislation to allow some "war brides" to enter the country, Asian women were initially barred and then only had limited access to these opportunities.[82] Officially, the marriage policy for members of the country team was explained in terms of security concerns. When Browne's relationship to Huoi finally became public, a memo from the ICA personnel office in Washington, DC, asked "has this relationship been a source of embarrassment to the USOM" and "whether there is any objection to the marriage from a security standpoint."[83] Being Asian, Huoi was suspected as a potential risk. Her dual Vietnamese and Chinese ancestry may have placed her under double suspicion, since her ethnicities could link her to both North Vietnam and communist China.

Browne must have understood that officially requesting permission to marry an Asian national would have placed him in a precarious situation in terms of his career. As Milton Esman explained years later, no one under his supervision ever asked to marry someone of Vietnamese ancestry.[84] Following Esman's departure from Saigon, there was at least one recorded request for marriage between an American man and an Asian woman, both employees of the U.S. country team. The request received approval, because there was "no security objection [to the] proposed marriage."[85] Within two weeks of their wedding ceremony, though, the American employee was stripped of his access to classified materials.

Esman believed that following his departure from Vietnam in 1959, his replacement discovered Browne's marriage and family and forced a resignation. It is also possible that Bob and Huoi decided to disclose their relationship. They may not have wanted to maintain their family life in such a closeted fashion. In addition, he became increasingly dissatisfied with U.S. policies in Vietnam and may have wanted a way out of Saigon.

In contrast to his respect and affection for Sihanouk, Browne expressed disdain for President Diem, who received extensive support from the United States but ruled his country in a corrupt and dictatorial fashion.[86] The opposition to Diem and to the United States became formalized through the founding of the National Liberation Front in 1960. The NLF, or the Vietcong, as Diem and the Americans began to call this opposition, executed raids and attacks in the countryside and in urban areas. During the year that Browne left Vietnam, two unsuccessful assassination attempts were made on Diem's life. In response to the growing violence, the U.S. country team issued increasing numbers of security memos to its personnel, instructing them not to travel in certain parts of the country, to be on guard especially around national holidays like Tet, and to more closely scrutinize the Asian servants in their homes.

Through his position at USOM, Browne had a front-row seat as he observed the escalating military and political conflict. He also understood the inadequacies of the U.S. economic mission. He recalled, "When I had signed on to work for Uncle Sam I had believed that I was joining a massive effort to alleviate poverty and improve the living conditions of deprived people. I think that most American workers in the aid programs of the fifties had such motivations. . . . As I became more politically savvy, however, . . . I began to realize that Washington's priority goals in Indo-China were not to raise peoples' living standards but to win points in the cold war."[87] The disproportionate amount of aid given to maintain the South Vietnamese military through the CIP was a significant indicator of this imbalance in priorities. As the ICA itself acknowledged:

> Since 1955, two-thirds of the dollars provided to Viet-Nam through ICA channels have gone to provide budget support to the Vietnamese armed forces and hence, have been spent for commercial imports. This heavy emphasis on budget support does not reflect anybody's judgment that such use of funds is the best way to restore Vietnamese agricultural production, foster industrial development, and bring about an early economic independence of Viet-Nam. It has been dictated by the fact that our primary objective has been to establish and maintain law and order within the country and create such a position of military strength as will deter communist infiltration and subversion and prevent overt attack upon this country by hostile military forces.[88]

The military aid did not deter opposition to Diem. Furthermore, the emphasis on commercial imports had "bad economic consequences."[89] Browne helped to author glossy USOM brochures, featuring hopeful stories and images of improvements in the transportation infrastructure, and education system, as well as the craft and manufacturing industries. In reality, these projects received 10–20 percent of the CIP counterfunds during the years that he was in Saigon. Both he and his supervisors at the ICA office in Vietnam clearly understood that the two goals of security and development directly conflicted with one another. The consequences of prioritizing the military goals and delaying the economic plans meant that the Diem government would indefinitely rely on the United States to prime its fiscal pump. The financial benefits of this relationship, though, only trickled down to selected circles within South Vietnamese society. Combined with Diem's unwillingness to institute political reforms, the situation would continue to facilitate the growth of opposition to Diem and necessitate increased U.S. military aid. Browne could see the beginnings of the U.S. quagmire in Southeast Asia.

His last major project with USOM drove home this point. As a result of the growing "unrest and disturbances in the countryside," Browne was asked to prepare a report analyzing the impact on the "rural aid projects" sponsored by ICA:

> We knew that public works of various sorts were being blown up, that crops were being burned, that many of our educational programs had been made inoperable because teachers were being terrorized and murdered, but the embassy wanted some quantification of the seriousness of it all. Working together with a State Dept. colleague over a three week period, I co-produced a report that, after aggregating the results of the numerous attacks to which our program had been subjected, essentially concluded that the effectiveness of our program, overall, had been reduced by a factor of as much as two thirds, depending on the region of the country. We had encountered a highly discouraging and starkly gloomy picture and we reported it as such. We had anticipated that the report would become a hot topic within the embassy family and were more than a little surprised when it was not even mentioned at the country team meetings. A week or so later, still confused by the silence, I undertook a little research to discover what was happening and was astounded to learn that the Ambassador had decided to "kill" our report in his office and not share it with Washington, presumably because it conflicted with the generally positive picture which the embassy had been reporting and too forcefully contradicted President Diem's assurances to Washington that he was in full control of the country. Truth was an early and regular casualty of the US experience in Vietnam.[90]

In Browne's memoir, he explained that he chose to leave the ICA because he became increasingly disturbed by the "absurdity of the Vietnam policy" as well as "growing rumors that the US was giving serious consideration to sending combat troops to South Viet Nam."[91] In Browne's official resignation request, he indicated that his marriage was the reason for his departure. In a letter dated 8 August 1960, he wrote, "In accordance with Manual Order No. 451.2, I herewith offer my resignation from the foreign service of the International Cooperation Administration. This is submitted in connection with my request for permission to marry a foreign national."[92]

Perhaps it was easier for Browne to leave the ICA by focusing on "personal" rather than "political" issues. In a sense, Browne's decision to prioritize Huoi and their family over his job was indicative of his politics. Other American men, of varying racial backgrounds, had relationships and children with Asian women during their stints abroad. A significant number of these men chose to discard these entanglements when they left Asia.[93] The famed opera *Madame Butterfly* by Giacomo Puccini and the more contemporary musical *Miss Saigon* both explore these themes of interracial romance and abandonment. Bob and Huoi no doubt became familiar with the storyline of the former, because they were regular patrons of opera.

In contrast to stories of American soldiers and diplomats deserting their Asian lovers and offspring, Bob assumed responsibility for his wife and children and facilitated their entry into the United States. Even as he left his ICA position, he made sure that Huoi and their children were officially listed as members of his family and hence eligible for health benefits under his appointment. Browne had to decide between a foreign service career and his Afro-Asian family. He chose the latter, for both personal and political reasons. His multiracial family reflected the affinity that he developed with Asian nationals over the course of his stay in Southeast Asia. In a sense, his family represented a personal version of the Afro-Asian alliance espoused in Bandung. Like the leaders who gathered in Indonesia in 1955, Browne returned to the United States eager to find a path beyond the binary politics of the Cold War and the racial hierarchies of global imperialism and domestic racism.

Chapter 3

Searching for Home and Peace

In the summer of 1961, Bob Browne, Huoi, and their four children left Saigon. Browne initially intended to take full advantage of their transpacific journey by making several stops along the way to see sights, visit friends, and slowly acclimate his family to the United States. Flying with three young children quickly changed his mind. Mai, Alexi, and Marshall were all under the age of four. Huo, then eleven, was no doubt enlisted to help take care of her siblings, evening the odds. There was one older caregiver for every younger child. Even so, there were numerous stresses to be managed: luggage, long flights, unfamiliar airports, real or feared communication barriers, and the anticipation of arrival. Rather than prolonging their journey, Bob decided to expedite their travels so that he could introduce his new family to his mother and his home neighborhood on the South Side of Chicago.

As they entered the United States, the Browne family faced the exciting yet challenging prospect of adapting to a new society. Huoi had a particularly steep learning curve as she grappled with a new language, strange foods, unfamiliar cultural practices, and even novel household appliances. Bob also experienced a new America when he returned to Chicago. It was a nation led by the young, charismatic John F. Kennedy. The recently inaugurated president faced intense international pressure as the Cold War continued to escalate. In the spring of 1961, Kennedy ordered the Bay of Pigs invasion in Cuba, which failed, and that summer, East Germany began constructing the Berlin Wall. Domestically, Kennedy confronted a moral crisis regarding race. Just the previous year, the Student Nonviolent Coordinating Committee (SNCC) formed and launched a more aggressive phase of the civil rights movement. These youths chose not to defer to the leadership of the NAACP, which prioritized legal strategies for integration, or to ministers like Martin Luther King Jr., who boycotted segregated facilities. Instead, they embarked on a series of sit-ins to integrate public facilities like Woolworth store lunch counters, libraries, theaters, and swimming pools. These young people and their supporters put their bodies and, at times, their lives on the line. They purposefully transgressed Jim Crow practices to draw public attention and compel the federal government to intervene and enforce desegregation laws in the South. The summer that Bob and his family came back, SNCC and the Congress of Racial Equality, a nonviolent direct action organization founded in Chicago, launched a series of "freedom rides" to integrate the interstate bus and railway system. Over a thousand volunteers, both black and white, participated. It was a far cry from the United States that Bob left in frustration nearly ten years earlier.

Over the course of the 1960s, Browne would discover his political voice and purpose. He was eager to support the civil rights movement and would eventually end the decade as a leading proponent of black power. For much of the 1960s, though, he primarily served as an ardent critic of U.S. diplomatic and military policies in Southeast Asia. Browne initially emerged as a public voice through a series of letters to the *New York Times*, written soon after his return to the United States in the early 1960s. Through his efforts to offer perspectives that were alternatives to those of the mainstream media and the U.S. government, he became part of a network of activists and intellectuals who were committed to peace and decolonization.

Browne's activism could be understood in three primary ways. First, his main method of political engagement was through public debate. His avenues of persuasion—through speeches and writings—reveal his fundamental belief in the power of ideas to change society. In other words, he operated according to the ground rules of a democratic society and made efforts to engage in socially sanctioned political activism.

Second, given the geographical and cultural distance of Vietnam from the United States, Browne attempted to convey the human costs of American policies in Southeast Asia. To cultivate a sense of empathy that transcended national boundaries, he emphasized his personal connections to Vietnam. In addition to his work experience with ICA in Southeast Asia, his ties through marriage and family lent Bob an aura of authenticity and credibility. His private life, previously hidden from view during his tenure in Southeast Asia, served as a valuable symbol to promote a sense of interconnectedness between Americans and Asians. Ironically, as Bob publicly evoked the personal for political purposes, a gendered and cultural gap emerged within the Browne household. Huoi learned to cope with the challenges of immigration by defining her role as a traditional housewife whose primary responsibilities focused on caring for her children. Her concentration on the family was crucial as Bob became a leading political activist during the 1960s, whose commitments took him throughout North America, Europe, North Africa, and back to Asia as well. As Huoi embraced the maternal, Bob broadcast his role as the paternal head of a multiracial family to advocate for peace.

Finally, Browne bridged racial and religious differences by working with whites, blacks, and Asians as well as with Christians, Jews, and Buddhists. Scholar Simon Hall has noted the relative absence of African Americans within the peace movement, despite the fact that blacks were on the whole more dovish than the general public.[1] His study tends to focus on recognized African American figures and leading black organizations. But Browne did not have the name recognition of Martin Luther King Jr. or Muhammad Ali. Browne also was not a spokesperson for organizations like SNCC or the NAACP. Nevertheless, he played a crucial, early, and visible role in the antiwar movement. Furthermore, Browne's blackness was significant for his political impact. One the one hand, he helped authenticate the predominantly white peace movement through his racial presence. On the other hand, he fostered an African American constituency and articulated a racial critique against the U.S. war in Vietnam.

The basis for Browne's political partnerships with both white and black activists was his embrace of Afro-Asian anticolonial solidarity and his efforts to introduce Vietnamese voices into American political debates. Studies of the U.S. antiwar movement have paid little attention to how Asian critics shaped the dialogue concerning American foreign policy.[2] A significant part of Browne's political legacy was his partnership with the Buddhist monk Thich Nhat Hanh. Together, they encouraged an end to the violence and suffering through the establishment of a democratic, peaceful society in South Vietnam that was not reliant on Washington, DC, or Hanoi. In essence, they promoted the possibility of a Bandung-like proposition, a "third solution" to the Cold War tragedy of the U.S. war in Vietnam.

Just as Browne's blackness and familial status had political significance, Hanh's identity as a Vietnamese Buddhist monk held symbolic value. In Jane Iwamura's study of representations of Asian religions in Western popular culture, titled *Virtual Orientalism*, she notes the emergence of the "Oriental monk" figure during the post–World War II era.[3] Characterized by "his spiritual commitment, his calm demeanor, his Asian face, his manner of dress, and—most obviously—his peculiar gendered character," the iconic Oriental monk offers Asian wisdom and enlightenment to rejuvenate the West.[4] This tendency to posit fundamental distinctions between the East and the West even while celebrating the possibilities of cross-cultural dialogue shaped the reception of Thich Nhat Hanh. In order to speak on behalf of Vietnamese people, he and his political allies had to persuade Americans of his cultural authenticity, his presumed differences from U.S. society. For both Browne and Hanh, their respective abilities to "speak" about peace for Vietnamese people were intricately connected to their perceived national and racial as well as gender identities. Browne's paternal masculinity as an African American man and Hanh's effeminate asexuality as an Asian monk contributed to their ability to communicate with audiences across cultural boundaries.

Bob and Huoi both went through a difficult period of adjustment after they arrived in the United States in the summer of 1961. As immigrants from Asia, Huoi and her children were anomalies. Asian people had been present in the United States since before the founding of the nation, when Filipino sailors aboard Spanish galleons abandoned their posts and settled with "natives" in what is now Louisiana. Large numbers of Asian immigrants only began arriving over the course of the mid-nineteenth century through the early twentieth century. Totaling approximately one million from such diverse countries as China, Japan, Korea, India, and the Philippines, these migrants primarily settled in California and Hawaii, where they built railroads, worked on plantations, farmed the land, canned salmon, established laundries, and worked as domestic servants. Although recruited and desired for their labor, Asian immigrants and their American-born children aroused the racial and class antagonism of whites who deemed them "cheap labor" and culturally alien. Beginning in the mid- to late nineteenth century and continuing through 1934, the United States passed a series of exclusion laws and issued a series of court rulings banning Asians from entering the country and denying them the right to naturalized citizenship. Asian immigrants, with the exception of Filipinos, who were under American imperial rule, were legally deemed "aliens ineligible for citizenship."[5]

The federal government eventually rescinded these laws because of the political necessities of World War II and the Cold War. Immigration and citizenship exclusion came to be at odds with U.S. needs to form alliances with Asian countries. Even so, the immigration quota allocated for Asian nations in the early 1960s was still miniscule and far below that of European countries. As Bob Browne noted in a 1961 publication, "One look at our immigration laws will reveal a broad field for improvement and rectification. Now that we are discovering that Orientals, too, are human, with ability to enrich or to destroy our happiness just as we can theirs, perhaps we will free ourselves from the self-imposed limitations of a less enlightened era. As presently constituted, our immigration quotas permit the annual entry of more than 149,000 persons from Europe as opposed to only 5,290 from Asia and Africa combined."[6] It was not until 1965, when the United States established the same quota for each nation in the world, that Asian immigrants began arriving again in large numbers. And it was not until the end of the Vietnam War that significant numbers of Vietnamese and other Southeast Asians, many of them refugees, entered the United States. In fact, three years after Huoi came to the United States, there were only 603 Vietnamese in America, most of whom were students, language teachers, or diplomats.[7]

Given the scarcity of Vietnamese and Asian people more generally in the United States, Huoi experienced cultural isolation and misrecognition. Wendelle, Bob Browne's half sister, recalled that when Huoi first arrived in Chicago, she wore Vietnamese clothing, which was "comfortable for her"; "people would stop . . . and ask . . . was she Japanese? They always wanted to know, 'Are you Japanese?'"[8] Residents of Chicago probably presumed that Huoi was Japanese for two reasons. First, African American soldiers tended to be stationed in the Asian as opposed to the European theater during the Cold War. Those few who persisted in circumventing the obstacles to interracial unions were more likely to marry Japanese and sometimes Korean women.[9] Second, there was an existing Japanese American community in the Windy City. Forced to leave their homes on the West Coast and to live in internment camps during World War II, approximately twenty thousand relocated to Chicago afterward. Being a despised and suspected group, some Japanese Americans worked with and lived alongside

African Americans. At times, the two groups competed for jobs and housing. In fact, Japanese Americans established a residential niche on the South Side of Chicago, close to Bob's family home.[10]

While Chicago residents found Huoi and her clothing fascinating, her youngest children were just as amused by their new surroundings and cultural practices. Their aunt, Wendelle, recalled that Mai, Alexi, and Marshall were particularly curious about women wearing pantyhose, a practice that was not prevalent in the tropical climate of Southeast Asia. The young children enjoyed running up to strange women and pulling their legs: "If it looked like it was a stocking they would die laughing."[11] The children's amusement may have stemmed from the fact that stockings, which give the appearance of skin and skin color, could be removed and changed at will. Wearing them was a flexible practice at odds with the color of "real" skin.

Hoa, then entering her teenage years, had a much more self-conscious transition to American society than her younger siblings. The Browne family eventually settled in Teaneck, New Jersey, to accommodate Bob's professional interests. Similar to the family's experiences in Chicago, Hoa recalled that they were the only Vietnamese people she knew. In New Jersey, they lived in a "mixed" community with white Jewish and black neighbors. None of them had even heard of Vietnam. As Bob recalled, when he explained that he had just returned from Vietnam, people would ask if it was located in East or West Africa. Hoa discovered that the children in the neighborhood were generally friendly but that they also laughed and made fun of her accent. Hoa may have stood out more than her younger siblings, not only because of language but also because of phenotype. Her siblings were multiracial and might have blended in better in their mixed neighborhood. Being young, though, Hoa eventually adapted to her surroundings.

In contrast, her mother had great difficulty, especially with learning English. Wendelle recalled that Bob tried "hard . . . to get [Huoi] into classes where she would at least get a knowledge of English," but Huoi played "hooky all the time. She'd sign up, never show up. Never wanted to learn English or anything that she knew would get her out of what was familiar."[12] Huoi's resistance to learning English stemmed from complex reasons. First, Huoi grew up with limited exposure to formal education and may have found the experience of learning a foreign language in a classroom rather daunting. Second, according to Wendelle, Huoi "had not wanted to leave" Asia. Although the decision was made for the benefit of their family, Huoi "was nervous and tense" about leaving behind her extended family and familiar surroundings. She had a very different temperament from Bob, who had a passion for exploring new worlds and meeting new people. Also, Huoi knew how to navigate Cambodian and Vietnamese societies. Unlike Bob, she spoke both Cambodian and Vietnamese. In Cambodia, she worked a variety of jobs and also had the support of her family and friends. In Vietnam, she and Bob employed servants to help take care of the kids and household.

In the United States, Huoi initially learned how to be a daughter-in-law in Chicago and then became the primary caregiver in a house filled with strange appliances and surrounded by a bewildering world. Bob recalled that in this initial period

> the most mundane aspects of American living were often perceived by my wife as sheer magic. This was especially true of the laundry equipment and the dishwasher, conveniences which we had not needed in Vietnam because it had been better for the local economy, as well as cheaper for me, to hire local manpower to assist us with the household chores. Television was new for my wife, and the scale of almost everything—of the city, of the traffic, of the markets and the shopping malls, of the office towers, of the bewildering choice of products of all sorts—was initially overwhelming.[13]

Even the home and family became sites of cultural battlegrounds. While in Chicago, Bob played mediator between his wife and his mother. Both women were well meaning but nevertheless encountered cultural and linguistic obstacles. Bob recalled:

> My homecoming had an almost fictional quality about it, dripping with drama. Each of the three adult players were under terrible strain and torn by emotion. There was my poor mother, anxiously waiting to meet her daughter-in-law and grandchildren and so very eager to please everyone. There was her prodigal son, returning home after a prolonged absence and presenting her with an instant daughter-in-law and four children, with none of whom she could have normal verbal communication. And finally, there was my wife. For her, the situation was probably the most bewildering, for she was being thrust into both a new family hierarchy and a new and strange culture. . . . The circus-like atmosphere which prevailed was highlighted at our first meal. I had taken pains to alert my mother that rice was our dietary staple, which certainly presented no problem to her inasmuch as she was herself a South Carolinian. . . . My mother proudly placed a bowl of rice in the center of the table and went back to the kitchen to

fetch a platter of meat. She returned just in time to see my wife daintily lifting the bowl of rice and placing it in the center of her plate, assuming it to be *her* portion. The look of horror which swept across my mother's face was unforgettable. . . . There were, of course, many other "moments of adaptation," some of them becoming quite loud, owing to the lamentable human tendency to respond to another's lack of comprehension by serially repeating oneself in ever rising decibels on the mistaken assumption that the listener has a *hearing* problem.[14]

To expedite Huoi's linguistic adaptation, Bob, who knew little Vietnamese, decided to stop speaking French at home. Although Huoi's French was limited, it was a language that she had in common with her husband. The strategy did not work as he had hoped. Huoi eventually developed a partial ability to communicate in English. With the exception of Hoa, none of her immediate family, including her three younger children, could speak to her in Vietnamese, the language in which she felt most comfortable expressing herself.

The cultural isolation that Huoi experienced parallels the experiences of other Asian women married to Americans. During the period between World War II and 1965, thousands of so-called military war brides arrived in the United States from Asia. They had met and married U.S. military personnel stationed in China, Japan, Korea, the Philippines, and eventually Vietnam. These Asian women even had their own immigration category as Congress passed legislation to exempt them, initially from the racially exclusive immigration laws and eventually from the discriminatory quotas in place against other Asian migrants. Most of these women crossed not only national boundaries but also racial and cultural ones as well. Like Huoi, they arrived in the United States and learned to adapt to their husbands' language, culture, and families. Because of the enormous strain involved, many of these relationships did not last.[15] Huoi and Bob eventually found a way to navigate these challenges. They held season tickets to the "Metropolitan and never miss[ed] a performance."[16] Their shared love of opera stemmed partly from a cultural and linguistic disconnect between them. As Bob explained, "It's the only form of entertainment we have where my wife isn't handicapped by the language. Neither one of us understand Italian."[17]

To adapt to the United States, Huoi embraced conventional gender norms and established her sphere of influence firmly in the home and neighborhood. Wendelle recalled that Huoi was "most secure in her home environment."[18] Perhaps it was because Huoi was a "very talented" cook. Seemingly unfamiliar with Western foods like bread and milk, she nevertheless quickly "learned to make American and Western dishes superbly." In fact, she became "better than anybody who lived" in the United States, in Wendelle's opinion. Even Bob's mother, "who could cook like a dream, said, 'I showed Huoi how to make hard rolls once, or how to make something once and the first time she was perfect."[19] Perhaps due to language differences, Bob's family underestimated Huoi's cultural exposure to Western foods. After all, she had worked as a chef in a French household in Cambodia. Also, over the eighty-some years of colonial rule, French food left an imprint on Southeast Asian cuisine. Even so, Huoi had not only a talent for cooking but also a wonderful memory. Perhaps due to her limited formal education, she never wrote down the recipes that she was learning. Yet she could reproduce the dishes perfectly. They "would look real pretty and she knew her own dishes too."[20] Despite his demands for linguistic assimilation, Bob appreciated Huoi's culinary diversity. He regularly escorted his wife, who never learned how to drive, to New York's Chinatown so she could purchase rice and other familiar foods. Huoi also became an avid gardener, seamstress, and embroiderer. These projects allowed her to use her creativity to care for her family and house. Huoi's abilities also alleviated some of her dependence on the outside world, since she could grow her own food and make her own clothes. She also found ways, despite her limited English, to connect with both Bob's family and friends in Chicago and their new neighbors in Teaneck. She learned new skills from these individuals and in turn shared the fruits of her labor with them.

While Huoi established herself in the private realm of family and home, Bob embarked on a quest in the public realm of work and politics. Having worked abroad in Southeast Asia for the previous six years in locations considered "hardship posts," Browne had accumulated substantial savings that allowed him the luxury of time to search for a position in keeping with his aspirations. After a summer-long visit with his mother in Chicago, he decided to return to the New York area because of his continued interest in international affairs. With his savings, he purchased the house in Teaneck. The establishment of a nuclear household might have helped Huoi by giving her a greater sense of security and authority.

Although Bob resigned from his post with ICA in Vietnam, he discovered that the agency continued to cast a shadow on his employment prospects. Despite his eagerness to acclimate his family to the United States, Browne's qualifications made him an attractive candidate for development positions abroad, this time in Africa. He pursued these opportunities, one with the Africa-American Institute (described by Bob as a "semi-government organization") and the other with the United Nations. These jobs required security clearances though, and Browne's application was repeatedly delayed. He suspected the ICA and its successor, the Agency for International Development, of blocking his opportunities. Browne wrote a series of letters to the State Department, the attorney general, and even to his senator, protesting this treatment:

> A year ago I was a solvent, well-qualified, multi-lingual person, eager to put my talents to good use and optimistic about my future. . . . During the past year, however, I have been the victim of such inconsiderate treatment on the part of the government that I can hardly believe that it is happening—and although it may well be unintentional and unpremeditated, this possibility serves rather to intensify than to assuage my rage, and in no way ameliorates the desperate economic straits to which I have been reduced. The operation (or lack thereof) of this loyalty board has cost me two jobs—the product of more than a year's searching.[21]

Browne suspected that the delay in the security clearance had to do with his public participation in political issues. As he detailed to the attorney general:

> In all honesty I can imagine no grounds for my being even suspected of any disloyalty unless it is for my outspoken criticisms, on the radio and in the New York *Times*, of certain administration policies in Southeast Asia . . . or for my activities on behalf of freedom riders and sit in movements. . . . If such activities lead to charges of disloyalty, then I want to be confronted with the charges so that they can be fought. I cannot, however, acquiesce in this niggling technique of "inaction" as a means to thwart my obtaining work in my professional field.[22]

Browne did not raise the suggestion that his marriage to a Vietnamese woman without receiving proper bureaucratic approval might have been a factor in delaying his security clearance. Despite his passionate pleas, he received no satisfactory response.

Unable to go abroad himself, Browne settled instead for working for the Phelps Stokes Fund, an agency based in New York City that sought to promote the involvement of African Americans in foreign service. As part of his responsibilities, he spoke regularly at historically black colleges and universities, many of them in the South, to recruit students for international careers.[23] Browne also decided to pursue his intellectual ambitions by enrolling in a PhD program in economics at the City University of New York. With his developing academic credentials and with previous experience teaching economics at Dillard University, he secured an assistant professorship at Fairleigh Dickinson University, located close to his home in New Jersey. Most of his energies from 1962 to 1968 were, in his words, "devoted . . . not to study, not to earning a living or teaching, but to the anti-war movement."[24]

Browne clearly aspired to be an active citizen, someone who participated regularly in political affairs by contributing to public debates. Even before he departed from Saigon, he had authored a booklet that was eventually published just as he arrived back in the States under the title of *Race Relations in International Affairs* (1961). In this work, he emphasizes the importance of understanding the underlying racial, as opposed to the overtly Cold War, dynamics of the post–World War II era. He characterized the anticolonial movements as the effort of "the colored peoples' wrenching of control over the world from the hands of the white man."[25] By drawing attention to these efforts for national liberation within the Third World, Browne highlighted the need to recognize and address racial aspirations and divisions. It is a theme that he would echo in his critiques of U.S. foreign policy in Southeast Asia.

Because Browne's booklet sold sparsely, he found other avenues to air his views. Soon after his return to the United States, he wrote a series of letters to the editor of the *New York Times* and to various politicians. His critiques of U.S. foreign policy in Southeast Asia centered on two main themes. First, he argued that America's "single-minded" tendency to view international politics through the lens of the Cold War led diplomats to misunderstand developments in Third World countries and to overlook valuable opportunities to gain the trust of these potential allies. In fact, U.S. policies actually resulted in cultivating anti-American and procommunist sentiment. In both Cambodia and Vietnam in the mid-1950s through the early 1960s, Browne believed that there were windows of opportunity for fostering pro-American opinion. However, U.S. "State Department single-mindedness led us into the same old 'you got to be for us or agin us' posture."[26] In Cambodia, this encouraged Prince/Prime Minister Sihanouk to pursue foreign aid funds from the Eastern bloc to deter U.S. influence on his country. In Vietnam, the United States staunchly supported the anticommunist but totalitarian and corrupt President Diem.[27] As a result, "the Vietnamese masses have made clear their indifference to an American victory by their ever-increasing support of the Viet Cong. The Vietnamese leadership, however, identifies its interest with American policy rather than with the wishes of the mass of Vietnamese people, who want peace—even if it means communism. . . . Paradoxically, our costly efforts to maintain a pro-western beachhead in Indo-China have had exactly the reverse of the desired effect."[28] .

Browne never strongly endorsed the North Vietnamese, the Vietcong, nor communism. Even so, he recognized the appeal that these forces had for the South Vietnamese populace, because they represented a nationalist alternative to U.S. interference. He recalled, "my tenure in Vietnam, government officials commonly refer[red] to the war as 'your war' (meaning the Americans' war)."[29] It is significant that this sentiment was expressed during the late 1950s and early 1960s, under the Eisenhower presidency and before presidents Kennedy and Johnson escalated financial and military commitment to Southeast Asia. In addition, the comment was made by a South, not North, Vietnamese government official, that is, from an ally, not a Cold War enemy.

Browne's second critique of U.S. conduct in Southeast Asia focused on race, a theme that he also developed in *Race Relations in International Affairs*. He argued that the ingrained American mentality of "white superiority" prevented politicians and mainstream Americans from recognizing the desire for self-determination among Third World people. As he subsequently pointed out in letters to the *New York Times*, the "white press" contributed to this racial arrogance by its "apparent inability . . . to resist detracting from the stature of any colored statesman by publicizing, with a subtle distastefulness, any unconventional trait which he may have in western eyes, whether it be of diet or religion, of fashion, of family, or other aspect. . . . It is one other example of our self-defeating prejudice, a luxury which America clings to at an excruciating price."[30]

In contrast to white America's inability to recognize the humanity and dignity of nonwhite individuals, Brown emphasized the racial bond between people of Asian and African ancestry. In another letter to the *New York Times*, he shared his sense of "racial brotherliness" which he experienced in his travels in Asia and Africa: "I have encountered a similar sentiment of kinship from non-white peoples in all portions of the world where colored people predominate. In Asia the basis seems to be more of a feeling of shared oppression at the hands of the whites whereas in Africa this sentiment is augmented by a feeling of common ancestry, but in both cases the bond's existence is undeniable."[31]

Browne began as an early and almost lone voice, but his consistent efforts to contribute to public discourse soon involved him in a broader network of political activists and organizations. His earliest and some of his most significant connections were made with predominantly white pacifist groups, such as SANE (the Committee for a Sane Nuclear Policy), Women Strike for Peace (WSP), Fellowship of Reconciliation (FOR), American Friends Services Committee (AFSC), and the Women's International League for Peace and Freedom (WILPF). These organizations tended to draw membership from the middle class and the middle aged. Cora Weiss, for example, was a key organizer within WSP. Some of the organizations, most notably FOR, AFSC, and WILPF, had developed their pacifist missions in the context of World War I and tended to have an elderly constituency. Others, like SANE and WSP, were created in the midst of the Cold War to promote dialogue and cooperation rather than escalation and annihilation; these groups attracted a younger but still relatively mature membership. While by no means richly endowed, these relatively established groups possessed institutional and economic resources to facilitate political mobilization. They monitored U.S.–Southeast Asian relations during the early part of the 1960s. They held public forums and congressional hearings. They also sponsored petitions among community members, religious leaders, and intellectuals. In addition, the groups published ads in the *New York Times* and the *Washington Post* to promote public understanding about U.S. policy and to advocate peaceful measures to diffuse the escalating tensions in Southeast Asia.

They recruited Browne to be part of their efforts, which intensified during the summer of 1964. In August of that year, an alleged attack by the North Vietnamese on a U.S. ship in the Gulf of Tonkin provided justification for President Lyndon Johnson to receive congressional approval to retaliate against enemy fire. Through Browne's connections with SANE, he was invited as one of three academics to present a petition bearing five thousand signatures to the 1964 Democratic National Convention in Atlantic City, New Jersey. Taking place just a few weeks after the Gulf of Tonkin Resolution, Browne argued the necessity of a nonmilitary solution to the political developments in Southeast Asia.

The 1964 Democratic National Convention has received historical attention because of the efforts of Fannie Lou Hamer and the Mississippi Freedom Democratic Party to unseat the all-white delegates of the regular segregated Democratic Party in the South. The presence of Hamer and the MFDP in Atlantic City represented the culmination of a summer-long and arguably lifelong campaign to challenge racial terrorism in Mississippi and throughout the South. Like Hamer's demands for justice, Browne's appeals similarly fell upon deaf ears.

Even as Browne tapped into existing organizations, he also helped to create new political partnerships. Given his academic credentials, he was well situated to play a leadership role among intellectuals and students. He helped inaugurate the teach-in movement on American college campuses in the spring of 1965 as President Johnson ordered the implementation of Rolling Thunder, a massive bombing campaign against North Vietnam. In fact, Browne often served as the lead-off speaker and shared the stage with prominent antiwar activists such as Professor Staughton Lynd and Doctor Benjamin Spock, as well as Students for a Democratic Society leaders Tom Hayden and Carl Oglesby. He traveled around the nation, giving talks at places like Michigan, Columbia, Berkeley, and other schools, including his alma maters, the University of Chicago and the University of Illinois, Urbana-Champaign. To sustain and develop the teach-in movement, Browne helped to create and promote the Inter-University Committee for Debate on Foreign Policy. The committee, which consisted mostly of faculty but also included graduate students, was dedicated to promoting public dialogue about political issues.

A second significant political network that Browne fostered was among African American students, intellectuals, community members, and political leaders. By the mid-1960s, black leaders like Martin Luther King Jr. and other civil rights activists had become widely regarded as the moral conscience of American society among their supporters. Consequently, the federal government and various mainstream political leaders exerted enormous pressures on black leaders not to speak out about foreign affairs.[32] As a counterbalance, white pacifist religious leaders, who also tended to support the civil rights movement, attempted to enlist the public support of King for the cause of peace. One of his closest African American advisers, Bayard Rustin, was a pacifist and a member of FOR. However, King would not make his famous condemnation of the Vietnam War at New York City's Riverside Church until April 1967.[33] Even SNCC, which tended to eschew establishment politics, did not criticize the war until the beginning of 1966. In contrast, Browne was an early and prominent critic of U.S. foreign policy.

Browne's credentials as an African American peace activist made him a highly desired spokesperson within both white and black political circles.

Because white antiwar leaders and organizers were conscious of the relative absence of blackness within their movement, they were invested in featuring African Americans. For example, Alfred Hassler, the executive secretary of FOR from 1960 to 1974, organized a 1965 delegation of clergy to South Vietnam to learn about the war. In recruiting participants for this tour, Hassler expressed his desire to include prominent black leaders: "Our first choice . . . would be Martin Luther King, Jr"; if he was unable to accept, "we want at least one Negro participant."[34] King did not attend, but African American civil rights leader James Lawson, who was a member of both FOR and its offshoot Congress of Racial Equality, apparently filled the "black" slot. In addition, Bob Browne was asked to serve as a consultant for this delegation, which traveled to South Vietnam just as the United States introduced ground troops there.

Given this propensity toward including black representation, which bordered on tokenism, Browne's relationships with white pacifists were not always smooth. FOR had a policy of noncooperation with communists that originated during World War II. Browne was not necessarily a supporter of communism. However, to facilitate the conclusion of the U.S. war, he was interested in establishing dialogue with the National Liberation Front (NLF) of South Vietnam, with the North Vietnamese if it could be done outside of North Vietnam, and with Third World independence movements more broadly. While Hassler wanted to send Browne to Saigon well before the arrival of the clergy delegation to establish political contacts, Browne insisted on traveling to Algiers to attend an Asian-African conference that was envisioned as a follow-up to Bandung. Although the meeting was eventually postponed due to the political instability following the Algerian Revolution, Browne also wanted to open lines of communication with the NLF and the North Vietnamese, both of whom had bases in North Africa.[35] Browne's "blackness" was a political asset to Hassler given the reluctance of mainstream civil rights leaders to support the peace movement. Yet Browne's political investment in Third World liberation in some ways marked him as "too black" for the FOR.

Among African Americans, Browne's racial identity and his political commitment toward Vietnam made him a desirable resource. Courted by African American antiwar activists, Browne published essays, gave talks, and even filmed a three-part television show, sponsored by WCBS-TV and Columbia University, that provided a black perspective on the Vietnam War and U.S. foreign policy more broadly. In an influential 1965 essay, "The Freedom Movement and the War in Vietnam," Browne again emphasized the connections between African Americans and Vietnamese people. He recalled that during his years in Vietnam, "Although I could never escape the obvious truth that I was a foreigner, the fact that I was a non-white, Vietnamese-speaking member of a Vietnamese family, frequently made me privy to conversations intended only for Vietnamese ears."[36] Following this statement, Browne indicated in brackets the comment, "Negro readers will readily understand what I mean."[37] Leaving aside his inflated claim to language fluency as well as his membership in a Vietnamese family, Browne's commentary suggests that African Americans, who had a history of experiencing marginalization and exploitation in the United States, would have an intuitive understanding of the connection with other "oppressed" and colonized groups. In fact, Browne recounts that during his 1965 trip to South Vietnam, "[when I first met] the venerable Tri Quang, leader of the Vietnamese Buddhists, I was momentarily thunderstruck at his appearance for, with his hair clipped short in the traditional style of the Buddhist monk, he looked exactly like any Negro whom one might meet on 125th Street in Harlem."[38]

The sense of commonality between African Americans and Vietnamese people led Browne to question why blacks were fighting in the U.S. war in Vietnam. African Americans tended to serve in the U.S. military in disproportionately high numbers throughout the Cold War. As historian Michael Cullen Green points out, participation in the military provided access to material benefits as well as symbolic recognition. These attractions were particularly compelling for African Americans who experienced economic, social, and educational disadvantages stateside.[39] In addition, as historian James E. Westheider argues, African Americans were drafted in disproportionate numbers because of their lack of representation on draft boards, minimal political power, and limited access to educational deferments.[40] Browne articulated critiques of the high representation of African Americans in the military and among those who suffered injuries from war. He kept track of this information by writing to American military and political leaders to acquire the data. He also publicized these findings by writing to mainstream as well as African American periodicals and journals about his racial concerns over the war. In addition, he gave public talks about this topic. In a speech titled "The Black Man and the War in Vietnam," given at the Black Anti-Draft Conference in New York City in January 1967, Browne stated,

> The tragic result today, so well known to us all, is that Black men comprise some 18 to 25% of the troops in Vietnam and some 20 to 29% of the

casualties—a figure which should be compared not merely with our 11 or 12% official proportion of the U.S. population, but more significantly, with our actual economic and political stake in this country: less than 2% of the representation in the Congress . . . ; exactly 1% of the representation in the Senate; and not more than 1/20 of 1% of the nation's purchasing power.[41]

Because of Browne's concerns about African American troops in Vietnam, he welcomed the opportunity to converse with black members of the military during his 1967 return trip to South Vietnam. His primary purpose for this journey was to observe the first presidential elections held since Diem came to power. The elections did little to change the political status quo though, since the United States supported the existing leadership's efforts to eliminate most of their opposition through questionable means.[42] By then, the U.S. military had reached its peak of half a million soldiers stationed in Vietnam.

An unidentified officer gave one of the most famous quotes about the war when he explained an American military attack on a Vietnamese village by saying, "It became necessary to destroy the town to save it."[43] The quote encapsulates the tragic irony of U.S. strategy in South Vietnam. To save the country from communism, American politicians and the military destroyed the land and its people. In total, U.S. pilots dropped more than three times the amount of bombs on Vietnam than all the bombs used during World War II. In fact, twice as many bombs rained down in the South, America's ally, than in the North, the designated enemy. The bombs were not just intended to destroy military targets, which included military sites or the manufacturing, transportation, and communication infrastructure. Despite U.S. government denials, eyewitness accounts by American travelers and international journalists indicate that residential areas, schools, hospitals, and dikes that could cause flooding and widespread famine were bombed repeatedly, either inadvertently through inaccuracy or consciously as targets. In addition, the U.S. military used cluster bombs, which did little to harm the physical environment but maximized human injury through the explosive dispersal of tiny bomb fragments that made extraction difficult.[44] Americans also deployed chemical warfare, utilizing Agent Orange and napalm, to defoliate Vietnamese forests and to burn down villages and harm their inhabitants. These biological weapons have had long-lasting effects on both the ecology of Vietnam and the people exposed to them. Seeking to contain the NLF and its supporters, the U.S. military and the South Vietnamese government designated certain villages and their surrounding countryside as "free fire zones." Any person living or working in these areas was considered a likely enemy. Residents were rounded up into "'strategic hamlets,' which the Vietnamese called concentration camps. These hamlets were surrounded by barbed wire and required passes for those leaving and entering."[45] As a result of these policies, an estimated four million people, approximately 25 percent of the South Vietnamese population, became refugees by the end of the war.[46] Those who did not evacuate from targeted areas and even those who did relocate, including the very young, the elderly, and women, were at times tortured, brutalized, and killed by American soldiers in search and destroy missions.

During Browne's 1967 visit, a U.S. security report was filed, alleging that he posted an inflammatory flier at the Tan Son Nhut Air Base.[47] The image offered a racial critique of the military. At the top, it declared: "Uncle Sam needs *you* nigger." The lower half featured the following commentary:

Become a member of the world's highest paid black mercenary army!
Fight for Freedom . . . (In Viet Nam)
Support White Power—travel to Viet Nam, you might get a medal.
Receive valuable training in the skills of killing off other oppressed people!
(Die Nigger Die—you can't die fast enough in the ghettos.)
So run to your nearest recruiting chamber![48]

It is not clear if Browne actually posted the flier. The security report also indicated that he "married his Vietnamese housemaid who was allegedly a Viet Cong (VC) or from a VC-connected family. Source advised Brown had an entry visa for North Vietnam, and had departed Saigon for Phnom Penh, Cambodia, en route to Hanoi." Neither of these latter allegations is substantiated. Huoi expressed little overt interest in politics, and Browne did not travel to Hanoi until after the U.S. war in Vietnam ended.

In 1966, Browne had carefully requested permission from the State Department to travel to the capital of North Vietnam. He explained this request by identifying himself as "a university teacher and an officer of an academic organization which encourages discussion, especially on university campuses, of foreign policy matters."[49] He did not hide his politics, which, he explained, "are quite critical of the Administration's policy." However, he offered to share his observations "with the White House" upon his return. He had participated in a similar debriefing when he traveled to Saigon in 1965. Although Browne did receive authorization from the State Department to travel to Hanoi, he also was warned that he would be "traveling at [his] own risk" and that "the Treasury Department prohibit [ed] all unlicensed transactions by Americans with North Viet-Nam or nationals thereof including payments for travel expenses, for accommodations, or for services."[50] In essence, the letter grudgingly gave Browne permission to travel to North Vietnam but warned that he could not legally pay for any transactions related to the trip. In the end, he did not make the journey.

Browne was certainly familiar with the content of the "Uncle Sam needs *YOU* nigger" poster as he retained a copy of it in the papers that he eventually donated to historical archives. Also, the sentiments expressed in the flier replicated his critiques of the war. As Browne stated in the speech given at the Black Anti-Draft Conference: "to me the racist character of this war is quite unmistakeable [*sic*]. . . . Firstly, in objective: I see the war as a preparation for all out war against the Chinese people, a war having the objective of restoring the white monopoly on nuclear weapons. . . . Secondly in technique: It is inconceivable to me that the U.S. would use, in Europe for example, the devilish weapons, gases and chemicals which it is using to deform and destroy the Vietnamese people. . . . Thirdly, in tactics," specifically the overrepresentation of African Americans in the military.[51] Consequently, he warned his audience, "We, dear Black brothers and sisters, are in the unhappy position of being caught right in the middle of this explosive juggernaut. The white man is using us as a major tool in his nefarious efforts to maintain and extend his control over these restless colored masses of humanity, and at the same time he is taking every step to insure that we are kept submerged and powerless here at home."[52]

Browne shared sentiments similar to those of historian Vincent Harding, who sent Browne a personal copy of his poem titled "To the Gallant Black Men Now Dead." In this work, Harding lamented the deaths of African American troops and questioned the reason for their sacrifice. He wrote:

> I weep for you.
> Hearing sounds of your death in the jungle
> performing great deeds of gallant savagery,
> I weep because. . . .
> we have been deceived
> again, black brothers,
> again.[53]

Browne's ability to play a significant role among white and black antiwar advocates was largely based on his access to a third political network, namely Vietnamese peace activists. His overall familiarity with Vietnam through his professional career, family ties, and political contacts served as crucial political assets. Collectively, they endowed him with authenticity and credibility.

The years that Browne spent living and working in Southeast Asia provided a valuable experiential base. Few Americans, particularly during the early part of the 1960s, had any firsthand contact with Vietnam or Vietnamese people. Browne's audience members might have had some misgivings or distrust of mainstream media representations and government sources. However, to hear from someone who actually lived in Vietnam and worked on behalf of the United States was quite compelling. As he recalled, "Between 1962 and 1964 I was virtually the only American in the country who knew Vietnam firsthand and who was prepared to talk honestly about what was happening there."[54] He could speak with authority about the detrimental impact of U.S. involvement in South Vietnam. In a 1963 talk in New York City for a forum titled Vietnam Aflame: What Are the Issues, Browne detailed how America's economic aid constituted "approximately $2 billion [since 1955]. This [came] to about $700,000 a day every day, including Saturdays and Sundays."[55] This vast amount of money did not create a more stable or democratic country. Instead, the wealth was horded by the existing elite, "Saigonese business men and high civil servants, including especially the President's family."[56] As Browne described, "no visitor to Saigon would ever suspect that he was in a country which was virtually bankrupt and living on the largesse of another. Rakish new French, German and British sports cars are everywhere in evidence. Fine restaurants and well provisioned shops abound, boasting imported wines, cheese, and perfumes . . . all thanks to America aid."[57] Browne reminded his audience, "Needless to say most of the Vietnamese are not so fortunate as to be riding around in foreign sports cars and motor boats. . . . It certainly seems to me that during my several years' residence in Indochina, the gap between the wealthy and the poor has actually widened rather than closed."[58] Such conditions generated dissatisfaction with the ruling elite and their American supporters. The disparity in wealth and repression of political reform fostered conditions for revolution.

When individuals who also claimed direct experience in Vietnam attacked American pacifist groups, these organizations turned to Browne to respond to criticism. In a 1964 letter to an American Air Force captain serving in Vietnam since 1961, Browne respectfully disagreed with the military officer's assessment of the nature of U.S. involvement in Southeast Asia. Browne ended his correspondence by expressing, "My heart goes out to our many U.S. servicemen serving in Vietnam, to their families and to the families of those who have died there. I only regret to say, however, that these men are dying for no good purpose—and indeed they die with the blood of immorality on their hands. That these trustworthy and enthusiastic young men should be so callously sacrificed and so cynically misled is beyond being a national tragedy. It is a national disgrace."[59]

It is particularly striking that Browne articulated this critique before the massive introduction of ground troops in 1965. Furthermore, he reminds the U.S. military officer that the tragedy is not just an American one: "Even more . . . does my heart bleed for the unnumbered thousands of Vietnamese who are being murdered and mutilated month after month, in part at least, because we insist that their country be a battleground for a struggle which we feel to be important. I suggest that it will be many years before America can wash the stains of this episode from our national face."[60]

Browne's ability to cite personal experiences of living and working in Vietnam, along with his skills as a public speaker, made him a powerful and persuasive antiwar orator. As one friend commented, "I was sitting in the next-to-last row at your Carnegie Hall appearance [in April 1965] lo these many years ago. You were very much the crowd pleaser of the night. The *charisma* came through like dynamite."[61]

In addition to emphasizing the years that he spent in Southeast Asia, Browne always publicly identified himself as marrying into a Vietnamese family. The selection of words is rather telling. First, Browne privileged the Vietnamese and maternal side of Huoi's ancestry. She could have been identified as Chinese due to her father's ethnicity or as Cambodian by virtue of being born and raised there or as a multiethnic or multinational person. No doubt, Bob's "ethnic choice" was made for strategic political purposes.[62] Second, Bob's often-repeated phrase contrasts with modern Western notions of marriage, which emphasize the union between two individuals and the husband's legal and cultural coverture of his wife's identity. Instead, Bob indicated that he became a member of Huoi's Vietnamese family. He could be referring to the fact that by marrying Huoi, he also assumed responsibility for a stepdaughter, Hoa. It is also possible that Bob was referring to his membership in an extended Asian kinship network. When they lived in Cambodia, Huoi relied upon her grandmother to help provide child care. Hoa recalled that her adopted father was very generous with her mother's relatives and attempted unsuccessfully to sponsor their migration to the United States.

While Bob announced his membership in a Vietnamese family as part of his political identity as an antiwar activist, Huoi herself was not engaged in these endeavors. She defined her primary responsibility as taking care of their children and household, especially since Bob traveled frequently for his political commitments. Some of his close political associates mention Huoi and their children in their correspondence, suggesting that she likely facilitated these relationships through acts of hospitality and personal friendship. She occasionally joined her husband in some functions connected with antiwar activities. There is no indication that she accepted the invitations of some women's peace groups who specifically requested her participation in their events and protests. Huoi probably declined some of these opportunities because of her limited English and more reclusive personality. In addition, she may not have appreciated being a token celebrity and a political symbol.[63] The publicity for one function, issued hastily, indicated that Robert Browne would be in attendance with "his Vietnamese wife."[64] Another organization asked that Huoi offer a few words of greeting in Vietnamese and also wear "a Vietnamese costume."[65] Initially misrecognized when she arrived in the United States, Huoi's Vietnamese identity became a political goldmine during the antiwar movement.

Just as Bob's years of living and working in Southeast Asia legitimated his views, his familial relationships also made him a more credible voice. A woman who served as the coordinator for the Martha's Vineyard Peace Center wrote to Browne in 1965, "Since you were there on our government-sanctioned business, stayed there for 6 years and married a Vietnamese girl will, I am sure make the people feel you are an authentic source of information."[66] In essence, Browne and his supporters publicly proclaimed his kinship connections to legitimate his critiques of American foreign policy.

This political use of kinship ties counters the dynamics that scholar Christina Klein identified in an earlier phase of the Cold War. Klein emphasizes how U.S. middlebrow culture sought to elicit sympathies from mainstream American audiences so that they might "save" Asian children from the evils of communism.[67] Instead, Browne suggests that true compassion should evoke the desire to save Asians from American political manipulation and militarism. In one of his speeches, he explicitly evokes the figure of a Vietnamese child in need of rescue. He begins with the statement: "I write of Indo-China more in sorrow than in anger—for rage cannot be sustained at a high intensity, but sorrow lingers long after the sun has set." Following his reflections about his early experiences in Southeast Asia and the subsequent destruction that Vietnam experienced as a result of American military intervention, Browne concludes this talk by asking:

> May I tell you about Thum? Thum is a little Vietnamese girl who came to live with us in New Jersey for a few weeks during 1968 and 1969. She had

been brought to the U.S. by a group of concerned Americans as part of a program to rebuild the bodies of Vietnamese children who had suffered serious physical mutilation by the war. Thum, who was 8 years old when we first saw [her], had lost her nose, her upper lip, and part of her chest in an attack which had also killed much of her family. It was hard to look at her at first, because she was so grotesque—and even after her face had been largely rebuilt at a New York City hospital, she still looked pretty frightening. My family, of course, grew fond of her after a while (she came to us between each series of skin graftings because she could speak only in Vietnamese and needed companionship) but whenever we took her out with us she inevitably aroused curiosity, sympathy, and repulsion. Perhaps some sense of guilt also. She was only one child; the program which brought her over reaches perhaps 20 children a year. But it is conservatively estimated that upwards of 200,000 children desperately need such treatment, and the number grows with each day the U.S. continues its war on these hapless people.[68]

In response to queries about why he focused his critiques on American-induced atrocities in Indochina and not on North Vietnamese acts of violence, Browne reflected: "The question always struck me as singularly curious inasmuch as my audiences were always comprised of Americans, not of North Vietnamese. It must be remembered that most peace activists were not seeking to score debating points but are engaged in a very serious business of attempting to convince their fellow Americans to stop killing off the Vietnamese people. We have neither access to nor responsibility for the crimes of other nations; only for our own."[69] Browne's depiction of Thum tended to emphasize her victimization, and his familial claims positioned him as a fatherly protector.

Browne also articulated the need for Americans to hear Vietnamese voices and to respect Vietnamese political agency. In a 1965 letter concerning a documentary on Vietnam produced by the Columbia Broadcasting Service, Browne wrote to the president of the company, John A. Schneider, "I applaud your effort. . . . I am, however, concerned lest your program, like most TV documentaries and discussion programs on this topic, fail to provide the public an honest presentation of the cogent reasons why our present policy is inadequate and the realistic alternatives open to us. As a member of a Vietnamese family myself I am also dismayed with the infrequency with which the Vietnamese people's views are included in the picture."[70]

Browne's primary efforts to help broadcast Vietnamese perspectives about the U.S. war in Southeast Asia revolved around his relationship with Nguyen Xuan Bao, who became better known as Thich Nhat Hanh. Bao was born in Hue, in the central part of Vietnam, in 1926, just two years later than Browne. Bao decided to become a Buddhist monk at a relatively young age. Even in Vietnam, he was open to ideas and influences beyond his native land. Initially educated under the French colonial system, he learned Western philosophy and religion as part of his Buddhist training. Bao eventually became part of a reform movement that promoted an "engaged" form of Buddhism, which adapted religious beliefs and practices to address contemporary worldly issues. During the First Indochina War, Bao supported the cause for national independence and became a public religious leader following the signing of the Geneva Peace Accords in 1954. Bao's reform efforts, which attracted a significant youth following, met with opposition from within the Buddhist religious establishment. When offered a fellowship from Princeton University, Bao came to the United States to study comparative religion and eventually became an instructor at Columbia University. In fact, Bao arrived in the United States in 1961, the same year that the Browne family left Saigon. Like Huoi, he falls outside of the established waves of Asian immigration. Bao was part of the Cold War migration of intellectuals, which has yet to receive substantial scholarly attention. He arrived before the 1965 Immigration Act, which opened America's gates to Asia. And he came to the United States before the entry of refugees from Southeast Asia in the mid- to late 1970s. In fact, Bao was the only representative of his faith from Vietnam in the United States when Thich Quang Duc (who previously resided at the same temple as Bao) deliberately set himself afire in Saigon on 11 June 1963 to protest the repression of Buddhism.[71]

The famous image of Thich Quang Duc's self-immolation sparked worldwide attention on South Vietnam. Duc's act followed an escalation of political conflict between Buddhists and the U.S.-backed and Catholic president of the Republic of Vietnam, Ngo Dinh Diem. Under his administration, Buddhism, which had the most pervasive religious influence on Vietnam, with an estimated following of 70–90 percent of the population, was officially designated an "interest group" rather than a state-recognized religion, like Catholicism. This bureaucratic differentiation had implications for a variety of political, civil, and economic rights for Buddhist sects and for their leaders, temples, and adherents.

Furthermore, Catholics tended to receive preferential treatment, so much so that non-Catholics were pressured to either convert or follow Catholic practices. Browne discovered this himself during his time in South Vietnam. He recalled one conversation with "a particularly dear South Vietnamese friend of mine, a Buddhist and bachelor." Because "he always demonstrated great interest in American customs, I thought to invite him to stop in late on Christmas eve to watch us decorate the tree." His friend's response surprised Browne:

> The scowl which swept across his face dripped with hatred.
> "I can't make it at that time," he muttered acridly. "I've got a command performance with Big Brother."
> "What do you mean?" I asked.
> "Mid-night mass," he grunted. "Every Christmas eve Diem holds midnight mass at the palace, didn't you know it?"
> "Yes, I do remember that there was a lot of ballyhoo about it last year. But you're a Buddhist. How does it affect you?"
> "I'm a Buddhist all right. But I'm also chief of my bureau. All bureau chiefs, department heads, commissioners—well, the top man in every major office of the government, is obliged to go to these masses. It doesn't matter whether he's Catholic, Protestant, Buddhist, or something else. Of course, most of the chiefs are Catholics and are proud to go. The rest of us go because we want to keep our jobs. This is the way Diem's democracy works."[72]

In contrast to the state mandate for Catholicism, Buddhism faced outright repression.[73] In 1963, tensions between Buddhists and the Diem government ignited. In May of that year, on the occasion of Vesak—the birthday of Buddha—a ban against the flying of Buddhist flags was enforced in Hue, a stronghold of Buddhist leadership. In contrast, Vatican flags were flown regularly at government-sponsored celebrations, including one held earlier that spring for the older brother of President Diem, Archbishop Ngo Dinh Thuc, the highest-ranking Catholic leader in Vietnam, who was also based in Hue. On Vesak, tensions between Buddhist supporters and the government escalated as protesters gathered in large numbers to demand equal recognition and rights for their religion. Blaming these public disturbances on the Vietcong, the military and police responded by opening fire, using bullets, grenades, and chemical weapons. Eight died following a demonstration on 8 May. The persistence of government repression, which included arrests and disappearances of Buddhist leaders, eventually led Thich Quang Duc and other Buddhist monks and nuns to conduct their very painful and very public acts of self-sacrifice.

As the only Vietnamese Buddhist monk in the United States, Bao felt a responsibility to educate the American audience about the events in his homeland. He was a reclusive and contemplative person, someone who was not inclined toward politics. Seeking advice about how to gain a public hearing in the United States, Bao sought out Browne because of his outspoken critique of American policies in Southeast Asia. In one letter, Browne describes the beginning of his relationship with Bao: "There is a Vietnamese Buddhist monk here in New York—the only one in America—and since the self-immolation of Quang Duc he has felt a great need to contribute to the Buddhist protest against the religious persecutions of President Diem. The local Vietnamese community here, to whom he is a sort of spiritual father, has been urging him to make some dramatic gesture of protest (short of cremation I hope!) and he has been coming to me for guidance."[74]

Over time, Browne and Bao became close political collaborators. Bao became a regular visitor at the Browne household and befriended Huoi as well as Bob. Using his contacts and communication skills, Bob found avenues for Bao to speak directly to the American people by arranging television and radio interviews. He also sought ways, not always successfully, to land Bao an audience with the Catholic President John F. Kennedy, his aides, and congressional representatives. Although Bao never met Kennedy, he had a brief audience with Defense Secretary Robert McNamara, who appeared rather disinterested. Even so, the Buddhist crisis of 1963 led the U.S. administration to withdraw support from Diem, eventually resulting in his assassination by military leaders seeking to take over the government. Not privy to these behind-the-scenes negotiations, Browne helped Bao and his associates to prepare an appeal to the United Nations to investigate human rights violations in South Vietnam. To sustain this transnational communication and political network between Buddhists in Vietnam and within the Vietnamese diaspora, Browne assisted in the creation of the Overseas Vietnamese Buddhist Association, which had branches in Europe and Asia as well as North America. Reflecting his political approach that sought to challenge American policy but within authorized constraints, Browne notified the Department of Justice of his work "on behalf of . . . foreigners" to ensure that his actions were legally defensible in the context of war.[75]

The summer of 1963 is perhaps best remembered for Martin Luther King's famous "I Have a Dream" speech, delivered on 28 August at the Lincoln Memorial. Browne boarded a bus from New Jersey to attend this historic event and was deeply moved by the experience. For Browne though, 1963 was even more profoundly associated with his involvement in supporting Bao and other Vietnamese Buddhists against Diem. As Browne expressed, "This has proved to be the summer of 'Vietnam' as well as of civil rights! I have been rather busy with the former."[76]

Following Diem's assassination in November 1963, Bao was summoned home to assist his Buddhist superiors to help rebuild their religious community. They had high hopes of genuine reform. Bao helped to establish Van Hanh Buddhist University in Saigon, and the School of Youth for Social Services. The school emphasized the philosophy of engaged Buddhism that Bao promoted. It did so by training monks, nuns, and laypeople to voluntarily enter peasant villages, the sites of military surveillance, conflict, and destruction, to assist these communities in educational, health, and economic projects. These support efforts were particularly difficult because Diem's successors, a string of military-backed leaders, persisted in waging war rather than seeking solutions for peace. They also continued the general policy of treating domestic opposition as an indicator of communist subversion. Browne maintained regular contact with Bao even as they lived on opposite sides of the world. One typical letter from Browne began, "Dear Bao, You are in my thoughts every day. . . . I so wish that I could be with you."[77] In fact, it was at Bao's request that Browne traveled to South Vietnam in 1965 and 1967.

The connections between Browne and Bao facilitated a transnational, cross-racial, and interfaith antiwar movement. The scholarship on the early 1960s tends to focus on either the black-white, Jewish-Christian coalitions of the civil rights era or the black separatist politics of groups like the Nation of Islam. Through his partnership with Bao, Browne expanded these political networks to include Vietnamese Buddhists based in North America, Southeast Asia, and France. As might be expected, the process of negotiating racial, national, and religious differences, which were also conceived in terms of gendered differences, was challenging as well as generative.

From Bao's perspective, the difficulties of organizing within South Vietnam made cultivating connections with peace advocates abroad absolutely essential. Bao sought to bring worldwide attention to the political and military developments in South Vietnam, hoping that this awareness would mobilize international public pressure on both the U.S. and South Vietnamese governments. Bao also hoped that communication with peace activists from abroad could help Buddhist leaders in South Vietnam advocate more effectively for peace. From Browne's perspective, the U.S. people and their government needed to hear Vietnamese voices to truly understand the human costs of their policies in Southeast Asia.

Bao, or Thich Nhat Hanh, was an ideal spokesperson for peace and in fact became the most recognizable Vietnamese voice in the West for this cause. As a religious leader dedicated to nonviolence, his outlook and goals were particularly attractive to Western Christian pacifists who were active in both the antiwar and civil rights movements. Browne facilitated the introduction between Hanh and the FOR during his 1965 summer trip to Vietnam. Founded in England in 1914 by Christian pacifists, the Fellowship of Reconciliation grew into an international organization that espoused interfaith cooperation. In fact, the FOR played a significant role in promoting Gandhian concepts of nonviolent resistance within the civil rights movement and had strong political connections to Martin Luther King Jr. As the United States engaged in war in Southeast Asia, FOR sought to use the moral authority of religious leaders both in the United States and internationally to condemn militarism and political repression. The organization cosponsored one of the earliest national protests against the U.S. war in Vietnam in December 1964 and initiated the formation of a Clergymen's Emergency Committee during the following spring.[78]

Establishing a political relationship with Hanh and promoting him as a spokesperson for peace fit in with FOR's practice of interfaith cooperation. In many ways, Hanh was groomed for Western recognition as a Vietnamese version of Gandhi. Both Asian male figures provided moral and spiritual guidance for Western audiences. The connections between FOR and Hanh were strengthened further when Browne arranged for the Vietnamese monk to visit the United States for a speaking engagement in 1966. The trip was a way to get Hanh out of the increasingly dangerous political environment of Saigon, when another round of Buddhist protest and persecution erupted that year. In contrast to 1963, the U.S. government firmly supported Prime Minister Nguyen Cao Ky. Buddhist leader Thich Tri Quang, whom Browne met the previous year, was placed under house arrest, and Hanh left South Vietnam for the United States. He had dared to publicly advocate for peace, a call regarded by the South Vietnamese government as pro-communist and hence treasonous.

Initially invited by Browne through the Inter-University Committee to speak at Cornell University, Hanh's travels eventually came under the sponsorship of FOR. FOR executive secretary Hassler and his assistants organized a speaking tour for Hanh, not only in the United States but also in Europe and Asia. They even made arrangements for Hanh to have an audience with Pope Paul VI. It was during this 1966 visit to the United States that Browne and FOR also made arrangements for Hanh to meet Martin

Luther King Jr.[79] Hanh had expressed interest the previous year in making contact with the famous civil rights leader, asking Browne to deliver an open letter to King about the war. Their eventual face-to-face meeting made a deep impression on King as he subsequently decided to nominate Hanh for the Nobel Peace Prize. In his 1967 nomination letter King stated, "I do not personally know of anyone more worthy of the Nobel Peace Prize than this gentle Buddhist monk from Vietnam. . . . Here is an apostle of peace and non-violence."[80]

Hanh was a particularly appealing figure among U.S. peace activists during this early phase of the war.[81] He not only represented a religious pacifist tradition but also advocated a "third way" or "third solution" for the conflicts in Southeast Asia. He clearly indicated that he was neither pro-Washington nor pro-Hanoi. He explained how his approach was different from that of the U.S. government. In order to stop the Vietcong, American military forces were killing the "Viet," the Vietnamese. The U.S. policy of "anti-commmunism mean[t] bombs, napalm, and wholesale destruction."[82] Instead, Hanh wanted to save the Viet and eliminate the "Cong" by deter-

Figure 3. Martin Luther King Jr., Thich Nhat Hanh, and Robert S. Browne. Personal collection of the Browne family.

ring the appeal of communism. The solution that Hanh advocated was nationalist self-determination. He believed that if the United States discontinued its support for the South Vietnamese government, as it did in 1963, the Vietnamese people would replace the existing leaders with those genuinely interested in seeking peace. The Vietcong, Hanh believed, achieved success only because the people of South Vietnam regarded the United States as an imperialist force and the existing political regime as a dictatorial force. However, if those who had the faith and support of the majority of the people could replace the government, the Vietcong would not be able to continue its fight. He explained repeatedly in his talks, "Communists want to save us from colonialism and under-development, and anti-Communists want to save us from communism. The problem is that we are not being saved, we are being destroyed. Now we want to be saved from salvation."[83] To achieve salvation for themselves, Hanh pointedly argued for political autonomy: "The non-Communist Vietnamese do not want to be the victims of negotiations between America and the Communists. They want to be represented in the negotiations themselves."[84]

In advocating for self-determination, Hanh occasionally had to negotiate with his white political partners with the assistance of Browne. Alfred Hassler increasingly assumed the role of a political "handler" for Thich Nhat Hanh. In presenting the Buddhist monk to American audiences, Hassler and the FOR balanced two conflicting goals. On the one hand, they sought to emphasize Hanh's authenticity as the voice of the suffering South Vietnamese masses. They did so by highlighting the cultural and religious importance of Buddhism as well as Hanh's close connections with Vietnamese peasants. On the other hand, Hassler had to reassure Western audiences that Hanh was not too Vietnamese, that is, too foreign and possibly incomprehensible or threatening to Americans.

In this balancing act between authenticity and accessibility, Hassler and the other white American FOR staff played a particularly crucial role in constructing Hanh's public identity and even crafting some of his political statements. In a letter to one such staff member, Hassler discusses his responsibilities in accompanying Hanh on speaking tours: "In the trip in Europe . . . my own activities included a considerable amount more of public comment on political issues involved in Vietnam, and in drafting statements to be used by Nhat Hanh. . . . Moreover, of course, the person who accompanies him is not infrequently put in the position of trying to interpret what Nhat Hanh has to say, sometimes in a preliminary meeting with government or other officers, sometimes on other occasions, and this creates a fairly sensitive situation."[85] Not only did Hassler speak for Hanh, he also guided his itinerary and therefore the range of his political contacts. Hassler cautioned:

> Very considerable astuteness and care are needed in dealing with Nhat Hanh, since we have here a man who both may be of some significance in the political configurations of southeast Asia, and one who is acutely vulnerable to a misstep. Examples of such possible missteps were the proposal we had from several sources that (1) he meet with representatives of the NLF in Paris, and (2) that he travel to some of the Communist countries in Europe during his trip. Such things cannot be seized on immediately because they are dramatic sounding but have to be evaluated very carefully in terms of what the total impact on Nhat Hanh and the Buddhist movement may be. In both these cases we concluded that the risk of damage was greater than any likely advantage would be and decided against them. Nhat Hanh himself is pretty wise on these things, but he can be influenced and we have to be extremely careful not to influence him in ways that are not carefully thought out beforehand.[86]

Even though Hassler and FOR publicly sought to promote Hanh as an autonomous alternative to both Hanoi and Saigon, these efforts to "influence" the Buddhist monk veered dangerously toward "control." Hassler's characterization of their relationship appeared to replicate the power that the U.S. government exerted over South Vietnam.

Hanh was not merely a pawn for Hassler and FOR. He asserted his ability to speak independently and directly to a Western audience. For example, Hassler worked closely with Hanh to author a book on Vietnam, Buddhism, and the war. Hassler read drafts of the manuscript, offered detailed advice about revisions, and negotiated with various presses for its release. Hill and Wang, the eventual publisher for *Vietnam: Lotus in a Sea of Fire*, sought to emphasize both the authenticity of Hanh's text and its accessibility. In a letter to Hanh, Hassler passed along the publisher's advice: "There must be some indication that the book had been written in Vietnamese and not in English. [The publisher's] first suggestion was that I [Hassler] be listed as translator."[87] Although Hassler indicated that he protested this description of himself, since it would imply that he knew Vietnamese, he agreed to a compromise that the book should be described as "translated by Alfred Hassler with the collaboration of the author."[88] This indication would legitimate the Vietnamese identity of the original author. In addition, the description also would bolster the credibility and accessibility of the ideas in the book by associating Hassler's cultural capital and in many ways his whiteness and Americanness with the work. Even though Hassler mentioned this detail as "one minor item," Hanh strongly but politely disagreed with this suggestion: "I think we should not put your name as translator. It is not true. I translated by myself, and you helped me with the English. I do not want friends and readers to have wrong impression that the F.O.R. is using my name to write a book."[89] In other words, Hanh desired assistance and collaboration but not political manipulation and control.

Hanh occasionally challenged Hassler and FOR more directly by utilizing other political resources, like Robert Browne. In a letter marked "personal-confidential" to Hanh, Hassler expressed concern that Browne and an associate of Hanh's, Tran Van Dinh, were drafting a public statement, a policy statement of the Buddhist Socialist Bloc in Vietnam, which indicated increasing Buddhist sympathies with the position of the NLF.[90] Hassler described in his letter that over the course of his conversation with Dinh, Hassler was able to persuade Dinh to change his opinion about this statement. However, Browne was on his way to visit Hanh in Paris, and Hassler did not want Browne to know that he was reporting this information to Hanh. Hanh responded to Hassler, saying Browne had "been a close friend of mine since 1963 when we . . . worked together to put an end to the dictatorship of Pres. Diem." Furthermore, the content of their political message came "from Paris" at Hanh's request. Hanh explained to Hassler, "[He] did not tell you about that before, because we had wanted to give you a . . . surprise."[91] Hanh's surprise for Hassler appeared to be the message that the Buddhist monk had a political will of his own and the ability to communicate these messages directly to an English-reading audience.

The racial, national, and political tensions among Hassler, Browne, and Hanh were reflected in the gender dynamics among the three men as well. All of them, in some ways, challenged traditional notions of masculinity. Hassler, a conscientious objector who rejected military service during World War II, stepped outside the accepted bounds of manhood and citizenship.[92] Browne, as an African American man, was never accorded the same opportunities and privileges as a white man. In addition, he consistently broadcast his membership in his wife's Vietnamese family. Finally, Hanh, as a slight man and a monk clothed in robes, reinforced the common perception of Asian men as deviating from the norms of white masculinity.[93] Although all three men challenged traditional concepts of manhood, they also varied in their gender personas largely as a result of their race and nationality.

Their differential gender presentations were crystallized during a highly successful "Town Hall" meeting sponsored by FOR in honor of Thich Nhat Hanh. The event, which was held on 9 June 1966 at New York University, was moderated by Hassler and featured an array of literary and religious figures who paid tribute to Hanh. All the people who spoke at the event were male, a phenomenon that reflected the gendered nature of the political and public realm. Although women were actively engaged in promoting peace and were symbolically evoked for political purposes, the overall movement still tended to be dominated by men in the mid-1960s.[94]

Despite the overwhelming masculine presence onstage at the Town Hall, Hanh, as the only Asian individual, was clearly linked to the oversized figures of a Vietnamese Madonna and Child, displayed prominently in a photograph above the podium. The Asian mother figure looked utterly hopeless and forlorn as she held a baby in her arms. Because the photograph had been enlarged, she appeared even bigger than the people onstage. In this context, Hanh performed the role of spokesperson for the mother and child, the victims of war who were themselves too helpless to speak on their own behalf. Even though Hanh as a man shared the masculine political sphere of public oratory, his attire, Asianness, and belief in nonviolence all combined to feminize him. He both embodied and served as the surrogate voice for the victimized women and children of Vietnam. Hanh's role was further reinforced by the circulation of an antiwar Christmas card during the winter of 1966 by the FOR. The card featured the same image of the Vietnamese Madonna and Child along with a poem and call for peace by Thich Nhat Hanh.

The stage also featured two other nonwhite individuals, both African Americans. Robert Browne, after reviewing the initial publicity for the program, offered to introduce Thich Nhat Hanh in order to highlight the role of the Inter-University Committee in bringing him to the United States.[95] In addition, Browne's presence onstage broadcasted his ties with the Buddhist monk, which began before Hassler and FOR. As the husband and father of a Vietnamese family, Browne also was connected to the image of the Asian woman and child. Unlike Hanh, Browne's relationship to these representatives of Vietnam was not based on racial, national, and gendered commonality but rather on heteronormativity. In other words, Browne's role as the political protector of his wife and children, and by extension of Vietnam, relied upon traditional conceptions of what it means to be a husband and a father.

Figure 4. A Vietnamese Madonna and Child. This image was displayed at the Town Hall meeting sponsored by the Fellowship of Reconciliation in honor of Thich Nhat Hanh on 9 June 1966 in New York City. It also circulated as a holiday card later that year and appeared on the cover of *Memo*, the newsletter for Women Strike for Peace, vol. 5, no. 4 (December 1966). Swarthmore College Peace Collection, Swarthmore, PA.

Browne's presence also was linked to that of Ishmael Reed. Reed, an African American writer, read a selection of Thich Nhat Hanh's poems as part of that evening's program. Reed was a member of the black writers' collective, Umbra. Key figures in this organization, including LeRoi Jones, also known as Amiri Baraka, would play an influential role in forming the Black Arts movement, which sought to develop a uniquely African American and African diasporic aesthetic.[96] The movement emerged alongside a black power movement that rejected integration as a goal and called for self-determination for African Americans. Like Browne, Reed helped to legitimate the antiwar movement through his blackness. Reed's presence was not associated with nonviolent civil rights leaders but rather gestured toward the black power movement, which emphasized the defiant reclamation of black manhood.[97] By reading Hanh's poetry, Reed symbolized the alliance between a black call for cultural nationalism and an Asian political and religious desire for self-determination. Along with Hanh, Browne and Reed visually symbolized an Afro-Asian antiwar alliance.

The black speakers, however, did not assume the same importance as the white male authorities on the program. Browne and Reed, perhaps as last-minute additions, were not listed in the brochure for the event and hence not officially commemorated. Instead, Hassler, along with Catholic priest Daniel Berrigan, Rabbi Abraham Heschel, poet Robert Lowell, playwright Arthur Miller, and John Oliver Nelson (the chairman of the executive committee of the FOR) constituted the recognizable political, religious, and literary figures in American society that authenticated Hanh's political message. Like Hassler, these individuals deviated from traditional understandings of manhood through their rejection of violence and, in the case of Berrigan, for his vow of celibacy. Even so, their collective whiteness and hence more normative masculinity in relation to Hanh, Browne, and Reed reinforced their status as cultural authorities.

The triangulation of Asian, black, and white gradations of masculinity reveal the subtle and complex dynamics underlying interfaith, multiracial, and international peace movements of the 1960s. The combined efforts of Thich Nhat Hanh, Robert Browne, and Alfred Hassler communicated an alternative message about war. Yet their relationship to one another also contained seeds of disagreement. Their alliances, which contributed to building an international community devoted to peace, nevertheless depended upon essentialized projections of racial, national, and gender difference.

An anecdote by Hassler provides insight into their combined efforts to build commonality despite conflicts. In June 1966, Thich Nhat Hanh and Alfred Hassler flew from the United States to Stockholm as part of a global speaking tour calling for an end to war in Vietnam. Hassler recounted that the flight to Scandinavia was rather unremarkable, except for the fact that they encountered a retired American physician with "great sympathy . . . and a penetrating voice. By the time morning came she had joined the FOR, but also involved about a third of the plane in the discussion with Nhat Hanh about the burning by the monks, of which she disapproved heartily and said so repeatedly. We had a minor public meeting at the Oslo airport, and people gathered around attracted by her voice, for a discussion with him."[98] The American woman who encountered Hassler and Thich Nhat Hanh on the plane could not comprehend why Buddhists in South Vietnam would burn themselves as an act of protest. Yet she was still willing to join FOR. Her perspectives and actions mirrored the efforts of Hassler and FOR. They tried to make Hanh and Vietnam more comprehensible to Western audiences, but they did so in part by emphasizing an essentialized Asian difference from Western norms. These imperfections and gaps in cross-cultural understanding help to explain not only why political cleavages developed but also the significance of individuals joining together in common purpose in spite of these divisions. Hassler, Browne, Hanh, the loud American physician, and others all came together as an affirmative act of faith, even as they recognized and acknowledged the inequalities and incongruity inherent in their efforts.

Unfortunately, the U.S. government rejected the proposal of a third solution by the Buddhists just as it rejected the NLF's advocacy for neutrality in the Cold War.[99] Hanh's public condemnation of the existing political leadership in South Vietnam and of the war there led to a life in exile. He decided not to stay in the United States because of the political implications of seeking refuge in the country that was mandating armed conflict in his home. Instead, he chose France as his base and continued to travel around the world, advocating for peace in Vietnam. Before he left the United States, though, Thich Nhat Hanh engaged in a dialogue, one of many, in which he was asked:

[INTERVIEWER]: In your heart of hearts, are you optimistic about the future of your country and your people?

NHAT HANH: I am not.

[INTERVIEWER]: Do you think the war is going to continue on its way until your country is literally a desert? Or . . .

NHAT HANH: I think that man has to hope, to have some hope in order to continue living.

[INTERVIEWER]: You haven't lost your hope, then?

NHAT HANH: No . . . I am still living, but it does not mean that I am optimistic. The majority of the Vietnamese people have no hope for peace through a military factory for either side. That means that only the United States can open the door for peace. That must be our hope.[100]

By the late 1960s, Browne had started to give up his hopes to end the war and shifted his political energies toward the black power movement. But he never stopped caring about the plight of Vietnam. In fact, Browne reconnected with Hanh in 1968, when Browne traveled to Paris as part of a delegation that included playwright Arthur Miller. This group, which had little political authority, attempted unsuccessfully to negotiate terms for peace with the NLF. Browne eventually left the antiwar movement out of frustration, because despite his tireless efforts, the conflict did not appear to have an end in sight. Instead, he redirected his political organizing skills and economic training to promote the emerging black power movement.

One of the turning points for Browne appeared to be the 1966 James Meredith March for Freedom in Mississippi. Martin Luther King Jr. had invited Browne to participate in this protest after the two had met through the occasion of Hanh's visit. The 1966 March for Freedom is best known for the introduction of the slogan "black power" by Stokely Carmichael and other SNCC organizers, who openly criticized the limitations of nonviolence as a strategy and integration as a goal. Instead, they advocated armed self-defense as well as black autonomy and control over their communities and their lives. Browne appeared to have some sympathies with these younger radicals, even as he tried to maintain his belief in pacifism. In a letter to Hassler on 30 June 1966, Browne explained:

> I have just returned from a couple of days of marching with the James Meredith Freedom March in Mississippi. It was an altogether disturbing experience in many ways. What concerns me most, however, is what I learned about myself and it is about that which I write you. . . . On last Thursday night, under the leadership of Dr. King, I was part of the group engaged in pitching a tent on the McNeil school yard in Canton, Mississippi. This tent was to become the local headquarters for the marchers on their stopover in Canton. At a given signal, a phalanx of state troopers fired tear and riot gas at us, the most recent in a series of provocations to which the marchers had been subjected. In that moment

of truth my impulses and reactions were not of the non-violent type which I feel is demanded of a pacifist. I realize with sorrow how unworthy I am to bear the label of pacifist at this time. For this reason, I refrained from volunteering for the Philadelphia, Miss. Confrontation on the folloint [*sic*] day, for it had been specifically requested that only those who could be sure of their commitment to non-violence should participate.[101]

Although Browne advocated for an end to U.S. violence in Vietnam, his personal encounter with the battlefields of the American South left his faith in pacifism and his personal capacity for nonviolent protest rather shaken. And, as the urban communities of Los Angeles, Detroit, and Newark, NJ, erupted in a series of racial riots, Browne discovered that he could play a leadership role in creating an economic and political agenda for black self-determination.

Browne's decision to commit himself more to the African American community at the expense of his antiwar activism also may have resulted from an aborted attempt to run for the Senate in 1966. Browne had not intended to campaign as a serious political candidate. The Democratic Council of New Jersey wanted to support a peace candidate for a Senate seat held by Republican Clifford P. Chase. The peace Democrats decided to nominate David Frost, a professor of biology at Rutgers University, for the party primary. The Democratic Council also asked Browne to run as an independent candidate in case Frost lost. Browne only committed to this plan on the condition that he would not run as a traditional candidate. He did not want to spend his time raising campaign funds or creating a political network to mobilize votes. Rather, he wanted to use the opportunity "to convert New Jersey in to a giant classroom and to lead a mammoth teach-in."[102] Before this plan could be put into effect, Browne felt pulled in different directions based on his antiwar politics and his racial affinities. Frost's nomination by the New Jersey Democratic Council came at the expense of an African American labor activist, Clarence Coggins. When Coggins lost the nomination, "he and about 30 follower[s] stormed out of the convention. . . . They shouted that the Council had killed the peace movement and lost the Negro vote."[103] The controversy shocked Browne. When publicly asked to run as a backup independent candidate, he "did not immediately accept the assignment. [Instead, he said,] 'I'd like your indulgence to postpone my acceptance speech for a few days until my thinking is a little clearer.' . . . He noted there were only three Negroes, including himself, left in the room after the Coggins Vanguard Democrats had left."[104] After some deliberation, Browne agreed to run for the Senate seat after Frost lost the primary to a pro-war Democrat. In the end, though, Browne decided to pull out of the elections. He publicly cited the lack of time and resources to truly pull off the "mammoth teach-in" through his campaign. Privately, he deplored the political factionalism within the anti-war movement.

Although Browne shifted his energies from Vietnam to black power, his commitment to both causes revealed a continuity in values. In the 1965 essay "The Freedom Movement and the War in Vietnam," written before his experience with the Meredith march or the Senate campaign, Browne argues that African American awareness of the importance of Vietnam could "introduce . . . a new and potentially revolutionary dimension into the civil rights movement. . . . Traditionally, the American Negro has been single-minded to a fault. . . . He has bestirred himself solely about problems directly involving his welfare *as a Negro.* Issues involving him only as a citizen."[105] This quote overstates the U.S. orientation of black politics. However, Browne goes on to argue that for the most part, African Americans of the Vietnam era felt a sense of kinship with

> wars of liberation. . . . American Negroes inescapably feel a pull toward this mass of colored people, even as they attempt simultaneously to win acceptance into American society, for they know that America will forever be a white society, and they are instinctively skeptical that their full acceptance into it can ever be achieved. Fearing that a move to Africa may demand too great an adjustment of them, but doubtful about achieving a satisfactory role in American society, Negroes are already groping toward some new cosmopolitan political arrangements which would relieve them of their dilemma.[106]

For Browne and others of the 1960s and 1970s, the struggles in Vietnam brought into relief the difficulties of self-determination and national liberation for Third World people not only in Asia but also in the United States.

Although Browne eventually chose to leave the antiwar movement and direct his political energies instead toward the black power movement, his activism was important. His advocacy for peace transformed him into a public figure. In addition, Browne illuminated the connections between the familial and the political as well as between people of diverse racial, national, and religious backgrounds. To do so, he and his political partners negotiated complex cultural assumptions regarding blackness, Asianness, whiteness, and manhood. In the end, Browne's efforts did not lead to a fundamental change in government policy. However, he helped to expand the range of political ideas in U.S. society and to shrink the emotional distance between Americans and Vietnamese people. Although Browne went on to make important contributions in other arenas, he believed, "there is no question that any success which I may have had in opening the public's eyes to our ill-advised policies in Vietnam constitutes the jewel in *my* crown, the activity of my life of which I am the most proud."[107]

American Studies scholar Daryl Maeda has provocatively argued that Asian American political and cultural activists during the late 1960s and 1970s, particularly Asian American men, performed black masculinity in order to formulate their own identities as racialized and resistant subjects.[108] The activism of Robert S. Browne and Thich Nhat Hanh during the early to mid-1960s poses an alternative way to understand multiracial political alliances and identity formation. First, Browne assumed and others projected onto him the responsibility of representing the experiences and desires of Vietnamese people to an American audience. In other words, his ties to Asia and Asian people provided political inspiration and legitimation for a global critique of American racism. While his own experiences as an African American predisposed Browne to understand white supremacy, both at home and abroad, Vietnam and its people served as a catalyst to launch his public political career. Most likely due to Browne's kinship ties as well as his advocacy to promote Vietnamese voices in Western civic debate, Tran Van Dinh, who worked as the American and Canadian affiliate for the Overseas Vietnamese Buddhist Association, said of Browne, "You are a Vietnamese as much as myself."[109]

Furthermore, as a member of a generation that was older than many of the activists of the mid- to late 1960s, Browne modeled a different type of masculinity than the image of the militant, lumpen proletariat epitomized by groups like the Black Panthers. Instead, his manhood and identity as an activist were based upon his status as an intellectual and social scientist as well as his roles as husband and father. While Browne's personal familial relationships appeared to replicate "traditional" gender patterns, he nevertheless performed a more humane version of paternal privilege and responsibility. He served as the political advocate for his "Vietnamese" wife, children, and by extension their symbolic kin in Southeast Asia.

Browne's political partner, Thich Nhat Hanh, also sheds new insight on Asian and Asian American activism. Hanh could best be characterized as a diasporic figure. He had political connections to the United States and consistently traveled to and from this country. Hahn was not making claims as a subject who had been excluded from political or cultural citizenship in the U.S. nation. Rather, he was advocating that Americans acknowledge and be accountable for their global dominance. Hahn represented a subject of U.S. empire who wanted autonomy from American militarization and neocolonialism.

Second, Hahn's pacifist politics are not in vogue with more recent efforts to recover Asian American radicalism. The early scholarship on the Asian American movement tended to posit a simplistic binary between good reformers inspired by the civil rights movement versus fractious radicals who turned toward Third World socialist ideologies.[110] More recent anthologies and scholars have highlighted significant individuals and groups who were influenced by revolutionary ideologies that originated both within the United States, such as the black power movement, and from the Third World, particularly socialist Asia.[111]

Thich Nhat Hanh partly fits in with this effort to reach beyond the U.S. nation. His identity as a diasporic subject and his engagement with the U.S. war in Vietnam shed light on how international developments inspired activism among people of Asian descent in the United States. In particular, his plea to stop the killing of Asian people and also his call for national self-determination resonated with the politics of the Asian American antiwar movement that would emerge in the late 1960s and early 1970s. Thich Nhat Hanh's political career also signals the importance of black freedom struggles for Asian American activism. His close collaborator, Robert Browne, and also Martin Luther King Jr. helped to launch Hanh as a significant public figure.

However, Thich Nhat Hanh's politics of peace, particularly his call for a third solution, challenges the identification that many Asian American radicals would eventually make with Ho Chi Minh, Mao Tse-tung, and socialist Asia more broadly. As an anticommunist, pro-nationalist, and nonviolent spokesperson, Hanh's outlook and goals were more attractive to Christian pacifists. His gender persona as a monk clothed in robes was a far cry from the gun-toting, leather-and-beret-wearing Black Panthers. Hanh's politics and embodiment modeled an alternative to the hypermasculinity associated with racial, nationalist, and internationalist defiance.

Together, Robert Browne and Thich Nhat Hanh crossed geographical, cultural, racial, and religious borders to communicate a message for peace, humanitarianism, and self-determination. As the African American father of a Vietnamese family and as a Buddhist monk, their Afro-Asian alliance utilized racial, national, and gendered differences to collaboratively make a call for peace.

Part II

Journeys for Liberation

Chapter 4

Anticitizens, Red Diaper Babies, and Model Minorities

As Bob Browne exited the antiwar movement for the black power movement, Black Panther Party (BPP) leader Eldridge Cleaver entered the global stage. A charismatic, flamboyant, and controversial figure, Cleaver co-led a delegation of American journalists and activists on a two-and-a-half-month tour of North Korea, North Vietnam, and Red China during the summer of 1970. He wrote about the journey in a poem titled "Gangster Cigarettes":

> I led the forbidden exploration
> To mysterious Asia Major
> By the U.S. Peoples
> Anti-Imperialist Delegation,
> A flock of peaceful geese
> Sowing seeds against the war,
> And resurrecting broken bridges
> Over broken faith between
> Wicked West and Inscrutable East.[1]

The "mysterious Asia Major" or socialist Asia was "forbidden" during the Cold War, because the U.S. government had prohibited travel to these countries to contain the spread of communism.[2] Even though Bob Browne received special permission to go to Hanoi, the warnings that accompanied this authorization help explain why he did not make the trip during the war. Even as Browne opposed U.S. policies, he was careful not to go too far beyond the pale.

The individuals who participated as members of the U.S. People's Anti-Imperialist Delegation were more radical critics of U.S. military and political policies.[3] The eleven-person delegation included representatives from a cross-section of American social movements, including the black liberation, antiwar, women's liberation, alternative media, and, significantly, Asian American movements. Appropriating President Eisenhower's concept of "people's diplomacy," they challenged the ability of the U.S. government to represent their interests.[4] Instead, they sought direct, people-to-people contact with socialist Asian societies.

The Anti-Imperialist Delegation both represented and departed from other journeys made by critics of the American war in Vietnam. In Mary Hershberger's study of these travels, she noted the regularity of these trips, which averaged approximately once a month by 1969.[5] Cora Weiss was the key antiwar activist responsible for organizing these journeys.[6] In large part due to her efforts, over two hundred Americans visited Hanoi during the war. The travelers included pacifist Dave Dellinger, Students for a Democratic Society (SDS) leader Tom Hayden, and actress Jane Fonda. Each delegation brought back eyewitness accounts of the widespread destruction wrought upon North Vietnam.[7] Their firsthand reports helped to generate skepticism of governmental and mainstream media accounts of the war. Their findings also fostered greater humanitarian compassion for the victims of U.S. military and technological might. In addition, the delegations made efforts to contact American POWs, to facilitate communication between these prisoners and their families, and to encourage North Vietnam to release them.

While the Anti-Imperialist Delegation also espoused opposition to the American war in Vietnam, the itinerary, political ideology, and composition of the group set them apart from previous travelers to Hanoi. They initially only intended to visit the Democratic People's Republic of Korea (DPRK), a country that was relatively unknown even within activist circles. At the time, Vietnam constituted the most visible hot spot of U.S. military engagement and stalemate. By 1970, the antiwar movement had gained both numbers and visibility through a series of local, regional, and national protests. The surprise attacks launched by the Vietcong against the South

Vietnamese and American forces during the 1968 Tet or lunar New Year was a major turning point. The Tet Offensive raised serious doubts among mainstream politicians, pundits, and the general public about whether the United States could successfully and quickly end the war, as Democratic President Lyndon B. Johnson and top military leaders claimed. Within a year of Republican President Nixon entering the White House, opinion polls indicated for the first time that a majority of the U.S. public favored withdrawal.[8] This position was in line with the goals articulated by the antiwar movement as well as Nixon's "Vietnamization" policy of shifting the fighting burden to South Vietnamese forces. Even though many American disapproved of the antiwar movement, they did not want U.S. forces to stay in Vietnam. Americans also were well aware of the People's Republic of China (PRC). The country was poised to become a political superpower with its vast population, geographical size, socialist ideology, and nuclear weaponry.

In contrast, despite the publicity generated by the capture of a U.S. spy ship, the USS *Pueblo*, by the North Koreans in January 1968, there was relatively little awareness about Korea.[9] Consequently, the members of the delegation sought to bring attention to the parallels between American policies toward Northeast Asia and Southeast Asia. The United States played a central role in dividing both Korea and Vietnam following the collapse of the Japanese and French empires in the aftermath of World War II. American diplomatic, economic, and military interventions also maintained these geopolitical boundaries in the context of the Cold War.

The destination of the Anti-Imperialist Delegation highlighted the motivation of the travelers. By consciously designating themselves anti-imperialists, the members separated themselves from pacifist activists. As one delegate, Alex Hing, explained, "If you have an anti-war movement, that might mean you would be against all wars, against the liberation wars of the people of the world, against all just wars. But if we take an anti-imperialist stand, then we clearly support the liberation struggles of the people of the world. In fact, we want the Vietnamese to win against U.S. imperialism, and we are against unjust wars of aggression."[10] In other words, the Anti-Imperialist Delegation was not, as Eldridge Cleaver claims, "a flock of peaceful geese." They were not the "loyal opposition," a term used by author James W. Clinton. A former career U.S. Air Force officer who supported the U.S. war in Southeast Asia, Clinton chose to interview antiwar activists who visited North Vietnam. Although he had previously regarded these individuals as treasonous, he concluded that they "are not, and were never, disloyal Americans but rather citizens who saw the war in different terms."[11] The motives of the Anti-Imperialist Delegation also differed from Mary Hershberger's analysis that for travelers to Hanoi "their domestic goal was reform, not revolution."[12] Rather, members of the Anti-Imperialist Delegation tended to view the U.S. government as fundamentally oppressive and supported the creation of alternative political, economic, and social systems. In essence, they constituted revolutionary travelers. They wanted to gain insight into a new socialist country. Their presence in the DPRK led to invitations to visit the Democratic Republic of Vietnam (DRV) and the PRC. In all three countries, the delegation learned about socialist Asia under hot and cold war conditions.

Finally, the Anti-Imperialist Delegation differed from previous groups due to its composition. Hershberger argues that "almost all of the travelers" to Hanoi "were white," because "black civil rights figures faced a dilemma that their white counterparts seldom encountered; the Johnson administration put heavy pressure on them to keep silent on Vietnam in return for official support for civil rights legislation at home."[13] Her characterization of the racial background of antiwar travelers highlights the significance of the Cleaver delegation, which was led not by a civil rights activist but by a black radical during the Nixon administration. In fact, a significant portion of the group, four of the eleven members, were people of color, specifically two African Americans—Eldridge Cleaver and Elaine Brown of the BPP—and two Asian American delegates—Alex Hing of the Red Guards, U.S.A. and Pat Sumi of the Movement for a Democratic Military.

Furthermore, a majority of the group—seven delegates—were female. The significant presence of women reflected their engagement and leadership in a variety of movements, including the civil rights, New Left, black power, and women's movements. Interestingly, only two white men participated in the Anti-Imperialist Delegation. One of them was Robert Scheer, a journalist and longtime collaborator of Eldridge Cleaver's who also served as the delegation's co-leader.

The politics and membership of the U.S. People's Anti-Imperialist Delegation provide an opportunity to examine four developments that emerged within activist circles by the late 1960s and early 1970s. First, the delegation offers a case study of how the experience of travel both confirmed preexisting beliefs in and promoted new forms of Third World internationalism, a sense of political solidarity with African, Asian, and Latin American countries. The 1955 Bandung Conference presented the Third World as a group of nations not aligned with either the United States or the Soviet Union.

However, as the Anti-Imperialist Delegation's destinations suggest, American activists who viewed their own government as an imperialist power were drawn to socialist Third World countries.[14] In the increasingly rich scholarship on black internationalism, Africa and Cuba tend to serve as the primary sources of inspiration for black activism.[15] The Anti-Imperialist Delegation provides an opportunity to consider the centrality of socialist Asia for American internationalists of varying backgrounds, including those of Asian ancestry.[16]

Second, the composition of the delegation offers a window onto the frequently complex, multiracial, and multiethnic dynamics of 1960s activism.[17] By the latter half of the decade, black activists, particularly the Black Panthers, were widely recognized both domestically and internationally as the revolutionary vanguard among U.S. radicals. Committed to empowering African Americans, the Black Panthers also developed political partnerships with a variety of communities. The white delegation members, a significant portion of whom were Jewish, reveal the crucial role that they played in supporting the vanguard status of the Panthers.

In contrast to both black and white activists, Americans of Asian ancestry were rendered largely invisible within movement circles. During the mid- to late 1960s, the mainstream media increasingly depicted Chinese and Japanese in the United States as "model minorities." The alleged ability of these Asian groups to achieve economic and educational success without resorting to political activism and demands for systemic change was explicitly contrasted with the plight and tactics of African Americans. A 1966 article in *U.S. News and World Report* offered the opinion that "at a time when it is being proposed that hundreds of billions be spent to uplift Negroes and other minorities, the nation's 300,000 Chinese-Americans are moving ahead on their own—with no help from anyone else."[18] Similar articles about Japanese Americans appeared as well, and together the two ethnic groups constituted nearly 80 percent of the Asian American populations in the United States in the mid-1960s.[19] In this context, the travels of Alex Hing, a Chinese American, and Pat Sumi, a Japanese American, reflected the emergence of a broader Asian American movement that challenged the popular depiction of their groups as apolitical accommodationists. Instead, they emphasized their status as racially oppressed peoples akin to African Americans.[20] The presence of Hing and Sumi on a tour led by Eldridge Cleaver symbolized the catalytic significance of black activism for Asian American radicalism. Yet the personal dynamics between individual travelers, which tended not to be aired publicly for the sake of political unity, offer insights into the difficulties of multiracial and multi-ethnic coalition building.

Third, the significant presence of women, including women of color, in the Anti-Imperialist Delegation also offers an opportunity to examine how men and women differed in their experiences and interpretations of their travels. The female delegates tended to be more interested in the roles of women in Asian socialist societies. They returned with heroic tales, particularly of Vietnamese women, who served as role models for their ability to fulfill their maternal and political responsibilities as well as their nationalist and feminist callings. However, the gender dynamics among the travelers also reveal the difficulty of implementing these more egalitarian ideals even within radical circles.

Finally, the ability of the delegation to travel throughout socialist Asia provides insight into how their Asian hosts cultivated internationalist political networks among American activists of varying racial, ethnic, and gender backgrounds. Historian Mary Hershberger points out that the North Vietnamese could not accommodate all the requests from Westerners who wanted to travel to Hanoi. Given the wartime context, the Vietnamese both were deeply concerned about the physical welfare of their potential guests and had limited resources to host these individuals. Even so, the DRV and the National Liberation Front (NLF) in the South recognized the importance of developing allies, not just at the state level but among ordinary people around the world. Both the DRV and the NLF posted communication officers and sent diplomatic missions to Europe, Asia, Africa, Latin America, Australia, and Canada.[21] These representatives communicated not only with heads of state but also with individuals and organizations seeking information about the war in Vietnam. Pham Van Chuong, for example, worked for the Liberation News Agency of the NLF. He was posted in East Berlin during the early to mid-1960s and then was sent to Prague in 1965. Because Czechoslovakia was relatively easy for those from the West to reach, Chuong met with religious and pacifist delegations both in Prague and in other European cities. He recalled meeting well-known antiwar activists Dave Dellinger, Tom Hayden, Staughton Lynd, and Stewart Meacham of the American Friends Services Committee, as well as entertainers Jane Fonda and Dick Gregory.[22] In both North and South Vietnam, organizations were established to foster these international relationships. The Vietnam-America Friendship Association was created in 1945, soon after the founding of the DRV. During the U.S. war in Vietnam, the organization became the Vietnam Committee for Solidarity with

American People or the Viet-My Committee. A similar organization was created by the NLF.

These citizen diplomacy efforts were perceived as a crucial part of the war effort. Trinh Ngoc Thai, a former delegate at the Paris Peace Talks and the former vice chair of the External Relations Department of the Central Committee of the Communist Party of Vietnam, explained that the Vietnamese conceived of fighting the war on multiple fronts. He quoted Ho Chi Minh, who identified two primary fronts: "the first front against the U.S. War in Viet Nam, and the second one is inside the U.S. . The American people fight from inside, the Vietnamese fight from outside."[23] Thai also quoted another Vietnamese leader who conceived of the war in three fronts: "one united front against the U.S. in Viet Nam; one united front of Indochinese nations against the U.S.; and one front formed by the people in the world against U.S. imperialism, for national independence, and peace."[24] In either the two- or three-front formulation, mobilization of American and worldwide public opinion was regarded as an important priority. As Thai notes, "the power of public opinions" could pressure American policy and military leaders. In addition, worldwide support served as "an enormous source of encouragement to the Vietnamese people and their armed forces in the battlefields. The world people's support was very valuable both spiritually and materially to the Vietnamese people."[25] The Cleaver delegation provides insight into how the North Vietnamese as well as the North Koreans and the Red Chinese attempted to court progressive world opinion to support their politics.

When Eldridge Cleaver, the minister of information for the BPP, initiated the formation of the Anti-Imperialist Delegation in the fall of 1969, he was already in exile from the United States and had been living overseas for nearly a year. His identity as a political refugee from his own country reflected both the particular status of the BPP by the late 1960s and more generally the status of African Americans as "anticitizens" in the United States. In an intellectual history of black freedom movements in the twentieth century, Nikhil Singh posits that African Americans, particularly African American men, have been relegated to a position antithetical of citizens.[26] Eldridge Cleaver's life, a sharp contrast with Bob Browne's, confirms this observation.

Born in Arkansas to a working-class family in 1935, Cleaver migrated west to California along with tens of thousands of other African Americans who relocated during the World War II period. He grew up in a predominantly working-class Mexican American neighborhood in Los Angeles, where he became involved in gang culture and crime. He eventually served nine years in prison, going in and out beginning in 1954 and finally being released in December 1966, for selling marijuana, attempted rape, and assault with intent to kill. As a member of the multiracial lumpen proletariat found in mid-twentieth-century Los Angeles, Cleaver was ripe for recruitment by black nationalist and revolutionary organizations, such as the Black Muslims and the Black Panthers. His transformation from hoodlum to activist brought him national and international fame as his autobiographical work, *Soul on Ice*, became a best-seller in 1968.[27]

Cleaver's conversion to political radicalism and his ascendancy in the BPP accentuated his anticitizenship status in the United States. Founded in 1966 in Oakland, California, the BPP was inspired by a philosophy of armed self-defense and black power. Members initiated community patrols against the police, seeking to monitor and deter police harassment of the predominantly black and working-class residents of Oakland. Their strategy included visibly carrying firearms and following local law enforcement officers in their neighborhoods. When the California State Legislature considered a gun control law to curtail these activities, the Black Panthers protested for their constitutional right to bear arms by appearing en masse in leather jackets and black berets and carrying shotguns at the state assembly in May 1967. Through such theatrical confrontations, the Black Panthers attracted the admiration and enthusiastic support of activists throughout the country. As historian Manning Marable has noted, "by the late 1960's, the Black Panthers had become the most influential revolutionary nationalist organization in the U.S."[28]

One of the converts to the BPP included Elaine Brown, who eventually served as the first female leader of the national organization. Born in 1943 in Philadelphia, Brown grew up in overwhelmingly poor and black neighborhoods, where she socialized with a "gang" of girls and flirted with the "youngbloods." Had she and Cleaver resided in the same area, they might have encountered one another in this urban street youth culture.[29] In contrast to Cleaver, Brown obtained a relatively privileged education. Her mother enrolled her in experimental schools for gifted children as well as an elite girls' high school. Brown excelled in these academic settings in which she was one of a few students of color. She acquired the cultural capital to be a model and refined citizen. She studied Latin and also learned classical piano and ballet. In recounting this period in her life, Brown also emphasized her sense of cultural negation. She desired to emulate the wealth and "whiteness" of her classmates, many of whom were Jewish. As Brown wrote in her 1994 autobiography, *A Taste of Power*: "There seemed to be a promise at [school]. . . . It was not in the victory of hitting a number. It was not in the success of stealing a new dress from a dress factory. It was not in a decent piece of meat for dinner or in songs played over a new RCA Victor record player. It was bigger than my mother's arms. It was a promise with wings that would lift me away from York Street forever and plant me in the security of a white world. I saw that promise and knew I had to join those white people."[30]

Brown's efforts to straddle the predominantly "white" world of school and the "black" world of poor housing projects eventually led to disillusionment and alienation. After a half-hearted attempt at attending Temple University, she relocated to Los Angeles in April 1965. Seeking a new start to her life, Brown found work as a waitress at a strip club that was popular with white celebrities and businessmen. She describes herself as oblivious to racial politics during the mid-1960s, even in the midst of the tumultuous Watts riot during the summer of 1965. In fact, her introduction to civil rights and black liberation politics came from her rich, married white lover, Jay Kennedy, a man whom she met at the strip club. He expressed admiration for African American activism and claimed to help organize and contribute funds to support their causes.[31]

Brown would personally become involved with the black freedom struggle by teaching piano to inner city youth. Through the process of engaging in community service, she met a variety of black activists and became attracted by their magnetism and vision. The Southern California chapter of the BPP was established by such charismatic leaders as "Bunchy" Carter, a former gang leader, as well as John and Ericka Huggins, described by Brown and others as black "hippies."[32] Brown became absorbed in the life of the party, especially after she had the opportunity to meet the noted author and Panther leader Eldridge Cleaver during one of his visits to Southern California in 1968. Brown focused her initial energies on organizing students at the University of California, Los Angeles, and negotiating university support for BPP community programs. These "serve the people" programs strived to meet the immediate needs of black Angelinos, such as free breakfasts for children and seniors, free health clinics and testing for sickle cell anemia, and free transportation for family members of imprisoned inmates. Through these interactions, Black Panthers sought to transform the political consciousness of those individuals whom they "served," thereby building a base of support within the African American community.

The BPP's combined agendas of "armed self-defense" and "serve the people" programs led the police and the FBI to label the BPP as the "most dangerous . . . of all extremist groups."[33] Through the COINTEL, or counterintelligence program, they targeted the organization for infiltration, manufactured and manipulated tensions within the group, and encouraged and executed violent confrontations against members. Eldridge Cleaver's departure from the United States resulted from this escalating campaign of state repression against the BPP. Two days after the assassination of Martin Luther King Jr., Cleaver was involved in a police shootout on 6 April 1968, which resulted in the death of seventeen-year-old Panther Bobby Hutton. The minister of information for the Panthers decided to leave the country rather than go back to prison for violating parole. Having experienced a cycle of imprisonment as a youth, Cleaver believed, "when they have you in their clutches, they proceed with what they want to do whether they have a right or not."[34] By then, the organization's cofounders, minister of defense Huey Newton and chairman Bobby Seale, were deeply entangled in the criminal justice system. Newton had been incarcerated for his involvement in a 1967 shootout that resulted in the death of a policeman. Seale became a defendant in two trials, as one of the Chicago 8 for the demonstrations at the Democratic National Convention in 1968 and as one of the New Haven 21, a group of Panthers accused of murdering an infiltrator/informant of the party.[35]

While living abroad, first in Cuba and then in Algeria, Cleaver took advantage of his exile status to develop connections with Third World socialists and to bolster an internationalist agenda within the BPP. The founders of the party had long been influenced not only by American black leaders such as Malcolm X and Robert F. Williams, but also by Third World revolutionaries like Frantz Fanon, Che Guevera, Fidel Castro, Ho Chi Minh, and Mao Tse-tung.[36] The Panthers had sold Mao's Little Red Book to Berkeley students to obtain funds to purchase their first weapons but became equally influenced by its content. When Elaine Brown joined the Panthers in 1968, she recalled being "given a *Red Book* to read, a collection of Mao Zedong's philosophical treatises and statements on revolution and revolutionaries. We were ordered to study his writings, to be prepared to recite portions of them on command, and to distribute his books to the masses."[37] A 1973 internal party memo confirmed the importance of this work, indicating that "50 percent of the morning political education classes concentrated on the 'little red book.'"[38] The FBI also noted the significance of Mao for the Panthers, recording in its memos about the organization that "Issues of 'The Black Panther' regularly contain quotations from MAO Tse-tung of the People's Republic of China and features Mao's statement that 'political power grows out of the barrel of a gun.'"[39] Mao's concept of "serving the people" also influenced the BPP to form their community survival programs. Absorbing the writings of Third World revolutionaries led the Black Panthers to adopt an anti-imperialist critique of American race relations and international policies. They regarded the status of African Americans and other peoples of color within the United States as being analogous to people of color suffering under colonialism.

As a fugitive of the American legal system and a leader of the foremost black radical organization at the time, Cleaver was both a magnet for Third World revolutionary leaders and a potential problem for his host countries. Cuba offered him asylum but, due to persistent concerns regarding American aggression, they also requested that the Black Panther leader avoid drawing public attention to his presence there. They did not fulfill his request for military training facilities to organize a revolutionary force against the United States. Cuban leaders also condemned hijackers who arrived in their country for the express purpose of joining Cleaver in exile.[40] Having escaped imprisonment in the States, he discovered that life in Cuba was not without its own kind of limits.

When Cleaver relocated to Algeria, he also experienced tensions with his host country but he gained much greater latitude and support to establish an open Black Panther base of operations there. Being in a socialist Third World nation with formal ties to other Third World countries, Cleaver came into contact with a variety of revolutionary movements, such as Yasser Arafat's Palestinian liberation movement, Al Fatah; various African liberation movements based in South Africa, Zimbabwe, the Congo, Guinea-Bissau, and the Cape Verde Islands; and the NLF of South Vietnam and the North Vietnamese government.[41]

The Vietnamese were particularly interested in establishing ties with the BPP. Given Cleaver's stature among American activists and his contacts with the radical press, he represented an important potential ally in their effort to influence American public opinion about the war. Pham Khac Lam, formerly on the secretarial staff of famed General Vo Nguyen Giap during the war against the French, became a member of the Press Department of the Central Committee of Propaganda and Training during the war against the United States. His responsibilities included hosting visitors from the West, such as Tom Hayden, Howard Zinn, and Joan Baez. He also focused his energies on reporting news about the United States for Vietnamese audiences. He reviewed American mainstream newspapers and magazines, seeking information about the U.S. political economy as well as about social protests. He would then write articles on these topics for newspapers in North Vietnam. His goal was to highlight the cleavages within U.S. society, to locate "signs of weakness," and to offer inspiration for the Vietnamese to continue their struggle for liberation.[42] Because of the status of African Americans in the United States, Lam was particularly interested in featuring Martin Luther King Jr. and the Black Panthers in Vietnamese news stories. By courting Eldridge Cleaver in Algeria, the Vietnamese hoped to shape how the war in Vietnam would be portrayed in the Black Panthers' influential newspaper. After all, Cleaver remained the minister of information even during exile, and the organization's publication was widely read by radical activists in the United States and even abroad.

In exchange, the Vietnamese helped to legitimize Cleaver's standing in the international arena. As he recalled, "The State Department was constantly identifying me as a fugitive from justice, a roving hoodlum or something. They made every effort to lock a criminal identity to my speeches and activities; the Vietnamese not only lent credibility to my overseas operation but intervened on our behalf when the Algerians clamped down."[43] The NLF and the DRV accorded Cleaver the status of a foreign dignitary by regularly inviting him and other members to attend diplomatic ceremonies. They also advocated to the Algerian government that the BPP be given official recognition as an accredited movement, thereby obtaining access to resources for their activities. Furthermore, when the NLF was given new embassy facilities upon the formation of the Provisional Revolutionary Government in 1969, the Vietnamese persuaded the Algerians to allow Cleaver the use of the vacated space as a Black Panther headquarters. Upon Cleaver's request, the Vietnamese agreed to offer a prisoner exchange; the release of American POWs for incarcerated BPP members, beginning with Huey Newton and Bobby Seale.[44] The U.S. government ignored the request, but when Newton eventually obtained his release from prison, he volunteered to send Black Panthers to fight on behalf of the NLF and the DRV.[45]

It was during his stay in Algeria that Eldridge first developed a relationship with North Korean officials. Motivated by similar considerations as the Vietnamese and recognizing the power of the antiwar movement in the United States, the DPRK ambassador invited Cleaver to attend the International Conference of Revolutionary Journalists, held in their capital of Pyongyang. Cleaver traveled throughout the country for nearly a month during the fall of 1969 to attend the conference, which attracted journalists from ninety countries. During his visit, Cleaver also studied how North Korea interpreted and applied Marxist-Leninist ideology to reconstruct their nation. He was particularly attracted to the concept of *juche*, roughly translated as self-reliance.[46] As a relatively small country, the DPRK was weary of "great power chauvinism" from the Soviet Union and China. Consequently, it sought to develop its own interpretation of socialist revolution. The North Korean innovations encouraged the BPP's efforts to reinterpret Marxist-Leninism in light of the conditions of the black urban poor in the United States.

In addition to these theoretical exchanges, the DPRK also offered material support for the families of the Black Panthers. The Korean Democratic Women's Union invited Kathleen Cleaver and Barbara Easley-Cox, both members of the BPP and the wives of Black Panthers Eldridge Cleaver and Don Cox respectively, to stay in their country to complete their pregnancies.[47] Kim Il Sung's wife even sent her private jet to escort Kathleen, her young son, and Barbara from Moscow to Pyongyang. She also visited them after the two women gave birth. In the DPRK, their hosts provided medical care, lodgings, a cook, housekeepers, and child care. Barbara, then pregnant with her first child, was more nervous about the prospect of giving birth than Kathleen, who was having her second. Barbara actually brought issues of *Time* and *Newsweek* magazines with articles about the latest medical care and technology for childbirth, hoping that the publications might be helpful for her North Korean doctors and nurses. She also carried a copy of the popular guide to child rearing by Dr. Benjamin Spock, who was an outspoken critic of the U.S. war in Vietnam. The two women and their children mainly stayed in the house that they were provided. When they did go out, they attracted attention with their big Afros and miniskirts.[48] The DPRK offer to support the formation of families among Black Panthers contrasted sharply with the inability of the same individuals to create a secure home and community in the United States.

Influenced by his stay in Korea, Eldridge used the party newspaper, the *Black Panther*, to educate members and readers about North Korea and

Figure 5. Kathleen and Joju Younghi Cleaver. Photo taken in the early 1970s at the children's nursery of the International section of the Black Panther Party in Algeria. Courtesy of Bill Jennings and It's About Time: The Black Panther Party Legacy and Alumni project.

to highlight Kim Il Sung's support for the black liberation struggle in the United States.[49] In fact, the image of Kim Il Sung would join the portraits of Ho Chi Minh, Che Guevera, and Congo Prime Minister Patrice Lumumba on the masthead of the international section of the newspaper; this section was created by Cleaver during his time in exile.[50] At some point

Figure 6. The International News masthead of the *Black Panther* newspaper, 3 October 1970. The face of Mao Tse-tung was added following the end of the Anti-Imperialist Delegation tour. Courtesy of Bill Jennings and It's About Time: The Black Panther Party Legacy and Alumni project.

in his 1969 stay in the DPRK, officials asked him to return with a delegation of American journalists to visit their country. They hoped to enlist the U.S. radical press to support their efforts to reunite North and South Korea.[51]

The U.S. People's Anti-Imperialist Delegation, which eventually traveled to the DPRK in the summer of 1970, reflected an array of political movements that had emerged in the United States and had developed relationships, however tangentially, with the BPP. Cleaver consulted with his long-time collaborator Robert Scheer to create the roster of travelers. Elaine Brown believed that Eldridge Cleaver personally requested her presence on the trip. Following the assassinations of Bunchy Carter and John Huggins in January 1969 by US, a black nationalist organization in Los Angeles, Brown had increasingly taken a leadership role in Southern California. Deemed "an effective party propagandist," she had become "deputy minister of information" for her chapter.[52] Although Brown had given birth just four months prior to the trip, she agreed to travel with Cleaver as the only other representative from the BPP.

Brown and Cleaver, targeted black activists within the U.S. context, sought inspiration and recognition by traveling abroad. They were not the only Panthers to do so. Other members of the organization journeyed to Europe, Africa, Latin American, Canada, Australia, and Asia to engage in political dialogue and pronounce international solidarity. Regarded as anticitizens at home, the Black Panthers were heavily courted as vanguard political activists globally.

If African Americans constituted anticitizens, the white members of the Anti-Imperialist Delegation were relatively privileged insiders who nevertheless embraced outsider status. Like other activists of the 1960s generation, the white delegates tended to be middle class, college educated, and young. Almost all of the travelers were in their midtwenties, while Cleaver and his co-leader Robert Scheer were in their midthirties. Although the

white delegates had racial and class advantages, they identified with out-
casts. They did so due to their ethnicity, politics, and/or gender.
In a poem about the Anti-Imperialist Delegation, Cleaver emphasized
the significant presence of Jewish activists in their group. He writes:

> In our Anti-War band
> meant to be a crosscut
> from each section of our land.
> There were four Jewish women
> And half a Jewish man.[53]

Robert Scheer, whose mother was a Jew from Russia and whose father was
a gentile from Germany, was the "half a Jewish man." The high proportion
of Jewish activists within the delegation reflected a broader phenomenon
within the civil rights and student movements of the 1950s and 1960s.[54]
Regardless of religious belief or practice, Jews of European ancestry in the
United States were subjected to anti-Semitism and did not necessarily have
the full privileges of "whiteness." Scholar Jack Salzman identified "the
lynching of Leo Frank in Atlanta in 1915 . . . as a painful reminder to many
Jews of both their own vulnerability and their need to struggle against racism."[55] For those who came of age in the aftermath of World War II, the
Holocaust was fresh in the collective memories of their families and communities. Recognizing this history of social ostracism and genocide, Jewish
Americans participated in significant numbers in protest movements for social justice. They supported and provided leadership for the NAACP. They
constituted "two-thirds to three-quarters of the white volunteers who went
south to ride busses through Alabama or organize Freedom Summer in Mississippi in 1964."[56] In fact, it was the outcry over the disappearance and
deaths of Michael Schwerner, Andrew Goodman, and James Chaney, "two
young Jews from New York and a Black from Mississippi," which attracted
national attention to the 1964 Freedom Summer.[57]
The political beliefs of the white activists, Jewish and gentile, also positioned them as societal outsiders. They broadly constituted members of
the New Left. The term conveyed their collective critique of and alienation from the existing American social order.[58] These 1960s activists constituted the "new" Left as opposed to the "old" Left of the 1930s. The old
Left, inspired by communist movements of the earlier period as well as
classical Marxist theory, primarily focused on labor organizing. In contrast,

the New Left emerged out of the era of civil rights, the counterculture, and Third World decolonization. They also critiqued capitalism and read Marxist-Leninist theory, but they focused more on issues related to race, empire, and culture. Interestingly, the white activists in the Anti-Imperialist Delegation tended to be "red diaper babies." They were children of parents who belonged to the old Left.

Robert Scheer, the co-leader of the delegation, exemplified and played a leading role in defining the New Left. Born in Brooklyn to immigrant parents who worked in the garment industry, Scheer studied economics as an undergraduate and graduate student at a series of institutions of higher learning that eventually landed him at the University of California, Berkeley. In the San Francisco Bay Area, he worked for City Lights Bookstore, famous for its association with writers of the Beat generation, like Jack Kerouac, Allen Ginsberg, and Lawrence Ferlinghetti. Fascinated by the Cuban Revolution, Scheer coauthored a book about the island in 1964. He traveled there regularly and cultivated relationships with political leaders like Fidel Castro. Scheer even asked the Cuban leader to write an introduction for the diaries of Bolivian revolutionary Che Guevara. Scheer arranged for the publication of the diaries, which quickly became a cult classic among American activists. These Cuban contacts became useful for Eldridge Cleaver, as Scheer assisted the Black Panther leader's efforts to seek refuge there.

The two became collaborators through their mutual association with the New Left Catholic publication *Ramparts*.[59] Founded in 1962, the magazine was an anomaly. It was a glossy yet alternative publication whose circulation reached almost three hundred thousand by 1970. *Ramparts* launched Eldridge Cleaver's writing career, publishing his essays while he was still in prison. These initial pieces formed the genesis of the best-seller *Soul on Ice*. Cleaver eventually assumed the position of senior editor for the magazine, even as he became the minister of information for the Black Panthers and eventually fled the country.

Ramparts also fueled the antiwar movement in the United States. The magazine published articles that exposed CIA covert operations in Vietnam, the role that Michigan State University's technical group played in supporting the war effort, and the widespread use and impact of napalm. From 1964 to 1969, Bob Scheer was at the center of these initiatives, first serving as the Vietnam correspondent, then a managing editor, and finally editor in chief for *Ramparts*.[60]

In many ways, Scheer was a kingmaker for Cleaver and other members of the BPP. Just as Scheer introduced Che Guevera to the American New Left, he arranged for Cleaver to work with Bobby Seale to write a biography of Huey Newton.[61] Scheer also maintained close contact with Cleaver during his exile. While visiting the Black Panther leader in Algeria, Scheer brought news of political developments in the United States and also encouraged Cleaver to continue his writing and publishing. These activities generated a vital source of income for the Cleaver family and their growing entourage of asylum seekers and political dissidents.[62] Scheer's efforts entailed some risk. The FBI sought various ways to neutralize Eldridge Cleaver, even during his time abroad, and attempted to freeze his financial assets. So when Scheer returned from Algeria, he "was promptly subpoenaed to appear before the Federal Grand Jury meeting in San Francisco, and ordered to turn over all records of activities performed on behalf of Eldridge Cleaver's legal defense."[63] Despite what Scheer described as a "general pattern of harassment," he assured *Ramparts* readers that Cleaver would serve as the "International Editor of this magazine and reports by him will appear regularly."

Given their partnership, it is not surprising that many of the Anti-Imperialist Delegation members had some connection to Bob Scheer and the New Left. Among the white delegates, a significant number had been politically active in the San Francisco Bay Area. Jan Austin was another editor at *Ramparts*. Andy Truskier was identified with the International Liberation School that was based in Berkeley as well as a member of the Peace and Freedom Party. Bob Scheer had run for the U.S. Senate in 1966 with the support of the party. Bob Browne, who had briefly run for a Senate seat in New Jersey, was aware of Scheer's campaign in California and kept track of his effort. The Peace and Freedom Party also nominated Eldridge Cleaver as a presidential candidate in 1968. Another member of the Anti-Imperialist Delegation, Regina Blumenfeld, described as a women's liberation activist, was likewise from Berkeley.

Members of the Anti-Imperialist Delegation not from the San Francisco Bay Area nevertheless had connections to the political movements that originated from that region. Another delegation member, Randy Rappaport, had lived with Gina Blumenfeld in what Rappaport characterizes as the "first political commune" in Berkeley. Inspired by the French Revolution, the members ironically called themselves "COPS . . . which stood for Committee on Public Safety."[64] Like Scheer, Rappaport was Jewish and came from Brooklyn. Her parents had been members of the Communist Party. Exposed to African American leftist cultural figures like Paul Robeson while she was growing up in a "very white . . . somewhat anti-Semitic" community, she eagerly engaged in civil rights activism in the Northeast, the South, and in California.[65] At the time of the delegation, she had relocated to Boston, where she became involved with the women's collective Bread and Roses. There, she befriended feminist activists, one of whom had traveled to Vietnam and others who eventually published the innovative women's health manual, *Our Bodies, Our Selves.* Although Scheer and Cleaver did not know Rappaport, they knew the same people. At the Berkeley commune, Rappaport met SDS leader Tom Hayden and countercultural figure Stew Albert, a close friend of Cleaver's who also visited him in Algeria.

Ann Froines, another Anti-Imperialist Delegation member, had political credentials similar to Rappaport's and even closer connections to the Black Panthers. Froines grew up in Chicago and, like Rappaport, she was a member of a "red diaper family."[66] Although not Jewish, she lived in a neighborhood and attended school in "quite a heavily Jewish community." She participated in the Warren Avenue Congregational Church, which was a seat of civil rights organizing that strived to create a multiracial and multiethnic community. She recalled that the "church had three pastors: a white, an African-American . . . and a Mexican . . . so there was services in Spanish." The political consciousness of her family and the institutions that they chose to support prepared Froines to become an activist at Swarthmore College, a school founded by the pacifist Quakers. She recalled, "By the end of [my] college career I considered myself part of the New Left and we had an SDS chapter on our campus very early because one of the [authors of the] Port Huron Statement [the founding document for SDS], Carl Whitman, was a member of my class at Swarthmore." She worked with others to improve the quality of education for African American students, who were experiencing de facto segregation due to racial and economic neighborhood stratification. Along with other members of her generation, she became aware of the "history of colonialism in Asia . . . [and] began to understand about American neo-colonialism."

Although Froines had solid New Left credentials, her invitation to the Anti-Imperialist Delegation stemmed more directly from her involvement in defending the Black Panthers from political repression. In 1968, when antiwar activists protested the Democratic National Convention in Chicago, Ann and her husband, John Froines, were spending the summer there with her family. Ann mainly busied herself with their young daughter, who was just six months old. John, also an activist, was slated to begin a tenure-track assistant professorship at the University of Oregon. That summer he "was organizing volunteer marshals in the city streets" to help stem the violent clashes between the police and protesters.[67] He eventually was indicted as one of eight activists charged with conspiring to incite a riot. It was not clear why John became one of the Chicago 8. The others tended to be nationally recognized figures, like pacifist David Dellinger, SDS leaders Tom Hayden and Rennie Davis, Yippie cult figures Abbie Hoffman and Jerry Rubin, and Black Panther Bobby Seale. Eventually, John Froines and Lee Weiner, both less known and less flamboyant individuals, were acquitted. As Ann assisted in the defense of her husband and the other members of the Chicago 8, she became particularly appalled by the treatment of Bobby Seale. He was a last-minute replacement for Eldridge Cleaver, who was unable to travel outside of California due to concerns about violating his parole. In fact, Bobby Seale had been in Chicago for less than twenty-four hours during the Democratic convention. At the trial, the judge ordered that the Black Panther leader, the only African American among the charged conspirators, be bound and gagged for his vocal protests during court proceedings. Following the Chicago 8 trial and the subsequent murder of Black Panther leader Fred Hampton by the city police in December 1969, Ann took a leadership role in the New Haven Black Panther Defense Committee. She believed that Bobby Seale, Ericka Huggins, and other members of the Panthers were facing politically motivated persecution. In response, Ann helped initiate a movement against what she described as "Racist and Political Oppression."[68]

The final member of the Anti-Imperialist Delegation, Janet Kranzberg, represented the Newsreel Alternative Media Collective, based in New York City. Founded in 1967, Newsreel was the East Coast film counterpart to *Ramparts*. The collective documented some of the most significant political protests, organizations, and individuals of that era, including the Chicago protests and the Black Panthers.[69] Its filmmakers had traveled to Cuba and Vietnam. Kranzberg did not know Bob Scheer or Eldridge Cleaver, although she was closest to them in age. In fact, she received the invitation almost by default because of an outbreak of mononucleosis among other Newsreel filmmakers. She had met Tom Hayden in Chicago in 1968 and knew Gina Blumenfeld and Randy Rappaport from attending a women's meeting at COPS. Like the other two women, Janet was Jewish. She recalled how the Holocaust had marked her consciousness. The awareness that she could have died, except for a fluke of history, fostered her belief in fairness, justice, and compassion.[70] She traveled to the DPRK, expecting to create a documentary film about their experiences.

The "white" members of the Anti-Imperialist Delegation were collectively connected to some of the most important New Left media sources, organizations, political movements, and individuals of the late 1960s and 1970s. Many of them also were "red diaper babies," with personal and intellectual connections to the old Left. In addition, the ethnic and gender composition of the delegation reflected the broader participation and leadership of both Jewish and female activists in the social movements of this era.

The remaining members of the Anti-Imperialist Delegation, Alex Hing and Pat Sumi, were just as excited as the others, perhaps even more so, by the opportunity to travel to socialist Asia with Eldridge Cleaver. Their presence on the tour symbolized the significant influence of black liberation struggles and sixties radicalism more generally on Americans of Asian ancestry during the 1960s and 1970s. While there was a history of activism within Asian American communities as well, both Sumi and Hing were effectively cut off from this past due to the combined legacies of Japanese American internment during World War II and the subsequent suppression of Chinese American leftists during the Cold War. Unlike the white travelers, many of whom had direct and personal connections to the old Left, Asian American radicals lacked political role models within their own community. Consequently, Sumi and Hing, like others who helped to form the Asian American movement in the late 1960s and 1970s, credited external political developments for transforming their political consciousness. Yet the ways in which Sumi and Hing were invited to join the delegation indicated their relatively marginal status within American activist circles.

During World War II and the 1950s, Chinese and Japanese Americans respectively obtained unprecedented legal rights in the United States. Over the course of the late nineteenth and early twentieth centuries, they had been designated "aliens ineligible for citizenship," subjected to racial segregation, and prevented from immigrating to the United States, owning land in many states, and marrying interracially. The World War II alliance with China and the Cold War alliance with Japan led to the removal of these legal restrictions and eventually a new image of Chinese and Japanese Americans as "model minorities."[71] These changes in legal status and cultural representation did not necessarily redress the historical and continued significance of racial discrimination.

Alex Hing was a far cry from the model minority image. Born in San Francisco's Chinatown in 1946, Hing grew up in a borderline middle-class family. His father worked as a magician in a nightclub that catered predominantly to tourists, and his mother worked in a department store and also occasionally helped her husband with his act. Although Chinatown was and is widely regarded as a tourist destination, the community throughout its history could more accurately be characterized as a segregated urban ghetto.[72] It boasted the second-highest population density in the country, the highest tuberculosis rate, and widespread substandard housing. Like Cleaver, Hing became involved with youth gangs and committed a number of crimes that eventually landed him in detention. Seeking to find direction in his life, Hing enrolled in San Francisco City College and sought to avoid his former friends. While in school, Hing developed his political consciousness by listening to Bob Dylan, reading revolutionary literature, and participating in civil rights and antiwar activities sponsored by students "who were red diaper babies."[73] He even registered voters to support Eldridge Cleaver's presidential campaign as a candidate for the Peace and Freedom Party in 1968.[74]

Hing recalled being particularly impressed by the Panthers. He thought "the Black Panther Party was really, really, really cool. I thought that they were really hip. These were a bunch of gangsters, just like us. . . . The people I grew up with—we all hated cops and they were having pitch[ed] battles with the cops and they were articulating everything that we felt. . . . They were speaking for us. So even though my involvement was through the antiwar movement, my heart was with the Black Panthers."[75] Hing's admiration for the political gangster persona of the Panthers resonates with the analysis of American Studies scholar Daryl Maeda. He suggests that Asian American political and cultural activists during the late 1960s and 1970s, particularly Asian American men, mimicked the performance of black masculinity in order to formulate their own identities as racialized and resistant subjects.[76]

Following the assassination of Martin Luther King Jr. in 1968, Hing decided to participate in a journey that took him from Oakland, California, to Washington, DC. Described as a "last chance for nonviolence," the trip was part of the Poor People's Campaign, a movement that King called for before his death to bring attention to poverty in American society. Hing was initially hesitant to join the effort, explaining, "I'm not a Martin guy, I'm a Malcolm guy." Since the Panthers also endorsed the campaign, Hing decided to get on the bus. During the summer of 1968, he traveled across the country learning about various political struggles. In New Mexico, Hing was exposed to Chicano struggles to regain land initially granted by the Spanish and lost as a result of Anglo conquest. In the South, they "went . . . from church to church rallying." The Ku Klux Klan attempted to stop their journey, placing bombs on their buses while they were at a gathering in Louisville, Kentucky. On the journey, Hing met Black Panthers, Chicano or Mexican American youth, and white students affiliated with the Communist Party, USA. He was familiar with these groups, having been exposed to their struggles and working with them on various causes. However, as a Chinese American, he was unfamiliar to other activists. When they arrived in Washington, DC, Hing recalled, "Everyone thought I was an Indian."[77]

After that summer, Hing returned to his community to organize. The group that he helped to form, the Red Guard Party, USA was heavily influenced by the BPP. Inspired by the Black Panthers' ten-point program, the Red Guards adopted a similar agenda and studied Mao's Little Red Book. Ironically, the Chinese American youth who formed the organization gained their first exposure to the Chinese leader through the Panthers. Bobby Seale invited them to participate in weekly study groups at Eldridge Cleaver's house, where they read and debated Mao's writings. David Hilliard, the chief of staff for the BPP who assumed leadership of the organization during the absence of Newton, Seale, and Cleaver, spoke at the founding rally of the Red Guard. The Panthers even encouraged the Chinatown group to adopt the name Red Guard to encourage identification with the youth movement and Cultural Revolution in China. Alex Hing, as the minister of information for the Red Guard Party, USA represented the Chinese American counterpart to Eldridge Cleaver.[78]

The disconnect between Hing as an American of Chinese descent from Mao's China was indicative of broader political legacies within the Chinese American community. Historically there had been an active and vocal Left within Chinese communities in the United States, especially during the late 1920s and 1930s.[79] During that time, Chinese Americans were inspired by the resilience of the Chinese Communist Party in fighting Japanese imperialism as well as the vibrancy of the Communist Party, USA. However, with the formation of the People's Republic of China in 1949, described in the United States as the "fall" of China, and the ensuing McCarthyist witch hunts in the 1950s, the Chinese American Left was driven underground or deported. The San Francisco Chinatown that Hing grew up in was politically dominated by the Kuomingtang (KMT) or Chinese Nationalist Party.

The KMT supported the Republic of China, which claimed to represent China although it was based only on the island of Taiwan. As an expression of their opposition to Mao's China, the nationalists cooperated whole-heartedly with FBI efforts to intimidate and silence leftist sympathizers. The Little Red Book, like other things associated with Communist China, was banned from sale in Chinatown stores.

Even though Hing gained his first exposure to Mao's words through the Black Panthers and not through people of his own ancestry, he had to "fight" his way into the Cleaver delegation. In contrast, Hing unexpectedly received support from the old Chinatown Left. When Hing heard about the trip to North Korea through the "movement grapevine," he persuaded David Hilliard to include a member of the Red Guards in the delegation. Until then, the group consisted almost entirely of white activists. He recalled arguing, "We should be in on this. We were really close to the Panthers. How dare they organize a trip of U.S. people to North Korea and not invite us?" Hing's statement indicates that even though he was based in a Chinese American organization, he was part of a broader movement that emerged in the late 1960s that advocated a pan-Asian consciousness, a sense of connection between people of Asian ancestry in the United States as well as with leftist Asian nations internationally. Hing finally received the invitation to join the delegation rather late in the process, when some travelers were already in Paris. Furthermore, he was responsible for raising funds for the trip. Hing recalled pondering, "Which bank are we going to rob now?" However, "the word got out" in the Chinese American community about his invitation, and "five thousand dollars' cash [was] delivered to me. . . . It turns out it came from the old Left in Chinatown that I had not a clue existed. . . . They were convinced that I would end up in China, too. So that I would be one of the first Chinese Americans to go to revolutionary China."[80]

The old Chinatown Left was not alone in their enthusiasm for the socialist Chinese government. The newsletter published by the Red Guard Party, USA had featured Mao's portrait as well as information about the PRC. They also sought to challenge the KMT stranglehold on political expression by openly flying Red China's flag and broadcasting their support for Mao at community rallies.[81] Consequently, even though the Anti-Imperialist Delegation initially intended to travel only to North Korea, Hing believed that he would find a way to get to Red China. Its status as a powerful and respected nation among U.S. activist circles helped to form Hing's identity. The small size of the Asian population in the United States, constituting approximately one million people, as well as its pan-ethnic demographic, held implications for the political aspirations of Asian Americans.[82] In contrast to African Americans, Chicano/as, and even American Indians, Asian Americans had difficulty viewing themselves as a separate nation with claims to territorial sovereignty on U.S. soil. While Asian Americans could forge a political identity as a racialized group, it was more difficult to argue that they constituted a "nation," similar to a Black Nation with rights to the territory of the American South or the Chicano Nation with its connection to the American Southwest.[83] Chinese American activists could at least claim Mao and the PRC as international beacons for radical socialism as well as nationalist sources of inspiration.

Although Pat Sumi's upbringing and views on socialist Asia differed from Alex Hing's, the black liberation struggle also played a central role in shaping her political consciousness and activism. Unlike Hing, Sumi grew up as a member of a relatively privileged Japanese American upper-middle-class family in the Los Angeles area. Her grandparents emigrated from Japan and achieved financial success by owning and operating a paper factory. Like other Japanese immigrants, they utilized their networks within the ethnic economy to establish a niche in the United States. Sumi's grandparents built their fortune by catering to the large numbers of Japanese Americans in agriculture and produce marketing. They succeeded so well that they were able to persuade Pat's father to marry into their family and to adopt the Sumi name after marrying their only daughter.[84] Despite their financial success, the U.S. government interned the Sumi family, along with other Japanese Americans living on the West Coast, during World War II. Due to their Japanese ancestry, they were regarded as enemies of the state. Pat Sumi was born in 1944, when her family was on furlough from camp and residing in Colorado.[85] With the support of their white neighbors and friends, the Sumis were able to maintain some of their financial assets and resume their previous status, something that was relatively rare among Japanese American internees. Even though Pat's father eventually abandoned his wife and two daughters, the wealth of the Sumi family offered Pat the opportunity to grow up in a privileged and protected environment.

In contrast to Hing, Sumi lived the role of the "model minority." She grew up in the Los Angeles suburb of Silverlake, where she excelled in predominantly white schools and was part of the "smart" crowd. Like Elaine Brown, Pat Sumi also learned and excelled in playing classical music, the violin rather than the piano. Throughout junior and senior high school, she participated in student government, journalism, and other activities that groomed her for civic leadership.[86] Sumi, in her senior high school photograph, looks like an Asian version of Jackie Kennedy. She sports a short but elegantly coiffed haircut and a pearl necklace.[87]

Like Hing, Sumi became increasingly radical due to the influence of the black liberation movement and the growing international attention regarding race and global inequalities. She first realized her lack of understanding about race relations in the United States when she traveled to Japan to visit relatives in 1963. When asked about the civil rights movement in the American South, she realized, "[I] could not explain my own country to someone who was asking me a halfway decent intelligent question."[88] As an extension of her liberal commitment to civic leadership, Sumi eventually traveled to Africa as part of Operation Crossroads, a program that promoted educational and cultural exchange similar to the Peace Corps. She also volunteered for civil rights work in the American South. She recalled, "This was in '66 and '67. Both summers I went and met people in CORE and SNCC, met people like Stokely Carmichael who had just begun using the slogan 'black power.' I attended the first Southern Christian Leadership Conference (SCLC) able to be held in the south because of the desegregation of public facilities."[89]

When Sumi returned to the West Coast, she became involved with the antiwar movement, which to her was also about issues of race. Not only were the "vast majority of the front line infantry . . . black and brown," but American engagement in the war also promoted "a hatred of the Vietnamese."[90] Sumi joined the Movement for a Democratic Military and focused her energies on organizing active-duty Marines stationed at Camp Pendleton in southern California.[91] She hosted "coffeehouses" where soldiers could hear speakers like Black Panther Angela Davis and actress Jane Fonda discuss their opposition to the Vietnam War. This was dangerous work, as Sumi and her co-organizers faced government surveillance, drive-by shootings, and police raids for their antiwar activities among Marines.[92] Pat Sumi, the model minority, had evolved in her political engagement to the point that she was directly challenging the state and encouraging soldiers to question their citizenship responsibilities to the nation. By then, Sumi was participating in study groups and becoming increasingly critical of capitalism. For her, the racial stratification of American society resulted from the "political economy that helped to create that division and continues that division and on whose survival that division must remain."[93]

Unlike Hing, who was focusing his activism on Chinese Americans, Sumi tended to work outside of her own ethnic, racial, and even gender group at this point in her political career. For a period of time, she lived in a "pacifist commune" that was "really upper, middle class, hippie. . . . She kept house for about eight men, cooked, did laundry for" them.[94] Even though Sumi rejected the role of being a "Japanese housewife," she recognized, "that was what I was basically into. I didn't want to. I felt bad, but I couldn't figure out what else to do about it, so I did it anyway."[95] Sumi found one avenue to critique male chauvinism through the GI antiwar movement. Scholar Heather Marie Stur points out that these activists emphasized "gender liberation—the liberation not only of women but of men as well."[96] They raised questions about the cultural expectations of "conventional masculinity" that led American men to regard the "military as a bastion of masculinity and male bonding."[97]

Sumi's initial disconnect from an understanding of her own racial and gender oppression stemmed partly from her class background but also from a conscious political amnesia within the Japanese American community.[98] The World War II internment of Japanese Americans was premised on the belief that this group constituted the racial antithesis of American citizens. While Sumi grew up with stories about the camps, she accepted the internment "as part of what happened during World War II, without necessarily questioning" why it occurred.[99] Like many other Japanese Americans during the postinternment era, which also coincided with the McCarthyist era, Pat's family resorted to individual strategies to regain their foothold in American society.

By the late 1960s, some Japanese Americans in Southern California had begun to reject these nonconfrontational approaches. The publication of the newspaper *Gidra* signaled the emergence of a "yellow power" movement, a phrase that underscored the significance of black power for Asian Americans.[100] While Sumi had participated in coalition efforts on behalf of Third World students in the San Francisco Bay Area, she did not appear to be particularly identified with the emerging Asian American movement in Southern California.[101] The BPP also did not view her as a representative of Asian Americans but invited her due to her antiwar work with the military. Just prior to the scheduled departure of the Anti-Imperialist Delegation, she traveled with a group of GIs opposed to the war to the BPP headquarters in Berkeley. She met chief of staff David Hilliard, who extended an invitation to her to join the delegation.[102] Sumi's "Asianness" was not completely absent from the consideration to include her though. She believed that her presence resulted from tokenism: the organizers "realized that this was a delegation to Asia, and there were no Asians in the group."[103]

Not only did Sumi not necessarily identify with the Asian American category, she did not approach socialist Asia with the sense of radical nationalism that inspired Alex Hing. As a person of Japanese ancestry, Sumi was inadvertently linked to that nation's colonial legacy. As she stated following her return from the delegation, "Being Japanese is very confusing, because my Mama was in a camp for 2 years. . . . At the same time, I know the Japanese were slaughtering millions of innocent people in Asia. So I couldn't identify with the American pigs, when they were putting my people into camps, but I couldn't identify with the Japanese pigs either."[104] The trip to socialist Asia—particularly to Korea, a former colony of Japan—consequently raised rather difficult issues for Sumi regarding her ethnic and national identity. Her dilemma was mirrored in the contents of the *Gidra* newsletter, a publication produced by a predominantly Japanese American staff. The periodical drew parallels between the dropping of atomic bombs on Hiroshima and Nagasaki during World War II and the massive destruction wrought on Vietnam by the American military.[105] At the same time, the newsletter also highlighted Japan's roles as a colonial aggressor and as a Cold War ally of the United States. For Japanese Americans like Sumi, their desire for international leftist solidarity necessitated a critique of cultural nationalism and Japanese militarism.

Sumi and Hing differed in how their class, ethnicity, and gender shaped their political transformations. Hing, who identified with working-class Chinese Americans, was drawn to the militant masculine personas of the Black Panthers. Sumi, in contrast, came from a more privileged middle-class background and struggled with conventional expectations of Asian femininity and American militarized masculinity. While Hing embraced Chinese socialist nationalism as well as pan-Asian solidarity, Sumi critiqued Japanese imperialism and had not yet identified comfortably with the emerging Asian American movement. Nevertheless, as American activists of Asian descent, Sumi and Hing recognized their commonality and their collective difference from the white as well as African American activists on the Anti-Imperialist Delegation.

The disparity between the importance of black activism and the relative marginalization of Asian Americans within activist circles was mirrored by the differential treatment that these two groups received from white American activists and socialist Asian nations. The dominant understanding of racial oppression in the United States was based on the experiences of African Americans. In contrast, Asian Americans were almost completely invisible on the political radar. In addition, even though both the BPP and Asian American movement publications featured articles on socialist Asian nations, only the BPP newspaper contained greetings, letters, and telegrams from leaders like Mao Tse-tung, Ho Chi Minh, and Kim Il Sung.[106] These socialist Asian representatives regarded the black movement in the United States as a vanguard revolutionary force. They courted leaders like Eldridge Cleaver and organizations like the BPP. They also established contacts with the white New Left and monitored the broader antiwar movement. In contrast, relatively little attention was paid to Asian Americans, despite their ancestral connections to Asia and their growing admiration for socialist Asia. Nevertheless, both Alex Hing and Pat Sumi regarded their travels to North Korea, North Vietnam, and Red China as profoundly moving and transformative experiences. They, along with other members of the Anti-Imperialist Delegation, were eager to journey halfway around the world to witness the accomplishments of socialist Asia.

Chapter 5

A Revolutionary Pilgrimage

To reach the Democratic People's Republic of Korea (DPRK), almost all
the members of the Anti-Imperialist Delegation crossed the Atlantic instead
of the Pacific. In early July, some met Eldridge Cleaver in Algiers while
others joined the group in Paris. They then flew to Moscow and on to
North Korea, arriving in the capital, Pyongyang, on 14 July 1970.[1] Because
the U.S. government forbade entry into the DPRK on American passports,
the travelers received visas on a separate piece of paper that they could
remove if necessary.[2] They were right to be cautious. Cleaver's FBI file
indicated that the U.S. State Department attempted to track the delegation's
movements and ordered investigations of each member for possible violations of national security.[3]

Despite the surveillance, the Anti-Imperialist Delegation broadcast their
intentions and their findings. On the eve of their departure from Moscow,
the group held a press conference explaining the purpose of their trip. In the
words of Cleaver, they sought to expose "a history of U.S. imperialism in
Korea."[4] The mainstream press quoted only Eldridge Cleaver and Robert
Scheer, both well-known figures. Alex Hing also conveyed his sense of anticipation by writing a letter to the Asian American movement publication
Gidra:

I am here in Moscow with Comrade Eldridge Cleaver, Minister of Information of the Black Panther Party, enroute to North Korea. . . . This is the first delegation to be invited from Amerika by the Koreans. . . . As this is the first such trip by Amerikans and because two Asian Amerikans are on the delegation—sister Pat Sumi from movement for a Democratic Military is with us—the information we will gather and our experiences with the Korean people and Korean culture should be extremely exciting.[5]

During the delegation's travels in the DPRK, they were hosted by the Committee for the Peaceful Reunification of the Fatherland. The committee had two primary goals: first to educate their visitors about the historic and ongoing intervention of the United States on the Korean peninsula; and second to gain support from the American antiwar movement to unify North and South Korea. As the interviews and writings of the travelers reveal, the visitors were eager to absorb the anti-imperialist message of their hosts. The sites that the delegation visited resulted from mutual consultation. As Hing recalled, "One of the first things we did was sit around with the North Koreans to plan an itinerary."[6]

The North Koreans, like the North Vietnamese and the Red Chinese, supported the premise of "people's diplomacy" and received the travelers like dignitaries. The delegates were treated to banquets and receptions.[7] They also had the opportunity to engage in conversation with top governmental officials. Tranh Minh Quoc, who worked for the Vietnam Committee for Solidarity during the war, regularly hosted international delegations in North Vietnam. He recalled that the Cleaver group was a "high-level delegation"; they "held him in high esteem" because of Cleaver's leadership position in the Black Panthers.[8] The access that the Americans had and the treatment that they received contrasted greatly with their status within the United States. As Elaine Brown expressed soon after her return to the United States, "We were welcomed with open arms. And as a matter of fact we were treated as delegates, as diplomats, representing the people as opposed to the government . . . of the United States. . . . For the first time in even our own lives we were treated as human beings and as respected members of the human race."[9]

The perceptions of the Anti-Imperialist Delegation provide an opportunity to explore the connections between Third World internationalism and the concept of radical orientalism. The travelers, like other U.S. activists of the time, continued an orientalist practice of cultivating ideas and fantasies about the Orient as the polar opposite of the Occident and using these projections to more clearly define themselves. Their romanticization of Asia differed from traditional Western conceptions of the feudal, stagnant, and exotic Orient. Instead, as radicals who identified with socialist Asian countries, they highlighted the progressive, revolutionary East and contrasted it with the capitalist and militaristic West, or, in Eldridge Cleaver's words, the "wicked West."[10] Consequently, the experience of traveling in Asia provided an opportunity for American activists to gain a different vantage point on themselves and their home nation. Socialist Asia stimulated the imagination of U.S. radicals by modeling alternative societies based on revolutionary cultural and political values.

Radical orientalism is part of a broader embrace of Third World internationalism by American activists during the 1960s and 1970s. Todd Gitlin, a former SDS activist as well as a sociologist, explains that activists of his generation believed that "America [had] forfeited our love. . . . [Consequently] we needed to feel that someone, somewhere in the world, was fighting the good fight and winning. . . . Increasingly we found our exemplars and heroes in Cuba, in China, in the Third World guerrilla movements . . . [and] most of all—decisively in—Vietnam."[11] As this passage conveys, the "linkage of spirit" between American radicals with Vietnam was part of a broader fascination with the decolonizing and socialist Third World.[12] Just as U.S. activists traveled to Vietnam to witness and understand the war, they also went on journeys to Cuba. Beginning in 1969, the Venceremos Brigades mobilized people from the United States and around the world to harvest sugar cane.[13] They came to help Cuba meet its economic production goals in spite of the U.S. economic blockade and bans on travel.

Even as American activists embraced solidarity broadly with the socialist Third World, Asia, particularly Vietnam, occupied a distinct status within the American radical imagination. Asia was both closer and more distant for Americans. Asia spawned the earliest successful national liberation movements during the post–World War II era with the formation of the PRC and DPRK. Cuba and many countries in Africa did not achieve independence until the mid- to late 1950s and 1960s. Asia also became the site of overt and massive U.S. military confrontation with the Korean and Vietnam wars. Finally, due to geographical distance, political restrictions, and cultural/linguistic differences, Asia was more difficult for Americans to access, especially compared to Cuba. Despite the difficulties of traveling to the island, thousands participated in the Venceremos Brigades. In contrast, only two hundred people journeyed to Hanoi over the course of the war. Even so, the heroism of Vietnamese people in resisting American military power made them symbolically and emotionally important to U.S. activists. As Gitlin explains, "Visits to 'the other side' started as explorations and diplomatic missions and became pilgrimages."[14] Politically motivated journeys offered the possibility of spiritually rejuvenating the souls of American radicals.

The interviews and speeches given by the Anti-Imperialist Delegation soon after their journey reveal how their desire for political insight and transformation shaped their experiences as revolutionary pilgrims. Despite the enthusiasm of the delegates, it is important to recognize that they spent a limited amount of time in each country. They stayed for a month in the DPRK, three weeks in the Democratic Republic of Vietnam (DRV), and a week total in the PRC. In addition, the travelers' overall lack of familiarity with these Asian cultures and languages led them to rely on their hosts for information about socialist Asia. In other words, the Anti-Imperialist delegates were in many ways "tourists," who received a packaged and staged version of revolutionary Asia. Several of the delegates, many years later, expressed the belief that they were presented with carefully crafted views of socialism, particularly during their stay in North Korea. However, their public pronouncements during and soon after their journey conveyed their excitement at seeing these new societies. They sought to reproduce their radical orientalist perspective by emphasizing the destructiveness of U.S. intervention in Asia, the modernity of Asian socialism, and the revolutionary capabilities of Asian women.

In *Imperial Eyes*, Mary Pratt analyzes the writing of Westerners, most commonly European bourgeois men, who traveled to colonized lands. She illuminates how these visitors from the "metropole" arrived with a sense of "innocence."[15] They did not perceive or understand that their very presence and ability to travel resulted from an ongoing history of diplomatic, military, economic, cultural, and social penetration by the West into the lands that would become the Third World. In contrast, the Anti-Imperialist delegates were eager to understand the destructive impact, the guilt, of Western imperialism in Asia.

The Korean War (1950–53) is often referred to in the United States as the "forgotten war."[16] To counter this cultural amnesia, the Anti-Imperialist travelers were inundated with the history and legacies of the war. In their excursions in the North Korean capital city of Pyongyang, Elaine Brown recalled that they were reminded of how "the U.S. devastated, completely bombed and leveled" the city.[17] On one of their earliest stops, the delegation visited the "'Museum of Anti-Japanese Revolutionary Struggle'

Figure 7. The Anti-Imperialist Delegation coverage in the *Black Panther* newspaper, 3 October 1970.

where the group viewed pictures taken during the United States war with North Korea and a display of American military debris."[18] The museum also memorialized atrocities committed by the United States, including the mass death of thirty-five thousand people within fifty-two days of war. In a series of radio addresses upon her return to the United States, Brown shared the profound emotional impact of these sites. In Sinchon County,

> 87% of the population was wiped out here. A somber crowd awaited us outside the museum. It was as if the entire village had come out to look at us—there were no salutes, cheers, or clapping here, as there had been every-where else we had visited. All of them had lost husbands and wives, children and parents and grandparents. The museum itself was modest and shabby—of whitewashed cinderblocks, I think. It had obviously been as-sembled by the people themselves and was full of, along with photos and other documented evidence, the scraps of the personal possessions of the dead.[19]

Both the physical remnants and the survivors testified to American atroci-ties. Brown recalled seeing

> the bomb shelters where women and children and old people were herded together and gasoline poured over them and they were burned alive. There are still scratch marks on the walls where they struggled to get out. . . . A woman, whose sister was one of the few survivors of the ordeal, told us that a US officer went to the warehouses and seeing the women and children together, he declared that they looked too happy. This was after they'd been there over a week without food and water. So they separated the women from their children; they put the children into one warehouse and the women in the other. They gave the children gasoline to drink telling them that it was water, so they got violently ill. Then the troops finally set fire to the warehouses, and killed almost ev-eryone in them.[20]

The recounting of the war from the perspective of the DPRK challenged the dominant narrative of the conflict in the United States. Americans criticized North Koreans for initiating military engagement through their incursion into South Korea in 1950 and justified U.S. intervention as a necessary means to deter communist expansion. In contrast, the DPRK argued that the conflicts in the region resulted from U.S. political and military policies that divided Korea after World War II. According to this interpretation, the United States denied the legitimacy of indigenous nationalist leaders, who tended to be more closely allied with the Soviet Union and the PRC. Instead, the Americans backed a "puppet" South Korean government and military, which would follow the lead of U.S. Cold War policy.

The accounts of the Anti-Imperialist delegates might appear propagandistic. However, historians Bruce Cumings and Michael Cullen Green document that while the North Koreans were certainly not blameless in their conduct, the United States did engage in particularly vicious forms of warfare. According to Cumings, "From early November 1950 on, [General] MacArthur ordered that a wasteland be created between the front and the Chinese border, destroying from the air every 'installation, factory, city, and village' over thousands of square miles of North Korean territory."[21] Consequently, "by 1952 just about everything in northern and central Korea was completely leveled."[22] In addition to conventional bombs, napalm and other chemical weapons were used as well. On the ground, U.S. forces "thought anyone in 'white pajamas,' which they called the Korean native dress might potentially be an enemy. . . . [Consequently] American forces began burning villages suspected of harboring guerillas, and in some cases burned them merely to deny the guerillas hiding places."[23] The racial attitudes of American troops justified these atrocities. One journalist witnessed "an American Marine kill[ing] an elderly civilian as if in a fit of absentmindedness, showing no sign of remorse"; the writer commented that GIs "never spoke of the enemy as though they were people, but as one might speak of apes," noting that even some correspondents' "dearest wish was to kill a Korean. 'Today, . . . I'll get me a gook.'"[24]

Green further elaborates that "use of the term 'gook' was ubiquitous" during the Korean conflict, demonstrating an American fighting mentality that viewed Korean people as less than human. He cites one journalist as saying that U.S. troops referred to "a dead Korean body of whatever sex, uniformed or ununiformed," simply as "dead Gook" or "good Gook." Green also notes that the usage of this term could be traced to other militaristic and imperialistic ventures in Asia: "A linguistic cousin of 'goo-goos,' which was employed by servicemen to refer to Filipino insurgents at the turn of the century, it emerged in its current form in Korea."[25] The perception of Korean allies and enemies as subhuman justified the dropping of "more than 30,000 tons of napalm on a peninsula about the size of Minnesota" as well as the military strategy of "destroying civilian targets to prevent their real or potential use by the enemy."[26]

These characterizations of the American war in Korea resembled those of the U.S. war in Vietnam. The Anti-Imperialist delegates had the opportunity to compare these experiences directly. The group visited the DRV embassy during their stay in Pyongyang to pay their respects and received an unexpected invitation to travel to Hanoi. All of the travelers had engaged in the antiwar movement in the United States. Some were reluctant to prolong their journey beyond the initially allotted time, though. Ann Froines, whose daughter was two and a half that summer, was anxious about being away longer than she originally anticipated. Elaine Brown, who learned that Black Panther Party (BPP) leader Huey Newton was finally released from prison after three years of an international campaign to "free Huey," also expressed reluctance to continue their travels. However, Eldridge Cleaver and Bob Scheer, as heads of the delegation, disregarded any reservations and decided that the group would accept the invitation. Going to North Vietnam was exciting for many of the political activists. Randy Rappaport explained that she "had friends . . . who had gone to North Vietnam and that was like Mecca."[27]

The Anti-Imperialist travelers had all read and heard stories of atrocities committed by American troops. Nevertheless, the impact of meeting someone who experienced the war firsthand was profound. Alex Hing recalled, "We interviewed this one man who was working in his rice field. There were no military targest [*sic*] anywhere near this rice field. And this U.S. sky rat flew his plane over and threw napalm on him and 2 of his buddies. One was killed, one slightly wounded, and he was completely deformed by napalm. His arms were paralyzed, his face was melted into his body, and he could barely talk. When the weather got a little too hot or cold, he would experience excruciating pain."[28] In addition to this human suffering, Hing noted the environmental impact of chemical warfare, particularly the widespread use of herbicides: "There are sections in Vietnam where not even a blade of grass can grow, and these sections are all in the Mekong Delta, formerly the most densely populated area in the whole world." Based on his travels, Hing described the American policy in Asia, not just in Vietnam, as one of "genocide and biocide, which is the destruction of all life."[29] Given the extensiveness of American destruction in Vietnam, visitors could easily witness widespread damage and meet individuals who suffered injuries or lost loved ones.

The Anti-Imperialist Delegation's tour deepened their understanding of the scope of American military incursion into Asia as a whole. In addition to being exposed to the wartime sufferings of the North Vietnamese, the American travelers also met with Laotian and Cambodian leaders during their stay in Hanoi and Peking. Shortly before the Anti-Imperialist Delegation left on their journey, President Nixon publicly announced on 30 April that the United States had invaded Cambodia to target Vietcong bases of operation there. He had in fact ordered secret bombings in Cambodia more than a year earlier. Nixon's April announcement sparked the largest antiwar demonstrations to date, including the Kent State and Jackson State protests that resulted in the death of six students. Laos, which had been subjected to bombing as early as the Johnson administration, also would be invaded in February 1971. The Anti-Imperialist Delegation learned of this escalation throughout Southeast Asia through conversations with Laotian and Cambodian officials. Pat Sumi recalled visiting the Laos Information Bureau in Hanoi, where they learned the history and ongoing struggles of the Laotians. They also received gifts: "not of gold and diamonds but of struggle. They gave us . . . revolutionary song books, and gifts made from the metal of destroyed American aircraft. . . . As he presented Eldridge Cleaver with a beautiful large vase made from American aircraft debris, the Laotian representative said simply that he was returning part of a death machine transformed into a symbol of life to his American comrade."[30]

While the delegation did not experience such emotionally laden encounters during their stay in the PRC, they had the opportunity to meet with Prince Norodom Sihanouk, who was living in exile there due to the political instability instigated by the United States in Cambodia.[31] As Alex Hing recalled, "The anti-war movement only saw Vietnam as totally unconnected to other struggles in Laos, Cambodia (when we were in China we learned there are liberation struggles going on at very high levels in Burma, Thailand, Indonesia, Philippines and India)."[32]

This pan-Asian analysis of U.S. imperialism was significant both for the delegation's Asian hosts and for the development of an Asian American political consciousness. In the three-front strategy that Trinh Ngoc Thai outlined, forming a united front among Southeast Asian countries was a key component of fighting the U.S. war.[33] Both the United States and the DRV recognized that their political and military strategies needed to cross national boundaries. This articulation of a pan-Asian resistance to American imperialism resonated deeply with activists like Alex Hing seeking to create an Asian American political identity. The category "Asian American" emphasized the commonalities between people of Asian ancestry who suffered racial oppression in the United States and also their imagined connection with Asian nations that challenged American imperial power globally.[34]

Because the American military represented such a destructive force in the eyes of the Anti-Imperialist Delegation, the travelers staged protests during their stay in Asia. While in North Korea, they journeyed to the demilitarized zone at Panmunjom, where delegation members demonstrated "in front of American military police."[35] Cleaver's FBI file indicates that photographs of the Anti-Imperialist Delegation were taken at the site on 24 July 1970.[36] In Hanoi, Eldridge Cleaver and Elaine Brown made two radio broadcasts on Voice of Vietnam radio. They urged U.S. troops, particularly African American soldiers, to stop fighting the Vietcong and even to turn their weapons against their own officers. As Brown explained: "What we said in essence is to put down their guns. We told them to desert. We told them that in fact the best thing they could do, if they wanted to, if they had the guts to, would be [to] turn their guns against the people who are giving them orders to kill innocent Vietnamese people, who have not done anything to them and who are not invading California or New York or anything like this."[37]

These radio addresses replicated the content of Eldridge Cleaver's articles that had already appeared in the *Black Panther*.[38] The FBI monitored these broadcasts and writings with particular interest. They sought to verify the statements and determine their impact in order to gather evidence against Cleaver for "attempting to cause insubordination, disloyalty, or refusal of duty by members of the Armed Forces."[39] The concern of the U.S. government no doubt stemmed from the fact that actual incidents of disobedience and even violence against commanding officers were taking place. Between 1969 and 1972, the Department of Defense documented 788 fraggings or attempted fraggings, while a congressional investigation reported 1,016 incidents during the same time period.[40] Furthermore, African American soldiers tended to be disproportionately targeted for punishment compared to white soldiers who engaged in similar behavior.

The BPP delegates who appealed to black soldiers to stop fighting the war acted with the endorsement of their Vietnamese hosts. Other African American visitors to North Vietnam also were invited to speak on Radio Hanoi. During their visits, civil rights activists Diane Nash Bevel and Reverend James Lawson also communicated messages of racial and anticolonial solidarity between African Americans and Vietnamese.[41] In addition, Vietcong forces and sympathizers encouraged black soldiers not to fight and promised to refrain from shooting them. According to historian James Westheider, "Stories attesting to such special treatment for blacks were widely circulated and were sometimes true."[42]

The radio broadcasts were intended not just for American soldiers. They also fostered the morale of the Vietnamese people. As journalist Pham Khac Lam recalled, his stories about the United States focused on revealing the "weakness" of the enemy "so that [his] people . . . [would] go on fighting" and have the belief that they could win.[43] The Anti-Imperialist Delegation's visit, therefore, held great symbolic importance for the North Vietnamese. In fact, they sponsored an "international day of solidarity with the black people of the United States" on 18 August during the delegation's visit.[44] The date had been selected by the Organization for Solidarity with the People of Africa, Asia, and Latin America to commemorate the 1965 Watts rebellion.[45]

These ceremonial displays of Third World solidarity were personally moving for members of the Anti-Imperialist Delegation. Eldridge Cleaver recalled that he felt a sense of kinship with the Vietnamese. He expressed a special fondness for Premier Pham Van Dong, who granted the delegation a three-hour audience:[46]

> At one reception he paid a personal tribute to me that I will never forget. . . . He did a play on words of the French translation of my book, *Soul on Ice.* When they put you in an American jail, the slang expression is that you are "on ice." And the title of my book meant that my soul was in prison—in jail. The French have a different expression for the same experience—a person is not on ice, but he is "in the shadows" (out of the sun). The French title of my book translated *Un Noir a l'ombre*—"a black in the shadows." A notable poet in his own right, the premier understood this nuance in the foreign translation and said at this party, "In the West you are a black in the shadows, but here you are a black in the sun." That touched me deeply—both his awareness of my writing and his sensitivity to my difficulties in being in exile.[47]

While the North Vietnamese, like the North Koreans and the Red Chinese, emphasized black-Asian solidarity, they also more broadly embraced the philosophy of people's diplomacy. They repeatedly conveyed to the delegation and to other visitors from the United States that their enmity was directed toward the U.S. government, not the American people. Consequently, they allowed the Anti-Imperialist Delegation the opportunity to bring back to the United States 379 letters from American POWs in North Vietnam, a mail service that other visitors to Hanoi also performed.[48]

This message of reconciliation was compelling. Pat Sumi had experienced discomfort and embarrassment when exposed to the legacy of Japanese imperialism in Korea. She recalled feeling reluctant to speak Japanese with one of her North Korean hosts, because she did not want to evoke the experience of colonization. In the spirit of the people's diplomacy, her Asian host focused on the responsibility of the Japanese and American governments in carrying out imperialist policies, not the guilt of the Japanese and American peoples. Alex Hing also reflected on the powerful impact of this message following his return from Vietnam: "Our country had committed so many despicable crimes in that country and yet these people were the warmest, the most loving people that you'd ever meet. They were really genuinely friendly. . . . They made it very clear that even though they took us to these museums and things, and they showed us these sites where we could see the devastation of what the U.S. did, that they harbored no ill feelings for the American people. . . . You go back after that and you dedicate your life to ending the war."[49]

Through their travels, the Anti-Imperialist Delegation gained a more visceral and profound understanding of the impact of American policies in Asia. The activists also developed a critique of imperialist worldviews by inverting assumptions regarding modernization and civilization. The gaze of the traveler from the metropole to the colony is frequently the view from an industrialized culture into an allegedly less evolved, more primitive society.[50] The socialist countries that the anti-imperialists visited, particularly the DPRK and the PRC, took pains to highlight the modernization of their economy and society. In fact, they modeled an alternative form of modernity, a socialist version that countered Western capitalism. Elaine Brown captured these perspectives in a speech she gave at the University of California, Berkeley, soon after her return to the United States. She reflected that in visiting socialist Asia, "one gets the feeling of being catapulted ahead in time and visiting some sort of future society."[51]

The idea that socialist Asia was ahead of Western development challenged fundamental beliefs that most Americans held about their own country and the world. In a radio interview after her return to the United States, Elaine Brown responded to a series of questions regarding North

Korea. The queries revealed assumptions regarding the lack of development in Asia, partly due to information that American travelers shared about North Vietnam. The radio interviewer asked, "What kind of a town is Pyongyang? It might as well be on the moon, you know, as far as anybody here knows about it. . . . Everyone who goes to Hanoi has expressed wonderment that this is really a sort of small town. . . . Is the agricultural sector of the [North Korean] country . . . still fairly primitive, as far as instruments and that kind of thing is concerned? . . . In North Vietnam the agricultural methods are still fairly simple and it's done in the traditional way as I understand it."[52]

In response, Brown emphasized the industrial, agricultural, and social development of the DPRK: "Pyongyang is a major, large city. It's a very beautiful city. There are many new buildings. . . . I don't have the exact figures. But it is a large city and you don't have the feeling that this is some underdeveloped country. This is a highly developed, industrial, agricultural state."[53] In contrast to the United States, "there were no homeless beggars on the streets of Pyongyang, no prostitutes, no hustlers. There were no gambling houses or cheap bars, no rundown houses or apartment buildings. Connected to every workplace were a free clinic and a free child-care facility or school."[54] Even in the rural regions, "the entire countryside has electricity, in all houses and so forth. . . . And in comparison to the United States . . . the people who live on cooperative farms actually live on a much higher living standard . . . because each person, for example, is provided already with health care and medical facilities, with childcare, with housing, with some clothing allotment, with a free educational system up through what we would call high school and even college education. So that the so-called peasant is not living at a low standard at all."[55]

Brown's statements sound propagandistic and no doubt reflect the selective experiences that she had during her stay in North Korea. Many years after the Anti-Imperialist Delegation, members expressed skepticism toward the constant references to Kim Il Sung, who was credited for all the positive developments in North Korea. However, some of Brown's impressions of the society and economy in the DPRK are corroborated by historian Bruce Cumings. Previously industrialized under Japanese colonialism, the country formulated economic plans throughout the 1950s and 1960s to focus on "reconstruction and development of major industries devastated by the war."[56] As a result, their "industry grew at 25 percent per annum in the decade after the Korean War, according to external observers, and about 14 percent from 1965–78."[57] The DPRK's economy actually outperformed its southern counterpart during this time period, despite the massive amount of U.S. aid given to South Korea's economy.[58] By 1965, "American economic and military aid still accounted for about 75 percent of the South's military budget, 50 percent of the civil budget, and nearly 80 percent of the available foreign exchange."[59] However, during "the period 1945–60 it was rare to find any American official who thought the ROK [Republic of Korea] would become 'economically viable.'"[60] In contrast to South Korea's dependency on the United States, the North Koreans accepted aid from the Soviet Union and China but mainly sought to create "an independent, self-contained economy," even from other socialist nations.[61] In its restructuring, the DPRK deprioritized consumer goods and focused on providing social welfare. According to Cumings, even the "World Health Organization and other UN agencies praise the delivery of basic health services; North Korean children are better vaccinated against disease by far than are American children."[62]

The Anti-Imperialist delegates were particularly impressed by the education and resources available for children in the DPRK. As Elaine Brown explained, "You notice that the Korean people put great emphasis on the youth because, of course, the youth are future generations to continue the society."[63] Her interest in children no doubt partly stemmed from becoming a new mother herself and partly from the Black Panthers' outreach to community children through their free breakfast and educational programs. Alex Hing described in detail their visits to "children's palaces," which were constructed "not only in the largest cities but also in the most mountainous, rural villages":

Children between the ages of 7–12 can attend these palaces, organize their own activities, for about 4 months at a time. Children go there after school, on weekends, and during vacations. One we visited in Pyongyang was as big as a large-size university building, and had an agricultural cooperative connected to it outside the city, and a zoo, too. . . .

By the time they reach 9 years of age, children are taught to play 3 instruments well enough to play for concerts. Children are taught to dismantle weapons, embroider, paint, sculpture, dance, sing, do mathematics, understand an entire economic system, and the entire production process of one factory. The worker in the U.S. has no conception of what his job is . . . all he knows is you put this bolt in this hole all day long. In Korea a child is taught the entire production process of 5 or 6 different products by the time he is 9. He learns to make vinylon, a Korean discovery, because they couldn't grow cotton, they make a synthetic out of rock. A 9 year old can explain the entire process of converting limestone into vinylon.[64]

This extensive system of child care and education that the DPRK created was part of their revolutionary goal of reformulating family and gender roles in order to create a new socialist citizenry. Kyung Ae Park argues that "as early as 1946, North Korea . . . instituted various policies regarding women's emancipation . . . aim[ed] at three basic goals: liberation from the patriarchal family and social system; liberation through social labor; and the creation of a socialist woman."[65] Kim Il Sung himself "advocated that the state should take steps to rear children under public care in order to encourage women to take part in public life."[66] As a result, the numbers of nurseries and kindergartens grew from 12 and 116 respectively in 1949 to the capacity for "almost 100 percent of the 3.5 million children" to "enter more than 60,000 nurseries and kindergartens" by 1976.[67] The new child care system enabled parental, particularly maternal, involvement in public life, especially in the realm of economic production. In addition, the educational system helped to create new socialist male and female subjects in the next generation.

In the DPRK, the Anti-Imperialist delegates encountered a society that was both modern and fundamentally different in values than the United States. As Hing gushed in a second letter to *Gidra* magazine at the conclusion of their stay, "So many stupendous things have happened to me here in Korea that cannot possible [*sic*] fit within the framework of this letter. Suffice it to say that the Socialist countries in Asia are probably the bastion of world civilization."[68]

The delegation's visit to the PRC reinforced the message that socialist Asia represented an alternative modernity to the United States. Traveling to China was particularly moving for Hing, who claimed to have initiated their trip there. When the Anti-Imperialist Delegation was asked where they would like to visit during their stay in the DPRK, he immediately requested to see the PRC embassy. His demand was a source of embarrassment for Eldridge Cleaver. Despite the popular understanding in the United States of the monolithic nature of communism, the DPRK and the PRC had ongoing tensions. Cleaver was concerned that Hing might have offended their North Korean hosts. However, as a result of Hing's request, the entire delegation not only visited the Chinese embassy but also received an invitation to visit the PRC itself.[69] They traveled through

China to visit North Vietnam but then returned for a lengthier stay on 3 September.[70] Hing recalled his exchange with the Chinese embassy in one of his letters to *Gidra*: "The representative of the People's Republic of China expressed solidarity with the anti-U.S. imperialist struggle with Amerika on behalf of the 700 million Chinese people. I, on behalf of the 300 thousand Chinese-Amerikans, expressed our wishes that Chairman Mao live ten thousand years!"[71] Hing remembered years later that when he arrived in his ancestral land, he "literally got off the plane and kissed the ground."[72]

The sheer size of the Chinese population impressed upon the delegates that this nation and its people would play an important role on the world stage. While the DPRK had approximately forty million people, the PRC was home to seven hundred million. As Elaine Brown reflected, with a nation that size, "you know that the Chinese people are not going to tolerate any kind of aggressive act by the U.S. imperialists."[73] Seeking to impress their Chinese hosts, Eldridge Cleaver attempted to exaggerate the number of African Americans. As he recalled, "The U.S. government used to say that there were 25 million blacks in the country. The Panther figure was 35 million—we wanted to have a power base, so we included the people who were passing as whites. But under these oriental circumstances, I said, 'About 40 million blacks in America.' The Chinese expert stared at me a minute and said quietly, 'Ah, we have some villages that size.'"[74] The Chinese representative no doubt exaggerated as well or perhaps they miscommunicated about numbers.[75] Even so, Brown recalled being impressed with the social organization of the sizable Chinese capital. She shared: "Peking is a tremendous city. I believe there's a population of about 6 or 7 million. That's almost the population of New York, and yet its [*sic*] not like New York, because the people are not squashed into housing. The land space is plenty enough for them to live comfortably. . . . If people were to be really concerned with each other and if governments were concerned with their people, of course, people wouldn't have to live like that."[76] Again, the delegates' limited stay in socialist Asia, particularly in China where they only visited for a week, gave them a rather selective view. In addition, their previous experiences with urban slums and rural poverty in the United States led the travelers to speak glowingly about alternative ways to organize society.

Even the underdevelopment of DRV did not deter the Anti-Imperialist delegates from celebrating the potential of socialist Asia. As Elaine Brown explained, "The main thing that you see is the fact that the Vietnamese people have been stifled in their growth. They achieved liberation, but yet they have not been able to move within, in terms of socialist construction . . . because of the fact they're of course occupied. . . . They cannot put their full emphasis and full concentration on developing the society in terms of agriculture and industry."[77] Even under conditions of war, Brown stressed that "they're building factories. . . . And they have cooperative farms, and hospitals."[78]

In North Vietnam, what most impressed the delegates was not necessarily their attempts to achieve modernity but their efforts to combat U.S. technological might with limited resources. As Pat Sumi reflected:

> One of the things that I learned from the Vietnamese is that you can win with superior thinking and not necessarily with superior technology. . . . When the bombers came [to one of the villages], it was just at first a shattering experience with the noise, the power of the bombs, the destruction, the killing, the strafing of livestock, and the strafing of old people, women, and children as they ran for cover. The use of napalm, and all of these things. . . . Certainly they [the villagers] had had to fight the French, but their total armaments consisted of a couple of ancient M-1 carbines, single-load carbines, where you put in one, you shoot it, pop it out, and put in another. When the bombers came, people were terrified, people were angry, and they immediately demanded [of] the party structure and the local government that the national government and the national party do something to protect them. They asked them to send the more arms and send them anti-aircraft weapons and so on, and the government said, "We will, as soon as we have them, but this is going to be a long time. You're going to have to find some way to do it yourself, because we don't have guns and we don't have anti-aircraft at this point, and such as we have we have around a hundred at Hai Phong to protect the big cities." . . . So I was told that this village had a big meeting about "What are we going to do? The government can't help us, right now. We're going to have to do something," and one old man told me "We adopted as our slogan, when the airplanes come, should we look up and study the airplanes or should we look down and run" and he said "We all decided to look up. The only way we could defeat the airplanes was by knowing more about the airplanes than we did, because we could not match them technologically.[79]

After observing the planes, the villagers developed a sense of the flight patterns, which allowed them to farm without fear of attacks at certain times of the day. They also tested their carbines and discovered the limited range of these weapons. Through the use of human decoys, some of whom lost their lives in an effort to lure the planes into range, the villagers ultimately shot down two American fighter planes.

The underdog status of these Vietnamese villagers underscored the message that the entire war conveyed to the American public. The DRV and the Vietcong lacked the technological weaponry of the U.S. military, but they were winning the war or at least fighting the United States to a stalemate. As Sumi explained, the Vietnamese "were successful because they used superior knowledge, courage and determination and love to do it."[80] When she praised them for their ingenuity and questioned whether she had the capability to replicate their revolutionary spirit, her hosts responded, "No, you're just like us, and we're just like you. Nobody would allow this to happen to their own country without fighting, by whatever means possible. Even with your bare hands you would fight."[81] While the DPRK and the PRC represented socialist alternatives to modernization, the DRV served as a reminder not to underestimate the seeming "primitiveness" and "backwardness" of Asian society.

The theme of the oppressed overcoming their oppressors was also embedded in the delegation's final method of subverting the imperialist gaze. In classic orientalist travel narratives, the colonial destination tends to serve as a site for interracial erotic conquest. As exemplified by the Madame Butterfly storyline, these interactions usually occur between Western male travelers and "native" women. These non-Western women offer food, medicine, and cultural knowledge as well as sexual companionship during the duration of the traveler's stay. All this, and these women have little power to protest when their Western lovers decide to leave.[82] This portrayal of eroticized cooperation and submission symbolically represents the geopolitical status of the colony in relation to the metropole. In contrast, the Anti-Imperialist Delegation and their socialist hosts highlighted the role of Asian women in liberating and rebuilding their motherlands.

The focus on revolutionary womanhood stemmed from the interests of both the American travelers and the socialist Asian societies that they visited. The predominantly female composition of the delegation and the emergence of the women's liberation movement in the United States by the late 1960s inevitably led to discussions among the travelers regarding gender roles. In fact, when the delegation was in Moscow, they "made tape recordings explaining their activist histories and why they believed traveling to North Korea was significant for them personally."[83] Ann Froines noted, "The taping session was the beginning of a 2-hour discussion which broke through a lot of shit, especially on the women question. The group felt closer, more coherent."[84] All of the female travelers were eager to learn more about women in socialist societies. Even before Elaine Brown's visit to Asia, she was exposed to the exemplary abilities of revolutionary Vietnamese women. Images and discussions of their accomplishments appeared in the *Black Panther* newspaper.[85] Furthermore, they were part of the BPP curriculum. When Brown first joined the BPP, she attended the mandatory classes taught by Ericka Huggins, who offered these instructions regarding the ideal female revolutionary: "Ericka told us point-blank that as women we might have to have a sexual encounter with 'the enemy' at night and slit his throat in the morning—at which we all groaned. She reminded us of the Vietnamese guerrilla women, who were not only carrying guns but using their very bodies against the American forces. . . . Our gender was but another weapon, another tool of the revolution."[86]

This portrayal of Vietnamese women as devious and sexual predators evokes popular depictions of Asian women as both "dragon ladies" and "prostitutes," representations that circulated both in the American public and among U.S. soldiers. As Heather Marie Stur points out, "the idea of the dragon lady" who is simultaneously seductive and deadly builds upon previous orientalist depictions of Asian women and reveals the ambivalence of the American military toward their role in Vietnam.[87] The image of the alluring yet dangerous Vietnamese woman symbolized the broader country. American troops were there to "protect" South Vietnam, but the inhabitants also had the potential to betray their masculine rescuers. The Black Panthers, according to Elaine Brown, renarrated this GI cautionary tale of seduction and betrayal to emphasize the revolutionary capacity of Vietnamese women.

The interest of the Anti-Imperialist Delegation in female roles was matched by the efforts of their hosts to emphasize the importance of women in socialist revolution. Each country had a specific organization, like the Vietnam Women's Union, that focused on women's issues and engaged foreign visitors in discussion about their status and concerns.[88] In fact, the union had a long history of establishing contacts with international women's peace groups.[89] Pat Sumi recalled the impact of their conversations: "In every country we went to, everyone kept telling us that women are half the population, and if we all rose up at once, the revolution would be over. So organizing women is very important."[90]

The women's organizations in socialist Asian countries did not reinforce the dragon lady depiction of Asian women but instead emphasized the revolutionary potential of peasant and working women. The Asian hosts focused on the importance of understanding that female liberation involved over-turning "triple oppression." As Sumi explained, women "were oppressed by the imperialists, colonialists (French, Japanese, etc.) and they were oppressed by the national bourgeoisie of each country which maintained capitalist op-pression over them, and they were also oppressed within their own families and cultures."[91] As a result of the overlapping nature of these hierarchies, the Asian socialists emphasized that "women cannot possibly be liberated until the whole country is liberated, not only from imperialism but also from capitalism." Consequently, "women have to organize each other about things that will enlighten women about the entire liberation struggle."[92] These Asian socialist critiques that embedded women's liberation within class and national liberations resonated with the analysis of the BPP and for women of color in the late 1960s and 1970s. They tended to view women's liberation in the United States as mainly a white, middle-class movement that did not take into account racial discrimination and class oppression.

By visiting established socialist countries like the DPRK and the PRC, the delegation observed how these societies enabled more equal participa-tion for women in society. Alex Hing recalled how "women in Korea and China have incredible day care centers. Every factory and collective farm or commune has a kindergarten and a nursery, where if a mother wants to, she can drop off her kid Monday morning and pick him up Friday night. In the U.S., if a mother has 3 kids she's washed up. . . . she has to take care of the kids, she can't work. In Korea and China, if a mother has 3 kids, she can work 6 hours and get paid for 8. During pregnancy in Korea, women get 66 days off, and in China I think it's 56 days."[93] In addition to day care cen-ters, Pat Sumi also noted the availability of services that made household chores more convenient for women: "In Korea, they have restaurants attached to the factory where you can order food in the morning and pick it up in the evening hot, and take it across the street for your family's dinner. So you don't have to spend 2 hours fixing dinner. You can do other things."[94] The comments of both Hing and Sumi suggest that these services were estab-lished to free women from the responsibilities of cooking and caring for children in order to engage in productive labor, such as working in a factory or on a farm. Their reports do not indicate that men should learn to share in these family responsibilities or that some women may choose not to marry or have children.

Scholars of North Korea also note the contradiction between policies that state the goals of female liberation and economic integration along with the persistence of patriarchal norms that construct women's roles primarily through maternity.[95] Soon after the DPRK was founded, legislation was passed to grant women economic rights, such as the right to own land, the right to work, and maternity benefits. After the widespread destruction of the Korean War, the North Korean government valued women as both producers and reproducers. Women contributed to the development of a new socialist economy, constituting "54.9 percent" of the labor force by 1965; in addition, "women in North Korea were under strong pressure to produce more children."[96] In 1970, the year that the Anti-Imperialist Delegation visited North Korea, the "Fifth Congress of the Korean Workers' Party (KWP) made freeing women from the heavy burden of the household a major goal of the party."[97] Even as the socialist state established service industries, like child care and food service, to alleviate some of the double burden, North Korean leaders still expected women to serve as the primary cultural reproducers of the family. As Kim Il Sung stated in 1971, "The mother has to bear the major responsibility for home education. Her responsibility is greater than the father's . . . because it is she who gives birth to children and brings them up."[98]

Due to the incomplete gender revolution in Socialist Asia, which prioritized "material liberation" or "the ability [of women] to work and do activities equal to men," the Anti-Imperialist Delegation were eager to observe how these societies promoted "cultural liberation," which strived to change people's understandings of gender roles.[99] In China, Pat Sumi credited the Cultural Revolution for challenging the social hierarchy and thereby transforming gender hierarchy. The Cultural Revolution

> liberated everyone from all the old, capitalist, bourgeois ideology and behavior patterns and established a whole new set which are infinitely more humane, equalitarian, democratic, and liberated than the old bourgeois patterns were. Every human being is a creative and beautiful and complete human being able to make collective contributions to the well-being of all the other human beings on the planet earth. Women in China have gone through this whole thing. They dress almost like men do, jackets and slacks, because it's more convenient. They have no fears in meetings about speaking up. It doesn't mean that all the difference between sexes have been erased or that romantic love has been erased. Politically and ideologically people are equal and united as a class.[100]

Sumi's perception of the Cultural Revolution reflected an idealized and limited understanding of this period of Chinese history. As the youthful

Red Guard and various factions within the political elite sought to transform Chinese feudal culture, they also caused widespread suffering and persecution.

At the time that the delegation visited the PRC, though, Elaine Brown also commented on the sense of political solidarity and equality that was conveyed by women and men dressing in a similar manner:

> The Chinese people are strong and they are determined to work toward world revolution. . . . The women all wear pants and they're not involved with clothing. They wear good clothing, very simple, very plain, and very pretty too. When we arrived back in New York, having left Peking not too long before that, it almost looked like walking into the snake pit. Because you see all kinds of madness. Everybody dressed in 15 different ways, and people looked confused. And when you're in China everything is clear, everyone is beautiful.[101]

Again, Brown's reference point was not just what she was observing in China but how her travels contrasted with certain practices and values that she associated with the United States.

Scholar Emily Honig notes the tendency to overlook the complex impact of gender during the Cultural Revolution. She points out that officially both "feminism and femininity were rejected. Feminism, or any discussion of women's specific problems, was declared bourgeois; femininity, or any assertion of a specifically female identity, was denounced."[102] Instead, the image of "the Iron Girls—strong, robust, muscular women who boldly performed physically demanding jobs traditionally done by men—were celebrated."[103] External visitors tended to applaud "the plain-colored loose-fitting clothes worn by men and women alike for preventing the sexual objectification of women that they so abhorred in their own countries."[104] Some Chinese women did experience empowerment through these public transformations of gender roles and gender presentation. However, they were encouraged to emulate masculinity in the name of gender neutrality. Also, various forms of gender inequality persisted, particularly in the familial and sexual realms.

Not all the women in the Anti-Imperialist Delegation were as enamored of what they learned on the tour. Ann Froines noted during her stay in North Korea:

> We do not have enough information to do a very good article on women. We've seen some remarkable women, seen women in roles very different

and "liberated," observed the remarkable benefits the state provides . . .
but—we don't know about women

1) in politics
2) in the family
3) in self-defense units, militia

Where are the Madame Binhs? It is very hard to say what women have to look forward to in the way of liberation.[105]

Froines's frustrations reflected the incompleteness of female liberation in North Korea. While women constituted a sizable portion of the economic workforce, they still lacked "equal 'power of property.'"[106] In addition, women in the DPRK constituted distinct minorities in the political realm and the military. Kyung Ae Park argues they lacked "power of position and the power of force."[107] While "a handful of women played a part in the political leadership hierarchy," their status "was not the institutionalization of women's power but a 'star system'" that recognized individual women.[108]

At the same time that Froines expressed disappointment, her query "Where are the Madame Binhs?" reveals her eagerness to learn from socialist female role models. Nguyen Thi Binh was the foreign minister of the Provisionary Revolutionary Government of South Vietnam (created by the National Liberation Front) and their chief negotiator at the Paris peace talks.[109] She was widely recognized among American female activists, mainly because she helped to initiate and maintain connections with U.S. women's peace groups. In addition, she served as a role model because she occupied such a significant position of leadership. Perhaps due to her greater visibility and influential position, Binh's "star power" was more convincing as an indicator of broader transformations of gender roles in Vietnam.

The female Anti-Imperialist delegates gave their highest praise to, and told their most adulatory stories about, women, not in the established socialist societies of the DPRK and the PRC, but in Vietnam, where they contributed centrally to the struggles for independence. As Pat Sumi explained: "Women in Vietnam have a tradition of being liberation fighters. . . . We met this 17 year old woman. In her village there was an all-woman guerilla unit that shot down 2 American airplanes, while taking responsibility for the rice fields around the battery where the anti-aircraft guns are. They produced more on that rice field than any other comparable plot in the village. And the whole group sang poetry and songs for us."[110] Sumi exalted these Asian female warriors, whom she portrayed as exemplary fighters, farmers, and folk artists. In contrast, Elaine Brown emphasized the tragic nature of the war in Vietnam, which forced "young women . . . sixteen and seventeen years old . . . [to spend their lives] watching the sky for U.S. planes to come back. When of course 16 and 17-year old women, girls here don't have to do that. . . . This shouldn't be part of a 16-year old girl's life—to have spent practically all of her life, from the time say since she was 10 years old, involved in watching the skies for planes coming over for possible bombings."[111] One widely circulated image in U.S. movement newspapers captures the sense of vulnerability and strength of Vietnamese women. Publications like the *Black Panther* and *Gidra* featured the same drawing of an Asian female peasant, cradling a rifle in one arm and a baby in the other.[112] She appears equally ready to engage in armed struggle and to nurture her child. In fact, the image suggests that in order to fulfill her role as a mother, the female peasant must take up arms. As a symbol of revolutionary womanhood and motherhood, she conveys the interconnectedness of multiple liberations: by fighting for her family, her class, and her nation, the female peasant also frees herself.

Figure 8. Peasant woman with baby and gun. Cover of *Gidra*, March 1970, reproduced in Steve Louie and Glenn Omatsu, eds., *Asian Americans: The Movement and the Moment.* Los Angeles: UCLA Asian American Studies Center Press, 2001, p. 17.

The transformation of gender roles appeared more complete in Vietnam, where women visibly and heroically obtained power of property, position, and force. Two arguments could be made to explain Vietnamese exceptionalism. First, the Vietnamese proclaimed a distinct nationalist tradition of female liberation fighters. They traced this legacy all the way to "the Trung sisters," who combated Chinese imperialism "in c.e. 40" and became nationalist "martyrs to the cause of Vietnam."[113] Sandra Taylor, in her interviews with Vietnamese women who fought in wars of liberation against the French and the United States, points out that these women "drew on their land's 2,000-year history as well as the very recent past."[114] In addition to this folk national history, which provided female role models of leadership, Vietnam was engaged in an ongoing hot war. A saying commonly repeated during the war was, "When war comes, even women have to fight."[115] Cynthia Enloe and other scholars have argued that wartime conditions commonly necessitate gender experimentation; in contrast, the postwar periods of societal reconstruction frequently result in gender regression.[116]

In the midst of the U.S. war in Vietnam, women were mobilized through nationalist folklore and wartime propaganda. The Vietnamese Communist Party encouraged women to do so by assuming three responsibilities. "She took responsibility for her household and raised her children, she carried on production so the soldiers could be fed, and she fought in place of her husband when he went off to war."[117] As a result of wartime demands, Vietnamese women at the grassroots and elite levels assumed a visible and highly valued role in their societies.

The anti-imperialist gaze of the delegation, which focused on American guilt, Asian modernity, and Vietnamese women warriors, tended to rely on radical orientalist logic to praise socialist Asia and to condemn the United States. In their eyes, Asia continued to represent the contrasting image of the West. However, it was a modernized and revolutionary Asia rather than an exotic, stagnant, mystical Orient. Furthermore, the travelers sought not only to portray socialist Asia but more importantly to point out the flaws of the United States.

The delegation's perceptions of decolonizing Asia resonated with their hosts' political agenda. Pham Khac Lam, who wrote about the United States to Vietnamese audiences, also met with international delegations to North Vietnam. He recalled organizing the itineraries with three goals in mind: "First of all, we want them to see . . . the aggression of war . . . [what] is happen[ing] to our people, so that they can . . . tell the situation to the American people . . . [of] the war crimes. . . . Secondly, . . . we want them to see the determination of the Vietnamese to resist the war of aggression. . . . The third thing we want . . . to . . . acknowledge is the peaceful life the Vietnamese want to live when there is no bombing."[118] These goals, in Lam's eyes, were not distortions of reality but "the real situation . . . the sufferings of the people" and their genuine desire for peace.[119]

The American travelers, however, had limited time and ability to develop a full and complex understanding of socialist Asia. They visited select sites. In addition, they followed an orientalist tradition of perceiving the East in relation to the West. As Pat Sumi expressed, "One of the things about being raised in an imperialist country is . . . somehow you are almost completely unconscious of your beliefs and values. . . . You think they are so normal that you are unconscious of them. What happens when you go in a delegation like that to a foreign country is you finally become acutely aware of what it means to be American and what it means to be a non-American."[120]

The Anti-Imperialist Delegation and the phenomenon of radical orientalism offer new insights into U.S. political movements of the 1960s and 1970s. First, Cleaver's pilgrimage reveals how socialist Asia served as a beacon of hope for American activists. As the most visible examples of Third World resistance against U.S. imperialism during the Cold War, North Vietnam, Red China, and to a lesser degree North Korea inspired the imaginations of American radicals.[121] The concept of radical orientalism can be linked to Bill Mullen's idea of Afro-orientalism, the political inspiration that decolonizing Asia offered for African Americans more broadly throughout the twentieth century. The "red East" also served as a particularly powerful symbol for activists of other racial backgrounds. Perhaps it resonated most profoundly for Asian American activists who otherwise would be relatively invisible in the American political landscape.

Second, not only did Asian American, African American, and other American activists turn toward socialist Asia for political guidance, they also sought inspiration from those whom they perceived to be the most disempowered. Along with Mao, Ho, and Kim, the figure of the peasant woman warrior also circulated widely within activist circles. The female guerrilla fighter resonated strongly with the growing women's movement but also with male radicals. She symbolized the ultimate underdog. After all, if female peasants in an underdeveloped nation could beat the most technologically advanced and wealthy country in the world, what might be possible for activists within the United States?

Finally, the political inspiration that socialist Asia and Asian individuals offered for activists globally resulted from a combination of Western desire for revolutionary role models and Eastern effort to foster international solidarity. North Korea, North Vietnam, and Red China consciously sought out allies among citizens of the world. They fought on the battlegrounds and negotiated with heads of state. They also understood the importance of engaging in personal diplomacy and the power of an international people's movement.

Chapter 6

The Belly of the Beast

As the Anti-Imperialist delegates celebrated socialist Asia and condemned the United States, they also developed intense conflicts with one another. As Pat Sumi reflected, "The only way to explain what it was like is for you . . . to spend every day for two and a half months with the same eleven people in a foreign country where you don't speak the language. . . . Every weird idiosyncrasy, eccentricity, twitch, habit, not to mention sexuality, power trips, egos, everything comes into play. . . . People had fights. People stopped speaking to each other."[1] These tensions, with one notable exception, were not publicly aired, either during the delegation's travels or immediately following their return. Aside from Elaine Brown's conflicts with Eldridge Cleaver, the volatile differences were expressed in documents that were more privately circulated at the time or from recollections long after the trip.[2] The deterioration of group dynamics generated multiple and at times contradictory accounts of what occurred.

Representing a cross-section of the U.S. radical Left, the Anti-Imperialist Delegation shared a revolutionary critique of America and an admiration for socialist Asia. However, the individuals on the delegation subscribed to different political goals, ideologies, and strategies. They also preferred diverse methods of communication and organizing. In addition, they were

Figure 9. Anti-Imperialist Delegation (arms raised) with Vietnamese women (wearing hats). Delegation members, left to right, front: Pat Sumi, Ann Froines, Randy Rappaport, Elaine Brown, and Jan Austin; back: Gina Blumenfeld, Bob Scheer, Eldridge Cleaver, Alex Hing, and Andy Truskier. Eldridge Cleaver Papers, BANC PIC 1991.078-PIC, Bancroft Library, University of California, Berkeley.

relative strangers who had distinct personalities. These political and personal differences, as Pat Sumi suggested, festered under the incubating pressures of living for an extended period of time in unfamiliar settings. Because of the delegation's limited ability to communicate or travel freely, they were forced to spend extensive amounts of time together.

Furthermore, the reach of the U.S. security state, even beyond American borders, heightened insecurities and divisions within the Anti-Imperialist Delegation. At the time, Eldridge Cleaver was in exile but still under surveillance. As the most recognized leader and as the person responsible for initiating the delegation, he imposed his authority on the group. Cut off geographically from his base in the United States, Cleaver's continued political relevance was in many ways dependent on his connections with the socialist Third World. In turn, his stature within these international networks relied on an actual or perceived ability to mobilize the political resources and contacts of the Black Panthers and the U.S. radical Left. Con-

Figure 10. Eldridge Cleaver with Vietnamese women. Eldridge Cleaver Papers, BANC PIC 1991.078-PIC, Bancroft Library, University of California, Berkeley.

sequently, Cleaver was deeply invested in the interactions and outcomes of the Anti-Imperialist Delegation. He was a charismatic and persuasive figure but also inclined toward demanding control and obedience. Bob Scheer, his co-organizer and confidante, literally served as second in command.

The power dynamics within the Anti-Imperialist Delegation need to be analyzed utilizing an intersectional framework.[3] The authority of Cleaver and Scheer held distinct gender implications. No female delegates could speak or make decisions on behalf of the group. In addition, the travelers at times formed alliances with or expressed hostility toward one another due to race, ethnicity, and sexuality. These difficult dynamics eddied around the figure of Cleaver. Some delegate accounts of the Black Panther leader and even fragments of his own writings portray Cleaver as a mercurial and abrasive person who expressed sexist, anti-Semitic, and even anti-Asian sentiments. He led a multiracial, multiethnic, cross-gender group to socialist Asia, but Cleaver also targeted members of his own delegation for humiliation and hostility.

The Panthers frequently described African Americans as residing within "the belly of the beast."[4] The beast symbolized, in their eyes, the militaristic, racist, and imperialist country of the United States. In fact, Cleaver referred to America as "Babylon," a site of corruption and iniquity. Being in the belly of the beast, African Americans had the revolutionary potential to tear down the corrupt system from inside. Yet Cleaver, like other radicals who challenged social norms, also had the capacity to reinscribe social hierarchies. They could reproduce the beast within themselves and in their interactions with one another.

Nevertheless, these portrayals of Cleaver, both by others and by himself, need to be carefully evaluated and contextualized. Certainly, the more public and negative narrations about the Anti-Imperialist Delegation, written by Elaine Brown and Eldridge Cleaver himself, surfaced in highly charged political circumstances. Brown's allegations about Cleaver justified a volatile split within the Black Panther Party (BPP) that emerged after the delegation returned from socialist Asia. Cleaver's autobiographical account of his political exile was published many years later, when he was brokering a deal to return to the United States. In other words, the experiences of the Anti-Imperialist Delegation could be interpreted and reinterpreted depending on the political needs of the narrators.

These accounts of the Anti-Imperialist Delegation and of socialist Asia, then, reveal the strength of traditional and not just radical orientalist thinking in two ways. First, the depictions of Asian and Asian American individuals at times evoked stereotypical representations of both Orientals and communists. Second, Asia once again serves as a blank canvas on which Western travelers can project their fears and aspirations in order to more clearly define their own identities.

Elaine Brown provided two troubling accounts of the Anti-Imperialist Delegation. Although she gave glowing public reports about her travels soon after her return, she offered much more critical assessments in her 1992 autobiography, *A Taste of Power*, and in a draft of an undated report, most likely written for Huey Newton soon after her return from socialist Asia. Newton was both a cofounder of the BPP and the organization's minister of defense. Like other leaders of the party, Newton experienced run-ins with the police and spent three years in prison. An international campaign helped to secure his release, which occurred just as the Anti-Imperialist Delegation received an invitation to travel from North Korea to North Vietnam. Newton's return soon ignited a public and violent division with Eldridge Cleaver.

The split within the Black Panthers resulted from a combination of external and internal factors.[5] The FBI made extensive efforts to foster suspicion and conflict within the group.[6] They targeted both Cleaver and Newton with misinformation campaigns, sending letters that made false accusations about each other's actions and loyalty. The fact that Cleaver was in exile and Newton was making a difficult and public readjustment to life outside of prison made them particularly vulnerable to these efforts. Cleaver, Newton, and their respective supporters also developed different political priorities. Cleaver, who was in daily contact with revolutionary leaders in the Third World, advocated for the importance of armed struggle for the BPP. Newton and other survivors of the systematic decimation of Panthers through state-sanctioned violence and incarceration searched for alternative strategies to maintain a foothold in the United States. By focusing on community service or survival programs and eventually on electoral politics, the Black Panthers hoped to build and mobilize a broader base of support within urban African American communities.

The conflicts of the BPP directly shaped Brown's autobiography and the account of her travels that she wrote for Huey Newton. Her reports of the Anti-Imperialist Delegation, both privately conveyed and in some cases publicly circulated through the Black Panther newspaper, provided ammunition for Huey Newton to criticize and eventually expel Eldridge Cleaver from the party. Brown's autobiography, published over two decades after the Anti-Imperialist Delegation's trip, offered justification for the actions of Newton and herself.

The title of Brown's document for Huey, "Hidden Traitor," was a direct reference to Eldridge Cleaver. In this piece, she states, "the defection of Eldridge Cleaver from the Black Panther Party had apparently begun sometime long before he organized, in exile from Algeria, the Anti-Imperialist Delegation to Korea. However, I became familiar with his disdain from the

BPP, and through the BPP, of course, for the people, at the time of the delegation's visit to the Democratic People's Republic of Korea."[7] In her 1992 autobiography, Brown recounts that Cleaver publicly announced an impending split in the BPP in Moscow, before the Anti-Imperialist Delegation arrived in North Korea and before the release of Huey Newton. According to Brown, Cleaver wanted the support of the delegation for his "left wing of the party" as opposed to "the right wing operating out of national headquarters, dominated by reformist David Hilliard and his nepotistic hierarchy."[8] Brown claimed that she was unaware of this political division within the party until then. She also was appalled that Cleaver would reveal internal issues of the BPP to people who were not black and did not belong to the organization. Brown portrays Cleaver as having lost touch with reality and as responsible for initiating the conflicts within the party. In her autobiography, she described her reaction to Cleaver's public airing of the BPP's dirty laundry: "Was he serious? . . . Had exile driven him so mad he did not see? Had he been given some new mind-altering drug that had erased the police raids and assassinations from his brain? He had obviously forgotten the detail of the party mandate, based on the teachings of Malcolm X, that no member speak against another outside the ranks."[9]

Brown elaborated on Cleaver's unstable and volatile personality by highlighting his hostile and chauvinistic behavior toward women—black, Asian, and white. Brown, who had a sexual relationship with Cleaver, claimed that he threatened violence and verbally assaulted her throughout the trip to enlist her support for his agenda in the BPP. In addition, Brown recounted his abuse of his wife, Kathleen Cleaver. In *A Taste of Power*, Brown writes:

> There was something sadly heroic about Kathleen. . . . There was her defiant acceptance of Eldridge's well-known brutality toward her. . . . What threw me back into a shell of fear was Eldridge's behavior on the visit to Kathleen. She was weak and less than one month from delivering. Nevertheless, Eldridge immediately launched into an attack on her about nothing in particular, something personal to them. Her listless response only increased his hostility to her. He did not feel shit about her condition, he told her, since the baby she was carrying was probably not his.
> When she tried to defend herself, he shouted her down. "Shut up! Shut up, bitch!" True to form, Kathleen hung on, chiding him with spitfire responses, pushing further with her high-bred intelligence. Incapable of shutting her up, he finally slapped her hard, right there in the pristine

orderliness of a North Korean hospital reserved for Communist Party leaders.[10]

In "Hidden Traitor," Brown suggests that Eldridge purposely sent Kathleen to the DPRK as a way to lock her away "under the guise of being a guest of the Korean people."[11] This charge that Eldridge was holding Kathleen hostage also surfaced in an article that Brown published in the BPP's newspaper after the split occurred.[12] In that article, Brown charges Eldridge with killing a man who briefly became Kathleen's lover when the couple returned to Algeria. Brown's efforts to discredit Cleaver for his hypermasculinity reflected a broader effort within the Black Panthers to address issues related to gender inequality.[13]

Kathleen Cleaver, the first woman to serve on the central committee of the BPP, has directly challenged the veracity of Elaine Brown's accounts, stating, "whatever she portrayed of my relationship to Eldridge is either fantasy or hallucination."[14] Barbara Easley-Cox, who was present with Kathleen in North Korea and Algeria, also discredits Brown's portrayal of the Cleavers. Kathleen and Eldridge did have a complex and at times difficult relationship. They first met when Kathleen worked as an organizing secretary for SNCC. She attended a 1967 conference at Fisk University, where Eldridge was an invited speaker. She recalled being immediately attracted to him: "I'm sitting there typing the agenda, and I spin around and see Eldridge Cleaver standing in the doorway staring at me. . . . He was huge, big as a door frame. He was a very stately and mesmerizing person. . . . He was very—what's the right word? Magnetic. You couldn't help but notice this person."[15] They fell in love and by December, they were married. Within a year, though, Eldridge fled the country and Kathleen, who discovered that she was pregnant a week after his departure, eventually joined him in exile. While abroad, she gave birth to two children, whose names reflected their travels. Their son, Maceo, was named after the Cuban revolutionary Antonio Maceo, and their daughter, Joju Younghi, was named in honor of her birthplace, North Korea. Kathleen admitted that Eldridge was a difficult man. In an interview given after their divorce, she recalled, "My life with Eldridge was very, very frustrating. I had always kept the vision that he was difficult because he was a man under difficult circumstances, and that if those circumstances changed, then he would be easier to live with. Those circumstances *did* change, but he didn't get any easier to live with: he was just as ornery and cantankerous and difficult."[16] Despite these personal conflicts, Kathleen was not held hostage by Eldridge or the North

Koreans. She was closely monitored by the FBI, but she could travel without the immediate threat of imprisonment. In other words, she chose to live and raise her family abroad in order to share Eldridge's life of political exile.

Kathleen's actions, writings, speeches, and interviews indicate that she understood their endeavors overseas in a very different way from Elaine Brown. Kathleen characterizes their initiatives as an intentional strategy to internationalize the BPP. Although born of circumstances not in their control, the Cleavers' life outside of the United States allowed them to make connections with revolutionary movements around the world. In fact, Kathleen believes that it was their presence on the global stage that further intensified FBI surveillance and infiltration:

> The whole idea of a conscious, political policy on an international scale that was being articulated within the Black Panther Party . . . was horrifying to the State Department. . . . There's a memo—not a memo, a directive . . . [that] talked about how they really have no interest in seeing any form of connection between what they called the militants in the United States, the black militants in the United States with Arabs outside the United States or Africans outside of the United States. And so, it's important to control the type of politics that, that develop within the black movement here because that will have an impact on what kind of relationship the United States can maintain in African countries. So . . . you might say that this [Anti-Imperialist] delegation is on the fringes of playing with fire.[17]

Kathleen believes that to put out this wildfire, the FBI authorized intensified infiltration within both the party and the Anti-Imperialist Delegation itself. Given the role that Elaine Brown played in spreading misinformation about the Cleavers to Huey Newton and in exacerbating divisions within the party, Kathleen believes that Brown was a government agent. She publicly made this accusation both in the aftermath of the split and in an interview given in 2006.[18]

Brown's charges against Eldridge extend beyond his abusive interactions with herself and Kathleen. She also questioned his relationship to the white activists on the delegation, specifically the choice of Robert Scheer as his co-leader and the decision to include so many white women on the delegation. These accusations in turn cast suspicion on Cleaver's commitment to the BPP and provided evidence of his lack of political integrity.

These criticisms emerge most forcefully in "Hidden Traitor" rather than in Brown's published autobiography.

To join the Anti-Imperialist Delegation, Brown traveled to Paris on the same flight as Bob Scheer. Their initial and subsequent interactions led her to regard him as a political opportunist, motivated by a shallow sense of adventurism toward the Third World. Upon meeting Scheer, it surprised Brown "to find that a person not of our Party, nor of our community, was more familiar with the inner-workings of our Party than certainly I was and that that person had subsequently even formulated certain opinions about the internal relationships in our Party. Robert Scheer began his discussion . . . by casually mentioning that he knew that David Hilliard was part of 'the Right Wing of the BPP.' "[19] Her surprise turned to disgust when he regaled her with stories of his and Cleaver's sexual conquests in Cuba: "He would even mention several of the women's names (most of whom were, by the way, white women) and he talk[ed] incessantly about how much he and Eldridge enjoyed the fine Cuban cigars, rum, and women (in that order!). Scheer's whole attitude toward . . . Cleaver's exile in Cuba seemed to be adventuristic."[20]

Brown cites Scheer to allege that Cleaver's departure from Cuba was not due to political differences with his hosts but rather "because of his Bacchanalian attitude . . . [which] forced [him] then to go elsewhere and remain in hiding."[21] Brown decided that Scheer was "no more than a typical American slob who was involved in variety of activities which had nothing whatever to do with the struggles of oppressed people. Because he is not a member of the Third World, of the oppressed world, he is afforded the luxury of a vicarious relationship with our struggles. The fact is, however, that he was permitted to enact such a relationship and to, in fact, exert influence over our struggle to whatever degree by E.C."[22]

Brown further charges that Cleaver's sexual desire for white women and Scheer's role as Cleaver's accomplice explain the demographic makeup of the Anti-Imperialist Delegation. As Brown observed, "Sexual relations between individuals had become a pre-occupation and an obsession with Eld.. [*sic*] It seemed, in fact, to be really his prime concern and prime motivation in everything that he did."[23] Eldridge Cleaver initially achieved literary fame for his "Letters from Prison," in which he admitted his obsession with "The Ogre—the white woman." As the ultimate sexual taboo for a black man, "the Ogre possessed a tremendous and dreadful power over me."[24] The reigning racial and gender order had "indoctrinated [him] to see the white woman as more beautiful and desirable than my own black woman."[25] To retaliate against the lynchings of black men in the name of protecting white womanhood and to exact revenge against white men who sexually abused black women, Cleaver "became a rapist"; in his eyes, "rape was an insurrectionary act. It delighted me that I was defying and trampling upon the white man's law, upon his system of values, and that I was defiling his women."[26] He began, though, by "practicing on black girls in the ghetto."[27] In this same essay, Cleaver also admitted that he was wrong: "I had gone astray—astray not so much from the white man's law as from being human, civilized—for I could not approve the act of rape."[28]

Although Cleaver publicly denounced his own acts of sexual violence, he readily pursued sexual relationships for various reasons, including personal pleasure and political advantage. He seduced an emotionally vulnerable white female coworker at *Ramparts* during a turbulent period in the magazine's office and subsequently learned significant insights about the power struggles through her.[29] On his long boat ride to Cuba as an exile, Cleaver passed the time having sex with a white female activist, a person he despised because of her politics but also someone whom he found physically desirable.[30]

It is likely Cleaver had sexual relationships with members of the Anti-Imperialist Delegation. In addition to Elaine Brown's retelling of their travels, Alex Hing also expressed the opinion that Cleaver "had sex with as many of the women on the delegation that he could."[31] The sexual "revolution" of the 1960s, with its emphasis on experimentation and "free love," likely shaped the behavior of some delegation members.[32] Also, the unexpected length of their travels and the sense of dislocation that they experienced might have fostered a desire for physical and possibly emotional intimacy. If Brown and Hing are accurate in their characterizations of sexual relationships, then members of the delegation did not challenge but in fact replicated the practices of other Western travelers who tended to view the East as a particularly appropriate location for erotic pleasure.

Did Eldridge Cleaver perceive women only as sexual conquests and disregard their roles as political activists? In a journal written during the Anti-Imperialist Delegation's trip, Cleaver proposed a unique role for white women:

> Within the White community in the U.S.A., White Women constitute the most revolutionary element. The problem posed above is for white women, who are simultaneously waging both a class struggle and a struggle for

women's liberation from oppression by men, to resort to the only solution to the problem: Revolutionary Violence. White Women must pick up the gun and the bomb and go into action against the hated system. They must be implacable in their resolve to destroy the system that is oppressing them and not waver in their firm resolve to carry the struggle forward to its bittersweet end.

The Conscious resort to revolutionary violence by white women will throw the ruling class into an unprecedented crisis. It would speed up the disintegration of the repressive forces into the hands and at the service of the ruling class—Army, National Guard, State & local police. There will be extreme differences of opinion amongst the troops over the question of murdering White Women. This goes to the heart of America. Many of the troops would turn their guns against their superior officers before carrying out orders to kill white women. Black troops will not be allowed to do it. A very interesting situation will be the result.[33]

This call to arms was being enacted in the United States by the Weather Underground, a group of predominantly white men and women that emerged in 1969 out of a faction within Students for a Democratic Society. Because political lobbying and nonviolent protest did little to stop the U.S. war in Vietnam, members of the Weather Underground turned to violence. They plotted to bomb symbolic physical structures, like banks and government buildings, including the Pentagon. They issued warnings before their attacks, because they did not intend to harm individuals.[34] None of the members of the Anti-Imperialist Delegation were affiliated with the Weather Underground, at least not publicly. Even if they held revolutionary beliefs, they did not in fact engage in armed struggle.

Cleaver's call for white women to take up revolutionary violence was written in a private notebook and was likely not a serious political position. What is striking about his musings is its resonance with his earlier argument for rape. Because white women are perceived as needing protection by white men, Cleaver believed that the mobilization of white women as literal shock troops could be detrimental to the existing social order. Rather than raping white women, he expressed a desire to enlist them on the front line of political battle. Both perspectives suggest that Cleaver regarded white women as tools, sexual and military pawns, in his larger political struggle.

The white female members of the Anti-Imperialist Delegation had diverse reactions to Eldridge Cleaver and Bob Scheer. Randy Rappaport recalled, "The sexism would just pour out of" them.[35] Cleaver, in her opinion, demanded complete abjection. She believed that Brown's description of his harangue in Moscow "catches the emotional tone" of his two- to three-hour speech: "What he was essentially, I think, trying to do at that point was to really put the fear of God into us and to sort of establish his absolute authority over us. . . . The basic message that came through is, you're all at my beck and call. I control your lives from here on in."[36] Cleaver reinforced this message of authoritarian control by monitoring the interactions of delegation members. Rappaport recalled being reprimanded for socializing with Cubans at their hotel in Hanoi. Scheer called her away from the bar for a special meeting with Cleaver. The Black Panther leader bullied and intimidated her to reinforce the message that she should not speak to anyone without his authorization, particularly people from Cuba, a country where he had recently fled. Rappaport recalled that it was not just the content of Cleaver's message but rather the explosive demeanor that he used to reinforce his power. In contrast, he behaved politely and diplomatically to their Asian hosts.[37] Rappaport subsequently reflected that Cleaver's authoritarian behavior had to do with his own sense of insecurity. "I mean, he came from a situation where people had been killed . . . that underneath there was just the fear of uncertainty of his life. . . . I think his biggest fear was being irrelevant and of wasting his talent."[38]

Cleaver's demand for submission had gendered implications, considering the power dynamics within the group. He was clearly the alpha male in the group, and Scheer was his beta. Rappaport described Scheer as "Eldridge's shadow. . . . He was more than a gopher. . . . He was the one who would do . . . Eldridge's dirty work."[39] While all the other delegates shared hotel rooms during their travels, Eldridge Cleaver, Bob Scheer, and Elaine Brown had private rooms. Brown believed that for the two male co-leaders, it was a form of privilege. She recalled that when their entourage traveled to visit various sites, Cleaver and Scheer almost always rode in a separate car while the rest traveled on a bus.[40] In contrast, Brown described the assignment of a separate room as a form of punishment, a way to isolate her from the other members of the delegation. The individuals whom I interviewed knew nothing of Brown's conflicts with Cleaver until they read her autobiography. Their lack of knowledge could testify either to Cleaver's skill in containing Elaine or to her skills in reinventing a believable past.

Ann Froines also described Cleaver and "Bob Scheer as being among the most chauvinistic men [she had] met in the movement or spent any time with."[41] The female members bonded through "one sort of outburst kind of discussion" in reaction to Bob Scheer, who "was making a lot of fun of women's liberation." In contrast, the two other men on the delegation, Alex Hing and Andy Truskier, were "soft spoken, respectful. . . . I thought of them as . . . men who could really sit around in a group that was majority women and participate in talk and not dominate."

In contrast, Cleaver and Scheer insisted on being front and center. Randy Rappaport recalled one particular incident that revealed their inability to allow female autonomy. In Vietnam, the Women's Union invited the female delegates for a separate meeting. Rappaport recalled, "The Vietnamese men were fine with this. . . . So we got there . . . [and] we're about maybe an hour into it and Eldridge and Scheer . . . burst through the door in this private meeting with the Vietnamese Women's Union. I mean, these were . . . high-level people . . . in the national liberation. . . . It was appalling male behavior and it was so obvious that he could not tolerate being left out or that he was afraid that we were gonna say things about him."[42] In addition, Rappaport believed that Cleaver's behavior reflected his inability to consider women as significant and independent political thinkers and actors.[43]

Delegation members did not openly criticize these gender power dynamics. Elaine Brown explained that she wanted to protect the BPP from outside criticism and felt little solidarity with the white women who traveled with her. In "Hidden Traitor," she characterized them as members of "bourgeois culture" who complained needlessly about the lack of physical comforts.[44] She also described these individuals as sexual accomplices of Cleaver.[45] She recalled that when she first learned of Huey Newton's release from prison, "all of us were gathered in one particular spot with the exception of Eld. and one of the women on the delegation. We finally found him in her private room; we had to literally beat on the door for almost 5 minutes before we could get his attention."[46]

White delegation members, like Ann Froines, stifled their criticisms of Cleaver and Scheer, because of the desire to "keep a kind of united front with respect to our hosts."[47] Delegation members were dependent upon Cleaver because of his status as the most recognized movement "celebrity" and as the leader of their tour. Any disagreements or unpleasantries had to be endured, partly because they had limited ability to complain or even communicate with their Asian hosts. In other words, their isolation as travelers in a foreign land made them susceptible to "power trips." In addition, the delegates also felt an obligation to promote an image of political unity. Given their commitment to racial equality, they were particularly concerned about publicly criticizing a well-known African American leader. Rappaport explained that this sense of solidarity had to do with their experiences as members of "old Left" families: "For those of us who grew up as red diaper babies, the feeling of loyalty and not speaking ill of comrades . . . is very powerful. . . . [It was] almost like a dictum from our families, because they had lived through the McCarthy period. The worst people in the world, in our families, were the people who had testified or who had given evidence in some way, or spies. . . . So it's taken me all these years . . . almost forty years to get to a point where I can even talk about this. Where I can even share with you the negative stuff."[48]

The difficult dynamics were not just internal to the Black Panthers or between white women and the male co-leaders. Lines of exclusion also were drawn for Jewish members of the delegation. Randy Rappaport, who had difficulty publicly discussing conflicts about gender, felt even more reluctant about raising the issue of anti-Semitism. She recalled, "As I've looked back on it that they were sort of an in-group, a semi-in-group, because nobody was really in except maybe Scheer. A semi-in-group and an out-group and as I analyze that . . . I think the out-group were the Jewish women and the two Asians."[49] Although Eldridge recognized that his closest white allies and supporters tended to be Jewish, he also resented their presence and political influence. The conflicts revolved around whiteness, Zionism, and gender.

Historian Cheryl Lynn Greenberg, in her study of black-Jewish relations during the twentieth century, argues against sweeping pronouncements of either solidarity or enmity between the two groups.[50] Instead, she posits the need to recognize the diversity among both African Americans and Jews as well as the need for historical contextualization to understand shifting relationships between communities. Greenberg argues that a sense of solidarity that had emerged over the middle decades of the twentieth century fell apart as the political platform of liberalism collapsed in the late 1960s and 1970s. She identifies four basic assumptions of liberalism: "First, rights accrue to individuals, not groups. Second, although achievement depends on the individual the state has a role to play in guaranteeing equality of opportunity (but not equality of outcome). Third, in a capitalist democracy, liberalism stresses reform rather than revolution, compromise rather than confrontation. Finally, as its goal for civil society, liberalism enthrones pluralism, the championing of difference within a broadly agreed-upon framework of what constitutes socially acceptable behavior."[51] Each of these goals was challenged by the tenets of black power and more broadly Third World socialist liberation movements. Black power activists demanded the recognition of historic and ongoing inequalities based on race. Consequently, they emphasized the need to redistribute resources based on group rights and to work toward achieving equality of outcome. Some black power advocates, like the Panthers, advocated revolution, not reform, and they demanded self-determination, not integration within a pluralistic society.

While some African Americans adopted black power to redress racial inequality, some Jews regarded this agenda as anti-Semitic. African American writer James Baldwin published a famous essay in 1967 titled "Negroes Are Anti-Semitic because They Are Anti-White."[52] Baldwin argues that African American resentment of Jews stemmed from the differential racial and socioeconomic positions that the two groups occupied in American society. Because of anti-Semitism, Jews tended to own property and run businesses in economically depressed and predominantly black neighborhoods. Even though both groups experienced marginalization, power hierarchies still existed between the two groups. As Greenberg states, "If Jews were not entirely white, they nonetheless often 'stood in' for whites in black people's minds. . . . Jews served this 'stand-in' function because so many worked in black neighborhoods as landlords, shopkeepers, and middlemen."[53] Also, in the post–World War II era, class differences increased between Jews and blacks, thereby heightening divergences of racial and political identification. In simplistic terms, Jews tended to become increasingly white, while African Americans identified increasingly as black.

Baldwin articulates this disconnect between the two groups:

> One does not wish, in short, to be told by an American Jew that his suffering is as great as the American Negro's suffering. It isn't, and one knows that it isn't from the very tone in which he assures you that it is. . . . The Jew's suffering is recognized as part of the moral history of the world and the Jew is recognized as a contributor to the world's history: this is not true for the blacks. Jewish history, whether or not one can say it is honored, is certainly known: the black history has been blasted, maligned and despised. The Jew is a white man, and when white men rise up against oppression, they are heroes: when black men rise, they have reverted to their native savagery.[54]

Baldwin qualifies some of his assertions, indicating that not everyone who holds power over African Americans is Jewish. He also concedes that not all Jews behave or think the same way. However, his language tends to assume and posit essentialized interpretations of Jewishness and blackness.

Baldwin's essay appeared shortly before the 1968 Ocean Hill–Brownsville conflicts regarding race and education. Throughout New York City at the time, "90 percent of the teachers . . . were white . . . [and] the majority of the teachers were Jewish."[55] In contrast, "more than half of the students were Black or Puerto Rican."[56] In the neighborhoods of Ocean Hill–Brownsville, the parents, inspired by black power politics, demanded community control and more resources for public education. They also called for greater diversity in the curriculum as well as the hiring of nonwhite teachers and administrators. Scholars of black-Jewish relations regard the volatile conflicts in Ocean Hill–Brownsville as a key turning point, which crystallized an emerging discord between the two groups.[57]

Eldridge Cleaver was familiar with Baldwin's work and even published a review of the author's writing in *Soul on Ice*. Cleaver, like James Baldwin, used a linguistic shorthand to characterize Jewish activists. Cleaver described the New Left as "Jewish controlled."[58] They constituted "the hard core of Jewish political manipulators—The Wienbergs, Rubins, the Savio-Rosenthals, the Mike Parkers, Burnstiens—all the way to Brooklyn and Tel Aviv. The Bob Scheers."[59] Although Scheer was Cleaver's right-hand man, the Black Panther leader regarded him with caution and disdain. In an essay about Scheer, titled "Enter the Devil," Cleaver refers to the journalist as "the Devil," who served as "the front man for the Jews."[60]

Cleaver also portrayed himself and other members of the BPP as being engaged in political maneuvers with Jewish members of the New Left. In one particular tense confrontation, he recalled, "The Jews were pissed off because we were a phenomenon in their midst which they could not control, and we were pissed off because we saw that they intended either to control us or sabotage us."[61] The most volatile issue of contention, as Cleaver perceived it, centered on the issue of Palestine and Israel.[62] Like other black power activists, Cleaver was an advocate of Third World liberation. He supported the Palestinian liberation movement and even met with Yasser Arafat during his stay in Algeria. Zionism, the call for a Jewish homeland, and the creation of Israel represented a form of imperialism in Eldridge's eyes. The charge of Jewish imperialism became particularly acute following the 1967 Six-Day War. In this brief war, Israel defeated and gained land from the bordering Arab countries of Egypt, Syria, and Jordan. Even though Cleaver worked with Jewish members of the New Left to critique

American policies in Vietnam, he charged the same individuals with ignoring Israeli imperialism. In Cleaver's words, "the Jews . . . at bottom . . . were all Zionists, and that what was wrong with the American Left was that it refused to confront the question of Palestine."[63]

On the one hand, Cleaver's accusations shed light on difficult political issues. On the other hand, his comments demonstrate a propensity to project a uniformity of belief and action on all individuals of Jewish heritage. Even the FBI, eager to find ways to undermine the Black Panthers, devised a plan to inform Jewish American organizations of Cleaver's anti-Zionism in order to neutralize cross-racial political alliances.[64] During the Anti-Imperialist Delegation's trip, Cleaver persisted in making sweeping statements about Jews and Israel. One of the Jewish female travelers, whom the Black Panther leader targeted with his contempt and intimidation tactics, nevertheless reminded him to distinguish between the Israeli state and Jewish people as well as between different individuals of Jewish ancestry.[65]

Similar to Jewish delegation members, Asian American activists also occupied an outsider position within the group hierarchy. Both Elaine Brown and Eldridge Cleaver wrote dismissively of Alex Hing and Pat Sumi. Cleaver particularly resented Sumi due to class, gender, and personality differences. Furthermore, the Black Panther leader's portrayals of the two Asian American travelers were conflated with his later denunciations of Asian socialism.

Although Elaine Brown has little to say about her fellow travelers, she specifically mentioned Alex Hing and Pat Sumi in her autobiography but in a trivializing fashion. Brown recalled, "Besides the whites, there were two Asians: a young, diminutive Japanese woman and a fellow from San Francisco's Chinatown, whose face was overwhelmed by acne."[66] Brown does not refer to Pat Sumi and Alex Hing by name, although she traveled with them for over two months; their individual histories and personalities are completely absent. Instead, they are described in purely ethnic and physical terms. Not surprisingly, both Hing and Sumi had negative reactions to Brown as well. They described her as self-serving and arrogant in interviews given many years after the conclusion of their journey together.[67]

Cleaver offers a similarly one-dimensional portrayal of the two Asian American activists. Published eight years after their travels to socialist Asia and after Cleaver renounced his former belief in socialism, *Soul on Fire* describes two incidents to highlight the condescension of the Asian people who hosted the delegation and the humiliation suffered by the Asian American travelers. Cleaver also does not name Hing but describes him as "a young Chinese man from California, with great enthusiasm for his ancestral homeland."[68] When Hing tried to speak to their guide-interpreter in Chinese, "she turned and glared at him; in words that cut to the bone, she said loudly, 'Comrade Brother, please speak English. We cannot understand your version of Chinese.'" Cleaver interpreted the exchange as representative of "Communist arrogance and insensitivity."[69] Hing, who grew up speaking English and had limited Cantonese language skills, remembered attempting to speak Chinese with one of their guides. Although most of their Chinese hosts spoke the official national language of Mandarin, Hing remembered having a positive interaction with one who did speak the Cantonese dialect.[70] His recollections of the exchange contrasted greatly with Cleaver's. In fact, although Cleaver claims to be sympathetic to Hing, his characterization of both the interpreter and the Chinese American activist focuses on their zealotry for communism.

Cleaver's description of Sumi also emphasizes her single-minded political devotion. He explained that there was another Asian American in the delegation, "a young radical Japanese woman from the West Coast really caught up in the righteous magic of this return to Asia. She was hard-boiled, seldom smiled, and was always most professional about her correct revolutionary stance."[71] Cleaver likewise recounts how Sumi was humiliated during the trip: "The youngster from the West Coast caught it on both cheeks—first for being Japanese, second for being American. The Koreans were not friendly to her; they had limited capacity to express the international solidarity of workers who were supposedly united. . . . The poison of racism hit her where she least expected it; but then, that is the Communist style."[72] Sumi recalled how her Korean hosts encouraged her not to feel a sense of personal guilt about Japanese colonialism. In contrast, in Cleaver's account, Sumi's treatment by their Korean hosts is used to depict the narrowness and inflexibility of Asian communists. In addition, Cleaver's description of Sumi reveals that he also viewed her as ideologically rigid.

Cleaver's portrayal of Asian communists and Asian American radicals reveals the force of traditional orientalist thinking. The charge that Hing and Sumi lacked emotion echoes stereotypes of Orientals as being expressionless or, in the words of Eldridge, as manifestations of the "inscrutable East."[73] Strikingly, Alex Hing and Pat Sumi are not criticized for being apolitical model minorities. Rather, they are depicted as being overzealous model revolutionaries. The portrayals of the Asian American delegates in turn provide an opportunity to criticize socialist Asia for its totalitarianism, for a single-minded devotion to communism. Alex Hing and Pat Sumi in some ways are depicted as being not fully Asian, either due to limited language abilities or to ethnic differences from their hosts. Simultaneously, Cleaver conflated Asian Americans with Asians by emphasizing their similar political beliefs and personalities.

These caricatured depictions of Asian communists and Asian American radicals in *Soul on Fire* can be interpreted as stand-ins for Cleaver's former self. Previously devoted to socialist revolutionary ideology, Cleaver sought to exorcise his past life and reinvent his identity in order to end his exile abroad. As the former minister of information for the Black Panthers, he was responsible for publishing Kim Il Sung's writings in the organization's newspaper. Also, Cleaver had led this highly publicized tour of North Korea, North Vietnam, and Red China. No doubt he felt pressure to renounce his former infatuation with socialist Asia to gain permission to reenter the United States. Following in an orientalist tradition, the Asian and Asian American revolutionaries served as foils for Cleaver to distance himself from his former beliefs and to recreate himself as an acceptable American.

Similar to their reactions to Elaine Brown, both Alex Hing and Pat Sumi had largely negative perceptions of Eldridge Cleaver. Hing recalled in a 2005 interview that during their travels in Socialist Asia, "my opinion of him very seriously deteriorated quite quickly. I thought he was really arrogant. And he would say things that I would never say or even believe. He would say that the 'masses are asses,' which is contrary to Mao Tse-tung thought, counter to everything that I believed in, and counter to what the Panthers were saying."[74] Sumi also expressed her intense dislike for Cleaver, specifically because he confiscated her travel journal. Throughout the tour, she had been recording the experiences of the delegation and her reflections about their travels. Cleaver explained that he wanted to protect the information from the U.S. State Department, a concern that was certainly legitimate given the FBI's careful monitoring of the delegation's travels and the efforts of the COINTEL program in targeting and sabotaging the organization. In "Gangster Cigarettes," a poem that Cleaver wrote about the delegation, he suggests that other dynamics also were at work: "We all began to fear her book / And some began to hate the girl / And call her Jap behind her back."[75] Cleaver suspected that Sumi was a government agent. Randy Rappaport observed this dynamic. She recalled that Cleaver "definitely did not trust Pat. . . . He decided that by the time we got to China, after Vietnam, that she was [a] CIA agent."[76]

Cleaver's dislike of Sumi stemmed from various reasons. Rappaport recalled that "Pat was a little more outspoken." Cleaver, who demanded obedience, particularly from women, likely did not appreciate Sumi's efforts to question him. Also, her middle-class upbringing and serious demeanor contrasted greatly with Cleaver's underclass background and performative political style. When Cleaver confiscated Sumi's notebook, he also humiliated her publicly in front of the delegation. Alex Hing recalled, "Eldrige [sic] disliked Pat and often mocked some of her petty bourgeois mannerisms and thinking. . . . After taking possession of Pat's journal, which included poetry and drawings, Eldrige read aloud to the delegation certain passages in a sarcastic manner."[77] In other words, Cleaver created an environment that fostered group hostility toward Sumi, a hatred that he characterizes as having racial overtones. It is unlikely that other members of the delegation called Sumi a "Jap." Given Cleaver's propensity for using ethnic slurs, it is likely that he used the racially pejorative term about her. As for Sumi's reactions to Cleaver, she stated years later that she would "never forgive him . . . never."[78]

Activists of the 1960s generation tended to perceive the world in dichotomous ways—the revolutionary Third World versus the imperialist West, the "people" versus "fascist pigs," the revolutionary vanguard versus the running dogs. The Anti-Imperialist Delegation, which represented a cross-section of the U.S. radical Left, illuminated the complexities of human beings. Being in the belly of the beast, they at times also reproduced the beast within themselves. They held contradictory ideas and behaved at odds with their stated values. In addition, their conflicts with one another indicate differences of political goals, strategies, and ideologies. Furthermore, their suspicions of one another as government agents and as political sellouts reveal the reach of the U.S. security state in fomenting psychological warfare and counterinsurgency against activists. Finally, the isolating experience of extended travel in relatively unfamiliar societies and cultures exacerbated these divisions and fueled a pervasive sense of insecurity and dislocation.

This airing of dirty laundry within the Anti-Imperialist Delegation exposes the fault lines between activists of varying racial, ethnic, and gender backgrounds. Yet there are also counternarratives that focus on the hopeful and genuine possibilities of cross-racial and international alliances. Even the most reviled individuals on this journey experienced moments of political inspiration and human connection.

Just as Anti-Imperialist Delegation members privately questioned Eldridge's behavior, they also noted the controlled and constructed nature of their travels, particularly in DPRK but also in the PRC. Even under these constraints, they experienced "emotionally intense" epiphanies. Randy Rappaport recalled that hearing about the burning of the warehouse of prisoners in North Korea "didn't feel like propaganda to me." In fact, she recalled writing in the guest book in the museum that the experience "just seared my heart."[79] Similarly, Pat Sumi reflected years later that despite what she learned about the Chinese Cultural Revolution since her 1970 visit, she could not deny the political inspiration of that movement:

> None of us really knew what was going on. We knew what we were told was going on, and we took it all at face value. When the Chinese told us that the Cultural Revolution was one of the greatest accomplishments of the Chinese Revolution I believed them. How could I not? Everywhere you go everyone is telling you what a great accomplishment the Cultural Revolution is. And you meet peasants who are in their eighties and they tell you—while they are waving their little red book—that the reason they believe in Mao Tse-Tung was that in the old days they would never have survived this long. You can't argue with that. . . . I believed him.[80]

The delegation experienced their most profound moments of political connection in the Democratic Republic of Vietnam (DRV). Compared to the other socialist countries, they found North Vietnam to be much more open and less scripted. The travelers could wander more freely and at times used French to have conversations with locals. Compared to the North Koreans and even the Chinese, the North Vietnamese were more familiar with Westerners due to the legacy of European colonialism. In addition, by 1970, the DRV was considerably more practiced at hosting American activists. The other socialist Asian countries were just beginning people's diplomacy efforts and learning how to do so effectively. Delegation members found the North Vietnamese to be more "warm" and "friendly." As Randy Rappaport recalled, "They wanted to know who we were as people and not just as comrades who could do something for them."[81]

An unanticipated detour in their travels demonstrated clearly the values of their Vietnamese hosts. The Anti-Imperialist Delegation had journeyed into the countryside by bus one day. Due to previous bombing attacks, their bus had to cross a river on a raft, which had to be dragged across on a rope. It had rained that day, off and on. Rappaport recalled that by the time they were prepared to return to Hanoi,

> The river was too swollen to cross. . . . They [the hosts] had to figure out what they were going to do with us for the night. . . . So they took us to a school in the mountains. . . . It was raining quite a bit too and going up the mountain . . . was a little bit scary. You know, in this very rickety bus— there was a bombing halt at that point but these roads were narrow. . . . It might have been like a Communist Party school 'cause I would say people were in their late teens and early twenties and everybody had a little room . . . [a] very tiny little desk . . . little bowl of water for washing your hands, and . . . a hard pallet . . . like a straw mat on it and some kind of pillow but it wasn't a soft pillow, it was like something hard. . . . They gave up their rooms for us. There was very little food there obviously and they gave us . . . warm condensed milk with some, maybe some kind of grain or something in it for a little bit more nutrition. . . . We had been eating very lavishly at the hotel, you know. . . . This country's at war, but you know, we were guests.[82]

The next day, when they attempted to cross the river again, the delegation was given a small lunch box of rice balls to share with each other: "They knew we were hungry, I guess. You know, we were big stocky Americans who . . . were used to eating a lot. And the whole group of them walked away about a hundred yards and stood and smoked cigarettes under some trees while we ate and . . . somebody actually said or maybe I just thought this, 'They're standing there because they don't want to embarrass us by being with us and not eating.' "[83]

Rappaport recalled feeling "this incredible sense of gratitude . . . and I think everybody felt [it]. . . . [Even] Eldridge was touched. . . . It would be very easy to just describe him in terms of . . . a bully. . . . But there was this other side to him. . . . He was genuinely touched."[84] Even after Cleaver later recanted some of his former radical politics, he would describe "the North Vietnamese and the Vietcong . . . [as] forever friends of the Black Panthers."[85] And, in her autobiography, Elaine Brown recognized, "the Vietnamese offered us their best, when they had so little."[86] By more fully understanding the difficulties of achieving solidarity, it becomes possible to appreciate the rare moments of mutual understanding and inspiration.

After the Anti-Imperialist Delegation left socialist Asia, the travelers pursued diverse political paths. Immediately after the tour ended, Eldridge Cleaver escorted the group to Algeria, where he pronounced the establishment of the international branch of the BPP on 13 September 1970.[87] His hopes for an independent and visible base outside of the United States were soon dampened by the public and violent split within the BPP and his expulsion from the party. Kathleen Cleaver believes that the timing of the conflict was not coincidental; precisely because Eldridge was officially establishing himself and the Black Panthers on the world stage, there were increased efforts by the U.S. government to foster conflicts between Panther leaders and their organization.[88]

Elaine Brown, despite Cleaver's alleged threats, safely returned to the United States with the rest of the delegation on 16 September. The FBI prepared for their return by ordering U.S. customs to search their bags at John F. Kennedy Airport in New York City.[89] They confiscated both the letters by POWs and the film footage of the delegation's travels. As Brown stepped off the plane, she met Huey Newton for the first time. She quickly became his lover and confidante. At Newton's request, they traveled to the PRC the following year to cultivate connections with Chinese leaders before the arrival of President Nixon. This subsequent journey to the East was made possible through the contacts that Brown had established during her previous trip with Eldridge Cleaver. When Newton eventually fled the United States to avoid another prison sentence, Brown became the first female chair of the BPP and transformed the organization through a focus on community programs and electoral politics.[90] She attributed the new Panther strategy to China and Huey Newton. In her autobiography, she explained, "China had been instructive. China's recent entrance into the U.N. was neither contradictory to China's goal of toppling U.S. imperialism nor an abnegation of revolutionary principles. It was a tactic of socialist revolution. It was a tactic, Newton concluded, that offered us a great example."[91] If China could become a legitimate political power in the United Nations, then perhaps the Panthers could maintain their revolutionary agenda and run for electoral office.

According to Pat Sumi, neither she nor Alex Hing wanted to leave socialist Asia. She recalled, "Alex and I volunteered to stay behind and bring reports," but "for whatever reason Cleaver made the decision that we would go back."[92] Upon their return to the United States, Hing and Sumi began another series of tours. Due to their association with movement celebrity Eldridge Cleaver and their experiences of traveling through the forbidden socialist nations of Asia, they became highly sought-after speakers, especially within the emerging Asian American movement. When Hing arrived back in San Francisco, he discovered the Red Guard on the point of dissolution. They faced both police harassment and financial pressures from landlords who disliked their politics. Consequently, the organization experienced a division similar to that of the Black Panthers with some members advocating the formation of an underground military contingent. Hing decided to focus on community organizing instead and joined I Wor Kuen, a revolutionary nationalist organization that eventually embraced Marxist-Leninism. Like the Red Guard, I Wor Kuen consisted predominantly of Asian American activists and named itself after a social movement in China, specifically the 1898 Boxer Rebellion that sought to repel Western imperialism.[93]

Following the Anti-Imperialist Delegation trip, Pat Sumi increasingly involved herself with Asian American issues. She became a staff member of *Gidra* magazine and contributed several articles based on her travels in socialist Asia. In her speaking tours, she had the opportunity to meet other Japanese American leftists, such as former Communist Party member Karl Yoneda and Harlem-based activist Yuri Kochiyama. She described the experience of discovering radicals from an older generation as being akin to meeting her political "parents."[94] Sumi became widely regarded not as a model minority but as a model revolutionary, especially for other Asian American women. Along with other female members of the Anti-Imperialist Delegation like Randy Rappaport, Ann Froines, Gina Blumenfeld, and Janet Kranzberg, Pat Sumi helped to organize the Indochinese Women's Conferences of 1971. These meetings, held in Canada, provided opportunities for North American women to meet face-to-face with Southeast Asian heroines.[95] During this period, Sumi exchanged her Jackie Kennedy look for a Mao suit, an attire that other Asian American activists also adopted.

Some of the white female activists, including Jan Austin, Gina Blumenfeld, and Ann Froines, maintained some contact with Eldridge Cleaver, and almost all of them continued their activism in some form or other. Froines stayed the course for a long time. She returned to New Haven to continue her support for Ericka Huggins and Bobby Seale during their lengthy trial, which lasted from October 1970 through May 1971. Both were acquitted and the charges dismissed. For these efforts, Ann, her husband, and their daughter experienced, she said, "a sudden spate of harassment. Lots of obscene telephone calls, threats to kidnap Rebecca. All the tires of my car have been slashed twice in the span of one week. . . . I think it's the pigs because

Figure 11. Pat Sumi on the cover of *Rodan*, an Asian American movement publication. Drawing by Saichi Kawahara, reproduced in Steve Louie and Glenn Omatsu, eds., *Asian Americans: The Movement and the Moment* (Los Angeles: UCLA Asian American Studies Center Press, 2001), p. 16.

they have gotten the car when it has been parked in different parts of the city."[96]

Froines remained dedicated, though, not only to the Panthers but to North Korea and North Vietnam as well. In November 1970, she organized a protest at the United Nations, demanding that this international body recognize and redress its role in supporting American aggression in Korea. She discovered, though, despite her efforts to arouse public interest, that "there was no receptivity really to the information about North Korea. There was no context in which people could act on it."[97] Froines also stayed in touch with Gina Blumenfeld, Randy Rappaport, Janet Kranzberg, and Alex Hing about a plan to open two People's Anti-Imperialist Centers, one on the East Coast and the other on the West Coast. These would serve as resource centers to promote a broader understanding of American policies in socialist Asia. However, it was difficult to rally human and financial resources for these endeavors. Instead, Froines found more common ground for antiwar activism. She became the Midwest coordinator of the Indochina Peace Campaign, an organization started by Tom Hayden and Jane Fonda.

Despite the persistence of this activist energy, the traumatic experience of the journey left its mark. Randy Rappaport recalled that she "was really in an emotionally very bad shape the year after the trip."[98] She withdrew from politics for a period of time. The Anti-Imperialist Delegation, though, did reignite her interest more broadly in Asian culture, religion, and people. She had previously studied Indian culture and language as an anthropology major. As she said, "I've often jokingly said to friends, I went to . . . Asia communist and I came back a Buddhist."[99]

The 1970 Anti-Imperialist Delegation was a product of and helped to fuel a larger social movement. From the mid-1960s through the early 1970s, American radicals who protested the war in Southeast Asia sought inspiration and political instruction from Third World socialist leaders. Asian revolutionaries also prioritized fostering these international relationships as part of their international and domestic strategies. Consequently, articles and images about Asia circulated widely within movement publications during this period. In addition, traveling to these forbidden lands offered the possibility of establishing personal contact and gaining more accurate information. Travel theorists remind us, though, that there is a need to "interrogate the notion that travel (i.e. 'seeing' other cultures) inevitably results in knowledge."[100] The interviews and writings of the delegates suggest that even as they cultivated an anti-imperialist gaze, their perception of Asia could still be refracted through an orientalist lens. In fact, as the conflicting accounts about what really occurred during the trip suggest, the depictions of socialist Asia and of people of Asian descent can be narrated and renarrated in response to the changing political and personal needs of the narrator.

Part III

Journeys for Global Sisterhood

Chapter 7

"We Met the 'Enemy'—and They Are Our Sisters"

In April 1971, approximately one thousand female activists from throughout North America gathered in Vancouver and Toronto, Canada, to attend the Indochinese Women's Conferences (IWCs). The U.S. and Canadian women originated from large metropolitan centers, small towns, and even rural communities to meet a delegation of women from North and South Vietnam as well as Laos. Some North American antiwar protestors, like Bob Browne and members of the Eldridge Cleaver delegation, had traveled to Southeast Asia. Others learned through the movement and mainstream press about the sufferings and the heroism of Vietnamese people. The 1971 IWCs, however, represented the first opportunities for large numbers of North American women to have direct contact with their Asian "sisters."[1]

The IWCs illuminate how women literally and symbolically crossed borders in order to build an international antiwar movement. As such, the organizing of the conferences and the experiences of those who attended shed light on the process of building "global sisterhood." Critics of the idea have argued that the call for female international solidarity represents another form of Western domination, this time by well-intentioned champions of women's rights who see themselves as the saviors of oppressed women in non-Western societies.[2] The IWCs provide an opportunity to rethink global sisterhood in two ways.

First, the conferences highlight the political multiplicity of North American women and the complex process of negotiation that occurred to foster an international peace movement. There were three North American sponsors of the IWCs: "old friends" or more "traditional" women's peace organizations; "new friends" or women's liberation activists; and "Third World" women or women of color in North America.[3] Within each group, the women ascribed to a variety of political viewpoints as well. Engaging in an international movement did not unify women in the West. In fact, the IWCs provided a forum to air and accentuate differences between North American women, particularly along the lines of ideology, race, sexuality, and nationality. Fractured by these differences, women from North America did not dominate the political agenda at the IWCs. Instead, they looked to women from Southeast Asia for leadership and inspiration. Thus, the IWCs reveal the political variety among women in the West and how these conflicts can ironically foster the growth of a global women's antiwar movement.

Second, while critics of global sisterhood emphasize the power and misperceptions of Western women, a focus on the Southeast Asian women demonstrates how women from outside the West deployed female internationalism. During the U.S. war in Vietnam, the Women's Union of North Vietnam and the Women's Union for the Liberation of South Vietnam (collectively referred to in this work as the VWUs, Vietnam Women's Unions) played integral roles in fostering a global women's peace movement. Through meetings, correspondence, and the circulation of print as well as visual media, the VWUs actively nurtured American women's interest in U.S. foreign policy and military activity in Southeast Asia. The Vietnamese believed that all human beings, and especially all women, could share a sense of commonality and purpose. To promote an international peace movement, Vietnamese women cultivated a belief in global sisterhood, projecting and cultivating a female universalism that simultaneously critiqued and transcended racial and cultural divides. It was not just an ideology imposed by the West but was promoted by women from the East as well.

The IWCs resulted from a longer history of North American and Southeast Asian women politically engaging with one another. They developed personal and political connections through face-to-face meetings that took place in Eastern and Western Europe, Asia, Cuba, Africa, Australia, and Canada. These conversations and partnerships in turn helped to shape the political content of Vietnamese antiwar appeals, which eventually circulated beyond the individuals involved to influence activist media portrayals of the U.S. war in Vietnam. In this campaign to promote a worldwide antiwar movement, the VWUs established relationships with individual women and with female organizations from a variety of political spectrums and backgrounds. The North American sponsors of the IWC—old friends, new friends, and Third World women—reveal the diversity of individuals engaged in fostering female internationalism.

The term "old friends" referred to the U.S.-based Women Strike for Peace (WSP), the Canadian Voice of Women (VOW), and the Women's International League for Peace and Freedom (WILPF), headquartered in Switzerland but with national sections throughout the world. These organizations were designated old not because of the age of their constituency, although all three did attract largely middle-aged to elderly women. Rather, the organizations were considered old friends because of the history of friendship that these North American women established with Vietnamese women. For example, WSP's contact with the VWU extended back to 1965, when two WSP members were among the first Americans to visit Hanoi after the commencement of U.S. bombing of North Vietnam. That same year, a ten-person delegation from WSP met with representatives from North and South Vietnam in Jakarta, Indonesia, to affirm women's unique abilities to cross Cold War barriers and foster peace.[4] These political and personal relationships continued to develop as WSP sent international delegations to Europe, Canada, Cuba, and North Vietnam throughout the remainder of the war.

Although differences existed among WSP, VOW, and WILPF, they could be characterized as maternalist peace organizations. For example, WSP originated in 1961 from the efforts of predominantly middle-class and middle-aged white women to protect their families from nuclear annihilation. As historian and former WSP activist Amy Swerdlow explained:

> On 1 November 1961 an estimated fifty thousand women walked out of their kitchens and off their jobs, in an unprecedented nationwide strike for peace. As a radioactive cloud from a series of Russian atom bomb tests passed over American cities and the United States threatened to retaliate with its own cycle of nuclear explosions, the striking women sent delegations to their elected officials. . . . They demanded that their local officials pressure President John Kennedy on behalf of all the world's children, to end nuclear testing at once and begin negotiations for nuclear disarmament.[5]

Figure 12. Timeline of international meetings of Women Strike for Peace, on the cover of *Memo* 6, no. 8 (November–December 1968). Swarthmore College Peace Collection, Swarthmore, PA.

This initial strike eventually led committed women to form Women Strike for Peace. The members of the organization, as historian Andrea Estepa has argued, had "wide-ranging professional identities," yet they chose to publicly identify themselves as "housewives and mothers."[6] These women proclaimed their right to condemn the threat of global and nuclear warfare based on the desire to protect their own and other people's families. They embraced gender difference to define a special role for women on the global stage.

VOW, founded just a year before WSP in 1960, was similarly inspired by a belief in women's unique abilities and responsibilities to foster peace. Following the failure of the 1960 Paris summit on disarmament between the United States and the Soviet Union, thousands of women across Canada decided to form VOW. They presented themselves as "respectable" and as maternal "protectors of the world's children."[7] One of the founding members and an eventual president of the group, Muriel Duckworth, explained that "Voice of Women founders had the idea of women as lifegivers," mothers who could not support acts of aggression and violence.[8]

The roots of this maternalist form of peace politics can be traced back to Victorian and Progressive era notions of gender difference as opposed to more modern beliefs in gender sameness. In fact, WILPF, the third organizational member among the old friends, was founded before American women achieved suffrage and in the context of World War I. Created under the leadership of Jane Addams, WILPF advocated for equal political rights for women because members believed that women had a propensity to promote peace. As suffragist and pacifist Carrie Chapman Catt explained, "War is in the blood of men"; inversely, peace was believed to be in the blood of women.[9]

This maternalist and gender essentialist justification for women's engagement in international politics held particular significance in the early Cold War period. In the midst of the Red Scare, critics of U.S. foreign policies were easily dismissed and ridiculed as communist sympathizers and political ideologues. In fact, members of WSP, VOW, and WILPF all endured anticommunist attacks. By proclaiming the political responsibilities of motherhood, these women presented themselves as "commonsense" or nonideological activists.[10] They sought to defuse global conflict and promote peace in order to protect "all the world's children."

With their similarities, the three organizations frequently collaborated with one another and shared ideas for promoting peace. Representatives of each group corresponded with one another and participated in each other's conferences and activities. The organizations also overlapped in membership. In addition, for all three groups, traveling across geopolitical borders and having face-to-face meetings with their nations' enemies were important strategies for their efforts to defuse global conflict. When Bob Browne revisited South Vietnam in 1965, two members of WILPF traveled as part of the clergy delegation that met with Thich Nhat Hanh. Representatives of WSP, following a series of exchanges with Vietnamese women, cosponsored with their Asian counterparts the historic Conference of Concerned

Women to End the War.[11] The conference was held in Paris in the spring of 1968, just a few weeks before the formal peace talks began. In attendance were representatives from countries involved in the war, including Japan, Britain, Australia, New Zealand, West Germany, and Canada.[12] One American participant recalled the impact of the meeting: "I have always been convinced that the women who come in contact with the Vietnamese women come back home changed. They seem to march to the beat of another drummer. They have a new sense of urgency. Now I know why. It has happened to me. When you are actually faced with the 'enemy' and realize that American sons and husbands are killing them—it's too much to bear."[13]

After attending the emotionally charged Paris conference, Kay MacPherson, president of VOW, visited Hanoi for the first time. She did so with a sense of trepidation as well as determination. Aware that she would travel in the midst of an ongoing bombing campaign by the United States, MacPherson wrote, "In case I get to Hanoi and end up with a bomb on top of me I want to put down one or two thoughts before hand. . . . Not many people are invited to go to Hanoi, though many wish to go. To have earned the trust of the Vietnam women is a very great honour. . . . We cannot treat such an honour lightly, nor, however reluctant I felt, would I dream of refusing to go."[14] Following MacPherson's journey to Southeast Asia, VOW sponsored a reciprocal visit by representatives of the North and South Vietnam Women's Unions to Canada in the summer of 1969. Members of WSP, including Jane Spock—wife of Dr. Benjamin Spock—attended this gathering. In fact, they staged a protest against the war on the Fourth of July as they crossed the U.S.-Canada border at Niagara Falls.[15] This 1969 exchange directly inspired the subsequent 1971 IWCs.

The members of WSP, VOW, and WILPF recognized the power of face-to-face communication with Vietnamese women and sought to provide similar opportunities for other individuals. Aware of their own demographic base, they made various attempts to involve younger and nonwhite activists. Cora Weiss, a leader in WSP as well as in the peace movement overall, played arguably the most central role in arranging American delegations to Hanoi during the U.S. war in Vietnam. Activism ran in Cora's family. Her father, Sam Rubin, was known for his humanitarian philanthropy in Africa and Israel. Her mother, Vera Rubin, was an anthropologist "whose research and educational projects brought her to the Caribbean, where she supported anticolonialist scholars."[16] Cora protested against the Red Scare during her college years at the University of Wisconsin, Madison. While in the home state of Senator Joe McCarthy, she petitioned for his recall of in a campaign called Joe Must Go. She also met her husband in college. Peter Weiss, a survivor of the Holocaust, joined with Cora as they participated in the civil rights movement and in support of African decolonization. During the war, Cora, who is fluent in French, went to Paris several times to meet with Vietnamese representatives. She also helped to organize the 1969 and 1971 women's conferences in Canada. She traveled to Vietnam a total of five times, the first time in December 1969 after the first Canada conference and the last time in 1978 with her close friend Bob Browne.

Weiss traveled to North Vietnam and organized the trips of others because she believed in the power of "citizen diplomacy." On her initial journey in 1969, she discussed with Vietnamese representatives the importance of facilitating communication between American POWs and their families. In keeping with the maternalist outlook of other old friends, Weiss was motivated by a sense of compassion for the soldiers and their families. In addition, she recognized the political impact such humanitarian gestures would have. During the late 1960s and early 1970s, President Nixon and the U.S. administration focused on American POWs and soldiers missing in action to justify extending the war.[17] Weiss and other antiwar activists sought to defuse this issue by facilitating communication for and the release of U.S. POWs. After her first trip in 1969, Weiss established the Committee of Liaison with Servicemen Detained in North Vietnam, which organized monthly visits to Hanoi to serve as mail carriers for American POWs and their families. On her second trip to Hanoi in 1972, Weiss negotiated with the North Vietnamese to release three POWs as a gesture of goodwill. The regularly scheduled trips, sponsored by the Committee of Liaison, not only delivered mail and packages to U.S. soldiers but also provided an opportunity to expose dedicated peace activists to wartime conditions in Hanoi.[18] In composing the membership of these monthly delegations, Weiss invited individuals from diverse racial, generational, and gender backgrounds to expand the range of people who otherwise would not have the opportunity to travel to North Vietnam. These journeys invariably reaffirmed and further motivated the travelers' engagement in the antiwar movement. The women from North and South Vietnam who cultivated and encouraged international contact with women from the West also articulated a unique gender role for women in the struggle for peace and national liberation. They represented women's organizations in their respective regions. The Women's Union of North Vietnam, based in Hanoi, traced its history back to the founding of the Indochinese Communist Party in 1930. The Women's Union for the Liberation of South Vietnam was founded in 1960, along with the National Liberation Front (NLF). The phrase "women's liberation" in the Western context referred to activists who sought to identify and subvert the workings of patriarchy. The VWUs conceived of women's liberation primarily through the lens of anticolonial struggles for national liberation. Because of the long history of political repression and anticolonial warfare, Vietnamese women had assumed a variety of political, military, economic and cultural roles. Consequently, they had a wider array of life experiences than did most of their Western counterparts. Yet, interestingly, the Vietnamese women also conveyed the arguments for peace in the name of protecting their families.

Nguyen Thi Binh, who was present at the 1965 Jakarta meeting with WSP as well as the 1968 Paris Women's Conference, became one of the most recognizable Asian female figures in Western women's political circles. Like WSP members, she came from a relatively elite and educated background. The granddaughter of nationalist leader Phan Chu Trinh and the daughter of a civil servant under the French, Binh became a political activist in the 1950s when she led a series of student protests against the French and the United States in Saigon.[19] Imprisoned for three years for these activities, she helped to found the NLF and the Women's Union for the Liberation of South Vietnam after her release. Unlike most WSP members, who were denied formal political power, Binh became an authorized leader as the foreign minister of the Provisional Revolutionary Government. WSP historian Amy Swerdlow noted the unequal status of the American and Asian women who met at international gatherings. While WSP publicly identified itself as consisting of "nonprofessional housewives, . . . the women who represented North and South Vietnam presented themselves as workers, students, professionals, and artists."[20]

Despite the disjuncture in status, Vietnamese women like Binh used a language of sisterhood and motherhood to establish a common connection with their old friends. In a fifteen-minute film produced in 1970 and intended for an American female audience, Binh explained:

> I am so happy as a South Vietnamese woman and mother to have the opportunity to speak to you. . . . May I express my sincere thanks to the Women Strike for Peace for its contribution to the anti-war movements and its sympathy and support to our people, particularly the South Vietnamese women. . . . Our aspirations for peace are all the more ardent for

Figure 13. Patsy Mink (first congresswoman of color), Madame Nguyen Thi Binh, and Bella Abzug (WSP member and congressional representative) meet in Paris. From *Memo* 2, no. 3 (Spring 1972), p. 31. Swarthmore College Peace Collection, Swarthmore, PA.

over 25 consecutive years now, our compatriots, we women included, have never enjoyed a single day of peace. Let me tell you that in my own family, several members have been killed while some others are still jailed by the Saigon regime. I myself have had not much time to live with my husband and my children. The moments my son and daughter were allowed to be at my side have become so rare and therefore so precious to them.[21]

Her emphasis on the destructive impact of warfare on family life reflected the actual experiences of women in Vietnam. Her appeal also resonated effectively with maternalist activists in the West who stressed the sanctity of motherhood and home life. Irma Zigas, who coordinated WSP's national antidraft task force, recalled meeting Binh for the first time at the Paris Women's conference: "Binh is a small woman with a gentle face, who speaks fluent French and who is desperately dedicated to bringing peace to her country. She had to wait 10 years before she married, because of the war, and now she is separated from her husband and children for months at a time."[22] Significantly, Zigas's impressions centered not only on Binh's personality, language skills, and political dedication but also on her forced separation from her family.

VWU initiated multiple international gatherings to facilitate personal contact with Western women. In addition, VWU circulated print materials to communicate how Vietnamese women both suffered from but also heroically resisted colonialism and military aggression. During the U.S. war in Vietnam, the VWU published a periodical in English and French titled

Women of Viet Nam. They also shared copies of Vietnamese Studies no. 10, a booklet called *Vietnamese Women (VW)*. This 1966 English-language publication was presented to U.S. visitors, both at international gatherings and during their travels to Vietnam. The portrayal of Vietnamese women in this work, numbering over three hundred pages, appealed to the political ideologies and sympathies of women from a variety of generations and backgrounds in the West.

VW consisted of eight sections, with chapters having titles such as "The Vietnamese Woman, Yesterday and Today," as well as more intimate and localized portrayals of either individual women or women from particular villages or regions. The overall effect was to personalize and humanize women in North and South Vietnam by providing a narrative of personal and social uplift through four historical stages: (1) Vietnamese women's lives under patriarchal as well as colonial oppression under French rule beginning in the mid- to late nineteenth century; (2) Vietnamese women's efforts to challenge traditional gender roles through involvement in national liberation movements, first against the French and then against the United States; (3) the transformation of Vietnamese women's lives through socialist reconstruction projects in the North after the end of the First Indochina War against the French in 1954; and (4) finally, how the opportunities for improving Vietnamese women's lives continue to be threatened by American imperialism and the Second Indochina War, which was being fought against the United States and the South Vietnamese government. Somewhat predictably, the publication argued that the oppression of Vietnamese women, particularly for the vast majority who were members of the peasantry, was centrally connected to class and national oppression. For Vietnamese women to achieve liberation and equality, then, they had to struggle not only against patriarchal family and societal norms but also for national independence and socialist revolution. The way this political message was conveyed, particularly through intimate portraits, appealed to Western women in various ways.

For maternalist peace activists who subscribed to "traditional" gender roles and justified their political interventions as part of their responsibilities as mothers and housewives, the destructive impact of war on heteronormative family life in Vietnam resonated most strongly. Numerous stories in *VW* emphasize how war separates, sometimes permanently, husbands and wives as well as mothers and children. The tragedy of war, then, was conveyed through heteronormative and maternal loss. One folksong quoted in *VW* expressed this longing of a young woman in North Vietnam and her fiancé who had departed to fight in the South: "Our destinies are bound together, I will wait for you / Even if I should have to wait a thousand years."[23]

Protecting their families and loved ones against colonialism and war required Vietnamese women to engage in or support acts of rebellion and violence. In their publications and in face-to-face meetings, they frequently quoted the traditional saying, "When the enemy comes, even the women must fight." They also cited historic examples of Vietnamese women who battled against foreign invasion, such as the Trung sisters, credited with leading the first national liberation struggle against Chinese domination in 40 AD. This Vietnamese female warrior tradition, which could be regarded as a transgression of traditional gender roles, was framed as a heteronormative or maternalist act of agency. For example, the publication *VW* featured a poem by Minh Khai, a famous revolutionary against the French who wrote on her prison cell before she was executed:

> A rosy-cheeked woman, here I am fighting side by side with you men!
> On my shoulders, weighs that hatred which is common to us.
> The prison is my school, its mates my friends.
> The sword is my child, the gun my husband.[24]

In this poem, instruments of violence are equated with members of a heteronormative family. The evocation of the sword as a child and the gun as a husband justifies the embrace of these objects as a means to fulfill traditional familial responsibilities. Given colonial and wartime conditions that do not allow for peaceful existence of kinship units, the female warrior bears the responsibility of defending her home and homeland in order to become a wife and mother.

Embracing familial roles provided practical as well as ideological support in the context of war. Mary Ann Tetreault cites Frances Fitzgerald to argue that the NLF adopted a "Children of the People" strategy. Because the NLF lacked the resources to wage a conventional war, its cadre relied upon cultivating local support. These liberation fighters "depend[ed] upon village residents to protect them. . . . Villagers became the 'parents' and the cadres their 'children.'"[25] Some of the NLF members had organic roots and kinship ties to the villages where they were stationed. Others claimed and cultivated these fictive relationships to claim reciprocity and protection.

Maternalist activists in the West embraced pacifism.[26] However, they could understand the fierce desire to step outside of accepted gender practices in the name of protecting their families. After all, to help end the war and stop nuclear annihilation, members of WSP, VOW, and WILPF also left the confines of the home to travel, lobby, and stage protests. Rather than condemning the Vietnamese women for fighting to save their loved ones, Western women peace activists demanded that the U.S. government end the war. As one slogan adopted by WSP pleaded: "Not Our Sons, Not Their Sons."

The model of revolutionary womanhood that Vietnamese women offered resonated differently for the new friends who cosponsored the IWCs. This designation generally referred to a younger generation of women who became politically active through the civil rights, New Left, and eventually the women's and sexual liberation movements. In contrast to the old friends who claimed their roles as housewives and mothers to justify their political interventions, the new friends sought to fundamentally challenge male domination over women. They demanded equal opportunities and rights for women in the legal and political system as well as the workplace. They identified inequalities in the home, naming the "second shift" that women worked as primary caregivers and housekeepers as well as the limited rights of women in marriage and divorce. They questioned the reproduction of gender roles through child rearing practices and socialization. They protested the sexual objectification and violence directed toward women and their bodies. And they challenged heteronormativity by claiming lesbianism as a sexual and political practice.

Although the individuals referred to as "new friends" differed and disagreed with one another, they collectively constituted members of the so-called second wave of feminism. The first wave crested with the attainment of suffrage in 1920, while the second wave is associated with women's activism of the 1960s and 1970s. Historians have increasingly challenged the waves analogy, because this framework tends to privilege certain forms of white middle-class women's activism as indicators of feminism. Scholars also are increasingly critical of differentiating distinct strands of feminism, such as liberal, radical, socialist, and lesbian. After all, individuals tend to evolve in their political understandings, participate in multiple organizations and collectives, and embrace diverse political views.[27] However, some of these terms do capture key distinctions that emerged within the collective group of new friends. For them, the experiences of Vietnamese women offered a range of possibilities to help second-wave feminists discover new political roles and identities.

For liberal feminists seeking access and equality for women in the realm of work and politics, the experiences of Vietnamese women provided

... will present each other at a triple-threat meeting on Tues. Mar 24 8ᴾᴹ
at Wm. Penn House, 515 E. Capitol, D.C. Each group will present
their program, history, purposes. To meet is to know is to understand
is to grow. All women — in, out, or in between — are urged to attend!

Figure 14. Triple threat: WILPF, WSP, and women's liberation. Charlotte Bunch Papers, Schlesinger Library, Radcliffe Institute, Harvard University, Cambridge, MA.

insight into the social reconstruction of gender roles. The *VW* booklet notes, "It is easy to inscribe the 'liberation of women' in the programme of a political party, it is much more difficult to get it into legislation, and more difficult still to integrate it into the customs and manners of the time."[28] Significantly, the publication did not regard women in the West as the vanguard of change, stating instead that "at present, women in all Western countries are still asking for equal salary and wages with men. . . . And they are not to get it very soon."[29] Strikingly, the authors regarded women in the West as being engaged in a similar struggle and perhaps even falling behind the so-called Third World. Because North Vietnam was in the process of constructing a new society, *VW* documented at length the rights and advances women had achieved under the Democratic Republic of Vietnam, such as suffrage, equal pay, and women holding prominent positions of political and economic leadership. At the same time, the publication also frankly acknowledged barriers to greater gender equity, conveying both advances and challenges through individual stories and charts with clear quantitative data.[30]

While the Vietnamese focus on women integrating the public arena might appeal to liberal feminists in the West, other aspects of the Vietnamese analysis resonated more strongly with women's liberation activists in the United States.[31] These individuals sought to identify and subvert the workings of patriarchy in all realms of life, not just in the public sphere of work and politics but also in the private sphere of personal, familial, and sexual relationships. For these women, the Vietnamese provided functioning examples of female communities. They organized all-women economic production teams, guerrilla units, and even regular military battalions, while leading hybridized and improvised family structures in the midst of war. Although products of emergency circumstances, these practices nevertheless offered empowering demonstrations of how women, through separatist institutions, could transform the society around them.

The VWU often used biographical examples of heroic women to offer political instruction. This "emulation campaign" was primarily directed toward the largely peasant constituency in Vietnam.[32] One of the prominently featured women was Nguyen Thi Dinh, a cofounder of the NLF and president of the Women's Union for the Liberation of South Vietnam. Unlike Nguyen Thi Binh, who came from a relatively elite family, Dinh was a peasant. Born in 1920, she began dedicating herself to fighting French colonialism at the age of fifteen. She eventually became a guerrilla fighter and a general in the People's Liberation Army. Like many other women engaged in the struggle for national liberation, described by the Vietnamese as "longhaired warriors," Dinh suffered imprisonment and separation from her husband and child, as well as the death of her loved ones. Dinh's life story as a female revolutionary leader engaged in armed struggle inspired new friends in the West who were trying to understand how they might fundamentally change their society. In addition, the Vietnamese use of the personal to offer political instruction corresponded strongly to one of the key mantras of the U.S. women's liberation movement: the personal is political.

Some second-wave feminists had the opportunity to learn from Vietnamese women through direct contact. Vivian Rothstein, who was a student activist at Berkeley before her involvement in the women's liberation movement in Chicago, met with Vietnamese women in Eastern Europe and then in North Vietnam in 1967. As a member of Students for a Democratic Society, she had been invited by Tom Hayden to participate in a significant gathering of antiwar activists in Bratislava, Czechoslovakia, in September 1967. Thirty-eight Americans attended the meeting, including representatives from religious pacifist organizations, the civil rights movement, the liberal and progressive media, and faculty and student anti-war activists. In Bratislava, they met with Vietnamese spokespersons from the North and the South, including Nguyen Thi Binh and other representatives of the VWU.[33]

Rothstein recalled that the Vietnamese women whom she met insisted on having women-only discussions with American representatives. This was unusual for her. She tended to work in mixed-gender settings as a student activist. Also, the Bratislava conference was attended by men and women. However, the women from South Vietnam wanted to convey how the war had a unique impact on women. Rothstein recalled that they discussed how militarization fostered the growth of prostitution in South Vietnam. In addition, they provided examples of how American soldiers threatened and utilized rape as well as sexual mutilation as military tactics. Shaken and moved by these meetings, Rothstein requested an audiotape version of their presentation so that she might share their "appeal to the American women."[34]

During the conference in Bratislava, Rothstein received an invitation from the VWU to visit North Vietnam. The trip to Eastern Europe was the first time she had left the United States, so traveling to Hanoi, which was then being bombed, was a "huge, terrifying" experience. Nevertheless, the journey profoundly touched Rothstein. In North Vietnam, she observed how the VWU inspired and mobilized women to protect and transform their society. The VWU had chapters at various levels, ranging from local villages to the national level and operating in schools, workplaces, health clinics, and government units. In all of these settings, the unions trained women for political leadership and advocated for their collective interests. VWU representatives conveyed to Rothstein "how important it was to organize the women . . . and how powerful American women could be" as well.[35] When Rothstein returned to the United States, she went back to the "little women's group" that she had participated in before she left. Inspired by her experiences in Czechoslovakia and North Vietnam, Rothstein proposed the formation of the Chicago Women's Liberation Union, a group modeled on the VWU.

Just as American activists learned from the Vietnamese, their hosts were eager to learn from the visitors. Charlotte Bunch-Weeks, a women's liberation activist based in the Washington, DC, area, traveled to Vietnam as part of a multiracial and mixed-sex group in 1970. Bunch-Weeks had a long history of engaging in international activism. Her parents initially planned to be missionaries in China. Due to her father's ill health, they resided in a small town in New Mexico instead. Unable to live overseas, her family brought the world to their home. They regularly hosted foreign exchange students. Inspired by the progressive Christian student movement, Bunch-Weeks first traveled abroad in 1964 to attend a YMCA program in Japan, titled Our Responsibility in a Changing Asia. It was her first "real-life experience of being in a minority," and the conference taught her "to understand that the world looks different depending on . . . where you are. . . . It sounds very mundane now, but at that moment it was like a paradigm shift in my head."[36] Despite the profound impact of this experience, Bunch-Weeks initially felt torn about leaving the United States. At the time, she was attending Duke University and had become involved in the civil rights movement. While Bunch-Weeks was in Japan during the summer of 1964, some of her friends participated in Freedom Summer in Mississippi. Following her graduation, Bunch-Weeks found a position with the Institute for Policy Studies in Washington, DC, a think tank that also employed Peter Weiss, Cora Weiss's husband. In DC, Bunch-Weeks continued her activism in civil rights and antiwar causes. In addition, she became invested in women's liberation.[37]

Like other travelers to North Vietnam, Bunch-Weeks returned with a deeper commitment to ending the war. She remembers one particularly profound exchange she had with a Buddhist nun. Her delegation had traveled south of Hanoi, where they viewed the countryside, villages, and towns that had been repeatedly bombed, regardless of whether they constituted strategic military sites. In Vinh, a major city on the Gulf of Tonkin, her group learned that "over 4,000 air attacks" occurred there from 1964 to 1968, "an average of two tons of bombs dropped" for each person residing there. One of these attacks resulted in the destruction of a Catholic cathedral and the deaths of a number of worshippers there. She recalled viewing "the remains of Vinh's churches, schools, hospitals, homes; all indiscriminately destroyed."[38] Outside of Vinh, her delegation visited a Buddhist pagoda, which was only partly standing. Their host, "a small, thin, quiet Buddhist nun in [a] brown habit," showed them around the facility and explained religious customs. Bunch-Weeks recalled feeling "very tired" and wanting to say goodbye, when

suddenly she leaned toward us, grew very intense, and grasped our hands. She said that she had been waiting many years to talk with American women. She was convinced that if the women of the US knew what was really happening in her country, they would make it stop. She told of her experience, of how children came crying to her for their mothers, but she knew their mothers had been killed. Finally she said, "We the women, must unite to stop this war. We must unite to stop the terrible things that are happening in this world. I would like you to take that message back to the women of America."[39]

Accepting this mandate, Bunch-Weeks returned to the United States and shared her experiences through talks and writings, which circulated in women's liberation and antiwar publications. She also cofounded the Women and Imperialism Collective in the Washington, DC, area and proposed to launch the National Women's Anti-War Program. Along with Cora Weiss, Bunch-Weeks served on the steering committee of the New Mobilization Committee to End the War in Vietnam (the new Mobe). The first Mobe or National Mobilization Committee to End the War in Vietnam had organized a series of national protests, including a large rally of over one hundred thousand in Washington, DC, in 1967, the follow-up March on the Pentagon, and the protests at the 1968 Democratic National Convention in Chicago. The new Mobe formed in 1969 and coordinated a series of local and national protests that culminated in two national moratoriums, general strikes to force the Nixon administration to end the war. Held on 15 October and 15 November of that year, the second moratorium attracted over half a million people to Washington, DC. The strong showing sought to challenge Nixon's 3 November appeal to the "silent majority" of Americans whom he believed supported his policies. The new Mobe continued its efforts into the spring of 1970 as Nixon's secret bombings and invasion of Cambodia, a neutral country, were made public.

Although Weiss and Bunch-Weeks played leadership roles in the new Mobe, they both recognized the limited authority and respect that women had within the male-dominated antiwar movement. Even though women performed crucial organizing work, their ideas and voices tended to be marginalized and at times publicly denigrated. To address these issues from within the movement, Bunch-Weeks, Weiss, and other female members on Mobe's national staff and steering committee formed a women's caucus. Their group identified three main goals: (1) "combating male supremacy" in the antiwar movement, (2) developing "ideological and programmatic clarity about how the struggle for the liberation of women is related to the struggles against racism and imperialism," and (3) connecting the "spring actions of the Mobe to their own oppression as women."[40] The Women and

Imperialism Collective as well as the Women's Caucus provided opportunities for female activists to organize with other women and to develop a feminist analysis of war and imperialism.

Bunch-Weeks did not just receive political inspiration from Vietnamese women. During her travels to North Vietnam, she received a request to give a presentation on the origins, status, and goals of the American women's liberation movement.[41] Her Vietnamese hosts were eager to learn from her. They wanted to understand political developments in the United States and how they might communicate better with American activists.

These conversations and international partnerships helped the VWUs develop effective antiwar outreach campaigns. Nguyen Thi Ngoc Dung, a member of the 1969 delegation that traveled to Canada, was stationed in Paris as part of the NLF's external relations division. Dung first joined the Vietnam Women's Union in 1945, focusing her efforts initially on eradicating illiteracy among women and children. Dung, although highly educated and fluent in French, never developed a facility in English.[42] When she was stationed in Paris, she befriended two women who both played crucial roles in assisting Dung's mission. Maria Jolas, a French woman who was more than seventy years old at the time, and Diana Jolston, an American expatriate, helped to translate and edit Dung's weekly newsletter.[43] When Dung became a member of the Paris Peace Talks delegation in 1968, Phan Thi Minh, a cousin to Madame Binh, assumed the responsibilities of disseminating information about the war in Vietnam and meeting with antiwar activists from the West. Minh eventually traveled throughout Europe with actress Jane Fonda to speak against the war. Jolas and Jolston tutored Dung and Minh about the nuances and divisions within the United States, including those who opposed the war. Together, they strategized about the most effective way to communicate and persuade their intended audience. In fact, Jolas played a central role in arranging the 1968 Paris Women's Conference, which was cosponsored by WSP. The partnership between Dung, Minh, Jolas, and Jolston enabled the development of an international women's antiwar network.

Vivian Rothstein, Charlotte Bunch-Weeks, and other women's liberation activists who met with Vietnamese representatives in Asia and other parts of the world became key organizers of the IWCs. Their face-to-face encounters inspired U.S. women profoundly. Alice Wolfson of the Washington, DC, Women and Imperialism Collective shared her impressions after a 1970 planning meeting for the IWCs that was held in Budapest, Hungary:

We have just had our first formal meeting with the Vietnamese & Cambodians. They are incredible out of sight people. Yesterday, when I first met them, I filled up with tears & wanted to take them in my arms & say "I'm sorry." . . . No matter how much you read & how much you know in your head what a monster imperialism is, it comes home to you with an emotional force that seems physical, meeting women who live under the threat of death. It seems impossible to think that I could ever, even for a minute, contemplate withdrawing or dropping out.[44]

By organizing the IWCs, women's liberation activists had the opportunity to recreate their political intimacy with Southeast Asian women for larger numbers of women who did not have the privilege or opportunity to travel to Asia and other parts of the world.

The final group of cosponsors of the IWCs were Third World women. These individuals from racially oppressed groups in North America identified their status in the West as being akin to the status of Third World peoples globally. Understanding themselves as internal colonial subjects, they expressed solidarity among themselves based on similar experiences of disfranchisement and marginalization within the United States. In addition, they allied with people in the Third World who were fighting for self-determination and national liberation from colonialism and neocolonialism. Given this identification with Third World people both domestically and abroad, women of color tended to distance themselves from the predominantly white old and new friends. Instead, racialized women in the "First World" turned to one another and to women in the Third World for political inspiration.

Both the old and new friends recognized that their groups consisted predominantly of white women. Consequently, they attempted to work with nonwhite women. WSP and WILPF cultivated contacts with Coretta Scott King and other African American women at a time when great pressures were being placed on male civil rights leaders to avoid making public statements about Vietnam.[45] In addition, both organizations also attracted women of Asian ancestry. Aline Berman, a Chinese American, attended the Jakarta and Paris meetings as a WSP representative. Her husband, Dan Berman, also was engaged in antiwar activism and worked with Bob Browne on the Inter-University Committee. In addition, Marii Hasegawa, a Japanese American, served as president of the U.S. Section of WILPF during the late 1960s and early 1970s.

The presence of women of Asian ancestry in mainstream women's peace organizations stemmed from these groups' engagement with domestic racism and international pacifism. Marii Hasegawa explained that WILPF was "one of the few organizations which had passed a resolution against the concentration camps in which Japanese and their citizen children were held in WWII" by the U.S. government.[46] To assist Japanese American internees seeking to resettle outside of the designated internment zones on the West Coast, WILPF supported a hostel in Philadelphia where Hasegawa found a place to stay after she left camp.[47] In addition to WILPF's concern about domestic racism, the group also promoted an international agenda to stem nuclear proliferation. WILPF sponsored annual commemorations of the bombings of Hiroshima and Nagasaki, along with other pacifist groups and Asian American organizations. WILPF also facilitated international exchanges with Japanese women's peace organizations. These reminders of Asia and Asian bodies as the victims of American foreign policy no doubt fostered the political involvement and leadership of Asian Americans. These antinuclear campaigns laid the basis for WILPF's eventual peace efforts on behalf of Vietnam and Vietnamese people.[48]

The category of Third World women, which could have described non-white individuals involved in mainstream women's organizations, tended to refer instead to women who became active during the late 1960s in racially based liberation movements. These activists identified as black, Asian American, Chicana or Mexican American, Puerto Rican, and indigenous or Native. For these individuals, the Vietnamese analysis of women's oppression as resulting from a confluence of patriarchy, colonialism, and capitalism held particular appeal. In the mid- to late 1960s and into the 1970s, women of color in the global North began to articulate an intersectional analysis.[49] Rather than seeing themselves only in terms of their race, gender, or class, they began to understand how multiple systems of social hierarchy operated simultaneously to shape their lives. Consequently, they turned to one another and to women in the Third World for political inspiration.

Like other antiwar activists, women of color also traveled to Vietnam. In 1970, the same year that Elaine Brown and Pat Sumi traveled to Hanoi as part of the Cleaver delegation, Betita Martinez also visited North Vietnam. She believes that she was the first Mexican American to journey there. In fact, she went on the same delegation as Charlotte Bunch-Weeks and like her fellow traveler was asked to introduce the movement that she was engaged in building in New Mexico.

Martinez grew up in Washington, DC, a member of an international and multiracial family. Her father, a dark-skinned Mexican, worked for Mexico's embassy, and her mother, a fair-skinned Scotch-Irish, worked for the Swiss embassy. Growing up in the racially polarized, black-white city of Washington, DC, Martinez found it difficult to socially locate herself as a multiracial person of Latino/a heritage. She recalled, "The composition of the neighborhood was either . . . black or white, or both, because that's the way Washington, DC, was. There was no Latinos around the street back then. It was a very lonely thing."[50]

In that environment, Martinez developed both a racial identification with African Americans and a global consciousness against Western colonialism. She inherited her father's dark skin and was treated as if she was black. Martinez recalled, "The girl next door was not allowed to play with me by her parents because I was too dark . . . and we passed for black often on the buses and got sent to the back of the bus."[51] Her parents, who became Spanish language and literature teachers, offered emotional support for their daughter. Her father, who arrived in the United States right after the Mexican Revolution, told her stories about how "the U.S. bombed Vera Cruz to stop the revolution."[52] His anger against American intervention planted seeds of political inspiration for Betita. After graduating from college and in the aftermath of World War II, she obtained a position with the United Nations, conducting research for a department on former European and American colonies. As she read reports about the Congo and South Africa, she became "completely disgust[ed]." She decided to leak information in the reports to a "progressive representative of the trusteeship council . . . [so] he could then announce and talk about [the information] . . . and embarrass the colonial powers." She admitted that it "was a completely subversive, incorrect thing for a staff member to do," but her life experiences collectively helped her to make a connection "very early between racism and colonialism."[53]

During the late 1950s and early 1960s, Martinez also became invested in supporting the civil rights movement. As a writer and editor based in New York City at the time, she recalled the visceral impact of the 1963 church bombing in Birmingham, Alabama, which killed four little black girls. She thought to herself, "[I] gotta go down there and shoot those guys, or something, do something."[54] Instead of engaging in retaliatory violence, she decided to volunteer for the Student Nonviolent Coordinating Committee. Appointed by James Foreman, she initially worked in Mississippi for the 1964 Summer Project. She then coordinated the New York office, where she raised funds and mobilized support for civil rights activities in the South. She also edited an important collection of letters about Mississippi

Freedom Summer under the name of Elizabeth Sutherland. In the predominantly black-white environment of the committee, Martinez felt
more comfortable using a non-Latino name. In the movement she was
known as "Liz," not Betita. She also chose Sutherland rather than Martinez as her surname, because "in my mother's past there was this Duchess
of Sutherland . . . the chief lady-in-waiting to the queen."[55]

Martinez's interest in Latino/a issues persisted, though, and her ethnic
consciousness eventually emerged. She traveled to Cuba repeatedly, the first
time after the 1959 revolution, and eventually published a book in 1967
about her observations of their new society. Also that year, she decided to
relocate from New York City to New Mexico. She initially lived with Beverly Axelrod, an attorney known for defending political activists like Black
Panther leader Eldridge Cleaver and a participant at the 1965 WSP-VWU–
sponsored meeting in Jakarta. Eventually, Martinez started an influential
Chicano/a newspaper, *El Grito del Norte*. Originally reluctant to leave the
East Coast, she recalled feeling an immediate sense of cultural familiarity
with the Southwest: "[Getting] off the plane late at night in Albuquerque,
I looked around, I felt the air. I looked at the mountains, I heard the Spanish" and thought, "mmmmm, this is interesting. . . . Suddenly . . . I felt at
home."[56]

When Martinez traveled to Vietnam in 1970, her sense of commonality
with the Vietnamese, particularly the women, was due not only to gender
but also to a comparable colonized status. Because of the heavy bombing
campaign ordered by President Nixon at the time, the plane that she and
Bunch-Weeks traveled on to Hanoi "landed on a totally dark airstrip in
a totally dark airport."[57] Martinez's reflections, though, quoted in a study
of the Chicano antiwar movement by scholar Lorena Oropeza, focused on
the positive spirit of the Vietnamese people:

> "There are mountains and valleys and caves and big skies and glowing sun-
> sets, as in New Mexico." . . . The Vietnamese were *campesinos* (literally,
> people of the *campo* or countryside) who loved their land. Eastern medicine
> was like our *curanderismo* (folkhealing). . . . "The spirit of the people was like
> a force of nature itself, creating life in the shadow of death. The white
> people of the West with their unnatural soul and their unnatural weapons
> are a death people. . . . The Vietnamese are a life people. And anyone who
> thinks that a life people can really be conquered is a fool."[58]

Martinez observed how the vast majority of Vietnamese people were
peasants, a status similar to the agricultural background of many Chicano/as

of New Mexico.[59] In addition, the Vietnamese were demanding the right to determine their political future, just like what the Chicano/a movement and other liberation movements in the United States and globally were demanding.[60] Finally, she admired the indomitable spirit of the Vietnamese people.

These reflections crystallized for Martinez on the trip to Vinh, the same journey that both she and Bunch-Weeks remembered for their encounter with the Buddhist nun: "We went with a translator and a driver . . . it must be like sixty miles. The trip [took] all day because the bridges were bombed out, the roads were bombed out. I mean, we had detours, like, nonstop because of the bombing and at the same time . . . it was spring and so the rice fields were in bloom with that beautiful green color they have. . . . It . . . just struck me as, well, the green is the spirit of Vietnam and they're not gonna bomb that away."[61]

When Martinez arrived at Vinh, she was struck by the utter destruction of the city and the hypocrisy of the United States: "After this long trip . . . there was only one building left standing in this big city. . . . I could visualize the whole flattened city and we sat on the steps looking at the city and on the radio . . . [which] picks up stations from around the world . . . there was [a U.S.] program on the air, glorifying that this was the first Earth Day. Earth Day was being celebrated for the first time by the United States. . . . It was enraging to hear that while looking at this devastation."[62]

In the midst of this destruction, Martinez recognized the resilience of Vietnamese people who were fighting against the United States: "Our translator was a . . . wonderful young woman. She was in the dark—we could hardly . . . see in the dark and . . . she was sewing and it looked like she . . . had . . . something stiff and white that she was sewing. . . . So I said, 'Excuse me, but could I ask what you are sewing?' 'Oh,' she said very happily, 'I'm . . . making your . . . boxes for your boxed lunch tomorrow.' . . . I thought, 'Jesus Christ. These people would go to no ends to treat us right . . . and look what our country has done.'"[63] As Martinez completed her journey in North Vietnam, she vowed, "I gotta go straight to Washington, DC, and tell that president, forget it, you're never gonna defeat these people. . . . Their spirit is too strong."[64]

The commonalities that Martinez identified between Vietnamese and Chicano/a people coalesced around the issue of land.[65] Just as the Vietnamese wanted to protect their country from military aggression and ecological destruction, the Chicano/a movement sought to assert the rights of Mexican Americans to lands of the Southwest. One of the key ideals in the Chicano movement was the reclamation of Aztlan, the mythical homeland of the Aztec people before Spain and then the United States invaded, colonized, and annexed the region.[66] Following the U.S.-Mexican War, the 1848 Treaty of Guadalupe-Hidalgo promised to respect the land rights of the existing Mexican residents. Through legal maneuverings, economic pressures, and at times outright violence, Anglos eventually dispossessed Mexican Americans as well as indigenous peoples of the vast majority of their holdings. During the late 1960s and 1970s, Chicano/a activists sought "to recover lands, the communal lands, not individually held lands . . . [which consisted of] huge areas of . . . thousands of acres of north New Mexico."[67] Martinez acknowledged that the movement to restore land ownership was a difficult one. These activists fought against privatized economic development policies advocated by entrepreneurs. In addition, their efforts to claim land based on the authority of Spanish grants raised questions about who constituted the original owners. After all, the land was "originally Pueblo land, you know, . . . Indian land," and therefore illegitimately given away by the Spanish to people who became known as Mexican Americans. Chicano/a activists who proudly proclaimed their descent from indigenous people eventually developed "a decent relationship . . . with some of the native groups . . . about supporting their [mutual] struggles for their land."[68] Martinez foregrounded these issues of colonization and land in *El Grito del Norte*, drawing comparisons between Chicano/a and indigenous people's movements to reclaim land in New Mexico with the efforts of Native people in Hawaii as well as with peasants in Japan, India, and Vietnam.[69] This global Third World consciousness was emerging more broadly in political movements during the late 1960s and 1970s. Martinez claimed that *El Grito del Norte* was at the forefront. She recalled, "There were about twenty Chicano newspapers . . . in the late sixties . . . in different parts of California, Texas, all over, Colorado . . . but ours was the only one that was completely international."[70]

After returning from Hanoi, Martinez did not in fact travel to DC but instead focused on sharing her insights with the Chicano/a community. She wrote articles in *El Grito del Norte* and also gave public presentations. She was one of the featured speakers at the Chicano National Moratorium. Held in Los Angeles on 29 August 1970, the moratorium was part of a nearly two-year effort to mobilize Chicano/as against the Vietnam War. Similar to African Americans, Mexican Americans tended to have lower socioeconomic status as well as fewer opportunities for career advancement and college admissions. Consequently, Chicanos tended to be overrepresented in the military.[71] Chicano/a activists like Martinez encouraged other members of their communities to question why they were fighting in the war. They formed the only "minority-based antiwar organization, called the National Chicano Moratorium Committee."[72] The National Moratorium attracted an estimated twenty thousand to thirty thousand protesters, including elderly and children; it was the "largest anti-war march by any specific ethnic or racial group in U.S. history."[73] The event, though, was brutally disrupted by the Los Angeles police force. Approximately 150 were injured that day, and three were killed. Martinez recalled, "[I was] standing there, ready to make a speech at the podium and I look up from my notes and I see police charging across the whole park with tear gas flying. So I said, 'I don't think I'm gonna make my speech.' I was out of there, man, and ran into the house across the street with a Chinese family that didn't know what was happening."[74]

Despite this aborted attempt, Martinez found other ways to encourage Chicano/as to understand the issues of the war. She was not able to replicate her own experiences of traveling to Vietnam. The people with whom she interacted in New Mexico lacked the financial means to do so. Also, some expressed reservations that their journey might taint them as communists. However, Chicanas from New Mexico did travel to Vancouver for the IWC. There they met with women from Southeast Asia and other women of color, including other Mexican, Mexican American, and indigenous activists from throughout North America.[75] Reporting in *El Grito del Norte,* Dolores Varela titled her article, "We Are People of the Land." The "we" in the article referred to herself, who was engaged in land struggles in New Mexico; Alison and Suzette Bridges, "who have been carrying on the Indian fishing struggle in Washington state for so long"; and Indochinese women who referred to themselves as "people of the land."[76]

Maternal peace activists, second-wave feminists, and women of color all developed profound political connections with Southeast Asian women. These alliances across national, cultural, and ideological boundaries provide an opportunity to reexamine global sisterhood in two significant ways. First, rather than regarding women in the Third World as oppressed recipients of Western benevolence and feminist rescue, it is important to emphasize the agency of Vietnamese women in initiating international partnerships and to recognize their role as political mentors for women in the West. In other words, global sisterhood as a political strategy was not just imposed by the West but also crafted and promoted by women in the Global South. Second, international sisterhood does not depend upon a monolithic, universal analysis of gender oppression that transcends time and space. Rather, the political messages that Vietnamese women conveyed through face-to-face meetings and the circulation of print and visual media suggest that a rich and diverse array of discourses could be transmitted and debated between women of varying backgrounds. Activists of the broader 1960s movements have been accused of a devolution toward "sectarianism" as the decade progressed. In contrast, as Vivian Rothstein noted following her travels to North Vietnam, what impressed her was the emphasis that the VWU placed on organizing a "majoritarian" movement. This approach focused on building broad political agreements and coalitions.[77] Literally engaged in a struggle for life and death, the women of Vietnam cultivated the widest possible range of allies.

Global sisterhood, then, was not intended to propose a rigid universal theory for understanding women's oppression. Rather, the VWU sought to involve women of varying backgrounds and political beliefs to engage in ideas with one another and to learn from each other's life experiences. Vietnamese women did want women from the West to help them end the war. Yet the women from Southeast Asia believed that they had a reciprocal and perhaps even greater ability to inspire the political imagination of women in the First World. The Indochinese Women's Conferences of 1971 represented a continuation of these efforts to build a global antiwar movement among diverse sisters.

Chapter 8

War at a Peace Conference

On the last night of the Indochinese Women's Conference (IWC) in Vancouver, North American women met for a "Criticism and Evaluation session of the Conference."[1] A guerrilla theater group set up a sign, announcing themselves as "C.U.R.S.E. (Canadian Union of Rabid Senseless Extremists)," and attempted to perform a skit to express their critique of the conference. The reaction of the audience reflected the tense atmosphere of the entire event:

> Immediately a woman stood up grabbing away the sign. She demanded the C.U.R.S.E. women leave. Other women then came forward shoving and pushing, trying to get the guerilla theatre woman out of the meeting. the CURSE woman linked arms and refused to leave. At this point, a couple of woman [sic] began beating on one woman in the theatre group, the other woman; in the skit shouted "Don't hit her she's pregnant." but the American women kept on slugging her shouting "She shouldn't be here then." The five CURSE woman then formed a circle so as to protect their pregnant sister.[2]

When the audience finally allowed the performance to take place, the skit featured a series of vignettes in the life of a woman. She experiences denigration in the male-dominated workplace, the double standard as well as sexual abuse in the home, and political repression as she protests for abortion. She is able to recover from each of these efforts to wound and humiliate her. She is not able to overcome the hostility that she faces from other women when she attends the IWC:

> [First, the] heroine is stopped at [the] door by a stern-faced security guard demanding her revolutionary credentials. The security guard begrudgingly lets her pass. She is met by three women mechanically chanting "Off the Pig." And raising their fists in synchronized time. She innocently offers her out [*sic*] out in friendship to a delegate wearing a sign saying "Third World."
>
>   The chanting stops as the Third World delegate screams "Racist" and then hits her with a sign reading "Guilt." Somewhat beaten, she timidly approaches the next delegate with "Gay Lib" on her T-shift, who says "Heterosexual!" Again she is clobbered with guilt. Beaten to her knees she crawls to the USA Women's Lib delegate but, as she reaches out to touch her, she's accused of being a "Liberal." This final blow of guilt knocks her flat to the floor where she drags herself offstage, completely beaten.[3]

The North American and Southeast Asian women who gathered in Vancouver and Toronto in the spring of 1971 came with hopes for dialogue and political unity. However, volatile factionalism, particularly among North American women, exploded both during the organizing process and at the actual conference. The C.U.R.S.E. theatrical performance illuminated three axes of difference—race, sexuality, and nationality—which served as flash-points of contention.

The conflicts that emerged at the 1971 IWCs illuminate the challenges of organizing international meetings for diverse constituencies. The selection of Canada as a site for the IWCs reflected a broader practice within the North American antiwar movement. During the course of the U.S. war in Vietnam, representatives from North Vietnam and from the resistance movement in South Vietnam could not enter the States. Canada, as an officially neutral party, not only provided refuge for U.S. draft dodgers but also served as a communication node that facilitated face-to-face contact between Southeast Asian anticolonial spokespersons and the North American antiwar movement.[4]

In fact, the idea of the 1971 IWCs emerged from a successful visit of Vietnamese women to Canada in 1969. This two-week visit, which took place during the hot month of July, was sponsored by Voice of Women (VOW) in collaboration with Women Strike for Peace (WSP). Through their organizational efforts, three Vietnamese women from North Vietnam, South Vietnam, and Paris, along with two male interpreters, met with North American audiences throughout the entire continental expanse of Canada.[5] The Vietnamese delegation arrived in Montreal, spent a day meeting with Canadian and American women on a farm just north of New Hampshire, participated in the Fourth of July protest at Niagara Falls, attended a discussion at the University of Toronto, met with a welcome delegation during a one-hour stopover in Winnipeg, visited wheat farmers in Regina, and participated in a two-day conference in Vancouver that drew three hundred people and a public meeting that attracted more than six hundred people before they finally toured the Houses of Parliament in Ottawa and engaged in an evaluation meeting on the entire visit. Despite the intensive schedule, the Vietnamese representatives were pleased with their reception and interactions with North Americans. They had wanted to reach a wide constituency. At a planning meeting held in Helsinki earlier that year, a VOW representative had the opportunity to converse with Phan Thi An, an officer within the Vietnam Women's Union and a frequent correspondent with Western women's organizations. The VOW member reported that the Vietnamese "are not interested in women only meetings and really want to meet workers, teachers, students and young people. Also she [Phan Thi An] asked for meetings with U.S. young men, draft resisters and deserters—as many as possible."[6]

The emotional and political impact of the 1969 tour led the Vietnam Women's Union to request a follow-up visit the next year. VOW organizers, exhausted by the effort of planning and hosting the delegation, requested more time to consider how a second visit could reap additional political benefits. Together, they decided to focus on reaching out to various female constituencies, particularly members of the women's liberation (WL) movement and Third World women, as well as family members of American GIs and women who were not politically active. To involve these new groups, VOW and WSP had to expand beyond their traditional membership base of middle-aged, middle-class, white maternalist women.

These outreach efforts were somewhat hampered by VOW's concerns about whether they could obtain entry visas for another delegation of Vietnamese visitors. Although Canada was officially a neutral country, the U.S. government still exerted political pressure on its northern neighbors. During the period between the 1969 and 1971 conferences, a group of

Vietnamese representatives were denied the right of entry into Canada. They had planned to participate via closed-circuit television in the 1971 Winter Soldiers Investigation, a three-day conference sponsored by Vietnam Veterans against the War in Detroit. Fearing that the Canadian government would turn down future visa requests as well, VOW asked their cosponsors not to publicize the IWCs in mainstream or movement newspapers. VOW wanted to prevent widespread publicity, particularly in the United States, since that might lead the American government to intervene in the visa process. In the end, VOW succeeded in obtaining visas only "with every known string being pulled—formally and informally."[7] To minimize attention, IWC organizers primarily used personal contacts and correspondence to foster interest and recruit participants for the conferences. The blanket publicity muzzle proved impossible, though.

The old friends could most easily involve new friends. Maternalist peace activists already had collaborated with women's liberation (WL) activists. However, the two groups still differed from one another in their goals, political beliefs, resources, and organizing styles. Although the old friends engaged in protest and civil disobedience, they tended to do so as "ladies," with a sense of decorum. At times, they literally donned gloves and hats as part of their political performance of respectability. In contrast, the new friends tended to question all social hierarchies and norms, not just particular policies of the U.S. government. WSP and VOW had existing political networks at the local, national, and international levels. WL activists tended to be more loosely organized and primarily locally based. Recognizing the differences between old and new friends, North American and Vietnamese planners suggested dividing each conference into two sections. That way, old friends and new friends could each have greater control over the content and interactions within their portion of the meetings.

Involving Third World Women as a third cosponsor raised even greater challenges. Both old and new friends had worked with nonwhite women before. After all, both maternalist and WL activists had participated in and supported the civil rights movement. WSP also had significant contacts with black women in the welfare rights movement. Under the leadership of Marii Hasegawa, WILPF, which had the most elderly constituency, even engaged in discussions about black power and reparations for slavery. In fact, the WILPF newspaper featured sympathetic articles about Angela Davis. A Black Panther, a member of the Communist Party, and a professor of philosophy at the University of California, Los Angeles, Davis was imprisoned and eventually acquitted for suspected involvement in a hostage situation and shooting of a judge. Her supporters argued that Davis's treatment did not reflect actual criminal behavior on her part. Rather, her imprisonment, like that of other activists, constituted political harassment and persecution. Despite the connections that existed between the old friends, new friends, and women of color, the IWCs required an elevated degree of collaboration between women who developed their ideologies and identities in very different ways from one another.

Unlike the old and new friends, Third World women were not initially and consistently part of the organizing process. When WL representatives gathered in New York City in September 1970 to select delegates to attend a planning meeting in Budapest, they discussed ways to avoid the exclusivity that characterized previous international delegations, especially those sponsored by the old friends. Representatives in the past were often selected "through personal contacts, choosing known individuals rather than groups, choosing friends, etc.," and they "felt it was of utmost importance to the success of the Canada conference to get away from this kind of elitism and to involve as many women as possible in the planning for the Conference . . . through broad, grass-roots representation and collective responsibility."[8]

In order to involve Third World women, WL organizers decided to contact two groups: the Third World Women's Alliance (TWWA), a New York–based African American and Puerto Rican organization that emerged from the Student Nonviolent Coordinating Committee; and the Black Panthers, whose national headquarters was in Oakland, California.[9] They invited these organizations to participate in planning the IWCs and specifically asked if they wanted to send representatives to Budapest with the financial support of WL groups. In a series of criticism/self-criticism statements following the conference, WL organizers acknowledged their good but misguided intentions in these efforts: "We knew early that we did not want to be put in the position of 'choosing' which third world women should go, be represented, etc. We even had trouble with our decision that we should contact the Third World Women's Alliance and the Panthers for we felt that we were making the organizational choices for third world women."[10]

The confusion of WL activists in deciding whom to contact among Third World women is understandable. Activists of color began calling themselves Third World people with increasing frequency during the late 1960s. Asserting solidarity with one another and with decolonizing nations was just one step in creating a new political identity. Activists of color, who tended to be more attuned to racial oppression, were likely to be based primarily in communities of their own racial background. In some locales, most notably in large metropolitan centers where concentrations of diverse populations resided, people of color also formed political coalitions with one another. Creating such alliances was a process. They had to develop relationships, identify commonalities of historical and contemporary experience, determine mutual goals, and provide support for one another. The fact that WL activists did not know whom to invite reflected their lack of substantive contacts among Third World activists, particularly at the national level. Like WL activists themselves, it was difficult to identify spokespersons for Third World women when the political category itself was in the process of being constructed.

Neither TWWA nor the Panthers sent representatives to the planning meeting for the IWC in Budapest. Members of TWWA did eventually participate in the organizing process, but they generally did so with other Third World women. As the WL activists noted, "[Initially] three or four third world women did attend New York planning meetings in the Fall. [However,] they finally stopped attending, probably because the WL women were struggling among themselves for the most part. [Instead] by December a number of third world groups were meeting separately and regularly in NYC. Sometimes third world representatives would come to the New York WL meetings."[11] Elaine Brown of the Black Panthers never responded to the letter sent to her. She had returned from visiting socialist Asia in the summer of 1970 to the volatile and contentious split between Huey Newton and Eldridge Cleaver. Other Third World women, particularly in Los Angeles and San Francisco where women of color had previously collaborated with one another, began meeting on their own to discuss the conference.

On the West Coast, the political determination and organizational efforts of Third World women eventually resulted in a decision to divide the Vancouver conference into three, not just two, segments. Third World women from Los Angeles, led by Pat Sumi of the Anti-Imperialist Delegation, demanded time in the conference schedule so they could engage with Indochinese delegates autonomously. As their statement explained, "since we have been denied an equal participation *with* white groups, we can only ask for equal but separate conferences. The possibility of a confrontation between Third World and white women's groups at a joint conference would be disrespectful to the Indochinese women and would further reinforce the tensions that exist among North American women."[12] Their proposal received the support of white women from Los Angeles, who explained, "Why should Third World women unify with white women who claim to recognize the need of self-determination for the Indochinese, but who do not recognize the right of self-determination of all peoples in this country, as manifested in the 'small' way of planning a conference for people instead of with them."[13]

There were similar suggestions for a separate conference for Third World women at the Toronto conference, but the effort did not appear to be as organized. Neither Third World women nor women's liberationists on the East Coast formulated an identifiable position statement acknowledging the need for political autonomy. Organizers of the Vancouver and Toronto conferences did communicate with one another, particularly in regard to the timing of their respective conferences. Because of the uncertainty of obtaining entering visas for the Indochinese women, it was not clear if and when the delegation would actually arrive in Canada. Although the East Coast and West Coast planners developed contingency plans and shared proposed schedules with one another, the Toronto organizers did not duplicate the three-way separation of the Vancouver conference. Only afterward, in another criticism/self-criticism statement, did WL organizers on the East Coast recognize:

> We didn't know and didn't consciously try to find out what third world women's needs might have been with respect to the conference. On some levels we always saw the conference as "ours" with third world "participation." . . . When we talked about joint sessions with the third world women we were mostly considering our interests—that is to force women's movement women to see their racism, to learn from third world women, etc., etc. We seldom were conscious of whether a joint conference would in fact meet their needs; whether in fact they had a reason or need to meet with us. In addition, our vision of the potential of women from different race and class backgrounds coming together and struggling together in a sisterly way was far ahead of our practice and the practice of third world women. If we had considered all these factors and if we had had some real practice with third world women at the time the conference was initiated, we might have decided then that the most useful arrangement would be for separate conferences of third world and white women with the Indochinese—that separate conference would be O.K. politically.[14]

On the East Coast, where activists tried to work across racial lines, and even on the West Coast, where a degree of autonomy was validated, tensions surfaced concerning the content of the conferences and the security for the events. On the East Coast, an elaborate committee structure was established to allow for democratic and equal participation. However, the decisions of these committees tended to be overturned as new women joined. To counter their previous exclusion from the organizing process, women of color made demands for additional time with the Indochinese women and the opportunity to make public presentations about Third World women's issues. So when Naomi Weisstein, a pioneer feminist scholar in psychology, and her Chicago Liberation Women's Rock Band appeared in Toronto to perform as part of the Cultural Exchange Night, she was informed that there was no interest in white women's culture.[15] Instead, the "evening would consist of presentations about the third world struggle to the Indochinese."[16]

Some WL activists attempted to challenge the efforts by Third World women to control the content of the conference. However, afflicted by a sense of white "guilt," the new friends tended to avoid conflict with women of color. WL activists also recognized that their commitment to an egalitarian process bordered on anarchism. They realized afterward that the lack of organizational planning and political control made the conference experience less effective:

> In the Women's liberation workshops, questions were random; often the same question was asked three times in one day. . . . After the conference was over and WL learned about how the third world women had structured their workshops (they held caucuses to decide what they wanted to know, collected all the questions in the beginning, organized them into a building process) we realized how we had cheated ourselves through our own passivity and through our thinking that freedom was individual autonomy. The resulting chaos was not very fruitful.[17]

Differing concerns about security constituted another key source of racial conflict. Given the destructiveness of COINTELPRO in targeting organizations like the Black Panthers, Third World women tended to be highly sensitive about potential harassment of themselves as well as the Indochinese delegation.[18] Angela Davis's opening statement of solidarity for the conference, sent from the confines of her prison cell in California, underscored the urgency of this issue.

The potential for political harassment was heightened for Americans, especially women of color, when they crossed the border into Canada. All

U.S. participants, regardless of race, were issued instructions to safely negotiate the crossing: "You should 1) be prepared to look as straight as possible
(there is no way of getting around this) 2) have $15 to $20 per day for the
length of time you are planning to stay. . . . 3) have good I.D. . . . 4) have
no dope. People are often thoroughly searched, stripped, etc. 5) no literature, especially anything pertaining to border crossing."[19] To avoid invasive
searches, detainment, or denial of entry, female political activists were
advised to perform a normative, apolitical identity. Third World women
received additional advice about getting into Canada and being safe there:

> All of us from the U.S. and Hawaii are foreigners in a nation colonized and
> exploited by U.S. imperialism. . . . Since the Indochinese are not guests of
> the Canadian government, the Third World advance group decided that
> delegates themselves would take on the responsibility for the safety for the
> Indochinese friends with no dependency on the Vancouver or national
> Canadian pig forces. . . . If your delegation is fairly large, break down into
> brigades of ten women each. Each brigade should have a leader who will
> be responsible for getting everyone up on time, and keeping track of sisters
> so everyone is accounted for at all times. . . . Don't go around by yourself.
> Always take someone with you. And don't wear your delegate card as a
> badge. Cnada [*sic*] has a large group of fascist racists who may gather around
> the conference to hassle delegates, so be careful.[20]

These concerns reflected the experiences of women of color with state
surveillance. Nina Genera, a Chicana antiwar activist from the Bay Area,
recalled that she crossed the northern U.S. border for the first time to attend
the conference. Born in Texas, she frequently traveled back and forth across
the southern border. Each of these journeys raised anxiety, because, she said,
"You never knew how INS [Immigration and Naturalization Service] was
going to react. . . . It did cross my mind when we crossed in to Canada and
there was that fear factor."[21] Even after successfully negotiating the border
crossing, women of color experienced continued scrutiny. An account in an
Asian American women's publication reported: "In Vancouver, we were reminded that racism is not confined to the United States. Throughout our
stay there, the Third World candidates were followed whenever we traveled
in our chartered buses. One night when we visited Chinatown, the delegates
were harassed by Canadian police for charges such as jaywalking."[22]

   The call for heightened security shaped policies for all conference participants. Third World women "wanted no personal cameras at all" since

photographs of conference attendees could be used to identify and target activists.[23] They also warned white women that they "must be prepared for agents and provocaturs [sic] in our midst." Finally, Third World women took their responsibilities on the security force seriously, too seriously for many of the other delegates. Naomi Weisstein recalled being body searched before her band was finally allowed to perform. She attempted to protest this action through humor. She recalled chanting, "Don't touch me unless you love me." Her efforts, though, were not well received.[24] In Vancouver, the policies instituted regarding security led women's liberation activists to "feel that in some ways the whole 'show' of security was a way for groups to flex their muscles and gain power positions at the conference. By the third day the disputes over security were becoming so divisive between the Third World and white women that it was decided (partly as a result of discussion with the Indochinese) that the security would be much relaxed. Immediately the tension was reduced."[25]

The differences concerning workshop content and security were particularly intense between women of color and WL activists because the latter believed in the principle of involving everyone in planning the conference. While the old friends agreed to cosponsor the IWCs, WSP, VOW, and WILPF had less direct contact with large numbers of women of color. The maternalists insisted that their segment of the conferences be scheduled first.[26] The old friends wanted to establish an orderly tone to the proceedings, before ceding control to the more radical women of color and WL activists. Even with reduced contact, the old friends expressed criticism of what they perceived as the militancy, arrogance, and dictatorial nature of Third World women's authority.[27] In turn, women of color criticized the manipulation that they perceived on the part of some white women who had "direct contact with the Indochinese women . . . [and] used this privilege as a source of power and status for their own groups. . . . Because we do not have the direct contacts ourselves, we have . . . been left dependent on the whim of groups who apparently disseminate information only if and when it is advantageous."[28]

The women of color and the white women perceived one another as seeking to assert "control" and "power." The tensions can be traced to profound differences between their histories of involvement in the conference planning as well as their diverse life experiences and political perspectives. Some women were able to engage in conversation across racial lines. Overall though, it was extremely difficult for larger groups and especially for those who were new to those encounters or unused to sharing authority to recognize and understand diverse political approaches. Instead, given the urgency of organizing and executing the conference, their tensions exploded into hostile and derogatory interactions.

Another set of volatile conflicts at the IWCs coalesced around sexuality, specifically whether lesbianism should be addressed at the antiwar gathering.[29] Similar to the racial liberation movements, a sexual liberation movement emerged in the late 1960s and early 1970s.[30] The debates concerning sexuality at the IWCs reveal the complex ways in which diverse women understood their relationship to colonialism and liberation.

In a memo issued to IWC attendees in Vancouver, members of the San Francisco branch of Radicalesbians criticized the organizers of the conference for dismissing the issue of lesbianism. The statement complained, "Lesbianism apparently is not seen as a primary or relevant subject at an Indochinese Women's Conference."[31] The conflict over lesbianism reflected broader tensions within the women's movement. In 1969, National Organization for Women president Betty Friedan infamously denounced lesbians as a "lavender menace" for providing "enemies with the ammunition to dismiss the women's movement as a bunch of man-hating dykes."[32] In response to these charges, which were echoed in movement circles, lesbians critiqued gay baiting as a form of false consciousness. The group Radicalesbians initially formed in New York City in 1970 under the name Lavender Menace to appropriate Friedan's derogatory term. Members authored the now-classic statement "Woman-Identified Woman," which the San Francisco branch reproduced for IWC attendees in Vancouver. The West Coast Radicalesbians also quoted passages from the statement in its own memo for the conference. For the Radicalesbians, "lesbianism is not a sexual preference but a lifestyle in which women get their love, identity, and support from other women."[33] In other words, lesbianism represented the ultimate expression of a separatist women's movement that sought to subvert male domination.[34] The Radicalesbians argued that lesbianism was particularly appropriate to discuss at a conference devoted to anti-imperialism. Using the colonial analogy, they argued that women constituted the original colonized subjects under male domination. By extension, lesbians as women-identified women were anti-imperialists due to their efforts to obtain female liberation from male control.

The idea of women as colonized subjects was also articulated in the "Fourth World Manifesto," a lengthy statement condemning IWC organizers

Figure 15. "Out now!" The phrase has a double meaning. Published in the radical lesbian newsletter *The Furies* (June–July 1972, p. 12), the slogan proclaims the need to "come out" as a lesbian and for the United States to get out of Vietnam. Charlotte Bunch Papers, Schlesinger Library, Radcliffe Institute, Harvard University, Cambridge, MA.

as "an Imperialist Venture Against the Women's Liberation Movement."[35] Issued by female activists based in Detroit, the thirty-one-page manifesto questioned the politics of conference organizers. It began by supporting the idea of global sisterhood, particularly the proposal for women "from all over the world getting together to overcome *male imposed boundaries* between us—territorial, national, imperialist or ideological barriers."[36] However, the authors criticized IWC organizers for describing themselves as "anti-imperialist" women seeking to involve women in autonomous women's movements. In their eyes, "all women who fight against their own oppression (colonized status) as females under male domination are anti-imperialist by definition." They charged that conference organizers, by using the anti-imperialist designation—a term commonly used within the New Left—were positioning themselves as the political vanguard. In reality, according to the manifesto writers, the organizers were "acting as colonial-native (female) administrators for the male defined Left in relationship to other women—in this case especially to Women's Liberation women."

The criticism that women active in the antiwar movement constituted "dupes" and "tools" of the male Left was a troubling one. Women in the peace movement had experienced both subtle and overt sexism. Being publicly shouted down and humiliated by male antiwar activists led some women to create alternative women-only political communities, ones that valued and respected their voices. Just as the Third World asserted its autonomy from the United States and the Soviet Union, women, described by the manifesto as the fourth world, sought self-determination and liberation. Within this framework, women who remained committed to antiwar activism could be interpreted as having false consciousness, of following the political leadership of sexist men. According to the "Fourth World Manifesto" authors, these women—the "dupes" of the male Left—were the ones promoting the IWCs.

Conference organizers, like Charlotte Bunch-Weeks, sought to refute these charges. After all, they were attempting to develop a feminist analysis about war and imperialism. Early on, the WL organizers recognized that not everyone who wanted to attend the IWCs could do so. The Canadians had limited housing and meeting space. Also, each attendee had to raise a set amount of funds to help equalize the transportation costs for all participants. That way, a conference delegate traveling from far away would pay the same amount as someone who lived close by. No limits were established for the number of old friends, who tended to have the necessary resources and contacts to attend. Also, all interested Third World women were encouraged to make the journey, with the offer of financial support if necessary. For the new friends, though, organizers decided to establish a quota system to ensure broad geographical representation. Cities with large activist communities, like San Francisco, Los Angeles, New York City, Boston, and Washington, DC, received higher allocations. Even for these cities, though, not everyone who wanted to attend could do so, because other spots were reserved for participants from smaller towns and from the interior and southern states. For all these locations, decisions still needed to be made as to who would actually attend the IWCs. In general, the new friends encouraged local organizers to give preference to less active women or those with less experience participating in international gatherings.

Cognizant of the limited numbers who could attend the IWCs, the new friends decided to use the conference as a platform for political education. They encouraged American women to discuss and analyze why ending the Vietnam War should be a feminist priority, regardless of whether they traveled to Canada to meet Indochinese women. To assist in this process, the new friends authored and circulated various position papers. These essays articulated theories about the connections between military conflict, economics, and the status of women. The new friend organizers then encouraged local women's groups to discuss, revise, and elaborate on these ideas. In other words, conference organizers encouraged organic and localized theorizing of political ideas. They also urged WL activists to hold public events, like the commemoration of the tenth anniversary of the founding of the National Liberation Front in December 1970 or International Women's Day in March 1971, to attract interest and promote discussion about women and war.

Despite these attempts to craft a feminist perspective about war, WL organizers had limited resources and ability to respond to their critics. Seeking to foster an egalitarian and democratic process, WL sponsors used a grassroots approach. They held planning meetings in New York City; Baltimore, Maryland; and Dayton, Ohio, to expand the regional reach of their political contacts. Those in more active locations, like Buffalo, Washington, DC, or Chicago, divided the responsibilities for planning the conference. Ideally, this type of decentralized yet coordinated structure would promote awareness about the conference and also foster the development of a national feminist antiwar movement. In reality, this fragmented structure allowed issues and concerns to slip through the cracks. Conference organizers received a copy of the "Fourth World Manifesto" during a regional meeting in February 1971. The Washington, DC, collective, in which Charlotte Bunch-Weeks participated, mailed copies of the statement to groups that could not attend the Dayton, Ohio, gathering. The DC collective also drafted a response but wanted to circulate it for discussion before sending it. WL activists in locations closest to Detroit, notably Cincinnati, Chicago, and Buffalo, declined to initiate conversation with the manifesto authors. In the end, only because Third World women on the East Coast repeatedly urged WL organizers to confront the issue did DC organizers finally get in touch with their critics in Detroit. After a failed attempt at a meeting, the original response letter was sent, six weeks after the new friends initially read the "Fourth World Manifesto" and just a couple of weeks before the conferences. In the meantime, misinformation about the organizers and the IWCs circulated within feminist networks.

The challenges that the new friends faced are understandable. They wanted to create a democratic movement that allowed for autonomy, particularly at the local level. Given the multiple demands on female activists, their varying understandings of the war, and their diverse organizing skills and approaches, it was difficult to create an efficient and accountable system. Ironically, these women who worked so hard to create a democratic movement were charged with elitism and with siding against feminist interests.

The criticism that IWC organizers ignored lesbianism replicated the "Fourth Manifesto" charge, namely that the conference planners suffered from false consciousness. Detractors charged that the promoters of the Canadian conferences unquestioningly accepted heteronormativity and prioritized the Vietnam War instead of understanding their own sexual liberation. Lesbian activists, in contrast, sought to assert their understanding of anticolonialism by inserting their agenda at the IWCs. To make an effective intervention, they called upon their supporters to disregard the quota system and attend the conference en masse.

Those who opposed addressing lesbianism at the conference ranged widely in their motivations. Some were no doubt fearful of lesbianism and dismissed the issue as irrelevant because of homophobia. The old friends who embraced their identities as housewives and mothers were not particularly inclined to discuss lesbianism, even though some later identified themselves as lesbians. The contingent of Third World women also tended to distance themselves from this issue. Although some women of color conference attendees were lesbians, the dominant perspective in these circles emphasized lesbianism and gender nonnormativity as white women's issues.

The divide was clear to Maria Ramirez. A Chicana antiwar activist from the San Francisco Bay Area, Ramirez traveled to the Vancouver IWC with Nina Genera and several busloads of women. She also eventually visited the People's Republic of China with Betita Martinez. Ramirez recalled that she and the other Mexican American women activists tended to be more traditional in their appearance. They experienced culture shock in being housed with WL activists in a large auditorium in Vancouver. While she and her Chicana friends were trying to put on makeup to get themselves "dolled up" for the conference, they saw "white" women sporting unshaved legs, fatigues, and combat boots.[37] This dichotomy between "femme" and "butch" gender presentations did not necessarily distinguish heterosexuals and homosexuals. However, in Ramirez's mind, these differences in body adornment were mapped onto racial divides.

Other Third World women did not comment on racialized, gendered, or sexual differences. Instead, they argued that lesbianism should not be a central issue for a conference focused on ending the war. In fact, they viewed the assertion of this topic as an expression of white women's chauvinism. Judy Drummond, an antiwar activist who was involved with the San Francisco Bay Area Chicano movement and traced her ancestry to Native American communities in California, recalled, "Some of the radical lesbians just pissed me off. They pissed everybody off. . . . They had asked if the [Vietnamese] women had sex together in the fields. . . . And it was, like, how rude. I mean, you know, these women are fighting for their lives and you're asking what we thought was a trivial question."[38] Drummond subsequently acknowledged that the question was not trivial, but at the conference, she and other women of color sought to silence these questions from radical lesbians. Drummond recalled that she did so at the request of the Indochinese female representatives, some of whom "walked off the stage . . . when they [the Radicalesbians] asked that question." "You know, you don't ask those kinds of questions to these women. It is sort of inappropriate. You need to think. . . . You have your own agenda but . . . we're here for their agenda." While the Radicalesbians regarded themselves as anti-imperialists, the Third World women from the United States and Indochina regarded debates about lesbianism as a form of white feminist imperialism.[39]

Even some self-identified lesbian antiwar activists had concerns about discussing sexuality at the conference. Charlotte Bunch-Weeks was in the process of coming out when she helped to organize the Toronto IWC. She recalled experiencing enormous pressure, particularly from her lover, Rita Mae Brown, to place lesbianism on the agenda. In fact, the year after the conference, Brown published a provocative essay titled "Hanoi to Hoboken, a Round Trip Ticket."[40] She questioned why activists had such "persistent enthusiasm for far away places and distant struggles with imperialism. . . . Why travel to Hanoi when you can go to Hoboken [New Jersey] and see the same show?" She responded by arguing that "visiting Hanoi or Havanna . . . is one way to legitimize our movement through participation in those areas that the white, middle class, male-left movement has designated as legitimate. It shows that women are reaching out beyond what the male left defines as 'womens' [sic] issues.'" As an alternative, Brown challenged women activists to focus their attention on the United States: "Here in Amerika many women are also fighting for their lives, there are no bombers but the struggle is just as relentless and deadly—we are the poor, the Black, the Latin and the Lesbian. We aren't exotic and we aren't remotely glamorous."

Brown's call to prioritize domestic and sexual oppression over the experiences of the Vietnamese directly criticized the efforts of her lover. Charlotte Bunch, who dropped the hyphenated portion of her last name after divorcing her husband, had traveled to North Vietnam and experienced the personal appeal by the Buddhist nun in Vinh. She had dedicated her political efforts to connecting women across geographical and cultural boundaries. Years later, Bunch recalled how difficult this time was for her: "I did not feel that it was the right time and place to try to raise lesbian feminism but I felt enormous guilt because I was just a new lesbian. . . . So what happened to me which I now understand . . . is that I got sick. . . . I couldn't handle it. . . . I couldn't see a way to make it better . . . and I just . . . withdrew from the process. . . . I felt very guilty about not going because I also felt like I should try and make it better, but I couldn't see any way to make it better and so my whole body just collapsed."[41] The tensions that exploded at the IWC literally imploded in Bunch. Just as different factions at the conferences could not reconcile their different interpretations of anti-imperialism and their diverse political priorities, Bunch could not intellectually or emotionally process her own conflicting understandings of what constituted liberation.

In addition to the conflicts surrounding race and sexuality, nationality constituted a third flash point at the IWCs. Although the conferences were held in Vancouver and Toronto, Canadian organizers and attendees criticized their U.S. guests for their chauvinistic and imperialist behavior toward their hosts. Canadian female activists, irrespective of their racial backgrounds, tended to identify themselves as colonized subjects in relation to their neighbors to the south. Canadian women, particularly WL activists, claimed a status akin to women from Southeast Asia but not necessarily with Third World women from the United States.

Because the U.S. peace movement encouraged travel and relocation across the forty-ninth parallel, some of the Canadian organizers of the IWC were in fact former U.S. residents and veterans of the civil rights, New Left, and women's movements in the States. Despite the existence of these international alliances and transnational connections, the Canadian organizers, particularly those who were identified as new friends, believed they were unequal partners in organizing the IWC. Fewer criticisms were raised by the old friends from Canada, most likely because VOW had worked closely with WSP. In contrast, the Canadian WL activists, especially those in Vancouver, who did not have a history of ongoing political partnerships with their U.S. "sisters," expressed a sense of frustration and imposition.

Liz Breimberg was born in England and had participated in the Berkeley Free Speech Movement before migrating to Vancouver. She recalled that the West Coast IWC was held in

> April of 1971 and we only heard of it in December of 1970. And we only heard of it by accident by a woman from . . . the United States, I think from California, [who] was up visiting someone here and came to one of our women's caucus meetings. . . . [She] told us . . . that this was being organized by women in the United States and it was like we were just being used. . . . They never even bothered to let us know. . . . The conferences were to be for the Indochinese people to meet the . . . women from the United States who were involved in the women's liberation movement. . . . I mean, we were treated as if we didn't exist.[42]

The lack of communication resulted partly from the difficulties of organizing across regional and national boundaries. Conference planners had limited human and financial resources to coordinate the efforts of women from Southeast Asia, the United States, and Canada. Some of these political networks were being created as part of the conference organizing process. Even so, the execution of the conference did reveal power inequalities. Breimberg recalled that she and other WL activists in Vancouver became responsible for arranging the venue and housing for four hundred to five hundred delegates. They also assumed much of the financial cost associated with this process. In other words, they performed much of the so-called grunt work for the conference, even though they had limited input in the decision-making process.

Although Canadian women served as hosts for the IWC, their presence remained marginal. The delegate quota system, established to ensure broad geographical representation, gave decided preference to women from the United States. They received 80 percent of the approximately two hundred slots reserved for the new friends portion of the IWCs. That meant that only forty Canadian WL activists could attend each conference, and they also had to ensure geographic distribution among their delegates. As Breimberg emphasized, the IWCs were primarily intended for U.S., not Canadian, women. At the time, this disproportionate emphasis on U.S. women could not be widely discussed and criticized due to visa concerns. The Canadian government had previously denied the right of entry for the Winter Soldiers Investigation delegation based on the argument that these Vietnamese visitors intended to address a U.S., not Canadian, audience. So IWC organizers, saddled with logistical and financial burdens without representation, had to suffer their indignities quietly.

To add insult to injury, the female activists from south of the border did not always recognize that they had crossed into another country. Breimberg remembered, "One of the problems we had with the whole thing was the total chauvinism of the United States delegation. It was just absolutely astounding to the point where . . . when they spoke in the conference they would talk about this country as if this country was their country."[43] In contrast, Breimberg and her Canadian co-organizers became painfully aware of the forty-ninth parallel. They crossed over to the United States in February 1971 for a preconference planning meeting in Portland, Oregon. Because they brought activist literature with them, the border patrol ordered a strip search, which took place in front of a giant poster of President Nixon. This experience sparked their decision to issue detailed advice to American activists about how to cross the border.

Based on these preconference interactions, Canadian WL activists anticipated the need to educate their U.S. sisters and to curb their sense of entitlement. Toward that end, organizers authored a cartoon history of their nation that highlighted women's issues. This forty-page publication, *She Named It Canada: Because That's What It Was Called*, was not completed in time for the conference but was subsequently distributed within activist circles.[44]

As a result of the dynamics between white American and Canadian women, the latter identified themselves as colonized subjects. Both they and the Southeast Asian women suffered from imperialism. This analogy was particularly apt for activists who supported the French separatist movement based in Quebec. Initially, the IWCs were to take place in three cities: Toronto for East Coast participants, Vancouver for West Coast activists, and Montreal for those from the Midwest. Advocates for the last site noted the similarities between Quebec and Vietnam as colonies seeking self-determination and liberation; they also highlighted the significant population of Afro-Caribbeans in Montreal and emphasized a sense of racial comradery with the black liberation movement in the United States.[45] In the end, the Montreal conference did not take place for a number of reasons. The U.S. WL activists made their initial contacts with English-speaking women in Montreal. Marlene Dixon, a former Chicago-based activist who subsequently taught at McGill University in Montreal, was a primary conduit for these efforts. Scholar Jill Vickers has argued that Dixon was a polarizing figure among Anglophone feminists, because she transplanted fractious forms of U.S.-based politics. In contrast, Vickers argues that Canadian feminists were less divisive. Although differences existed, there was a "willingness to engage in debate" across political differences with less suspicion and greater "belief in dialogue."[46] In addition, Dixon failed to fully involve French-speaking activists in Montreal, which led to their sense of marginalization. They subsequently decided not to participate in the IWC and instead focused on the Quebec movement for sovereignty. In 1970 the escalation of their protest efforts resulted in increased government repression and the imposition of martial law. In a letter that was published by the Chicago Women's Liberation Union in late January 1971, women in the Front de Liberation Quebecois (FLQ) explained the political context: "Over 3000 [police] raids have been carried out, most of them in Montreal. Over 400 have been detained for questioning and about 100 are still in jail. People speaking sympathetically [toward the FLQ] are losing their lobs and/or being watched."[47] In this context, French-speaking organizers could not spare any additional resources or personnel to plan the conference. Also, the state of martial law raised concerns about security for the Vietnamese delegation.[48] Interestingly, the announcement to cancel the Montreal conference emphasized the similarities between the political persecution of the FLQ and the sufferings of the National Liberation Front in South Vietnam. Instead of a full conference, a smaller gathering of approximately one hundred people attended a series of discussions and meetings in Montreal.[49]

Even as white Canadian women, English and French speaking, portrayed themselves as colonized subjects, women of color in Canada distinguished themselves from their white counterparts. Gerry Ambers, a Native Canadian or First Nations activist, recalled that she and other members of her community received a request from IWC organizers to cook for the

Indochinese delegates.[50] Ambers was practiced in international political solidarity. She became active during the 1960s, forming alliances between indigenous nations in both Canada and the United States. They collaborated with one another to obtain fishing rights for Native Americans in Washington State, to bring attention to the sexualized violence directed against indigenous women, and to reclaim native land. During the Vancouver IWC, the Indochinese delegates expressed a deep appreciation for the meals that Ambers and other First Nations women prepared. They served foods "traditional" to their community, such as salmon and other seafood. In Ambers's mind, it was not just a coincidence that these items were familiar to and well liked by the Vietnamese. Their dietary similarities symbolized a deeper rapport between the First Nations and the Third World. In contrast, Ambers recalled that the white Canadian women offered unpalatable food, like raw carrot sticks. These items were both unfamiliar and difficult to digest, especially given the poor dental health of some of the Southeast Asian representatives who resided in rustic revolutionary base camps. Ambers also recalled that she and the white Canadian WL activists differed with one another as to who should be allowed to attend the conference. While Ambers and other indigenous women wanted to include First Nations men because of their mutual opposition to imperialism, the white women drew "a hard line at gender."[51] The differences between First Nations and white Canadian women suggest that the former did not readily accept the latter's claim to being colonized subjects.

Although Canadian women of varying cultural and racial backgrounds identified with Indochinese women, they had mixed feelings about the Third World women from the United States. Some Canadian new friends thought of themselves as occupying a status similar to Third World U.S. women, since both groups suffered from the chauvinism and colonial mentality of the American WL movement. However, they also resented how Third World women questioned Canadian WL activists' security measures and exacted demands. In an assessment of the Vancouver conference, one organizer expressed this sense of ambivalence: "The struggle of Third World women against racism, poverty and oppression could be directly related to the genocide in Vietnam. The attitudes they brought with them, their total disregard of our Canadian rights, and the imposition of their own realities on to the Conference were a great strain on the already taut fibre of our endurance and resources. . . . However, it was obvious that they *did* have a strong cohesive group of many racial origins."[52]

Figure 16. Vietnamese woman with gun evokes indigenous female iconography. *Georgia Straight*, Special Supplement for the Vancouver Indochinese Women's Conference, April 1971.

People of color in Canada also had complex relationships with women of color from the United States. In an article published in a Chinese Canadian newsletter, Peter Lee expressed his admiration for the Third World U.S. contingent, which included "Afro-Americans, Chicanos, Native and East Indians, Chinese and Japanese. There was noticeably more harmony among the members, a closer unity of purpose and thought in the third world group." He also recalled the eloquence of "our Chicano sister from Mexico. Her speech was full of the vigor, strength and will of all the third world."[53] U.S. Third World women also expressed a sense of solidarity across national lines. Maria Ramirez recalled how touched she was to discover that First Nations women helped to organize the conference. Afterward, she tried to track down documentary evidence, "pictures or any articles," so that their efforts could be included in the historical record.[54] In contrast, some Canadians did not find evidence of Third World solidarity across the Americas. One white organizer recalled, "In Canada efforts were made to involve people of the 'Third World,' but . . . no such united group was found to exist."[55] This assessment likely reflected her lack of contact with such groups. It is also possible that racialized groups had not yet created a sense of political commonality. IWC organizers tended to find that Canadians of color identified with their particular communities rather than across racial or national boundaries.

Given these cumulative difficulties, Canadian organizers questioned whether they should in fact continue these international efforts with Americans. Even VOW expressed the opinion that "Canadian women and sensitive ex-Americans became *very* conscious of 'American Imperialism,' not only the usual kind but 'of the Left.' Our visitors from below the border tended not to remember that Canada is still—a separate country, and our hospitality and patience were often tested. Some of our people questioned the wisdom of trying to collaborate with Americans on any project at this time. Americans are unhappy, upset and disturbed by so many pressures and problems which only they can solve."[56] Rather than focusing their energies on providing a forum for American women, Canadian women wanted to prioritize the development of their own antiwar movement.

The North American activists who traveled to Vancouver and Toronto aspired to create an international community of women. However, the conference provided a setting for emerging political ideologies and factions to ferment and explode among women of varying backgrounds. In an assessment of the IWCs, one attendee reflected on the overall absence of "sisterhood at the conference":

> The thing which disturbed me most at the Conference was the attitude of
> distrust and alienation among women. Prior to the Conference, labels like
> "feminists," "radical lesbians," and "anti-imperialist women" (whatever
> that means—it seems to imply some women in the Women's Movement
> are *for* imperialism?) were thrown around a lot, creating divisions before
> women even began to arrive. Women became catagories [*sic*], not people.
> What about a woman who might be a feminist or lesbian who was also
> "anti-imperialist?" The conference seemed designed to preclude such
> possibilities, and women began to polarize.[57]

Ironically, the desire of North Americans to espouse a sense of sisterhood with Indochinese women was greater than their ability to generate
solidarity among themselves.

The conference occurred at a historical moment in which different
strands of political ideologies and movements were just emerging. The
birthing of these new formations involved painful acts of separation.
Singer, lesbian feminist, and antiwar activist Holly Near did not attend the
IWC. She participated in similarly contentious meetings, though, and offers an insightful analysis of the political process:

> It's a long journey to really learn how to do coalition politics. . . . Because
> we all began somewhere. . . . I was homophobic at the beginning and I
> needed to be brought along. I was not a feminist at the beginning; I
> needed to be brought along. And none of us came into this with all of our
> pieces of the puzzle put together. . . . I have been at conferences . . .
> when I first was discovering lesbianism and there was a huge amount of
> rage coming forward with what had happened to gay people and the op-
> pression that had taken place. And when I first became a feminist and I
> started looking at statistics of abuse and my anger came in the room first
> and it was, it was dominating my thought process and so it made me in-
> sensitive to the fact that someone else might be walking in who lost a
> child to napalm and they would see my particular issue about talking
> about sexuality [as] really out of place in relationship to their loss. So, ob-
> viously losses, and grief, and oppression there—it shouldn't be a competi-
> tion but . . . I've learned over time that there is a time and a place to let
> someone else's story, or pain, or loss, or horror take precedence over what
> might be on my plate at the moment. . . . I learned this from Dr. Bernice
> Johnson-Regan [civil rights activist and singer]—you don't have to leave

yourself at the door. You can bring your whole self in but you don't necessarily have yourself be the center of attention.[58]

At the IWCs, the North American female activists had not yet learned
how to bring their whole selves into the political tent while not demanding the center ring of attention.

Chapter 9

Woman Warriors

As much as the North American women critiqued one another, they expressed adulation for their Indochinese sisters. The delegation to the Indochinese Women's Conferences (IWCs) from Southeast Asia consisted of three teams of two women and one male translator each for North Vietnam, South Vietnam, and Laos.[1] Vo Thi The, a fifty-year-old professor of literature at the University of Hanoi and an officer in the Vietnam Women's Union (VWU), had visited Canada in 1969. Given her seniority and experience, she served as an overall leader of the 1971 delegation. Nguyen Thi Xiem, a forty-year-old gynecologist and obstetrician, was the vice president of the VWU. Forty-six-year-old Dinh Thi Huong, a housewife, and thirty-one-year-old Phan Minh Hien, a teacher, represented the Women's Union for the Liberation of South Vietnam. Two additional teachers, forty-seven-year-old Khampheng Boupha and twenty-nine-year-old Khemphet Pholsena, represented the Laotian Patriotic Women's Association.[2] A fourth delegation from Cambodia planned to attend as well but was unable to do so. Due to war conditions, it was even difficult for the South Vietnamese women to travel to Canada. One of the delegates, Hien, walked with a forty-four-pound pack from her base in the South to the North so that she could take a flight out of the country. She was a slight woman, weighing just eighty-six pounds. Her journey took three months.

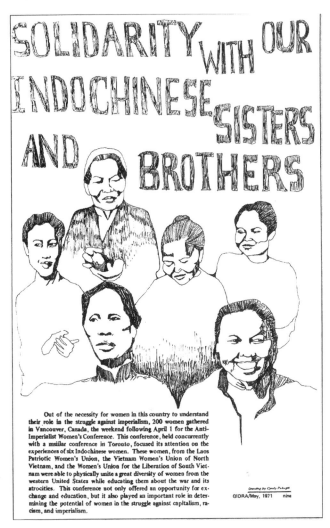

Out of the necessity for women in this country to understand their role in the struggle against imperialism, 200 women gathered in Vancouver, Canada, the weekend following April 1 for the Anti-Imperialist Women's Conference. This conference, held concurrently with a similar conference in Toronto, focused its attention on the experiences of six Indochinese women. These women, from the Laos Patriotic Women's Union, the Vietnam Women's Union of North Vietnam, and the Women's Union for the Liberation of South Vietnam were able to physically unite a great diversity of women from the western United States while educating them about the war and its atrocities. This conference not only offered an opportunity for exchange and education, but it also played an important role in determining the potential of women in the struggle against capitalism, racism, and imperialism.

Drawing by Cindy Fukagai
GIDRA/May, 1971   nine

Figure 17. The delegates from Indochina. Left to right, front: Dinh Thi Hong and Phan Minh Hien; middle: Nguyen Thi Xiem, Khampheng Boupha, and Khemphet Pholsena; back: Vo Thi The. Originally published in *Gidra* (May 1971) and republished in *Asian Women's Journal*. Drawing by Cynthis Fukagai. Source: Cynthia Sugawara and UCLA Asian American Studies Center Press, Los Angeles.

The women from South Vietnam, North Vietnam, and Laos presented themselves to North American women in large plenaries, smaller workshops, and discussions over meals. Since the conversations occurred via translation, some North American women questioned why the Indochinese chose to send male interpreters. Other women thought little of this gendered division of labor, because the Indochinese women made such a powerful impression. They did so through presentations and responses to questions but also through their sense of humor and expressions of affection. As one Canadian conference organizer recalled:

> Most remarkable about these women were their gentle dignity, self command, and deep concern for others, both individually and as nations. They laughed often with the women they met, hugged them when they felt common feelings, wept a little as they heard of each others' sufferings, and comforted us when (as too often happened) we ran late with the program or failed with the conference arrangements. Although their competence and dedication awed us, we felt that we, too, might cope better in future, as women and as citizens, for having met them.[3]

The Indochinese delegates shared both the inhumane suffering that the war caused as well as their sustained efforts to fight for liberation. The newspaper coverage of the IWCs and the personal reflections of the attendees offer insight into how North American women responded to their message. Reflecting past approaches of global sisterhood, some women from the United States and Canada expressed a desire to "rescue" their Indochinese sisters from the atrocities of the war. Others articulated a radical orientalist perspective, portraying the women from Southeast Asia not as victims but as exemplars of revolutionary womanhood. These Asian female warriors offered an image of hope and humanity that contrasted with the oppressive gender roles and fractious politics in North American societies. Consequently, the Indochinese women helped female activists in the West to redefine their political aspirations.

This productive tension between a binary sense of opposition between the Orient and the Occident as well as an identification with radical Asia was particularly acute for Asian American women. Due to their marginalization within American political movements, women of Asian ancestry in the United States aspired to connect with their revolutionary Asian sisters in Southeast Asia. Their sense of sisterhood recognized the disparate subject positions of Asian and Asian American women and yet was premised upon a sense of commonality rooted in racial, gender, and political likeness. Inspired by these encounters, both groups of women formulated innovative critiques of war and colonization that foregrounded the experiences and bodies of Asian women in understanding U.S. militarization and empire.

The delegates from Southeast Asia who tended to receive the most attention in activist publications were the women who either suffered traumatic abuse or who could testify to wartime atrocities. Their testimonials conveyed how war and political persecution had gendered implications for women, their bodies, and their ability to perform responsibilities of motherhood. These dramatic accounts of atrocities invited women from the West to work in political solidarity with women from the East to end the war.

Dinh Thi Huong made a powerful impact on conference delegates. A housewife from South Vietnam, Huong had not been politically engaged in the movement for liberation before she was imprisoned. Suspected of supporting the opposition to the South Vietnamese government, she was detained and tortured in a series of the most notorious prisons in the South. The detailed account of her experiences appeared in several movement publications produced by the New Left, Third World, and women's organizations. In her autobiographical narrative, she said, "Pins [were planted] in my fingertips, . . . electrodes . . . [were] attached to my ears and to my fingers, nipples and genitals . . . and [I was] tortured with electricity until I was unconscious." In addition, her interrogators, she said, "forced water, lye and salt into my stomach and trampled on my stomach until I vomited blood and was unconscious."[4] These dramatic episodes illustrated the visceral and sexualized nature of torture.

Huong's accounts also conveyed the dehumanizing day-to-day indignities of trying to survive in crowded cells with inadequate facilities and either little food or "rotten rice." One cell that measured approximately nine feet by four and a half feet held "15 to 32 people at a time—women and men in the same cell. In this cell the prisoners eat, go to the bathroom. Prisoners could only stand. I was not allowed to bathe from November 1955 to August 1956."[5] After nearly six years, Huong was finally found not guilty and released. During that time, her weight dropped from 108 to 78 pounds.[6] In addition, other family members of hers had died or were imprisoned. Following her release, Huong decided to "join my people to fight against the Americans and puppets."[7] As she surmised, "the more barbarous the army is, the stronger the struggle of the people."[8]

Huong's experiences provided a powerful example of the political persecution and lack of civil rights in South Vietnam, a condition that was supported by the United States. This message had been conveyed to women
in the West prior to the conference, particularly through Ngo Ba Thanh
and the Right to Live Campaign. Thanh, a lawyer who was trained at Columbia University and in Paris, led a women's peace movement in South
Vietnam. Like Thich Nhat Hanh, she and her organization represented an
independent force in opposition to the war. Because petitioning for peace
constituted treason in South Vietnam, Thanh was repeatedly imprisoned
beginning in 1965.[9] In the summer of 1970, Thanh cofounded an urban
women's movement in Saigon to protest for peace and against political
persecution. Calling themselves the Movement of Women's Actions for
the Right to Live, this organization reached out to female organizations
internationally.

Both new and old friends featured stories about Thanh and the Right to
Live movement. Women's liberation activists in Boston introduced the
organization in a flier calling for solidarity with women in Vietnam. The
poster explained, "When particularly brutal attacks on women occur in the
countryside, these women immediately go out marching in the streets of
Saigon. We in the US live under very different conditions and our struggle
takes different forms. But our Vietnamese sisters follow our movement with
great interest. Let's find new ways of supporting them and demonstrating
our solidarity with them!"[10] To express their connection with this movement, women's liberationists in the United States used variations on the
slogan "Right to Live" to promote feminist understanding of women
and war. Echoing Betita Martinez's observations about Vietnamese society, a memo from the Washington, DC, Women's Liberation Anti-
Imperialist Collective argued, "We use the word 'life force' to symbolize
a life-oriented movement, a politics based on people's determination to
live free lives and to build a new society. We see this life force, rather
than a death-oriented politics, as the key to bringing the monstor [*sic*] to
its knees."[11]

Old friends also made connections to the Right to Live movement, particularly through their mutual investment in maternalist politics. WILPF, for
example, reprinted an open letter from Vietnamese women in this movement
written to Vice President Spiro Agnew.[12] The group attempted unsuccessfully to meet with him during his 1970 visit to South Vietnam. Addressing
him as a "father [who has] deep love towards [his] children," the letter was
signed by "representatives of Mothers whose children are being detained in

the various prisons throughout South Vietnam, in the Tiger Cages, in the Disciplinary Cells . . . without trial or tried by unconstitutional Courts or have served their jail-terms or have been arrested during military operations (US, V.N. Allied)."[13] Twenty mothers signed the letter and gave the names of their missing children. The maternalist appeal of the Right to Live movement resonated strongly with the old friends.

Presentations at the IWC also addressed the destructive impact of war on families. Dr. Nguyen Thi Xiem, a physician with the Hanoi Institute for the Preservation of Mothers and Newly Born Children, provided analysis of the widespread and long-term effects of bombing on Vietnamese people and land. North American attendees recalled:

> Dr. Xiem presented an account, including pictures, of the Vietnamese wounded by pellet bombs, napalm and defoliants. Tremendous pain and mutilation, as well as death, have resulted from the use of bombs that release thousands of tiny pellets to become embedded in vital organs—napalm that burns and suffocates—defoliant sand that cause[s] blindness, genetic damage and other destruction to human beings, in addition to . . . devastating the countryside. 44% of the forests and cultivated land of South Vietnam have been affected by toxic chemicals.[14]

Xiem's status as a physician, devoted to the care of women and children, gave her report an air of professional authority. She also underscored that expert forms of testimony were not always necessary. When asked about the psychological effect of bombing on young children, the doctor replied, "This bombing is not suitable for their development. It is not necessary to make an analysis. Our experiences as mothers should indicate this. Thank you for your attention to our baby children."[15] These accounts of atrocities reminded North American women of the horrific nature of the U.S. war in Southeast Asia. While many antiwar activists no doubt had absorbed similar information through movement publications, the impact of hearing these stories in person was much more profound. It was difficult not to be moved by personal testimonies, recounted by women who had experienced or witnessed these atrocities and who traveled from the other side of the world in order to communicate with their "sisters" in North America.

North American reception to these accounts of war was shaped by the timing of the IWC, which began just after Lieutenant William Calley had been convicted for his role in the My Lai Massacre. On 16 March 1968,

Calley had commanded one of three platoons that entered a village suspected of supporting the Vietcong. Army intelligence actually had mis-
identified the hamlet. In the aftermath of the Tet Offensive on urban
military and political outposts throughout South Vietnam, U.S. soldiers
became determined to hunt down and punish communist sympathizers.
Practiced in violent search-and-destroy missions, American troops executed over five hundred residents in My Lai in one day. They murdered
women, the elderly, and young children, none of whom shot at the Americans. GIs also sexually abused and raped women before torturing and executing them. A soldier recalled, "I cut their throats, cut off their hands,
cut out their tongue, their hair, scalped them. I did it. A lot of people were
doing it, and I just followed. I lost all sense of direction."[16]

Among the soldiers, Calley was "responsible for killing the most Vietnamese," allegedly slaughtering "over 100 Vietnamese civilians."[17] In addition to ordering his men to "waste" individuals who were clearly non-
combatants, Calley also herded prisoners to a water ditch and began firing
indiscriminately into the group. Several GIs saw him run "after a bloody
but unhurt two-year-old boy who had managed to crawl out of the ditch,
throw him back in, and shoot him."[18] In addition, witnesses recalled that
Calley killed a Buddhist monk. When questioned repeatedly about the
Vietcong, the monk denied their presence in the village and "kept putting
his hands together in a praying position and bowing his head."[19] Calley
initially hit him with the butt of the rifle and then "took his rifle at point
blank and pulled the trigger."[20]

The military superiors of the three platoons made no attempt to stop
the massacre. However, army helicopter pilot Hugh Thompson observed
the atrocities from above. Outraged by what he saw, he landed the plane,
confronted Calley, and ordered his backup to train "his machine gun on
the American troops surrounding the bunker."[21] Thompson then placed
his body between U.S. troops and Vietnamese civilians to stop the killing and evacuated some of the survivors. Within the ditch, "the only
person they found alive was a small child, who had been shielded from the
hail of bullets by the body of a young woman, who had probably been its
mother."[22]

Afterward, the military attempted to cover up the massacre and described it initially as a victory over the Vietcong. News photographer Ronald Haeberle, who witnessed and documented the violence, challenged this
heroic interpretation. In addition, Ronald Ridenhour, who served in a

reconnaissance unit, sent letters to Washington politicians based on reports that he received about the massacre. Still, it took over a year before an investigation was initiated and nearly three years before Calley was finally found guilty of mass premeditated murder and assault with intent to commit murder.

Scholar Michal Belknap argues that Calley's defense team lacked a coherent legal strategy. They considered the insanity plea as well as the argument that Calley was merely "following orders" and that others were engaged in similar behavior. Calley and his supporters eventually condemned the trial and its outcome for scapegoating him. A vast majority of the U.S. population agreed, as did President Nixon and the army leadership. Calley's sentence, which could have been as severe as the death penalty, was set at lifelong imprisonment and hard labor but was reduced by the commander in chief. In the end, Calley only served "a few months in a military prison and a few years confined to his apartment."[23] All of the other defendants, including his commanding officer, were found innocent.

The mainstream press repeatedly asked the Indochinese delegation about the My Lai Massacre and Calley's sentence. In fact, the opening plenary at the Vancouver IWC took place on 1 April 1971, two days after the trial verdict was announced. Conference attendees, after hearing the emotional testimonies of the Indochinese women, learned that Nixon had released Calley from the stockade to house arrest.[24] Asked repeatedly about Calley, the Indochinese delegation used the occasion to highlight the level of violence and destruction the U.S. military committed every day in Southeast Asia. Without acquitting Calley for his role, Phan Minh Hien, the delegate who spent three months walking in order to meet North American women, stated, "While Calley is the person who gave the order, he was merely carrying out the orders of the U.S. administration." For Hien, Calley's crimes were America's crimes, since "the U.S. administration sent U.S. troops into Vietnam, 'that is why the U.S. youths commit crimes against our country . . . why the Vietnamese people have to fight . . . and why U.S. youths get killed.'"[25] To stop this cycle of violence, the Indochinese women stressed, the United States must immediately and unilaterally withdraw from the war and end its support of the South Vietnamese government.

The Laotian representatives at the IWCs, less practiced in these international settings, did not receive as much press attention as the other delegates. However, the information that they conveyed was new for most of the North American conference attendees. The inclusion of the Laotians and the intended presence of Cambodians reflected a pan-Indochinese anticolonial strategy that was increasingly necessary as the U.S. war in Vietnam escalated in all parts of Southeast Asia. The United States had long considered these nations in relation to one another as part of an overall American Cold War strategy. Just as the United States supported Diem, it initiated political and military campaigns in Cambodia and Laos as well. As early as 1960, "the U.S. Central Intelligence Agency (CIA) had recruited a secret army of 30,000 Hmong tribesmen in mountainous northern Laos to fight against a Lao communist insurgency."[26] These troops would eventually go directly into battle near the Lao border, alongside the military of South Vietnam. In fact, one major campaign against the North Vietnamese occurred in February 1971, just two months before the IWC. Nixon's policy of "Vietnamization" increased the number not only of South Vietnamese troops fighting the war but also of Laotian soldiers. While the president called for a de-escalation of U.S. troops, he and his advisers increased air support for the South Vietnamese military, expanded the scope of the bombings, and mandated that Asian soldiers take leadership in the ground war. Seeking to destroy North Vietnamese base camps and supply lines into South Vietnam, Nixon ordered secret bombings of the neighboring countries. Beginning in 1969, approximately 100,000 tons of bombs were dropped on Cambodia over a period of fifteen months, killing an estimated 150,000 civilians. In Laos, almost five million tons rained down over four years.[27] The U.S. directives in Cambodia came to light when Nixon ordered an invasion of the country in the spring of 1970. The American role in Laos did not receive the same level of public scrutiny.

The Laotian delegation of the IWC sought to expose these "secret wars." Khampheng Boupha, the more senior member of the Laotian team, shared the difficulties of living and teaching in time of war: "Since the U.S. bombardment began, about 2,000 schools have been destroyed. . . . The classes must be divided. We teach in small groups, sometimes in the jungle, under the shade of the trees. . . . The children have learned to leave their studies, to be ready to aid their family in rebuilding their home or help the peasants with their crops."[28] Despite these challenges, she expressed pride in her responsibilities: "That is my small contribution to my people—educating the children." Khemphet Pholsena, the youngest of the six delegates, was also a teacher as well as a mother of a ten-month-old baby. She shared that her father, who served as a minister of foreign affairs in 1963, followed a policy of neutrality, similar to what Cambodia attempted. She believed that

CIA agents killed her father because of his political beliefs and also severely wounded her mother in April 1963. Following these attacks, her injured mother and their remaining family joined the socialist-controlled Liberated Zone in Laos.

These personal accounts of war-related atrocities and political persecutions highlighted the gendered impact of American policies throughout Southeast Asia. Chandra Mohanty has critiqued the construction of a monolithic, victimized "Third World woman" in Western feminist discourse.[29] Strikingly, the Indochinese women who came to North America used individual experiences to convey an analysis of the similarities of U.S. policies throughout North Vietnam, South Vietnam, and Laos. They provided personal examples so that they might illuminate patterns of gendered violence. In other words, the Indochinese representatives were invested in constructing a categorical understanding of Southeast Asian women. They offered models of resistance, however, and not just evidence of victimization. In addition, the Indochinese women emphasized that the war harmed those in the West, including those in the American military who enacted atrocities.

These cumulative testimonials of violence made a profound impact upon North American female audiences. Their reactions reflected two main tendencies. Some maternalist peace activities expressed a sense of moral obligation that resembled a politics of rescue. As women from the West, they wanted to save the women from the East. Other activists, including maternalists, women's liberationists, and Third World women, placed the Indochinese women on an idealized political pedestal for their ability to endure and struggle. Asian American women, in particular, became inspired by the experiences and political leadership of Asian women to develop a transnational and intersectional analysis of American militarism.

Following the conference, the newsletter of WSP, *Memo*, published a series of letters from its readers. One statement, authored by Voice of Women president Muriel Duckworth, appeared under the headline "They Must Be Saved."[30] The phrase positioned North American women as the potential saviors of Asian women. Reinforcing this message was an image widely circulated among peace activists that appeared on the cover of *Memo* in December 1966. Featuring a Vietnamese mother holding a young child in her arms, the image portrayed the mother as utterly hopeless and forlorn. As she gazes down and away, three white angels descend toward her to offer solace, evoking the role to be played by women of the West. Published during the Christmas season, the Vietnamese Madonna image underscored a maternalist message, calling for the salvation of a fellow mother and, perhaps more important, her child, whose gaze connects directly with the viewer (see figure 4).

The mother and child photograph published by *Memo* replicated the image that circulated as a Fellowship of Reconciliation antiwar Christmas card in 1966, featuring a poem by Thich Nhat Hanh. In fact, the same image had been prominently displayed onstage at a public antiwar meeting held during that summer which featured Hanh and Bob Browne. Not coincidentally, the old friends, the maternal peace activists, tended to be political allies of Browne in his early efforts to foster awareness of U.S. policies in Southeast Asia. Chapters of WSP and WILPF frequently invited him to give talks about Vietnam. Given their investment in maternalist politics, they expressed particular interest in Bob's marriage to Huoi and his claim that familial responsibilities gave him added authority to speak about U.S. foreign policies. The sense of "paternalistic" materialism conveyed by the Vietnamese Madonna image and by Duckworth's letter resonated with the political and cultural orientation of older peace activists.

In contrast, the Indochinese women, although extremely modest in their claims and presentation styles, nevertheless highlighted their own political agency in resisting the war. They also emphasized that the U.S. war victimized Americans and damaged U.S. society as well. From their perspective, it was not a matter of the West rescuing the East. Rather, the Asian women were seeking to encourage those in the West to recognize that they had a role to play in stopping such a destructive war. Third World women, women's liberation activists, and maternalist peace advocates all noticed the contrast between their own engagement in the politics of "blame," their divisiveness and factionalism, compared to the Indochinese, who, they said,

> never let us feel guilty of the crimes they described. Furthermore, they expressed sincere compassion for the suffering the war has brought to Americans. These women, whose families were scattered by our armies, whose villages were leveled, whose loved ones were murdered, these women recognized that "young Americans are scapegoats" forced to fight the war. Over and over the Indochinese women reiterated their confidence that if the American people only knew what was going on in Indochina, Americans would demand an end to atrocities and the war.[31]

The Indochinese ability to forgive and to distinguish between the American people and their government led many conference attendees to regard them as model revolutionary figures. North American women tended to "place them on a pedestal because of their revolutionary courage, spirit and warmth."[32] For Third World women in particular, the opportunity to interact with and learn from nonwhite female leaders was especially empowering. Chicana activists Maria Ramirez and Nina Genera recalled that it marked their first opportunity to witness and interact with Third World women in the vanguard of an ongoing revolution.[33]

Asian American women expressed a special affinity for the women from Southeast Asia. In fact, the conference played a significant role in the political development of an entire generation of Asian American female activists. According to a Japanese American delegate, 120 Asian Americans and Asian Canadians attended the Vancouver IWC.[34] If this number is accurate, Asian North Americans constituted a significant and perhaps even majority constituency of the approximately 200 to 250 Third World women at the West Coast conference. Because Asian Americans resided predominantly in the U.S. West, they likely attended in smaller numbers in Toronto, which was intended for residents of the East Coast and the Midwest. Those who could not travel to Canada could read extensive coverage of the IWC in *Asian Women's Journal*, a pioneering and widely circulated publication devoted to Asian American women's issues. Originally issued in 1971, the same year as the conference, the journal was eventually reprinted three times. It included biographies of the Southeast Asian women who participated in the IWCs as well as personal testimonies, poetry, and artwork by attendees. Significantly, the publication also featured an interview with Pat Sumi, described as a movement "superstar."[35]

The IWCs attracted the interest of Asian American women because female revolutionaries from Southeast Asia crystallized three main tenets of Asian American women's emerging political identity—their racial, international, and gender consciousness. Donna Kotake, a Japanese American who attended the Vancouver conference, recalled the political inspiration that the Indochinese women offered. Raised in a farming community in San Francisco's South Bay and attending San Jose State University in 1971, she was undergoing a political awakening. Growing up in the United States, Kotake explained,

> your whole identity was not Asian. Your identity was just, like, you wanted to be a white person. . . . So, to us at that point, . . . identifying ourselves as Asian Americans, wanting to learn more about our own histories, and,

you know, being proud of the histories . . . and I think really hooking up with other nonwhites was a really big deal. . . . So, you know, there's the identity going on as being Asian and there's a Third World coming, coalitions coming together, and there's this international thing with Vietnam, and at the same time people talking about China and seeing what a shining example of, you know, what it could be like to be free, people who care about . . . people and a country that provides . . . for everyone.[36]

Kotake and other activists of her generation were discovering their racial identity as Asian Americans.[37] Instead of desiring whiteness, she recognized herself as a member of a resistant panethnic group that had a distinct history and culture connected to Third World struggles in the United States and around the world.

With her political consciousness raised through the Asian American movement press and conversations with individuals like Pat Sumi, Kotake experienced a profound connection with the Indochinese women in Vancouver. They shared her racial and gender status and her anti–imperialist politics. When asked how the IWC influenced her, Kotake responded, "Just feeling the strength of the women and realizing how much women can do and it really made me feel incredibly proud about being a woman."[38] Another Asian American woman who attended the conference emphasized that the presence of Asian female bodies enhanced the political message of the Indochinese delegates: "Their physical presence had tremendous impact on the hundreds of Third World and white women. Here were six Asian women—physically small, sincere, friendly often appearing extremely tired. Yet, whenever one spoke, it was with such clarity and with a background of personal involvement that the meaning of a people's revolution became a reality."[39]

At the time of the conference, Asian American women were developing a gendered and racialized analysis of the war that emphasized the transnational connections between Asians in Vietnam and in the United States. Activist Evelyn Yoshimura articulated this perspective in an essay titled "GI's and Racism," which first appeared in the Asian American movement newspaper *Gidra* and then was reprinted in the *Asian Women's Journal*. Yoshimura argued that the U.S. military relied upon and reproduced racial hatred for Asians to motivate American soldiers to fight in Asia. By promoting the "view of Asian people as sub-human beings . . . the U.S. military . . . can instill the values and mentality that is necessary to become effective killers."[40] U.S. soldiers carried and reproduced these racial attitudes, which were cultivated during basic training on the U.S. mainland and then on military tours in Southeast Asia, back and forth across the Pacific.

The figure of Asian women played a central role in the racial education of U.S. military personnel. As Yoshimura put it, U.S. soldiers learned to regard "Asian women as a symbolic sexual object."[41] Through the systematic creation of red light districts in Asian countries where U.S. troops were stationed, the U.S. military institutionalized the practice of American GIs frequenting Asian prostitutes.[42] Not limited to individual excursions, these practices became integral to military culture and discourse through the ritualized retellings of these experiences. An Asian American Marine recalled of his boot camp experience:

> We had these classes we had to go to taught by the drill instructors, and every instructor would tell a joke before he began class. It would always be a dirty joke usually having to do with prostitutes they had seen in Japan or in other parts of Asia while they were stationed overseas. The attitude of the Asian women being a doll a useful toy or something to play with usually came out in these jokes and how they were not quite as human as white women . . . how Asian women's vaginas weren't like a white woman's, but rather they were slanted, like their eyes.[43]

Such racialized and sexualized depictions of Asian women, used to foster male bonding among U.S. soldiers, guided American military policies and practices in Southeast Asia—in the brothels and in the general prosecution of war.[44]

In addition, Vietnam veterans brought these beliefs and practices back to the United States. Evelyn Yoshimura reminded readers of her article, "GI's and Racism," "We, as Asian American women, cannot separate ourselves from our Asian counterparts. Racism against them is too often racism against us. . . . The mentality that keeps Suzy [*sic*] Wong, Madame Butterfly and gookism alive turns human beings into racist murdering soldiers and also keeps Asian American from being able to live and feel like human beings."[45] This analysis of how racialized sexualization travels across borders emphasizes the mutually destructive impact of the war on Asians and Asian Americans. Suzie Wong and Madame Butterfly are both fictive representations of Asian women who engage in sexual and romantic relationships with Western men. Suzie Wong, created by novelist Richard Mason and immortalized on screen by actress Nancy Kwan, is a prostitute with a heart of gold who caters to British and American sailors in Hong

Kong during the Cold War. Madame Butterfly, the title of Giacomo Puccini's 1904 opera, is a Japanese woman named Cio-Cio-San who marries an American naval officer and has a child with him. When he abandons her for a white American woman, San not only gives up her child to the father and surrogate mother but also commits suicide. Yoshimura connects both of these representations of Asian women, which emphasize their sexual availability and vulnerability to Western military men, to gookism. The term "gook," which initially referred to a low-class prostitute, has historically been utilized by the American military as a racial epithet to refer to Asian enemies. It was used during the U.S.-Philippine War, fought by Americans to prevent Philippine independence; the term surfaced again during the Korean War, in which the United States attempted to prevent the reunification of Korea under socialist leadership; finally during the U.S. war in Vietnam, "gook" became widely used to refer to Vietnamese enemies, both real and imagined.[46] By linking Suzie Wong, Madame Butterfly, and gookism, Yoshimura emphasizes the connections between sexual and racial dehumanization of Asian people by the U.S. military. She also stresses that these perceptions have implications for Asian people globally, both for those in Asia and for people of Asian ancestry in the United States. As the appellation "Third World women" suggests, racialized women in the United States recognized how colonization and gender oppression operated in tandem both abroad and at home.

The IWC provided a counterexample of how ideas and practices could critique and transcend national boundaries. The political leadership of Indochinese women inspired an array of American sisters to combat American militarism and imperialism. Women of Asian ancestry in the United States were particularly attracted to Southeast Asian women as political role models. The alleged model minority status of Asian American women was compounded by projections of hypersexuality and submissiveness, rendering them invisible among movement circles and in fact the antithesis of political activists.[47] In contrast, Indochinese women were hypervisible revolutionary leaders.

The idealization of Southeast Asian women, which was expressed broadly among the North American attendees and not just among Asian Americans, reflects a radical orientalist sensibility. The revolutionary social movements of the late 1960s and early 1970s tended to endow the most oppressed with the greatest political capital. The Indochinese women, as targets of Western militarism, imperialism, racism, and sexism, represented the ultimate underdogs. Yet they fought against nearly impossible odds with a sense of strength, clarity, and unity. As warm, dedicated, revolutionary heroines, the Southeast Asian representatives reminded North American women what was possible to achieve both individually and collectively. After all, women of color, lesbians, and Canadians all utilized the colonial analogy to conceptualize and resist oppression. Following in an orientalist tradition, the imagined East helped to redefine the imagined West.

In response to the tendencies to perceive Indochinese women as either victims or heroines, the women from Southeast Asia encouraged their audience to view everyone as equally capable of political struggle and achievement. The North American women were eager to learn from the Indochinese representatives and asked questions not only about the war in Vietnam but also how women in the West might engage more effectively in activism. The Indochinese women responded by emphasizing the importance of forging political unity.

In contrast to the identity-based politics that created such negative dynamics at the conference, the Southeast Asian women stressed the need for self-sacrifice and developing alliances. Lacking the resources to fight a conventional war, the Vietnamese who resisted the Americans and the South Vietnamese government turned to guerrilla warfare, a tactic that necessitated cultivating political support among the "people." As one representative explained, "Cadres must make the masses love them," a representative explained at the IWC. "This is a question of principle. If the masses love the cadres, they will listen to what they say and give them protection." That love, she continued, flowed from shared sacrifice. "That is why you must be exemplary. You must be exemplary in sacrifices. You must be the first to give your life, and the last to get rewards."[48]

For the Indochinese delegates, their strategy of building a political base was applicable to struggles beyond armed conflict. In response to a question as to whether the antiwar movement should pursue violent forms of protest, the women from Southeast Asia explained, "Revolutionary force is in two parts: (1) political force and (2) armed force. When we say political force we refer to the consciousness of people. . . . You need this political force. . . . The force must be large and strong, of people determined and courageous, who can take repression. When one is killed or jailed, another takes the place."[49] Instead of recommending armed resistance for the U.S. peace movement, the Indochinese women explained that they had no choice but to fight militarily. "We need military force to drive out the aggressors and take the power. In different stages of struggle, sometimes political force is to the forefront, sometimes military force. But always military force must be combined with political force." The military ought to be inseparable from the people, they argued, since "isolation in the fight is very dangerous."[50]

The Indochinese emphasis on developing broad-based political awareness and support contrasted with the approaches of American war supporters as well as the extreme elements of the antiwar opposition. Some apologists for the Vietnam War blame the loss of the conflict on U.S. political leaders, the antiwar movement, and/or the liberal media for their meddling in military affairs. In their eyes, the military should have had a freer reign in executing the war. In contrast, the Indochinese women prioritized the importance of political understanding in the waging of armed conflict. For them, there should not be a strict separation between military strategy, diplomacy, and public opinion mobilization. Rather, the National Liberation Front and the North Vietnamese strategized to win the "total war," which took place not only through armed conflict but also in the hearts and minds of local peasants as well as in world public opinion.

The importance of cultivating broad political support also challenged the actions of some antiwar activists who engaged in violence or utilized strategies that alienated the American public. As the Laotian delegates explained, "the policy of the United Front . . . is to win more supporters and isolate the administration. It is a tactical policy, a policy of increasing our friends and decreasing the enemy."[51] The Vietnamese delegates also shared that they had

> followed anti-war activities in Canada and the U.S.A. We have taken note of the demonstrations, petitions, and many other actions. They all help in our struggle against U.S. aggression. The most important thing is to mobilize larger forces to undertake these actions. If we are larger and more united, we can achieve greater success. We need unity and solidarity between the many groups. . . . As Ho Chi Minh said, "Unity, unity, larger unity; success, success, bigger success." The greater the difficulties, the broader must be the force in order to defeat the enemy. The more we consolidate, the more we weaken and divide the enemy.[52]

The IWC provided a venue to articulate and pursue a common, transpacific struggle against U.S. imperialism.

In response to the frustration expressed by antiwar activists that their organizing efforts achieved little result, the Indochinese encouraged patience and persistence. The Vietnamese and Laotian delegates, regardless of their ages, proposed a broader historical consciousness that recognized and built upon previous generations' struggles. The Indochinese encouraged their American counterparts to do the same, addressing a tendency among some young American activists to search constantly for new political ideologies, strategies, and identities. They explained, "We must also be prepared for all the struggles to take a long time. Actions must go on, but the results may not be seen for a long time. . . . We say to you: Be patient. Be flexible. Be vigilant. And wage a *persistent* struggle."[53]

Ironically, these words of advice led North American women to regard the Indochinese women with awe and to view themselves even more critically for their failure to create unity and commonality of purpose. As an Asian American delegate pondered in a poem about the conference:

-How can your people maintain such discipline, understanding and humanity?
-One million soldiers have been killed or wounded
three million civilians have been killed or wounded
one hundred fifty thousand children are orphaned
fifty thousand people are imprisoned
thirty nine thousand women over the age of twelve are prostitutes
six thousand American bombers have been shot down.[54]

In the poem, the Asian American author expresses a sense of separation between the Southeast Asian women and herself and presumably other North American attendees of the IWC by asking how "your people" could endure and resist such violence and upheaval. Despite a sense of racial and gender affinity, she recognizes her subject position as a person of Asian ancestry in the West. She is geographically distanced from the direct site of colonial and military conflict. In addition, she ascribes a romanticized identity to the Vietnamese, depicting them as a collective people heroically suffering under and resisting American oppression.

The same poem, however, suggests that the Indochinese emphasized a nationalist and internationalist collective identity that transcended radical orientalist binaries. The voice of an Indochinese woman responds to the question addressed to "your people" by stating:

For twenty five years we have been defending our land. What our fathers began we continue. What we do not finish our children will continue and even their children's children until the enemy is driven out.
Until the People win. Until there is peace.[55]

The evocation of "we" is a collective call, an open-ended coalition that included multiple generations of Vietnamese people as well as a broader global community of "the people" struggling for peace. Another Asian American delegate recalled that through their words and actions, the Southeast Asian women reminded their North American audience that the Indochinese "were not too different from ourselves as women. We need not have false feelings of inadequacy."[56] By working together, women around the world might achieve liberation and peace.

The North American activists who traveled to Vancouver and Toronto aspired to create an international community of women. The racial, sexual, and national differences among American and Canadian women were particularly intense, perhaps because they lived and worked in closer proximity to one another. In contrast, they encountered briefly a very select group of female political leaders from Indochina who could fulfill and exceed their romantic visions of victimhood and heroism. As much as the North American delegates brought home stories of conflict with one another, they also carried with them hopes for political change. While some became disillusioned by the tensions among North American women, others became even more dedicated to exposing and ending the horrors of the war in Southeast Asia. At both the Vancouver and Toronto conferences, Southeast Asian and North American women issued joint declarations, affirming their mutual desires to end the U.S. war in Indochina. Individuals also signed the People's Peace Treaty, an initiative to assert the voices of ordinary citizens into top-down diplomatic and military decisions.

In addition, the conference inspired North American women to increase their efforts for feminist empowerment. Some individuals arrived at the IWCs with a political awareness of female oppression and the necessity of challenging these gender hierarchies. Others left with this sensibility. Nina Genera, who crossed the U.S.-Canadian border for the first time to attend the IWC, had been inspired to engage in antidraft activism because her brother was drafted and her husband nearly so. When busloads of young men arrived at the Oakland induction center, she and other Chicano/a activists would "be out there at 4:30, 5:00 in the morning . . . chanting our mantra that they shouldn't, you know, go fight a war that they didn't know why it was being fought and for what. And we'd literally pulled [Mexican American] guys aside—you know, there would be enough people to where they would at least want to listen to us and we'd talk to them about, you know, the possibility of being able to get out on legitimate deferments and then . . . we'd work with them long term."[57]

Maria Ramirez, Genera's co-organizer, was known for her antiwar theatrical performances. She and others in her group performed in community and public settings, including the culture night at the Vancouver IWC.[58]
Ramirez recalled that she and Genera were "strong women," but they
viewed their activism not as a separate women's cause but rather as part of
"our people's struggle."[59] Genera described female activists like herself and
Ramirez as "the workhorses . . . of the organizations. I think the men
took the credit at being, you know, in the forefront carrying the signs that
we had made. . . . But in the end . . . it was the women who still did the
bulk of the organizing." Genera in particular was extremely shy and preferred not to speak publicly in meetings. She recalled, "I was raised very,
very traditionally." When she returned from the IWC, she learned that a
"handful of Latino guys" in her husband's law school made fun of him
because "he let his wife go on a trip like this, by herself with, you know, a
bunch of women, a bunch of lesbos, a bunch of dykes, a bunch of . . . crazy
women. . . . I remember . . . walking into the law school, like, the following week after I'd gotten back and one of the guys was making fun of my
husband in front of me and I just walked right up to him, and I knew him,
and I knew his wife, and I just walked up to him and I slapped him in the
face in front of all the other men."[60] For Genera, it was a "line of demarca-
tion," transforming her into a more empowered and vocal woman. Following the IWC and the confrontation, she and other Chicana activists decided
to meet regularly to discuss their concerns as Mexican American women.[61]
The feminist awakening for Genera occurred at a time when Chicanas
around the country were discovering their need for a collective political
voice and vision. A month after the IWCs, approximately six hundred women
met in Houston, Texas, for the first national conference devoted to women
of La Raza, a Chicano/a phrase meaning "the people."[62]

A similar transformation occurred for women's liberation activists in
the Vancouver, BC, area. Various local newspapers covered the IWC. One
of them was *Georgia Straight*, an underground publication primarily authored by male countercultural and New Left activists. Shortly after the
conference, the headline "Indochinese Women—Their Personal Stories"
appeared on the front page of *Georgia Straight*. The cover also featured a
large drawing of a headless nude female torso with a Jesus Christ figure
crucified between her legs.[63] Women's liberation activists in Vancouver were
outraged by the image for its sexual objectification and denigration of
women. They were further incensed by the drawing's association with the
Indochinese conference. The women from Vietnam and Laos had such

dignity and had suffered for so long from the sexualized brutality of the war. Their testimonials, however, were retold in a publication that purported to oppose the war but in actuality supported the underlying logic of misogynistic contempt. In retaliation, women's liberation activists took over the press. After a long and tense meeting, the *Georgia Straight* staff agreed to four demands:

> 1) The creation of a newspaper for the people, which will present news to help us deal better with the problems of society and our lives rather than alienate us from them. . . .
> 2) Staff salaries and money received from our issue to be given to us for the formation of a women's defense fund. . . .
> 3) One issue per month [to] be produced by the women's collective on which two regular male staff members will be allowed to assist so that they can learn about women's lib.
> 4) Equal editorial control by women to veto all exploitation of women and men.[64]

The IWCs served as both the culmination and the catalyst for women's activism for peace and liberation. Women of different racial, sexual, and national backgrounds embraced diverse strategies for ending the war and held varying understandings of what constituted freedom. Nevertheless, they discovered some common ground for unity, particularly at the local and global levels.

One final indication of the importance of female internationalism can be gleaned by a celebration in Hanoi that marked the official end of the U.S. war in Southeast Asia. On 19 January 1973, the Washington, DC, branch of WILPF received an urgent cable from the VWU. The message, written in French and translated into English, invited a small delegation from WILPF to visit the capital of North Vietnam for a week, beginning on 27 January.[65] Even though the American travelers had only eight days to prepare for their journey and were not provided with a reason for their visit, WILPF accepted the invitation. Upon their arrival, the American delegates, headed by U.S. section president Marii Hasekawa, discovered that they were joined by "five women representing the Women's International Democratic Federation, one each from Argentina, Russia, India, France, and the Republic of Congo. To our knowledge, we were the only two visiting Americans in Hanoi for the signing of the Peace Accord."[66] The staging of this international female celebration to mark the end of the

U.S. war in Vietnam conveys the significance of women's peace activism. The invitation from the Vietnamese indicates how much they valued and consciously nurtured global female networks as part of their broader campaign to obtain national liberation and reunification. The acceptance of the invitation by WILPF representatives, given the limited information provided to them and the enormous resources necessary to travel across the world with such short notice, reveals how much American women believed in the profound possibilities of global sisterhood.

Legacies

Journeys of Reconciliation

The Vietnam War haunts America. U.S. veterans and their families perhaps experience this in its greatest intensity. Nina Genera's brother was serving in Vietnam when she attended the Indochinese Women's Conference in Vancouver. After much effort, she and her husband secured his release from the military, eight months into his term. She recalled that he flew back to the States on a plane that carried "the dead, the injured . . . the tanks and all the other stuff that had to be repaired back home. . . . He, like, curled up. He said, 'By that time, we had to learn how to curl up like the Vietnamese . . . into a little ball, you know, to hide.' And that's the way he made the, something like the eighteen- or twenty-two-hour trip back home."[1]

When he called Nina to be picked up, he was still wearing his fatigues: "He hadn't showered, like, in two weeks—[he] took this long shower in our . . . bathroom and when he got done, I mean, that thing was backed up because so much red dirt, you know, at the bottom . . . like two inches of red dirt."[2] But the experience of Vietnam could not just be washed off. Nina remembered, "His back was just horrible. . . . It looked like he had some kind of a rash on his back, which is all I could see but he said it was all over his body. And I guess it was from the Agent Orange." Vietnam left traces not only on his body but on his mind. Speaking in 2007, more than thirty-five years after her brother's return, Nina reflected:

> It cost him his marriage. He'd get up in the middle of the night and grab his wife at the time and, you know, throw her underneath the bed. You know, that whole duck and cover thing. And . . . [he] would have nightmares where he thought that she was the enemy . . . so she just couldn't put up with it. . . . He doesn't talk much about it now. . . . Just every once in a while—this last time we were together he said something about Vietnam. But . . . you don't want to, like, ask him questions because you don't know if it's gonna crack him or what.[3]

How do individuals, families, communities, and nations come to terms with the full "costs" of war? Supporters of the U.S. war in Vietnam have expressed anger at those whom they feel are responsible for the "loss" of the war: the antiwar movement, the liberal media, "soft" politicians, and, of course, the sneaky Vietnamese opposition too cowardly to fight a "real" war. Like the North American antiwar activists at the Indochinese Women's Conferences, war advocates continue to engage in a politics of blame.

But what does a "victory" in war mean? For the precious freedom to rule their own nation, Vietnamese anticolonial revolutionaries engaged in protracted wars against the French, the Americans, and the South Vietnamese government from 1945 to 1975. During this thirty-year period, millions of lives were lost, communities destroyed, survivors dislocated, and the landscape scarred. Vast amounts of unmarked and undetonated mines, an estimated 600,000 tons, continue to kill and injure Vietnamese people, long after the United States withdrew its troops.[4] The biochemical weapons, which also left their mark on U.S. soldiers, have had long-lasting ecological and genetic effects on Vietnam and its people.

During the war, the Vietnamese attempted to face the widespread destruction of their society with determination, ingenuity, and optimism. As Elaine Brown recalled, "They were passionate, unabashedly weeping as they spoke of the horrors of the war, and able to laugh with equal vigor—even about the war. Every time the United States dropped bombs on them, they told us, a big crater was created. The most efficient thing to do with the deep holes the bombs made was fill them with water. Then they became 'lakes.' 'We have many lakes in Vietnam,' they laughed."[5] Following reunification, the Vietnamese government and nongovernment organizations

have attempted to draw international attention and to solicit aid to address ongoing issues related to the war.

Unlike its actions following other conflicts, the U.S. government has
refused to provide reconstruction aid, although President Nixon promised
to do so. As demonstrated by the results of the William Calley trial, the
American state denies responsibility for acts of war. In fact, even after the
Paris Peace Accords of 1973, presidents Nixon and Ford continued to
pledge military aid to South Vietnam until funds were finally cut off by
Congress. To protest this military support as well as the lack of reconstruction aid, Ann Froines and other members of the Indochinese Peace Campaign persisted in their efforts to raise awareness among the American public
about the ongoing U.S. hostility into the mid- and even late 1970s.[6] Only
in 1994 did the United States lift an economic embargo against the Democratic Republic of Vietnam (DRV) and only in 1997 did the two countries
normalize political relations.

During the 1970s, most Americans showed little inclination to offer assistance to Vietnam, especially in the context of the stagflation economic
crisis. Even the arrival of refugees from Southeast Asia aroused mixed reactions. The first wave of approximately 130,000 Vietnamese came in
1975, shortly after the fall of Saigon in April of that year. They tended to
be educated, urban, and Christian, with economic and political ties to the
French and the Americans.

In addition to these evacuees, over three thousand children were airlifted
from orphanages and adopted by families around the world. This widely
publicized "baby airlift," designed to save these children from communism,
proved controversial. Not all the children were in fact orphans. Some parents had placed their children in social service agencies and religious
institutions because of the hardships of war. Pat Sumi enlisted legal support in the United States to protest the separation of these children from
their parents and to restore their families. Nancy Stearns—one of the legal experts, a friend of Sumi's, and a colleague of Cora Weiss's husband,
Peter—recalled:

> What happened was adoption agencies just emptied themselves out and
> brought the kids here, but adoption agencies in Vietnam at that point
> were . . . functioning like day care centers. . . . So, you had a real mix of
> kids plus there were women who worked at the agencies who were ter-
> rified of what was gonna happen to their kids because of the fact that
> they were working with Americans. Some of them put their kids on the

planes hoping to get them to relatives in the United States. Some of the Vietnamese women who worked for the agencies were going to try to follow and get their kids when they got here. . . . Some were what they called half orphans—you know, that had one parent alive and one parent not alive. . . . And some were kids who had American GI fathers and Vietnamese mothers and the mothers were afraid of what was gonna happen to their mixed-race kids.[7]

After a lengthy court battle, which lasted several years, the challenge to the orphan airlift was dismissed "in the best interest of the children." Stearns recalled, "It was a very painful case to work on."[8]

An additional wave of more than half a million Vietnamese refugees arrived in the late 1970s and onward. These individuals escaped on boats and suffered attacks by pirates off the coast of Thailand. A substantial portion were ethnic Chinese Vietnamese, like Bob Browne's wife. They faced persecution because they had developed an economic niche within the retail trade in Vietnam and because of the outbreak of war with China in 1979. Compared to the first wave, the second wave had less contact with Western people and culture as well as fewer opportunities to transfer their assets to the United States. Consequently, they faced a more difficult time adjusting to American society.

These waves of Vietnamese were joined by approximately 140,000 from Laos and over 100,000 from Cambodia. They fled their respective countries as a result of the political and military dislocation connected to the war in Vietnam. They tended to come from rural areas and had less access to education than the Vietnamese. The Hmong, an ethnic group within Laos that had been recruited by the American CIA to fight against communists, came from a preliterate culture. They discovered that the United States is "another kind of jungle—a technological and bureaucratic jungle."[9] Previously engaged in farming and soldiering, they had limited economic skills to survive in the United States. Consequently, they initially relied on low-wage jobs, social services, and welfare to get by. Like other veterans and survivors of war, they also suffered psychologically, emotionally, and physically. While some Americans welcomed their former allies, others resented their presence. The Southeast Asian refugees constituted a racial other, now on American soil, making demands again on American resources.

They arrived as the political landscape was shifting from the radical internationalism of the "long" 1960s to the "Me Decade," a phrase coined by writer Tom Wolfe to describe the 1970s.[10] The contrast is perhaps overdrawn, since not all activists abandoned their political commitments and became focused on self-transformation. However, there were changes in the ways American radicals perceived decolonizing Asia.

Previously, Vietnam was the most visible and successful site of resistance to American military and political aggression. Whether represented by Buddhist leader Thich Nhat Hanh, National Liberation Front spokesperson Madame Binh, DRV president Ho Chi Minh, or the iconic peasant woman warrior, the Vietnamese were heroic underdogs, struggling for the right of self-determination. They captured the political imagination of American activists invested in peace, liberation, and sisterhood. Although North Korea had less recognition among U.S. political circles, the People's Republic of China and Chairman Mao also stirred leftist, anticolonial, and Third World–identified activists. Disillusioned by their country's inhumane acts of war and increasingly aware of racial and gender inequality, American radicals turned to decolonizing Asia for political inspiration during the 1960s and early 1970s.

This book brings attention to this radical orientalist imaginary to enhance the existing scholarship on the long 1960s. Seeking to go beyond a black-white and domestically bounded framework for understanding U.S. history, this work foregrounds instead the importance of global political dialogue between American nonstate actors of varying racial and ethnic backgrounds and Asian political leaders and spokespersons. In addition, this book underscores the significance of gender in framing these international dialogues and relationships.

The radical orientalist sensibilities of American activists, which peaked during the U.S. war in Vietnam, declined during the mid- to late 1970s. The realpolitik of nation formation and international diplomacy increasingly challenged heroic perceptions of Asian nations. The Cold War détente between the United States and China that occurred in the early 1970s, the denunciation of the excesses of the Chinese Cultural Revolution that emerged in the mid- to late 1970s, the process of political consolidation in Vietnam following reunification in 1975, and the continued obscurity and isolation of North Korea throughout that period combined to lessen the romantic appeal of these socialist powers. As one of Cora Weiss's peace activist colleagues said to her after the U.S. war in Vietnam ended: Vietnam is now a country, not a cause.

James Meriwether, in his study of African American relationships to Africa during the middle decades of the twentieth century, noted a similar phenomenon. Blacks in the United States tended to "focus on countries embroiled in national liberation struggles, as opposed to countries that already had gained independence."[11] Doing so "enabled African Americans to continue building transatlantic bridges while finessing the task of addressing the complexities of contemporary Africa."[12] By the late 1970s, the Vietnamese were no longer heroically resisting Western imperialism. Instead, the DRV, PRC, and North Korea faced the challenges of running their governments and economies while negotiating complex domestic and international conflicts. There were no clear-cut revolutionary champions and capitalist villains.

In this context, some activists of the long 1960s generation, like Eldridge Cleaver, renounced their former politics. Other radicals, like Pat Sumi, continued to embrace idealistic beliefs about the egalitarian promise of socialism, regardless of the actual conduct of socialist states. As she said, twenty-seven years after the Anti-Imperialist Delegation, "I believe in our naiveté."[13] In fact, a leftist movement among Third World people in the United States persisted and even found organizational form in the mid- to late 1970s. The League of Revolutionary Struggle, a Marxist-Leninist organization, was created in 1978 out of a merger between I Wor Kuen (the predominantly Asian American organization of which Alex Hing was a member), the August 29th Movement (an organization named after the Chicano Moratorium and that worked with Betita Martinez), and the Revolutionary Communist League (formerly a black nationalist organization led by artist Amiri Baraka). Still others recognized the profound impact of antiwar politics on their lives and identities, without necessarily subscribing to a particular political ideology. Maria Ramirez, writing in 2011, reflected that she and her friend Nina "were forever changed by our involvement against that unjust war. . . . It has made us want to be better human beings."[14]

As diverse individuals processed the meaning of their activism in light of changing political developments, some channeled their radical orientalist sensibilities to become academic orientalists. During the 1960s and early 1970s, travelers to socialist Asia constructed knowledge about these societies for the West through movement writings, drawings, and speeches. They did so with the assistance of Asian and European partners. For example, Pham Van Chuong, the National Liberation Front correspondent based in Eastern Europe, published a weekly four-page newsletter in English for Western audiences.[15] He had limited resources to accomplish his tasks. He shared the facilities, equipment, and distribution network of the Czech News Agency in Prague. His routine included receiving news from a teleprinter provided by the office. Using a typewriter on stencil paper, he typically worked through the night to produce the newsletter. While he could send approximately five hundred copies to various individuals and organizations in North America, he relied upon his supporters in Prague to make all of the copies and disseminate newsletters among their circulation networks in Europe. Chuong developed the mailing list in North America by meeting with U.S. antiwar activists who visited him in Prague. These individuals, in turn, communicated what they learned from Chuong to their constituencies through interviews, essays, and articles published occasionally in the U.S. mainstream press but most often in alternative newspapers affiliated with their respective organizations.

After the end of the U.S. war in Vietnam, activists like Ann Froines and Charlotte Bunch continued their role as interpreters of Asia for Western audiences. Along with other radicals who became academics, they offered some of the first university classes and also authored articles and books on women, peasants, and revolution in Asia. In fact, Bunch became a leading activist-scholar of international and transnational feminism.

The questions of how diverse women might engage in meaningful dialogue and form political coalitions, topics raised by the 1971 Indochinese Women's Conferences, continue to be debated in feminist conferences, movements, and intellectual circles today. In particular, the controversies about whether and how to address sexuality would recur as women from the global North met with those from the global South.[16] Despite the difficulties of forming international alliances, women who became politically active during the Vietnam era recognize the importance of building these bridges. Even though leftist decolonizing movements conceived of women's liberation as integrally linked to national liberation and socialism, achieving independence did not eliminate gendered forms of inequality. In some cases, gender disparities have worsened due to globalization, a form of economic imperialism. Today, the Vietnam Women's Union continues to function. It helps to document the important contributions that Vietnamese women made to their country's liberation. In addition, the union seeks to address contemporary women's needs and partners with feminist organizations around the world to do so.[17]

As the political cachet of Third World socialism both waxed and waned, and as the investment in global sisterhood endured, the Western fascination with Asian culture and religion has fermented. The career of Thich Nhat Hanh provides insight into this phenomenon. Following his successful 1966 world tour, Hanh used Paris as his political base to continue his efforts to bring peace to his home country. While Bob Browne began to reduce his involvement in the antiwar movement in order to devote himself to black power causes, the Fellowship of Reconciliation continued its collaboration with Hanh well into the 1970s. Linda Forrest, whose husband, Jim, was assigned to travel with the Buddhist monk in 1968 on behalf of FOR, described their relationship in a memo to the FOR staff: "I've accumulated enough interesting bits and pieces from Jim's letters to give you all some brief comments about the tour. . . . A typical quote from Jim's letters: 'Nhat Hanh is now watching TV without the sound, something he greatly enjoys. . . .' From the tone of the letters, I should say that Jim is becoming something of a Buddhist, and Nhat Hanh something of a hippie. They're a hard act to follow."[18] Hanh began his public career in the West as an "authentic" spokesperson for the cause of peace in Vietnam. As the quote foreshadows, he would emerge as a leading figure in the New Age movement, someone who could distill and translate the insights of Eastern religion for a Western audience seeking peace and reconciliation. To this day, Thich Nhat Hanh promotes engaged Buddhism through meditation retreats, speaking tours, and publications. He continues to travel, engage in dialogue, and encourage self-reflection in the hopes that the values of nonviolence and compassion might speak beyond human-made barriers and transform individuals as well as their governments.

As the "Me Decade" came to an end, Cora Weiss and Bob Browne made their final trip to Vietnam in the name of international humanitarianism. In 1978, Weiss organized a private mission on behalf of Church World Service (CWS). This Protestant organization began working in Vietnam as early as 1954, providing refugee assistance at the end of the First Indochina War against France. During the U.S. war in Vietnam, CWS offered food, medicine, and educational resources to ameliorate the sufferings of war.[19] After the Paris Peace Accords of 1973 and after the reunification of Vietnam in 1975, the organization raised funds to rebuild bombed hospitals and reconstruct schools. It also sent food, a necessity for an ecologically devastated country attempting to rebuild its economic infrastructure. In 1978, as Vietnamese refugees fled on boats, Weiss organized a delegation to deliver a shipment of wheat, to be consumed and planted for future crops. Because the U.S. government refused to help, Weiss continued her service as a citizen diplomat and stepped in to provide aid.

Even though CWS was a Protestant organization, it had a history of practicing interfaith cooperation. And Weiss, although Jewish, had a long history of working with humanitarian activists of varying religious backgrounds.

In 1967, she had been part of an interfaith team that strategized to convince Martin Luther King Jr. to speak out about the Vietnam War. She gathered with the group at the apartment of John and Anne Bennett. John was the president of the Union Theological Seminary in New York City at the time. He and his wife, a member of WILPF, had visited Saigon in 1965 on a delegation with Bob Browne. At the 1967 meeting, the others present included Catholic priest Dick Fernandez, who served as the executive director of the Clergy and Laity Concerned about Vietnam, Rabbi Abraham Heschel of the Jewish Theological Seminary of America, and Reverend William Sloane Coffin of the Riverside Church in New York. Coffin would eventually travel with Weiss to North Vietnam in 1972 to bring back three American POWs, released to them as a gesture of goodwill. The interfaith group in 1967 discussed various ways to persuade King that now was the time to publicly declare his opposition to the war. They telephoned him and offered the venue of Riverside Church, where Martin Luther King Jr. eventually gave his famous antiwar speech.[20]

For the 1978 visit, Weiss, one of two women on the delegation, invited her longtime friend and antiwar colleague, Bob Browne, the only African American in the group. It would be his first visit to Hanoi and his first opportunity to revisit Saigon, now named Ho Chi Minh City, since his travels there eleven years earlier. As an economist, Browne was eager to observe the new policies being introduced by the DRV. Even after reunification of the country, the government had moved cautiously to consolidate the economies of the North and the South. However, in 1978, a new national currency was introduced and efforts were made to bring the previously "free wheeling, consumer-oriented economy of the South into some sense of equilibrium with the austere, government-controlled economy of the North."[21] As Browne noted, because Chinese Vietnamese "were disproportionately involved in commerce in Vietnam, many were economically squeezed in this process, giving rise to a new wave of refugees."[22] These economic reforms would be reversed eight years later, as Vietnam adopted *doi moi*, or a socialist version of a free-market economy.

In 1978, Browne recognized that consolidating a new nation meant hardships for those who had previously benefited under the Republic of Vietnam. The "re-education centers," where obstructionists of the new state were sent, were reputedly closed by 1978. Even so, Browne found "it difficult to locate his pre-war and war time Vietnamese friends," concluding "that such persons have been removed from positions of influence (if they did not flee to exile)."[23]

Among the dislocated, Browne found two of Huoi's brothers, who had moved to Vietnam from Cambodia due to the political turmoil in that country. Both nations suffered from food shortages. Browne recalled that his "two brothers-in-law in Vietnam . . . begged [him], with tears in their eyes, to help them get out of Vietnam—not because of political ideology but simply because they couldn't get enough food to feed their families."[24] Browne attempted to sponsor their migration, but was unsuccessful, perhaps because they were economic and not political refugees. He did write to the U.S. mainstream media, including the *New York Times*, to demand that America pay its "Overdue Debt to Indochina":

> My God, when is America going to overcome its adolescent pique at losing the Vietnam War and begin to display some common sense and genuine compassion for the beleaguered Indochinese people rather than a transparent posturing over the plight of the boat people? . . . What I did see was a Vietnam unable to feed itself and which clearly but with dignity was asking the U.S. to help to rebuild at least the food-producing potential which the U.S. military had quite effectively destroyed. Having spent $100 *billion* to deliver unconscionable terror and destruction to these two little nations [Vietnam and Cambodia], we certainly should be honest enough with ourselves to swallow our pride and send them at least $100 million worth of food.[25]

On his 1978 trip to deliver wheat to Vietnam, Browne traveled with religious, cultural, and economic leaders. His companions included a man from Kansas, representing American farmers who were donating their crops. When the ship left the dock in Texas, a church spokesperson from Houston expressed their goals for the journey: "We sail this ship as a sign of hope for peace and unity, and for the day when people will beat their swords into ploughshares, and we will create a world community with each sharing as equals."[26] Thirteen-year-old Susan Ross of Houston expressed a similar sentiment more simply, when she said, "I give this wheat because the children of the world are friends."[27]

Prime Minister Pham Van Dong met the delegation upon their arrival. In 1970, Eldridge Cleaver recalled the eloquence and empathy of this political leader, whose life spanned almost the entirety of the twentieth century. Born in 1906, Pham Van Dong cofounded the Indochinese Communist Party and served as the prime minister of North Vietnam through both the first and second Indochinese wars. He frequently met with American antiwar

Figure 18. Premier Pham Van Dong greets Cora Weiss and other members of the Ship of Wheat delegation in Hanoi, May 1978. Tranh Minh Quoc, who hosted the 1970 Anti-Imperialist Delegation, is second from the left. Bob Browne is third from the left. Donated to author's personal collection by Cora Weiss.

Figure 19. The Ship of Wheat delegation with Cora Weiss (middle of the front row) and Bob Browne (third from the left in the back). Photo taken in Ho Chi Minh City (formerly Saigon), 28 May 1978. Personal collection of Cora Weiss.

activists during the U.S. war in Vietnam, treating them as dignitaries. In the spring of 1978, Dong demonstrated once again his poetic command of language. He welcomed the Ship of Wheat and his American guests by saying, "You are the swallows who bring the spring."[28] The analogy is a moving one. Like swallows, internationalists such as Weiss and Browne find ways to move beyond human-made borders. Arriving at a time of rebirth and renewal, they brought seeds for food and hopes for peace.

Acknowledgments

This project weaves together multiple facets of my life. In college, I became a student activist, working with people of varied backgrounds—white, black, Chicano/a, Native American, Asian American, and international students. We advocated for more courses that examined race and inequality in American society, and we also called for more institutional support for ethnic student service centers so that students of color might feel more at home on the university campus. My best friend at the time was Vietnamese American, a comrade-in-arms in our activist endeavors and a great companion for food adventures, too. She introduced me to pho and Vietnamese coffee in excursions to San Jose. Her family, though, had been separated by war and relocation. Her dad and most of her siblings successfully made it to the United States as refugees. Her mother and younger brother were not as lucky. I remember driving her to the airport one day so that she could reunite with her mom after a separation of more than ten years.

As I found my identity and a sense of community through political organizing, I also discovered the joys of academia. My favorite undergraduate class was on the History of the Vietnam War. Taught by Gordon Chang, who eventually became my graduate adviser, the course presented an exciting new view of history to me. Rather than absorbing a series of recorded dates and events, we debated ideas and diverse interpretations of the past. Consequently, I decided to try my hand at research. Drawn to the topic of activism, I focused my honors thesis on social movements in San Francisco Chinatown during the 1960s and 1970s. It was during this initial foray into historical research that I first interviewed Alex Hing and discovered the Red Guards, U.S.A., the Anti-Imperialist Delegation, and the Indochinese Women's Conferences in Asian American activist newspapers. Spending a year working at the Martin Luther King, Jr. Papers Project after college confirmed my decision to pursue graduate studies in history.

For *Radicals on the Road,* I analyzed a range of archival printed materials, including letters, memoirs, speeches, government documents, movement publications, visual art, and newspaper and journal accounts. I also utilized oral history extensively. Even though these interviews occurred many years after the fact, they are invaluable sources. The oral histories provide insight into how my interview subjects remembered the past. That is, their accounts shed light on what they found significant about their travels, experiences, conversations, and activism as well as how these interpretations of international travel shaped their identities. Regardless of their accuracy, the interviews reveal what my subjects wanted to communicate about the past to a researcher like myself. In some instances, their recollections meshed well with the archival materials that I collected. In others, the interviews raised new perspectives that I had not gleaned from the printed sources. The interviews sometimes supported and at times contradicted one another as well as written sources. In these cases of divergence, I tried to ask questions of my subjects as well as my findings to understand why such differences might exist.

My interest in Robert S. Browne emerged from a fishing expedition to the Schomburg Center for Research in Black Culture. The staff there recommended that I examine his papers given my interest in African Americans who traveled to Vietnam. Browne had passed away by the time I began this research, but his voice and personality came alive through his writings. He deposited papers not only at the Schomburg but also at the Swarthmore College Peace Collection, which contains a treasure trove of information for anyone interested in pacifism. This institution holds papers of significant peace organizations like the Fellowship of Reconciliation, Women Strike for Peace, and the Women's International League for Peace and Freedom. In addition to conducting archival research in Philadelphia and New York City, I also examined government records at the National

Archives in College Park, Maryland, to understand the International Cooperation Agency and the U.S. Overseas Mission in Cambodia and Vietnam. To supplement these written sources, I conducted interviews with Robert Browne's family, including his daughters, Hoa and Mai; his wife, Huoi; and his half-sister, Wendelle. I also interviewed Browne's friends and colleagues, including those who continue to operate the Twenty-First Century Foundation. The foundation shared with me Browne's unpublished autobiography and put me in contact with his family.

My sources for the Anti-Imperialist Delegation came from the mainstream press, like the *New York Times*, and activist publications, like the *Black Panther, Getting Together*, and *Gidra*. In addition, I researched archival collections like the Steve Louie Asian American Movement Collection at the Asian American Resource Center at the University of California, Los Angeles; the Dr. Huey P. Newton Foundation Collection at Stanford University; the Eldridge Cleaver Papers at the Bancroft Library in Berkeley; and the Elaine Brown Papers at Emory University. Also, the extensive collection of FBI materials on Eldridge Cleaver, available through Freedom of Information requests, shed light on how he, other Black Panthers, and Anti-Imperialist Delegation members were tracked by the U.S. government. Oral histories were vitally important for this portion of the manuscript as well. I am grateful to those who agreed to speak to me, particularly Kathleen Cleaver, Ann Froines, Alex Hing, Randy Rappaport, and others, including those who chose to remain anonymous. Also, a special thanks to Daryl Maeda, Sean Malloy, Suzanne McCormack, and Ryan Yokota, who generously shared their research with me.

For the Indochinese Women's Conferences, I conducted archival research in various locations in the United States and Canada. In addition to the rich materials at the Swarthmore College Peace Collection, significant papers related to women's antiwar activism and the Indochinese Women's Conferences are also housed at the Chicago History Museum, the Schlesinger Library, Simon Fraser University in Vancouver, the Library Archives Canada in Ottawa, the Third World Women's Alliance Archives in Oakland, and the Wright State University's Special Collection. Also, many of the women whom I interviewed in person or over the phone shared their private archives, which include newsletters, pictures, mementos from travel to Vietnam, literature that they received during their journeys, and other movement documents. I particularly want to thank Charlotte Bunch, Nina Genera, Betita Martinez, Maria Ramirez, and most especially Cora Weiss for their generosity and support. They have dedicated their lives to social justice, and they continue to be an inspiration. I also thank Agatha Beins, Jessica Frazier, and Ann Koblitz for sharing their research and interpretations with me.

Most of my research focused on "Americans" who traveled abroad, but I also was able to gain insight into the perspectives of Asian activists. During August 2010, I traveled throughout Vietnam with the support of the Vietnam-USA Society. Founded in 1945, this organization was active during the U.S. war in Vietnam in hosting American antiwar activists. They continue these educational and citizen-diplomatic initiatives today. Through their assistance, I interviewed various people (diplomats, journalists, members of the Vietnam Women's Union, and veterans) who played significant roles in developing political dialogue with those in the West. I do not speak or write Vietnamese. These interviews occurred either through translation or in English, depending on the desires of the interview subjects. In addition, I visited museums and historic sites, like the village that became known for the My Lai Massacre, to understand how the war is documented and presented to the public. My special thanks to Nguyen Lien-Hang for putting me in contact with the Vietnam-U.S.A. Society and to Mr. Bui Nghi and Ms. Quynh Phan for hosting and translating for me.

I have incurred many intellectual debts in completing this project. I have benefited enormously from the encouragement and critiques offered by Mark Bradley, Paul Kramer, and Michael McGanty. I am honored to have this work become part of Cornell University's United States in the World series, and I want to thank the anonymous reviewer for taking the time to offer such helpful feedback. I also want to acknowledge Sarah Grossman, who sent such encouraging e-mails and helped me through the process of obtaining permissions for this book. And I appreciate the care with which Karen M. Fisher, Barbara Goodhouse, and Karen Hwa copyedited my manuscript.

My colleagues, students, and research assistants at the Ohio State University have provided me with tremendous intellectual support. My thanks to Leslie Alexander, Dan Amsterdam, Greg Anderson, Curtis Austin, Kevin Boyle, John Brooke, Cindy Burack, Jill Bystydzienski, Alice Conklin, Theresa Delgadillo, Theodora Dragostinova, Elsadig Elsheikh, Lilia Fernandez, Vicky Getis, Ken Goings, Donna Guy, Susan Hartmann, Mary Hershberger, Hasan Jeffries, Cricket Keating, Brian Kennedy, Mitch Lerner, Bob McMahon, Lucy Murphy, Joe Orser, Joe Ponce, Paul Reitter, Amy Shuman, Stephanie Smith, Wendy Smooth Mytheli Sreenivas, David Stebenne, David

Steigerwald, Maurice Stevens, and Monica Trieu for their advice and insights. I also want to thank my research assistants for their hard work: Katie Bausch, Wenjuan Bi, Zel Caldwell, Zachery Fry, June Kang, Duo Li, Brena Tai, Jeffrey Vernon, and Yan Xu. The students in my women's history research seminar during fall 2010–winter 2011 are a special group. Along with some interested guests, they helped me to complete the first draft of this work. Best wishes to all of them (Joseph Arena, Gregory Freitag, Seung-hyun Hwang, Nicole Jackson, John Knight, Kimberly McKee, Perry Miller, Lindsay Peiper, Peggy Solic, Tyran Steward, William Sturkey, Jeffrey Vernon, and Adrienne Winans) as they embark on their academic careers. And a special thanks to Lynn Demyan for her exceptional transcription skills.

I have benefited from the mentorship and insights of many colleagues and friends outside of OSU, including Rick Baldoz, Tani Barlow, Rosalyn Baxandall, Charlotte Brooks, Nick Calluther, Melanie Castillo-Calluther, Paul Chamberlin, Derek Chang, Gordon Chang, Tina Chen, John Cheng, Jeremy Clarke, Kathy Coll, Frank Costigliola, Maria Cotera, Nancy Cott, Bruce Cumings, Nina Dayton, Prasenjit Duara, Mary Dudziak, Angela Earnest-LeBlanc, Augusto Espiritu, Judith Ezekiel, Michael Flamm, V. P. Franklin, Estelle Freedman, Diane Fujino, Van Gosse, Beverly Guy-Sheftall, Eric Hayot, Nancy Hewitt, Emily Hobson, Madeline Hsu, Jane Hunter, Ryan Irwin, Joan Johnson, Waldo Johnson, Gregory Jue, Moon-ho Jung, Amy Kesselman, Ginah Kim, Suzy Kim, Anna Krylova, Scott Kurashige, Emily Lawsin, Christopher Lee, Jessica Lee, Jo Lee, Shelley Lee, Ian Lekus, Karen Leong, Tessie Liu, Mary Lui, Daryl Maeda, Tracye Matthews, Caroline Merithew, Edward Miller, Pablo Mitchell, Francesca Morgan, Donna Murch, Mae Ngai, Rodney Noonan, Franny Nudelman, Jeffrey Ogbar, Jolie Olcott, Christopher Phelps, Steve Pitti, Renee Ramono, Dave Roediger, Vicki Ruiz, Leila Rupp, Robert O. Self, Nayan Shah, Naoko Shibusawa, Nico Slate, Gregory Smithers, Robyn Spencer, Jack Tchen, Akinyele Umoja, Penny Von Eschen, Kim Warren, Lora Wildenthal, Ara Wilson, Shelley Wong, Steve Yao, Kathleen Yep, Henry Yu, and Ji-Yeon Yuh.

My work has been enriched and strengthened by the opportunity to present at the American Crossroads: Migration, Communities, and Race Conference at the University of Texas, Austin; the American Historical Association Annual Meeting; the American Studies Association Annual Conference; the Asian American Studies Workshop at the Stanford University Humanities Center; the Association for Asian American Studies Conference; the Association for the Study of the Worldwide African Diaspora Biennial Conference; the Bandung and Beyond: Rethinking Afro-Asian

Connections during the Twentieth Century Symposium at Stanford University; the Berkshires Conference of Women's History; the CIC Asian American Studies Workshop held at Pennsylvania State University; the Communist Feminism(s): A Transnational Perspective Workshop, cosponsored by the Chao Center for Asian Studies at Rice University and the Department of History at Duke University; the Critical Ethnic Studies and the Future of Genocide Conference held at the University of California, Riverside; the Diasporic Counterpoint: Africans, Asians, and the Americas Symposium held at Northwestern University; the From Bandung to Tehran: Transnational Networks in the Postcolonial World Conference held at Williams College; the National Women's Studies Association Annual Conference; the New World Coming: The Sixties and the Shaping of Global Consciousness Conference held at Queen's College, Kingston, Canada; the Newberry Seminar on Women and Gender in Chicago; the Organization of American Historians Annual Conference; the Out of the Margins: Asian American Movement Building Conference at the University of Michigan, Ann Arbor; the Race, Radicalism, and Repression on the Pacific Coast and Beyond Conference at the University of Washington, Seattle; the Reproduction of Race and Racial Ideologies Workshop sponsored by the Center for the Study of Race, Politics, and Culture at the University of Chicago; the Race, Roots, and Resistance: Revisiting the Legacy of Black Power Conference sponsored by the African American Studies and Research Program at the University of Illinois, Champaign-Urbana; the Religious Crossings in Literature, Art and Practice Symposium at the Ohio State University; the Sequels to the 1960s Summer Seminar held at the Schlesinger Library; the Society for Historians of American Foreign Relations Annual Meeting; and the War, Intimacy/Trauma and Asian American and African American Crossings Forum at Wesleyan University. I also benefited from the opportunity to present and receive feedback at Arizona State University; the Claremont Colleges; Cornell University; Duke University; Hamilton College; Indiana University, Bloomington; Middlebury College; Oberlin College; Rice University; the University of Dayton; the University of Michigan, Ann Arbor; and Yale University.

I would not have been able to complete this project without generous financial support provided by the Arts and Humanities Publication Subvention grant given by the Ohio State University; the Coca-Cola CDW Faculty Research Grant administered by the Women's Studies Department at OSU; the College of Humanities Seed Grant at OSU; the Emory University Short Term Fellowship sponsored by the Robert W. Woodruff Library;

Mershon Center for International Security Studies; the National Endowment for the Humanities Summer Stipend; the Schlesinger Library Research Support Grant given by Radcliffe Institute for Advanced Study; the Senior Postdoctoral Fellowship given by the Center for the Study of Race, Politics, and Culture at the University of Chicago; the SHAFR Diversity/International Outreach Fellowship; the Special Research Assignment given by the College of Humanities at OSU; the TELR Research-on-Research Student-Faculty ePartnerships Grant given by the OSU Digital Union; and the Virginia Hull Research Award at OSU.

Earlier versions of this work have appeared in the following publications: "An African-Vietnamese American: Robert S. Browne, the Anti-War Movement, and the Personal/Political Dimensions of Black Internationalism," *Journal of African American History* 92 (Fall 2007): 491–515; "Journeys for Peace and Liberation: Third World Internationalism and Radical Orientalism during the U.S. War in Viet Nam," *Pacific Historical Review* 76, no. 4 (November 2007): 575–84; and "Rethinking Global Sisterhood: Peace Activism and Women's Orientalism," in *No Permanent Waves: Recasting Histories of U.S. Feminism*, ed. Nancy Hewitt (Rutgers University Press, 2010), pp. 193–220. I also am in the process of completing two additional essays and have benefited from anonymous reviewers as well as the editorial guidance of Moon-Ho Jung and Gregory Smithers. In addition, I want to recognize Christopher Lee for his thoughtful insights and suggestions.

Finally, I want to offer my deepest gratitude to the people who have given me the personal support to complete this project. My parents, John and Betty Wu, always ask how my work is going, even when I don't really want to talk about it. But they are just as eager to celebrate and be proud of their daughter, even when I don't deserve it. My tennis friends offer wonderful companionship and fun exercise. Some of them even read what I write! Christel, Manfred, Andrea, and Juniper Walter (my family-in-law) are always eager to welcome us into their homes in North Carolina and play with our rambunctious kids. By the time this book is published, Konrad will be nine and Langston will be five. They live every day as an adventure, and I hope they will travel through life with this spirit. Their father, Mark, is a patient, hardworking person who envisions a green, sustainable future. He deconstructed and rebuilt our home with thoughtfulness and love. Despite his busy schedule, he always makes time to take care of us. I look forward to more time together to share our life journeys.

Notes

Introduction

1. James W. Clinton, "Cora Weiss," in *The Loyal Opposition: Americans in North Vietnam, 1965–1972* (Niwot: University Press of Colorado, 1995), p. 169.

2. Ibid.

3. Ibid.

4. Cora Weiss, interview with author, Brooklyn, NY, 7 April 2006.

5. Ibid.

6. Cora Weiss and Peter Weiss, interview with author, New York City, 9 April 2006.

7. Benedict Anderson, *Imagined Communities: Reflections on the Origin and Spread of Nationalism*, rev. ed. (London: Verso, 1991), p. 6.

8. Images of the Underground: Underground Newspapers of the 1960s and 1970s. Wisconsin Historical Society, www.wisconsinhistory.org/whi/feature/underground/.

9. Edward W. Said, *Orientalism* (New York: Vintage Books, 1979).

10. Christina Klein, *Cold War Orientalism: Asia in the Middlebrow Imagination, 1945–1961* (Berkeley: University of California Press, 2003). For other scholarship on American forms of orientalism, see Helen Heran Jun, *Race for Citizenship: Black Orientalism and Asian Uplift from Pre-emancipation to Neoliberal America* (New York: New York University Press, 2011). Robert G. Lee, *Orientals: Asian Americans in Popular Culture* (Philadelphia: Temple University Press, 1999); Karen J. Leong, *The China Mystique: Pearl S. Buck, Anna May Wong, Mayling Soong, and the Transformation of American Orientalism* (Berkeley: University of California Press, 2005); Melani McAlister, *Epic Encounters: Culture, Media, and U.S. Interests in the Middle East, 1945–2000* (Berkeley: University of California Press, 2001); Bill V. Mullen, *Afro-Orientalism* (Minneapolis: University of Minnesota Press, 2004); John Tchen, *New York before Chinatown: Orientalism and the Shaping of American*

Culture, 1776–1882 (Baltimore, MD: Johns Hopkins University Press, 1999); Judy Tzu-Chun Wu, *Doctor Mom Chung of the Fair-Haired Bastards: The Life of a Wartime Celebrity* (Berkeley: University of California Press, 2005); Mari Yoshihara, *Embracing the East: White Women and American Orientalism* (New York: Oxford University Press, 2003); and Henry Yu, *Thinking Orientals: Migration, Contact, and Exoticism in Modern America* (New York: Oxford University Press, 2001).

11. For an analysis of how imperialist forms of orientalism shaped U.S. Cold War epistemologies toward Asia as well as the Soviet Union, see Jodi Kim, *Ends of Empire: Asian American Critique and the Cold War* (Minneapolis: University of Minnesota Press, 2010).

12. Linda K. Kerber, *No Constitutional Right to Be Ladies: Women and the Obligations of Citizenship* (New York: Hill and Wang, 1998).

13. Sara Evans, *Personal Politics: The Roots of Women's Liberation in the Civil Rights Movement and the New Left* (New York: Vintage, 1980).

14. Sara Evans, *Tidal Wave: How Women Changed America at Century's End* (New York: Free Press, 2004); Leila J. Rupp, *Worlds of Women: The Making of an International Women's Movement* (Princeton, NJ: Princeton University Press, 1997); and Amy Swerdlow, *Women Strike for Peace: Traditional Motherhood and Radical Politics in the 1960s* (Chicago: University of Chicago Press, 1993).

15. See Rupp, *Worlds of Women*; Inderpal Grewal, *Transnational America: Feminisms, Diasporas, Neoliberalisms* (Durham, NC: Duke University Press, 2005); Chandra Mohanty, "Under Western Eyes: Feminist Scholarship and Colonial Discourses," *Feminist Review* 30 (Autumn 1988): 61–88; Judy Tzu-Chun Wu, "Journeys for Peace and Liberation: Third World Internationalism and Radical Orientalism during the U.S. War in Viet Nam," *Pacific Historical Review* 76, no. 4 (2007): 575–84.

16. Mary Hershberger, *Traveling to Vietnam: American Peace Activists and the War* (Syracuse, NY: Syracuse University Press, 1998).

17. Robert K. Brigham, *Guerrilla Diplomacy: The NLF's Foreign Relations and the Viet Nam War* (Ithaca, NY: Cornell University Press, 1999).

18. William J. Duiker, "The Foreign Policy of North Vietnam," in *Light at the End of the Tunnel: A Vietnam War Anthology*, 3rd ed., ed. Andrew J. Rotter (Lanham, MD: Rowman and Littlefield, 2010), pp. 172–90.

19. Both Hershberger and Weiss refer to this concept of citizen diplomacy, which suggests that American travelers also identified with this role. Clinton, "Cora Weiss," p. 169; and Hershberger, *Traveling to Vietnam*, pp. xx–xxi.

20. Examples include Todd Gitlin, *The Sixties: Years of Hope, Days of Rage* (New York: Bantam, 1987); and James Miller, *Democracy Is in the Streets: From Port Huron to the Siege of Chicago* (New York: Touchstone, 1987).

21. Political scientist Claire Jean Kim proposed the concept of racial triangulation to analyze how African Americans and Asian Americans are comparatively racialized in the United States. Claire Jean Kim, "The Racial Triangulation of Asian Americans," *Politics and Society* 27, no. 1 (1999): 105–38. For a recently published study on the intertwined movements of African American civil rights and Indian decolonization, see Nico Slate, *Colored Cosmopolitanism: The Shared Struggle for Freedom in the United States and India* (Cambridge, MA: Harvard University Press, 2012).

22. Max Elbaum, *Revolution in the Air: Sixties Radicals Turn to Lenin, Mao, and Che* (London: Verso, 2002); Daryl J. Maeda, "Black Panthers, Red Guards, and Chinamen: Constructing Asian American Identity through Performing Blackness, 1969–1972," *American Quarterly* 57 (2005): 1079–1103; Daryl J. Maeda, *Chains of Babylon: The Rise of Asian America* (Minneapolis: University of Minnesota Press, 2009); Lorena Oropeza, *¡Raza Sí! ¡Guerra No! Chicano Protest and Patriotism during the Viet Nam War Era* (Berkeley: University of California Press, 2005); Laura Pulido, *Black, Brown, Yellow and Left: Radical Activism in Los Angeles* (Berkeley: University of California Press, 2006); Cynthia A. Young, *Soul Power: Culture, Radicalism, and the Making of a U.S. Third World Left* (Durham, NC: Duke University Press, 2006).

23. Some notable examples include: Cynthia Enloe, *Maneuvers: The International Politics of Militarizing Women's Lives* (Berkeley: University of California Press, 2000); Kristin L. Hoganson, *Fighting for American Manhood: How Gender Politics Provoked the Spanish-American and Philippine-American Wars* (New Haven, CT: Yale University Press, 2000); Ian Lekus, "Queer Harvests: Homosexuality, the U.S. Left, and the Venceremos Brigades to Cuba," *Radical History Review* 89, no. 1 (2004): 57–91; Joane Nagel, *Race, Ethnicity, and Sexuality: Intimate Intersections, Forbidden Frontiers* (New York: Oxford University Press, 2003); Naoko Shibusawa, *America's Geisha Ally: Reimagining the Japanese Enemy* (Cambridge, MA: Harvard University Press, 2010); and Heather Marie Stur, *Beyond Combat: Women and Gender in the Vietnam War Era* (Cambridge: Cambridge University Press, 2011).

24. Joan Scott, "Gender: A Useful Category of Historical Analysis," *American Historical Review* 91, no. 5 (1986): 1067.

1. An African American Abroad

1. St. Clair Drake and Horace C. Cayton, *Black Metropolis: A Study of Negro Life in a Northern City* (New York: Harcourt, 1945); Maren Strange, *Bronzeville: Black Chicago in Pictures, 1941–1943* (New York: New Press, 2003).

2. Wendelle Browne, interview with author, Chicago, 21 May 2006.

3. For an earlier version of my analysis of Browne, please see Judy Tzu-Chun Wu, "An African-Vietnamese American: Robert S. Browne, the Anti-War Movement, and the Personal/Political Dimensions of Black Internationalism," *Journal of African American History* 92 (Fall 2007): 491–515.

4. Browne would return to a government position in the early 1980s. He relocated to Abidjan, the capital of the Ivory Coast, to serve as the U.S. executive director at the African Development Fund. Robert S. Browne, "Dance as if No One Is Watching: The Memoirs of Robert S. Browne" (unpublished manuscript), chap. 8, p. 1.

5. In the late 1960s and early 1970s, Browne founded the Black Economic Research Center and the Emergency Land Fund, which subsequently combined to become the Twenty-First Century Foundation, currently based in Harlem, New York. He also established the journal *Review of Black Political Economy*, which is still being published.

6. Simon Hall, *Peace and Freedom: The Civil Rights and Antiwar Movements in the 1960s* (Philadelphia: University of Pennsylvania Press, 2005); Simon Hall, *Rethinking the American Anti-War Movement* (New York: Routledge, 2012).

7. Kalamu ya Salaam, "In the Black: A Portrait of Economist Robert S. Browne," *Black Collegian* (September–October 1978): 32. Browne's comment is slightly exaggerated, since he and Bayard Rustin also crossed paths during this period.

8. James H. Meriwether, *Proudly We Can Be Africans: Black Americans and Africa, 1935–1961* (Chapel Hill: University of North Carolina Press, 2002), p. 6.

9. Ibid., p. 7.

10. In his memoirs, Browne also recounted that his family lived for five years, 1930–1935, in the predominantly white West Side of Chicago. When Browne returned to the South Side at the age of ten, he recalled, "I quickly learned that I had a bit of catching up to do in terms of acquiring some understanding of what it meant to be a Negro." Browne, "Dance as if No One Is Watching," chap. 1, p. 7.

11. Browne, "Passport Application," 15 February 1952, Department of State, FOIA Documents.

12. Robert S. Browne Papers, "Biographical Sketch," p. 1, box 1, folder 1, Schomburg Center for Research in Black Culture, Manuscripts, Archives and Rare Books Division, the New York Public Library.

13. Wendelle Browne, interview.

14. For an analysis of the significance of patronage politics among African Americans in Chicago, see Beth Tompkins Bates, *Pullman Porters and the Rise of Protest Politics in Black America, 1925–1945* (Chapel Hill: University of North Carolina Press, 2000).

15. Wendelle Browne, interview.

16. Ibid.

17. Browne, "Dance as if No One Is Watching," chap. 1, p. 9.

18. Ibid., chap. 1, pp. 9–10.

19. Ibid., chap. 3, p. 5.

20. Ibid., chap. 1, p. 10.

21. Ibid., chap. 1, p. 2.

22. Ibid., chap. 1, p. 1.

23. James N. Gregory, *The Southern Diaspora: How the Great Migrations of Black and White Southerners Transformed America* (Chapel Hill: University of North Carolina Press, 2007).

24. Wendelle Browne, interview.

25. Ibid.

26. Drake and Cayton, *Black Metropolis*, quoted in Strange, *Bronzeville*, p. xiii.

27. Drake and Cayton, *Black Metropolis*, 522.

28. Browne, "Dance as if No One Is Watching," chap. 1, p. 1.

29. Ibid.

30. Wendelle Browne, interview.

31. Ibid.

32. Ibid.

33. Browne, "Dance as if No One Is Watching," chap. 1, p. 13. Browne combined his good social skills with an entrepreneurial spirit. He delivered the *Chicago Defender*, groceries, and even the mail; he sold binoculars at Comiskey Park, shoes at a local store, and Christmas cards all year around. Wendelle recalled, "There he is working on his Christmas card deal in between . . . you know, the social life. . . . Like a good businessman he'd give you something, you know, free" to regular customers. His earnings allowed Browne to make small yet spectacular gestures of thoughtfulness. Wendelle remembered when she and two adult neighbors "dropped in" one hot summer day to socialize with the Brownes; it was "one really dismal afternoon . . . [when] all the windows were up, fan was going." In "those days people could drop in and they'd stay as long as . . . dinner." When one of the visitors prepared to leave, Browne said, " 'You're not going right away are you?' And she said, 'Robert, I should be going.' . . . [But] he said, 'Hang around,' . . . and in about twenty minutes he came back with huge rainbow ice cream cones." Wendelle Browne, interview.

34. Browne, "Dance as if No One Is Watching," chap. 1, p. 13. All the members of Browne's cohort graduated from a local public high school that was integrated because it drew students both from Bronzeville and from a predominantly white neighborhood adjacent to the community.

35. Ibid., chap. 2, p. 18. For Lorraine Hansberry's critique of the materialism exhibited by her family, particularly her mother, see Lorraine Hansberry, *To Be Young, Gifted and Black: Lorraine Hansberry in Her Own Words*, adapted by Robert Nemiroff (Englewood Cliffs, NJ: Prentice-Hall, 1969).

36. Browne, "Dance as if No One Is Watching," chap. 1, p. 6.

37. Ibid., chap. 1, p. 9.

38. Salaam, "In the Black," p. 28. The NLRA or Wagner Act provided federal protection for workers in private industry to unionize, engage in collective bargaining, and strike. However, agricultural and domestic workers were exempt from the legislation, and these two occupations tended to have heavy concentrations of African Americans.

39. Ibid., p. 28.

40. Drake and Cayton, *Black Metropolis*, pp. 516, 515.

41. Charles H. Wesley, *The History of Alpha Phi Alpha: A Development in College Life, 1906–1969* (Chicago: Foundation, 1969).

42. Browne, "Dance as if No One Is Watching," chap. 1, p. 16.

43. Ibid., chap. 1, pp. 18–19.

44. Ibid., chap. 1, p. 17.

45. Albert R. Lee, "The University of Illinois Negro Students: Data Concerning Negro Students at the State University," 25 June 1940, p. 3, Negro Matriculants List, Record Series Number: 2/9/1, box 1, University of Illinois Archives.

46. Browne completed basic training at Keesler Field, Mississippi, and was permanently stationed at Yuma Army Airfield in Arizona. He also was admitted to Officer Candidate School at Fort Knox, Kentucky, but chose not to complete his training when the war ended.

47. Browne, "Dance as if No One Is Watching," chap. 1, p. 16.

48. Michael Cullen Green, *Black Yanks in the Pacific: Race in the Making of American Military Empire after World War II* (Ithaca, NY: Cornell University Press, 2010).

49. Browne, "Dance as if No One Is Watching," chap. 1, p. 19.

50. Ibid., chap. 2, p. 3.

51. Ibid.

52. Ibid., chap. 2, p. 2.

53. Ira Katznelson, *When Affirmative Action Was White: An Untold History of Racial Inequality in Twentieth-Century America* (New York: W. W. Norton, 2005).

54. Browne, "Dance as if No One Is Watching," chap. 2, p. 4.

55. Ibid.

56. Salaam, "In the Black," p. 28; and Browne, "Background Paper for Ebony," 14 December 1972, p. 1, box 1, folder "Biographical Information," Robert S. Browne Collected Papers, Swarthmore College Peace Collection (SCPC).

57. Browne, "Dance as if No One Is Watching," chap. 1, pp. 19–20.

58. Salaam, "In the Black," p. 28.

59. Browne, "Dance as if No One Is Watching," chap. 2, p. 13.

60. Ibid.

61. Browne, "Biographical Sketch," p. 1.

62. Browne, "Dance as if No One Is Watching," chap. 2, p. 15.

63. Ibid.,

64. Arvarh E. Strickland, *History of the Chicago Urban League* (Urbana: University of Illinois Press, 1966).

65. Salaam, "In the Black," p. 28.

66. Ibid., p. 30.

67. Ibid.

68. Browne, "Dance as if No One Is Watching," chap. 2, pp. 20–22.

69. Robert S. Browne, *Race Relations in International Affairs* (Washington, DC: Public Affairs Press, 1961), pp. 1–2.

70. Salaam, "In the Black," p. 30.

71. For a discussion about the importance of the black press in fostering internationalism, see Robin J. Hayes, "'A Free Black Mind Is a Concealed Weapon': Institutions and Social Movements in the African Diaspora," in *Transnational Blackness: Navigating the Global Color Line*, ed. Manning Marable and Vanessa Agard-Jones (New York: Palgrave Macmillan, 2008), pp. 175–88.

72. Meriwether, *Proudly We Can Be Africans*, p. 7.

73. Lizabeth Cohen, *A Consumers' Republic: The Politics of Mass Consumption in Postwar America* (New York: Vintage, 2003).

74. Browne, "Dance as if No One Is Watching," chap. 2, p. 1.

75. Christopher Endy, *Cold War Holidays: American Tourism in France* (Chapel Hill: University of North Carolina Press, 2004).

76. For critiques of how Cold War politics shaped these academic fields, see Frederick Cooper and Randall Packard, eds., *International Development and the Social Sciences: Essays on the*

History and Politics of Knowledge (Berkeley: University of California Press, 1999); and Bruce Cumings, *Parallax Visions: Making Sense of American–East Asian Relations at the End of the Century* (Chapel Hill: University of North Carolina Press, 1999).

77. Endy, *Cold War Holidays*, p. 35.

78. See Thomas Borstelmann, *The Cold War and the Color Line: American Race Relations in the Global Arena* (Cambridge, MA: Harvard University Press, 2001); Mary L. Dudziak, *Cold War Civil Rights: Race and the Image of American Democracy* (Princeton, NJ: Princeton University Press, 2000); Brenda Gayle Plummer, *Rising Wind: Black Americans and U.S. Foreign Affairs, 1935–1960* (Chapel Hill: University of North Carolina Press, 1996); Penny M. Von Eschen, *Race against Empire: Black Americans and Anticolonialism, 1937–1957* (Ithaca, NY: Cornell University Press, 1997); and Penny M. Von Eschen, *Satchmo Blows Up the World: Jazz Ambassadors Play the Cold War* (Cambridge, MA: Harvard University Press, 2004).

79. Kenneth Osgood, *Total Cold War: Eisenhower's Secret Propaganda Battle at Home and Abroad* (Lawrence: University of Kansas Press, 2006).

80. Browne, "Dance as if No One Is Watching," chap. 2, p. 24.

81. Ibid., chap. 2, pp. 24–25.

82. Ibid., chap. 2, p. 25.

83. *Kent v. Dulles* 357 U.S. 116 (1958).

84. Carol Anderson, *Eyes off the Prize: The United Nations and the African American Struggle for Human Rights, 1944–1955* (Cambridge: Cambridge University Press, 2003); Dudziak, *Cold War Civil Rights*; Meriwether, *Proudly We Can Be Africans*; Plummer, *Rising Wind*; Von Eschen, *Race against Empire*.

85. Browne, "Dance as if No One Is Watching," chap. 3, p. 1.

86. Endy, *Cold War Holidays*, pp. 7, 128. Partly inspired by the release of the film *An American in Paris* in 1951, nearly four hundred thousand Americans visited in 1953, and the number would double by the end of the decade.

87. Browne, "Dance as if No One Is Watching," chap. 3, p. 7.

88. Ibid., chap. 3, p. 4.

89. Browne, "Application for Federal Employment," 30 May 1955, United States International Cooperation Administration, National Personnel Records Center, St. Louis, Missouri.

90. Browne, "Dance as if No One Is Watching," chap. 3, p. 8.

91. Ibid., chap. 3, p. 7.

92. Ibid.

93. Ibid., chap. 3, p. 6. Browne's portrayal of Wright resonates with biographical depictions of the author. Michel Farber describes Wright during the early 1950s as having "a well-established group of friends, admirers and literary acquaintances"; while Wright "avoided formal gatherings . . . he adored discussing politics and literature with Blacks of all nationalities . . . in . . . his regular cafes." Michel Fabre, *The Unfinished Quest of Richard Wright*, trans. Isabel Barzun (Urbana: University of Illinois Press, 1993), p. 382.

94. Browne, "Dance as if No One Is Watching," chap. 3, p. 5.

95. Ibid., chap. 3, p. 10.

96. Browne, *Race Relations in International Affairs*, p. 2.

97. Browne, "Dance as if No One Is Watching," chap. 3, p. 7.

98. Browne, *Race Relations in International Affairs*, p. 2.

99. Browne, "Dance as if No One Is Watching," chap. 3, p. 40.

100. Ibid., chap. 3, p. 42.

101. Ibid., chap. 3, p. 43.

102. Ibid., chap. 3, p. 45.

103. Quoted in Scott Laderman, *Tours of Vietnam: War, Travel Guides, and Memory* (Durham, NC: Duke University Press, 2009), p. 66.

104. Browne, *Race Relations in International Affairs*, p. 2.

105. Ibid., chap. 3, p. 55.

106. Ibid.

107. Ibid., chap. 3, p. 69.

108. Browne, "Background Paper for Ebony," p. 2.

109. "Charter of the United Nations," chap. 1, 26 June 1945, www.un.org/en/documents /charter/chapter1.shtml.

110. Browne, "Dance as if No One Is Watching," chap. 4, p. 3.

111. Ibid.

112. Anderson, *Eyes off the Prize*.

113. Browne, "Dance as if No One Is Watching," chap. 4, p. 3.

114. Ibid., chap. 4, p. 4.

115. Browne, "Biographical Sketch," p. 2.

116. Browne, "Dance as if No One Is Watching," chap. 4, pp. 5–6.

117. Cora Weiss and Peter Weiss, interview with author, New York City, 9 April 2006.

118. Browne, "Dance as if No One Is Watching," chap. 4, p. 10.

119. Ibid., chap. 4, p. 11.

120. Browne, "Application for Federal Employment."

121. Browne, "Dance as if No One Is Watching," chap. 4, p. 11; Browne, "Biographical Sketch," pp. 1–2; Salaam, "In the Black," p. 30.

122. Michael L. Krenn, *Black Diplomacy: African Americans and the State Department, 1945– 1969* (Armonk, NY: M. E. Sharpe, 1999).

2. Afro-Asian Alliances

1. Browne, "Dance as if No One Is Watching," chap 4, p. 16.

2. Ibid., chap. 4, p. 12.

3. The scholarship on the Vietnam War is vast. For a sample, see Mark Philip Bradley, *Vietnam at War* (New York: Oxford University Press, 2009); Stanley Karnow, *Vietnam: A History* (New York: Penguin, 1983).

4. Bill V. Mullen and Cathryn Watson, *W.E.B. DuBois on Asia: Crossing the World Color Line* (Jackson: University Press of Mississippi, 2005), p. viii.

5. Marc Gallicchio, *The African American Encounter with Japan and China: Black Internationalism in Asia, 1895–1945* (Chapel Hill: University of North Carolina Press, 2000); Gerald Horne, *Black and Red: W.E.B. DuBois and the Afro-American Response to the Cold War, 1944–1963* (Albany: State University of New York Press, 1986); Reginald Kearney, *African American Views of the Japanese: Solidarity or Sedition?* (Albany: State University of New York Press, 1998); Yuichiro Onishi, *Moving in a Racial Groove: How Afro-Asian Solidarity was Found in Black America, Japan, and Okinawa* (New York: New York University Press, 2013); Slate, *Colored Cosmopolitanism*.

6. Mullen, *Afro-Orientalism*. Also see Jun, *Race for Citizenship*.

7. Ibid., p. xiv.

8. Kim, "The Racial Triangulation of Asian Americans."

9. Browne, untitled speech beginning, "I wrote of Indo-China more in sorrow than in anger," box 1, folder "Writings/Speeches/Statements," Browne Collected Papers, SCPC.

10. William J. Duiker, *Ho Chi Minh* (New York: Hyperion, 2000).

11. Quoted in Bradley, *Vietnam at War*, p. 9.

12. Quoted in David G. Marr, *Vietnam, 1945: A Quest for Power* (Berkeley: University of California Press, 2005), p. 263.

13. Mark Atwood Lawrence, *Assuming the Burden: Europe and the American Commitment to War in Vietnam* (Berkeley: University of California Press, 2005).

14. Seth Jacobs, *America's Miracle Man in Vietnam: Ngo Dinh Diem, Religion, Race, and U.S. Intervention in Southeast Asia* (Durham, NC: Duke University Press, 2004).

15. The literature on the postwar decolonization movement in Southeast Asia and the Bandung Conference is large. For a selection, see David Chandler, *The Tragedy of Cambodian History: Politics, War, and Revolution since 1945* (New Haven, CT: Yale University Press, 1991); Matthew Jones, "A 'Segregated' Asia? Race, the Bandung Conference, and Pan-Asianist Fears in American Thought and Policy, 1954–1955," *Diplomatic History* 29, no. 5 (2005): 841–68; Jason Parker, "Cold War II: The Eisenhower Administration, the Bandung Conference, and the Reperiodization of the Postwar Era," *Diplomatic History* 30, no. 5 (2006): 867–92; Robert D. Schulzinger, *A Time for War: The United States and Vietnam, 1941–1975* (New York: Oxford University Press, 1995); Azza Salama Layton, *International Politics and Civil Rights Policies in the United States, 1941–1960* (New York: Cambridge University Press, 2000); Plummer, *Rising Wind*; Brenda Gayle Plummer, ed., *Window on Freedom: Race, Civil Rights, and Foreign Affairs, 1945–1988* (Chapel Hill: University of North Carolina Press, 2003); Odd Arne Westad, *The Global Cold War: Third World Interventions and the Making of Our Times* (New York: Cambridge University Press, 2005); Richard Wright, *The Color Curtain: A Report on the Bandung Conference* (Cleveland: World Publishing, 1956).

16. Von Eschen, *Race against Empire*.

17. Browne, *Race Relations in International Affairs*, p. 53.

18. Browne, "Dance as if No One Is Watching," chap. 4, p. 12.

19. Ibid., chap. 4, p. 13.

20. Ibid., chap. 4, p. 15.

21. Said, *Orientalism*.

22. Robert McClintock, Foreign Service Despatch No. 114 from Embassy, Phnom Penh to the Department of State, Washington, 25 September 1956, Record Group 469, E. 1115 box 4, folder "Limited Distribution, 1956," NARA, College Park, MD.

23. Browne, "Dance as if No One Is Watching," chap. 4, p. 18.

24. "Report on AID Programs in Cambodia," November 1956, Record Group 469 E. 1115 box 6, folder "Reports—General 1956."

25. "Special Study Group Report on Cambodia," p. 7, Record Group 469 E. 1115, box 6, folder "Study Group, 1956."

26. Browne, "Dance as if No One Is Watching," chap. 4, p. 15.

27. Ibid.

28. Chandler, *The Tragedy of Cambodian History*, p. 86.

29. McClintock, Foreign Service Despatch No. 114, p. 7.

30. Chandler, *The Tragedy of Cambodian History*, p. 86.

31. McClintock, Foreign Service Despatch No. 114, p. 8.

32. For a study of how African American military personnel were positioned in relation to the U.S. state and its global mission, see Green, *Black Yanks in the Pacific*.

33. The dates of Browne's promotions and transfer to Vietnam are from his ICA personnel file.

34. Milton Esman, telephone interview with author, Ithaca, NY, 26 October 2005. All the quotes attributed to Esman derive from this interview and are based on my notes from the session.

35. For a more critical view of race relations and practices, see Krenn, *Black Diplomacy*.

36. William J. Lederer and Eugene Burdick, *The Ugly American* (New York: W. W. Norton, 1958).

37. Elbridge Durbrow, letter to Eric Kocher, 18 December 1958; Elbridge Durbrow, memo to Secretary Robertson, 3 January 1959; and Arthur Z. Gardiner, letter to Raymond T. Moyer, 17 December 1958, Record Group 84 E. 3340 B box 2, folder "Economic Matters 1956–58."

38. Browne, *Race Relations in International Affairs*, 3. Browne goes on to say, "I don't adhere to the belief that going abroad necessarily transforms people in any perceptible way, although it certainly does appear to have a liberalizing effect on many of them. There is, however, a degree of subjective selectivity operating in the recruitment of personnel who go abroad to work; a high percentage of them tend to be more broad minded and more adaptable than their stay-at-home countrymen."

39. Ed Smith, interview with author, Honolulu, HI, 25 April 2009.

40. Kathleen Cleaver, interview with author, New Haven, CT, 22 February 2006.

41. Satoshi Nakano, "South to South across the Pacific: Ernest E. Neal and Community Development Efforts in the American South and the Philippines," *Japanese Journal of American Studies* 16 (2005): 181–202. I thank Kathleen Cleaver and Augusto Espiritu for bringing the work of Prof. Satoshi Nakano to my attention.

42. Despite the greater opportunities for racial mixing abroad, Cleaver recalled that her experiences of growing up in Asia and witnessing the development of newly independent nations did not necessarily lead her to promote integration in the United States but rather advanced her support for black nationalism. As she stated, "I lived in India in the '50s after the British had gone, and lived in the Philippines after the Americans had gone. So it was very clear to me that Brown people, colonized people, could run their own country; they don't really need white supremacy; they don't really need white government. So it was obvious to me that Black people in the United States don't need to be controlled by white people. They're perfectly capable of running their own lives, running their own schools, running their own states, running their own cities. So it kind of repudiated [white supremacy] completely, blew it away." Aaron Shuman, "A Sit-Down with Kathleen Cleaver," *Bad Subjects* 60 (April 2002).

43. Browne Papers, "Biographical Sketch," p. 2, box 1, folder 1, Schomburg.

44. Browne, *Race Relations in International Affairs*, p. 49.

45. Browne, "Dance as if No One Is Watching," chap. 4, pp. 15–16.

46. Ibid., chap. 4, p. 16.

47. Ibid., chap. 4, p. 20.

48. Ibid., chap. 4, p. 16.

49. Ibid., chap. 4, p. 21.

50. Ibid.

51. Ibid.

52. These critiques were articulated by members of USOM in both Cambodia and Vietnam during this time period.

53. Browne, "Dance as if No One Is Watching," chap. 4, p. 20.

54. Ibid., chap. 4, pp. 21–22.

55. Browne Papers, "Resume," box 1, folder 1, Schomburg. There are several résumés in the Browne papers. This one appears to have been written right after Browne's return to the United States in 1961.

56. Browne, "Dance as if No One Is Watching," chap. 4, p. 37.

57. "Far East Regional Data Book," 7 March 1956, Record Group 469 E. 1115 box 6, folder "Reports—General 1956."

58. "ICA Personnel Strength," 31 August 1955, Record Group 469 E. 1113 box 7, folder "Personnel—General 1955." In August 1955, the number of ICA employees in Cambodia was thirty-one and in Vietnam was 142.

59. "FY 1955 Funds for Allocations, Allotments, and Obligations, by Region and Type of Assistance," 15 June 1955, Record Group 59, E 1113, box 5, folder "Funds." For the fiscal year from June 1954 through March 1955, the aid allotment to Cambodia was 32.6 million while Vietnam's allotment was 293.5 million.

60. Seth Jacobs, " 'No Place to Fight a War': Laos and the Evolution of U.S. Policy toward Viet Nam, 1954–1963," in *Making Sense of the Vietnam Wars: Local, National, and Transnational*

Perspectives, ed. Mark Philip Bradley and Marilyn B. Young (New York: Oxford University Press, 2008), pp. 45–66.

61. Browne, "Dance as if No One Is Watching," chap. 4, p. 39.

62. Ibid.

63. Ibid., chap. 4, p. 38.

64. D. Bosley Brotman, letter to Gerald Windfield and Wallace Gade, 28 June 1956, Record Group 469 E. 1115 box 4, folder "Personnel—General—1956."

65. Hoa Browne, conversation with author, New York City, 3 May 2005.

66. Houi Browne and Hoa Browne, conversation with author, Teaneck, NJ, 1 December 2006.

67. For a study of how American understandings of race are exported and integrated within Asian countries, in this case South Korea, see Nadia Y. Kim, *Imperial Citizens: Koreans and Race from Seoul to L.A.* (Stanford, CA: Stanford University Press, 2008).

68. Browne, "Dance as if No One Is Watching," chap. 4, p. 41.

69. Ibid., chap. 4, p. 42.

70. Esman, telephone interview.

71. For a study on how American military families are expected to serve as international role models, see Donna Alvah, *Unofficial Ambassadors: American Military Families Overseas and the Cold War* (New York: New York University Press, 2007).

72. Edward Guinane, memo, 24 September 1959, and Arthur Gardiner, memo, 7 October 1959, Record Group 469 E. 430 box 44, folder "Vietnam—Security-Inspection."

73. L. Metcalfe Walling, "Memorandum on Reckless Driving of USOM Vehicles," 20 December 1956, Record Group 469, E. 1113, box 15, folder "Subject—Personnel, General 1956."

74. Maria Höhn and Seungsook Moon, eds., *Over There: Living with the U.S. Military Empire from World War Two to the Present* (Durham, NC: Duke University Press, 2010); and Susan Zeiger, *Entangling Alliances: Foreign War Brides and American Soldiers in the Twentieth Century* (New York: New York University Press, 2010).

75. "Official Mission Post Report, Phnom Penh," p. 4, Record Group 469 E. 1113, box 7, folder "Subject—Personnel Post Reports 1955."

76. Cynthia Enloe, *Bananas, Beaches, and Bases: Making Feminist Sense of International Politics* (London: Pandora, 1989); Katharine H. S. Moon, *Sex Among Allies: Military Prostitution in U.S.-Korea Relations* (New York: Columbia University Press, 1997); and Ji-Yeon Yuh, *Beyond the Shadow of Camptown: Korean Military Brides in America* (New York: New York University Press, 2002).

77. Nagel, *Race, Ethnicity, and Sexuality*, p. 191.

78. Laderman, *Tours of Vietnam*, pp. 33–35.

79. Smith, interview.

80. Browne, "Biographical Sketch," p. 2.

81. Browne, "Health Benefits Registration Form," ICA Personnel File.

82. For a discussion of the obstacles experienced by U.S. military personnel who wanted to marry Asian women, see Green, *Black Yanks in the Pacific*.

83. J. J. Riley, "Memorandum Regarding Robert S. Browne," 23 December 1960, Record Group 469 E. 430 box 58, folder "Vietnam—Personnel."

84. Esman, telephone interview.

85. Freeman Smith, "Memo," 29 March 1960, Record Group 469 E. 430, box 58, folder "Marriage."

86. Jacobs, *America's Miracle Man in Vietnam*.

87. Browne, "Dance as if No One Is Watching," chap. 4, p. 44.

88. "USOM Comments on Evaluation of Vietnam Program," 24 January 1958, p. 1, Record Group 469 E 430 box 41, folder "Vietnam—Program Evaluations."

89. Ibid., p. 6.

90. Browne, "Dance as if No One Is Watching," chap. 4, pp. 49–50.

91. Ibid., chap. 4, p. 50.

92. Robert S. Browne to A. Z. Gardiner, 8 August 1960, ICA Personnel File.

93. For a discussion of African American soldiers' decision making regarding interracial relationships with Asian women, see Green, *Black Yanks in the Pacific*.

3. Searching for Home and Peace

1. Hall, *Peace and Freedom*.

2. Hall, *Rethinking the American Anti-War Movement*; Daryl J. Maeda, *Rethinking the Asian American Movement* (New York: Routledge, 2012).

3. Jane Naomi Iwamura, *Virtual Orientalism* (Oxford: Oxford University Press, 2011).

4. Ibid., p. 6.

5. Ronald Takaki, *Strangers from a Different Shore: A History of Asian Americans*, rev. and updated ed. (Boston: Little, Brown, 1998).

6. Browne, *Race Relations in International Affairs*, p. 56.

7. Takaki, *Strangers from a Different Shore*, p. 448.

8. Wendelle Browne, interview.

9. Green, *Black Yanks in the Pacific*.

10. Charlotte Brooks, "In the Twilight Zone between Black and White: Japanese American Resettlement and Community in Chicago, 1942–1945," *Journal of American History* 86, no. 4 (2000): 1655–87, and Matthew M. Briones, *Jim and Jap Crow: A Cultural History of 1940s Interracial America* (Princeton, N.J.: Princeton University Press, 2012).

11. Wendelle Browne, interview.

12. Ibid.

13. Browne, "Dance as if No One Is Watching," chap. 5, p. 2.

14. Ibid., chap. 5, pp. 1–2.

15. Yuh, *Beyond the Shadow of Camptown*; and Green, *Black Yanks in the Pacific*.

16. Nora Kerr, "Vietnam's Closer to Their Hearth," *Sunday Record*, 8 February 1970.

17. Ibid.

18. Wendelle Browne, interview.

19. Ibid.

20. Ibid.

21. Browne, "Letter to the Honorable Attorney General of the United States," 24 January 1963, box 1, folder 4, Browne Papers, Schomburg.

22. Ibid.

23. Salaam, "In the Black," p. 32.

24. Ibid.

25. Browne, *Race Relations in International Affairs*, p. 7.

26. Browne to *New York Times* editor, 3 October 1961 and 22 October 1962, box 20, folder 1, Browne Papers, Schomburg.

27. Browne to *NYT*, 15 February 1962, box 20, folder 1, Browne Papers, Schomburg; Robert S. Browne, "FDU Prof. Visits Vietnam," *Tarrevir*, 25 October 1967, p. 3.

28. Browne to *NYT*, 23 March 1964, box 20, folder 2, Browne Papers, Schomburg.

29. Ibid.

30. Browne to *NYT*, 3 October 1961, box 20, folder 2, Browne Papers, Schomburg.

31. Browne to *NYT*, 6 February 1962, box 20, folder 1, Browne Papers, Schomburg.

32. See Borstelmann, *The Cold War and the Color Line*; Dudziak, *Cold War Civil Rights*; Plummer, *Rising Wind*; Von Eschen, *Race against Empire*; Von Eschen, *Satchmo Blows Up the World*.

33. Martin Luther King Jr., "Beyond Vietnam: A Time to Break Silence," The King Center, 4 April 1967, www.thekingcenter.org/archive/document/beyond-vietnam.

34. Alfred Hassler to Mildred Olmsted, 28 May 1965, Series II, G, box 9, folder "Trips to South Vietnam, Clergymen's Visit to Vietnam, 1965, Correspondence: Preparations," Fellowship of Reconciliation Records (FOR) (DG 013), SCPC, Swarthmore, PA. Coretta Scott King appeared frequently as a substitute for her husband in the peace movement. For more information about the goals and experiences of the 1965 delegation, see Hershberger, *Traveling to Vietnam*, pp. 15–21.

35. Bob Browne to Al Hassler, 18 June 1965, Series II, G, box 9, folder "Trips to South Vietnam, Clergymen's Visit to Viet Nam, 1965, Correspondence, Preparations," FOR.

36. Robert S. Browne, "The Freedom Movement and the War in Vietnam," in *Vietnam and Black America: An Anthology of Protest and Resistance*, ed. Clyde Taylor (Garden City, NY: Anchor Press, 1973), p. 61. Originally published in *Freedomways* 5, no. 4 (1965).

37. Ibid.

38. Ibid., p. 75.

39. Green, *Black Yanks in the Pacific*.

40. James E. Westheider, *Fighting on Two Fronts: African Americans and the Vietnam War* (New York: New York University Press, 1997); James E. Westheider, *The African American Experience in Vietnam: Brothers in Arms* (Lanham, MD: Rowman and Littlefield, 2008).

41. Robert S. Browne, "The Black Man and the War in Vietnam," *Newsletter*, Coordinating Committee of Black Organizations against the Draft, no. 1 (April 1967): 5. Over the course of the U.S. war in Vietnam, over 2.5 million Americans served in the military, and three hundred thousand of them were black (Westheider, *The African American Experience in Vietnam*, p. xix). In response to critiques of racial overrepresentation, black death rates declined from "more than 20 percent of American combat deaths, about twice their portion of the U.S. population," to "12.5 percent" for the entire war. Christian G. Appy, *Working-Class War: American Combat Soldiers and Vietnam* (Chapel Hill: University of North Carolina Press, 1993), p. 20, quoted in Natalie Kimbrough, *Equality or Discrimination? African Americans in the U.S. Military during the Vietnam War* (Lanham, MD: University Press of America, 2007), p. 81.

42. For more information about these elections, see Brigham, *Guerrilla Diplomacy*, p. 70.

43. Peter Arnett, "Major Describes Move," *New York Times*, 8 February 1968.

44. For more about these military strategies and how American travelers documented their impact, see Hershberger, *Traveling to Vietnam*.

45. Ibid., p. 104.

46. Bradley, *Vietnam at War*, p. 118.

47. Report, 22 August 1967, box 8, folder 12, Browne Papers, Schomburg.

48. "Uncle Sam Needs YOU Nigger," box 20, folder 15, Browne Papers, Schomburg.

49. Browne, Letter to the Director of the Passport Office, 28 July 1966, Passport Application File, Department of State, FOIA materials.

50. Director, Passport Office, letter to Robert S. Browne, 3 October 1966, Passport Application File, Department of State.

51. Browne, "The Black Man and the War in Vietnam," p. 5.

52. Ibid., p. 4.

53. Vincent Harding, "To the Gallant Black Men Now Dead," box 20, folder 14, Browne Papers, Schomburg.

54. Salaam, "In the Black," p. 32.

55. Browne, "Address at the Forum 'Vietnam Aflame: What Are the Issues,'" Community Church, New York City, 30 June 1963, p. 1, box 1, folder "Writings/Speeches/Statements," Browne Collected Papers, SCPC.

56. Ibid., p. 2.

57. Ibid., p. 1.

58. Ibid., p. 2.

59. Robert S. Browne, letter to Captain John R. Spey, 6 November 1964, p. 3, box 1, folder "Correspondence 1964," Browne Collected Papers, SCPC.

60. Ibid.

61. Bill to Bob Browne, 24 September 1966, box 2, folder "Correspondence 1966 (Jan.–May)," Browne Collected Papers, SCPC.

62. Hoa Browne indicates that the designation "Vietnamese" may also reflect the personal identity of her mother, who spoke Vietnamese and was given her mother's last name. Hoa Browne, conversation with author.

63. In contrast, Hoa became involved with antiwar activities and also enjoyed the attentions that she received as public consciousness about Vietnam increased.

64. Interestingly, the invitation was issued by Mary "Yuri" Kochiyama, the veteran Asian American activist who was based in Harlem. She did apologize for not knowing Huoi's name before the flyer was printed.

65. Hilda Osborne to Mrs. Browne, 28 February 1967, box 2, folder "Correspondence 1967 (Jan.–May)," Browne Collected Papers, SCPC.

66. Mary E. Macy to Robert S. Browne, 27 January 1965, box 1, folder "Correspondence 1965 (January–May)," Browne Collected Papers, SCPC.

67. Klein, *Cold War Orientalism*.

68. Browne, untitled speech, box 1, folder "Writings/Speeches/Statements," Browne Collected Papers, SCPC.

69. Browne, untitled statement, 26 October 1972, p. 5, box 20, folder 9, Browne Papers, Schomburg. The statement begins, "In 1962, a few months after returning to the U.S."

70. Robert S. Browne to John A. Schneider, 2 March 1965, box 1, folder "Correspondence 1965 (January–May), Browne Collected Papers, SCPC.

71. Robert H. King, *Thomas Merton and Thich Nhat Hanh: Engaged Spirituality in an Age of Globalization* (New York: Continuum, 2001), pp. 72–77.

72. Browne, unpublished manuscript on Vietnam, chap. 4, p. 5, box 20, folder 3, Browne Papers, Schomburg.

73. Robert J. Topmiller, *The Lotus Unleashed: The Buddhist Peace Movement in South Vietnam, 1964–1966* (Lexington: University of Kentucky Press, 2006).

74. Robert S. Browne to William Vanden Heuvel, 18 July 1936, box 1, folder "Correspondence 1962–1963," Browne Collected Papers, SCPC.

75. Nathan B. Lenvin on behalf of J. Walter Yeagley, letter to Robert S. Browne, 24 May 1967, box 2, folder "Efforts Re: Visit of Thich Nhat Hanh (Buddhist Monk), 1966," Browne Collected Papers, SCPC.

76. Robert S. Browne, letter to Roy Bennett, 9 September 1963, box 1, folder "Correspondence, 1962–1963," Browne Collected Papers, SCPC.

77. Robert S. Brown, letter to Bao, 21 June 1966, box 2, folder "Effort Re: Visit of Thich Nhat Hanh, 1966," Browne Collected Papers, SCPC.

78. For a historical overview of the FOR, see "Fellowship of Reconciliation: Historical Introduction," SCPC, http://swarthmore.edu/Library/peace/DG001-025/DG013/dg13for histintro.htm.

79. Robert S. Browne to Martin Luther King Jr., 9 April 1966, box 2, folder "Efforts Re: Visit of Thich Nhat Hanh (Buddhist Monk), 1966," Browne Collected Papers, SCPC; Robert S. Browne to Tran Quang Thuan, 15 April 1966, box 2, folder "Correspondence 1966 (Jan.–April), Browne Collected Papers, SCPC.

80. Martin Luther King Jr., letter to Nobel Institute, 25 January 1967, The King Center, www.thekingcenter.org/archive/document/letter-mlk-nobel-institute.

81. Hershberger, *Traveling to Vietnam*, pp. 20–21, 61–63.

82. "The Third Solution: A Neutral Coalition," *Vietnam: Matters for the Agenda* (Santa Barbara, CA: Center for the Study of Democratic Institutions) 1, no. 4 (1968): 7.

83. Ibid.

84. Thich Nhat Hanh, *Vietnam: Lotus in a Sea of Fire* (New York: Hill and Wang, 1967), p. 83.

85. Alfred Hassler, interoffice memorandum to Ray Gould, 6 October 1966, G-6, box 17, folder "Far East, November–December, 1966," FOR.

86. Ibid.

87. Alfred Hassler to Thich Nhat Hanh, 14 November 1966, p. 4, G-6, box 16, folder "Correspondence with Hassler," FOR.

88. Ibid.

89. Nhat Hanh to Al Hassler, 22 November 1966, G-6, box 16, folder "Correspondence with Hassler," FOR.

90. Alfred Hassler to Nhat Hanh, 23 June 1967, G-6, box 16, folder "Correspondence with Hassler," FOR. For more information about the collaboration between Browne and Dinh, see box 3, Folder "Involvement with Buddhist Socialist Bloc," Browne Collected Papers, SCPC.

91. Nhat Hanh to Al Hassler, 30 June 1967, G-6, box 16, folder "Correspondence with Hassler," FOR.

92. "People of the Fellowship: Alfred Hassler," International Fellowship of Reconciliation, www.ifor.org/fellowship%20people.htm; and Alfred Hassler, *Diary of a Self-Made Convict* (London: Victor Gollancz, 1955).

93. Lee, *Orientals*; Gary Okihiro, *Margins and Mainstreams: Asians in American History and Culture* (Seattle: University of Washington Press, 1994); Jennifer Ting, "Bachelor Society: Deviant Heterosexuality and Asian American Historiography," in *Privileging Positions: The Sites of Asian American Studies*, ed. Gary Y. Okihiro, Marilyn Alquizola, Dorothy Fugita Rony, and K. Scott Wong (Pullman: Washington State University Press, 1995), pp. 271–80.

94. Swerdlow, *Women Strike for Peace*; and Judy Tzu-Chun Wu, "Rethinking Global Sisterhood: Peace Activism and Women's Orientalism," in *No Permanent Waves: Recasting Histories of U.S. Feminism*, ed. Nancy Hewitt (New Brunswick, NJ: Rutgers University Press, 2010), pp. 193–220.

95. Bob Browne to Al Hassler, 6 June 1966, G-6, box 17, folder "Speaking Tours, May–June 1966," FOR.

96. Robert Elliot Fox, "About Ishmael Reed's Life and Work," in *The Oxford Companion to African American Literature*, ed. William L. Andrews, Francis Smith Foster, and Trudier Harris (New York: Oxford University Press, 1997), www.english.illinois.edu/maps/poets/m_r/reed /about.htm; and Kaluma ya Salaam, "Historical Overviews of the Black Arts Movement," in *The Oxford Companion to African American Literature*, ed. William L. Andrews, Francis Smith Foster, and Trudier Harris (New York: Oxford University Press, 1997), www.english.illinois. edu/maps/blackarts/historical.htm.

97. Jeffrey O. G. Ogbar, *Black Power: Radical Politics and African American Identity* (Baltimore, MD: Johns Hopkins University Press, 1994).

98. Alfred Hassler, "Notes of Trip with Nhat Hanh," 14 June 1966, Section II, Series C, box 6, folder "Travels in Europe with Nhat Hanh, Vietnamese Monk, June–September 1966," FOR. The same episode appears in the opening of Hanh, *Vietnam*.

99. The NLF was dominated by Vietnamese communists but also included noncommunists who supported the cause of national self-determination. When the NLF was first founded, it emphasized its goal of neutrality in the Cold War to argue for the need for political self-determination. As Robert Brigham points out, this call for neutrality generated both international recognition and American suspicion. Brigham, *Guerrilla Diplomacy*, pp. 19–39.

100. "The Third Solution," p. 11.

101. Robert S. Browne to Alfred Hassler, 30 June 1966, box 2, folder "Efforts Re: Visited Thich Nhat Hanh (Buddhist Monk), 1966," Browne Collected Papers, SCPC.

102. Robert Comstock, "Peace Candidate Browne Quits Senate Race," *The Record*, 29 September 1966, box 18, folder 4, clipping in Browne Papers, Schomburg.

103. "Democratic Unit Backs Frost for Senate," *The Record*, box 18, folder 4, clipping in Browne Papers, Schomburg.

104. Ibid.

105. Browne, "The Freedom Movement and the War in Vietnam," p. 67.

106. Ibid., p. 73.

107. Browne, "Dance as if No One Is Watching," chap. 5, p. 32.

108. Maeda, "Black Panthers, Red Guards, and Chinamen."

109. Tran Van Dinh to Robert S. Browne, 11 May 1967, box 3, folder "Involvement with Buddhist Socialist Bloc in Vietnam, 1967," Browne Collected Papers, SCPC.

110. Sucheng Chan, *Asian Americans: An Interpretive History* (Boston: Twayne, 1991); and William Wei, *The Asian American Movement* (Philadelphia: Temple University Press, 1993).

111. Diane Fujino, *Heartbeat of Struggle: The Revolutionary Life of Yuri Kochiyama* (Minneapolis: University of Minnesota Press, 2005); Diane Fujino, "Who Studies the Asian American Movement? A Historiographical Analysis," *Journal of Asian American Studies* 11, no. 2 (2008): 127–69; and Diane Fujino, *Samurai among Panthers: Richard Aoki on Race, Resistance, and a Paradoxical Life* (Minneapolis: University of Minnesota Press, 2012); Maeda, *Chains of Babylon*; and Maeda, *Rethinking the Asian American Movement*.

4. Anticitizens, Red Diaper Babies, and Model Minorities

1. Originally self-published in a chapbook series in 1984 and reproduced in Eldridge Cleaver, *Target Zero: A Life in Writing*, ed. Kathleen Cleaver (New York: Palgrave Macmillan, 2006), p. 225.

2. Although there were no congressional restrictions against such travel, the State Department decreed that U.S. passports were not valid for travel to select countries. China was placed on the banned list in 1952, and North Korea and North Vietnam were included in 1955. Hershberger, *Traveling to Vietnam*, pp. 32, 33.

3. The official name for the group was the "United States Peoples' Anti-Imperialist Delegation." Clyde H. Farnsworth, "Black Panthers Open Office in Algiers," *New York Times*, 14 September 1970, p. 2; and Ann Froines, "Know Your Enemy," *Liberation* 15, no. 9 (1970), p. 20.

4. "People of the World Unite: An Interview with Alex Hing and Pat Sumi," *Getting Together* 1, no. 5 (September–October 1970): 11.

5. Hershberger, *Traveling to Vietnam*, p. xv.

6. Cora Weiss and Dave Dellinger established a regular mail service for POWs and their family members and arranged monthly trips to Hanoi to facilitate the communication. See their interviews in James W. Clinton, "Cora Weiss," in *The Loyal Opposition,* pp. 25–61, 165–82; Hershberger, *Traveling to Vietnam*; and Cora Weiss, interviews with author, New York, 7–8 April 2006.

7. Clinton, "Cora Weiss"; and Swerdlow, *Women Strike for Peace*.

8. Hall, *Rethinking the American Anti-War Movement*, pp. 42, 114.

9. Mitchell B. Lerner, *The Pueblo Incident: A Spy Ship and the Failure of American Foreign Policy* (Lawrence: University Press of Kansas, 2002).

10. "People of the World Unite," p. 12.

11. Clinton, "Cora Weiss," p. xi.

12. Hershberger, *Traveling to Vietnam,* p. 67.

13. Ibid., p. xvii.

14. Elbaum, *Revolution in the Air*; Pulido, *Black, Brown, Yellow and Left*.

15. Dudziak, *Cold War Civil Rights*; Sudarshan Kapur, *Rising Up a Prophet: The African American Encounter with Gandhi* (Boston: Beacon, 1992); Robin D. G. Kelley, *Freedom Dreams: The Black*

Radical Imagination (Boston: Beacon, 2002); Robin D. G. Kelly and Betsy Esch, "Black Like Mao: Red China and Black Revolution," *Souls* (Fall 1999): 6–41; Minkah Makalani, *In the Cause of Freedom: Radical Black Internationalism from Harlem to London, 1917–1939* (Chapel Hill: University of North Carolina Press, 2011); Ogbar, *Black Power*; Plummer, *Rising Wind*; Nikhil Pal Singh, *Black Is a Country: Race and the Unfinished Struggle for Democracy* (Cambridge, MA: Harvard University Press, 2004); Slate, *Colored Cosmopolitanism*; Timothy B. Tyson, *Radio Free Dixie: Robert F. Williams and the Roots of Black Power* (Chapel Hill: University of North Carolina Press, 1999); Von Eschen, *Race against Empire*; Von Eschen, *Satchmo Blows Up the World*.

16. For a wonderful analysis of Eldridge Cleaver's political orientation toward socialist Asia, see Sean Malloy, "Uptight in Babylon: Eldridge Cleaver's Cold War," *Diplomatic History* (forthcoming). Also see Mullen, *Afro-Orientalism*.

17. Pulido, *Black, Brown, Yellow and Left*. Also see Fujino, *Heartbeat of Struggle*; Fujino, "Who Studies the Asian American Movement?"; and Fujino, *Samurai among Panthers*; Maeda, "Black Panthers, Red Guards, and Chinamen"; Maeda, *Chains of Babylon*; Vijay Prashad, *Everybody Was Kung Fu Fighting: Afro-Asian Connections and the Myth of Cultural Purity* (Boston: Beacon, 2001).

18. "Success Story of One Minority Group in U.S.," *U.S. News and World Report*, 26 December 1966, reprinted in *Roots: An Asian American Reader*, ed. Amy Tachiki, Eddie Wong, Franklin Odo, and Buck Wong (Los Angeles: UCLA Asian American Studies Center, 1971), p. 6.

19. Takaki, *Strangers from a Different Shore*, p. 420.

20. Yen Le Espiritu, *Asian American Panethnicity: Bridging Institutions and Identities* (Philadelphia: Temple University Press, 1992); Estella Habal, *San Francisco's International Hotel: Mobilizing the Filipino American Community in the Anti-Eviction Movement* (Philadelphia: Temple University Press, 2007); Fred Ho, with Carolyn Antonio, Diane Fujino, and Steve Yip, eds., *Legacy to Liberation: Politics and Culture of Revolutionary Asian Pacific America* (Brooklyn, NY: Big Red Media, 2000); Lon Kurashige, *Japanese American Celebration and Conflict: A History of Ethnic Identity and Festival in Los Angeles, 1934–1990* (Berkeley: University of California Press, 2002); Steve Louie and Glenn Omatsu, eds., *Asian Americans: The Movement and the Moment* (Los Angeles: UCLA Asian American Studies Center Press, 2001); Maeda, *Chains of Babylon*; Linda Trinh Võ, *Mobilizing an Asian American Community* (Philadelphia: Temple University Press, 2004); Wei, *The Asian American Movement*.

21. Brigham, *Guerilla Diplomacy*.

22. Chuong also served as a representative and interpreter for important international peace conferences, including the 1967 Bratislava meeting and also one in Paris where he had, in his words, "the privilege and also the heavy task of translating for" African American comedian Dick Gregory. Because of Gregory's use of black vernacular, the best that Chuong could do was to tell the Vietnamese-speaking audience members, "He must have spoken something very funny, but I did not understand!" However, that comment drew such a positive response from his audience that Gregory complimented Chuong on his translation abilities. Pham Van Chuong, interview with author, Hanoi, Vietnam, 12 August 2009.

23. Trinh Ngoc Thai, "The World People's Front in Support of Viet Nam: The Paris Agreement Negotiations Period," in *The Historical Negotiations* [in Vietnamese, trans. Quynh Phan] (Hanoi: Nha Xuat Ban Chinh Tri Quoc Gia, 2009).

24. Ibid.

25. Ibid.

26. Singh, *Black Is a Country*.

27. Eldridge Cleaver, *Soul on Ice* (Waco, TX: Word Books, 1978).

28. Manning Marable, *Race, Reform and Rebellion: The Second Reconstruction in Black America* (Jackson: University Press of Mississippi, 1991), p. 110, quoted in Charles E. Jones, ed., *The Black Panther Party Reconsidered* (Baltimore, MD: Black Classic Press, 1998), p. 7.

29. The biographical information for Elaine Brown mainly comes from her autobiography, *A Taste of Power: A Black Woman's Story* (New York: Anchor Books, 1994).

30. Ibid., p. 31.

31. Some former Black Panthers have alleged that Brown was an FBI informant. They suggest that Kennedy was a government operative who most likely recruited Brown. In Brown's autobiography, she hints at autobiographical aspects in her lover's novel. In that work, the protagonist is a white male CIA operative in love with a black woman who has become a black power radical. However, Brown also suggests that Jay detested the CIA, despite his choice of characters. Ibid., pp. 103–104, 94.

32. Ibid., p. 132; and Tracye Matthews, conversations with author, Chicago, IL, winter 2006.

33. "F.B.I. Brands Black Panthers 'Most Dangerous' of Extremists," *New York Times*, 14 July 1970, p. 21.

34. Eldridge Cleaver, "Address," *Ramparts* 7, no. 9 (14–28 December 1968), p. 6.

35. Ward Churchill, " 'To Disrupt, Discredit and Destroy': The FBI's Secret War against the Black Panther Party," in Kathleen Cleaver and George Katsiaficas, eds., *Liberation, Imagination, and the Black Panther Party: A New Look at the Panthers and Their Legacy* (New York: Routledge, 2001), pp. 78–117.

36. Michael L. Clemons and Charles E. Jones, "Global Solidarity: The Black Panther Party in the International Arena," in Cleaver and Katsiaficas, *Liberation, Imagination, and the Black Panther Party*, pp. 20–39.

37. Brown, *A Taste of Power*, p. 137.

38. Clemons and Jones, "Global Solidarity," p. 30.

39. Memo from San Francisco to the Director, FBI, 2 August 1970, p. 10, Section 18, Eldridge Cleaver FBI File, 100-HQ-447251.

40. In January 1969, Byron Booth and Clinton Smith hijacked a plane to Cuba but were imprisoned by the authorities. They escaped from a rural labor camp to join Cleaver in Havana. James "Akili" Patterson also hijacked a plane to bring himself, his wife Gwen, and their daughter Tanya to Cuba. Kathleen Neal Cleaver, "Back to Africa: The Evolution of the International Section of the Black Panther Party (1969–1972), in Jones, *The Black Panther Party Reconsidered*, pp. 221–22; and Ruth Reitan, "Cuba, the Black Panther Party, and U.S. Black Movement in the 1960s: Issues of Security," in Cleaver and Katsiaficas, *Liberation, Imagination, and the Black Panther Party*, pp. 164–74.

41. Cleaver, "Back to Africa," p. 223; and Clemons and Jones, "Global Solidarity," p. 33.

42. Pham Khac Lam, interview with author, Hanoi, Vietnam, 12 August 2009.

43. Cleaver, *Soul on Fire*, p. 149.

44. Cleaver, "Back to Africa," pp. 234–35; William Klein, "Eldridge Cleaver on Political Prisoners," *Black Panther*, 1 November 1969, p. 12.

45. Huey P. Newton, "To the Courageous Revolutionaries of the National Liberation Front and Provisional Revolutionary Government of South Vietnam We Send Greetings," *Black Panther*, 29 August 1970, p. 13. For the Vietnamese response, see "Dear Comrades," *Black Panther*, 9 January 1971, p. 11.

46. Cleaver, "Back to Africa," p. 226; Clemons and Jones, "Global Solidarity," p. 30; Kim Il Sung, "The Decisive Factor in Victory in the Struggle against Imperialist Reaction, Is the Internal Forces of the Country Concerned!" *Black Panther*, 3 January 1970, p. 18; "Kim Il Sung on the Question of Firmly Establishing 'Juche' and Thoroughly Implementing the Mass Line," *Black Panther*, 10 January 1970, p. 12.

47. Robin Haynes, conversation with author, Chicago, 9 January 2006; and Barbara Easley Cox, excerpts from interview with Robin J. Haynes, Philadelphia, PA, 22 July 2005. I thank Robin Haynes for generously sharing her research with me.

48. Barbara Easley Cox, telephone interview with author, Philadelphia, PA, 21 December 2006.

49. Kim Il Sung's portrait appeared on the front cover of the *Black Panther*, along with a picture of Cleaver, on 25 October 1969. Articles about Kim's political philosophy and North Korea appeared regularly in the newspaper in the fall of 1969 and 1970.

50. The first issue of the *Black Panther* that featured an "International News" section was dated 6 September 1969. A headshot of Kim became part of the masthead on 6 June 1970, shortly before the delegation departed on their travels.

51. Cleaver, "Back to Africa," p. 231.

52. Brown, *A Taste of Power*, p. 201.

53. Eldridge Cleaver, "Gangster Cigarettes," in *Target Zero*, p. 225. Cleaver goes on to describe "two white women / with Anglo-Saxon roots," so the number of Jewish women might be three rather than four (p. 226).

54. Jack Salzman and Cornel West, eds., *Struggles in the Promised Land: Toward a History of Black-Jewish Relations in the United States* (New York: Oxford University Press, 1997).

55. Ibid., p. 1.

56. Jonathan Kaufman, "Blacks and Jews: The Struggle in the Cities," in Salzman and West, *Struggles in the Promised Land*, p. 110.

57. Ibid., p. 111.

58. Terry H. Anderson, *The Movement and the Sixties: Protest in America from Greensboro to Wounded Knee* (New York: Oxford University Press, 1995).

59. Dwight Garner, "Back When Ramparts Did the Storming," *New York Times*, 6 October 2009, www.nytimes.com/2009/10/07/books/07garner.html.

60. "About Robert Scheer," Truthdig, www.truthdig.com/robert_scheer#bio. Scheer is editor in chief of Truthdig.

61. "Selections from the Biography of Huey P. Newton by Bobby Seale, with an Introduction by Eldridge Cleaver," *Ramparts* 7, no. 4 (7 September 1968), p. 21.

62. Eldridge Cleaver Papers, BANC MSS 91/213 c, Bancroft Library, University of California, Berkeley.

63. Robert Scheer, editorial introduction to Eldridge Cleaver, "The Black Moochie: A Novella, Part I," *Ramparts* 8, no. 4 (October 1969), p. 21.

64. Randy Rappaport, interview with author, Columbus, OH, 7 July 2007.

65. Ibid.

66. Ann Froines, telephone interview with author, 21 December 2006.

67. Ibid.

68. Ibid.

69. "History," Third World Newsreel, www.twn.org/twnpages/about/history.aspx.

70. Anonymous, conversation with author, Berkeley, CA, 21 March 2007.

71. For overviews of Asian American history, see Chan, *Asian Americans*; and Takaki, *Strangers from a Different Shore*.

72. There are a number of works on the history of San Francisco's Chinatown. For a selection, see Victor Nee and Brett de Bary Nee, *Longtime Californ': A Documentary Study of an American Chinatown* (Stanford, CA: Stanford University Press, 1972); and Nayan Shah, *Contagious Divides: Epidemics and Race in San Francisco's Chinatown* (Berkeley: University of California Press, 2001).

73. Alex Hing, interview with author, New York City, 19 March 2005.

74. Fred Ho and Steve Yip, "Alex Hing: Former Minister of Information for the Red Guard Party and Founding Member of I Wor Kuen," in Ho et al., *Legacy to Liberation*, pp. 279–98.

75. Hing, interview.

76. Maeda, "Black Panthers, Red Guards, and Chinamen."

77. Hing, interview.

78. Hing, interview; Ho and Yip, "Alex Hing," pp. 279–96; Laura Ho, "Red Guard Party," *Gidra*, May 1969, pp. 4, 7; Maeda, "Black Panthers, Red Guards, and Chinamen"; Ogbar, *Black Power*; "Red Guard Rally," *AAPA Newspaper* 1, no. 4 (1969), pp. 1, 4; "Red Guard," *Black Panther*, 23 March 1969, p. 9; Vivian and Carol, "AION Finally Arrives," *Gidra*, April 1970, p. 31.

79. Him Mark Lai, "The Kuomingtang in Chinese American Communities before World War II," in *Entry Denied: Exclusion and the Chinese Community in America, 1882–1943*, ed. Sucheng Chan (Philadelphia: Temple University Press, 1991); Nee, *Longtime Californ'*; Renqiu Yu, *To Save China, to Save Ourselves: The Chinese Hand Laundry Alliance of New York* (Philadelphia: Temple University Press, 1992).

80. Hing, interview.

81. Maeda, "Black Panthers, Red Guards, and Chinamen."

82. Espiritu, *Asian American Panethnicity*.

83. Pulido, *Black, Brown, Yellow and Left*.

84. Anonymous, telephone interview with author, 18 January 2006.

85. Pat Sumi, interview by Ryan Yokota, 1 July 1997, transcript, p. 1. I want to thank Ryan for generously sharing his research with me. Ryan interviewed Pat Sumi twice, once on audiotape on 19 June 1997 and the second time on videotape on 1 July 1997. The second interview session was transcribed, and an edited version of that interview was published in Louie and Omatsu, *Asian Americans*, pp. 16–31.

86. Frances Fournier, conversation with author, Vancouver, Canada, 31 October 2005; and anonymous, telephone interview with author, 18 January 2006.

87. Jim Hurst and Sam Weaver, eds., *Barrister 1962: John Marshall High School* (Los Angeles, 1962). My thanks to Frances Fournier for sharing her memories and her yearbooks.

88. Sumi, interview by Yokota, p. 1.

89. Ibid., p. 2.

90. Ryan Yokota, "Interview with Pat Sumi," in Louie and Omatsu, *Asian Americans*, pp. 19–20.

91. For information about the Movement for a Democratic Military and about antiwar coffeehouses, see Hall, *Rethinking the American Anti-War Movement*, p. 124; Stur, *Beyond Combat*; and Westheider, *Fighting on Two Fronts*.

92. *Investigation of Attempts to Subvert the United States Armed Services*, "Hearings before the Committee on Internal Security," House of Representatives, 92nd Congress, 1st session, 20, 21, 22, 27, and 28 October 1971; and 2nd sessions 9 and 10 May, and 1 and 20 June 1972 (Washington, DC: U.S. Government Printing Office, 1972). My thanks to Daryl Maeda for sharing these materials with me.

93. Pat Sumi, interview by Ryan Yokota, 19 June 1997.

94. Cindy Takemoto, "Pat Sumi: Off the Pedestal," *Asian Women's Journal* (1971; 3rd printing, 1975), p. 109.

95. Ibid.

96. Stur, *Beyond Combat*, p. 187.

97. Ibid., pp. 186–87.

98. Caroline Chung Simpson, *An Absent Presence: Japanese Americans in Postwar American Culture, 1945–1960* (Durham, NC: Duke University Press, 2001).

99. Sumi, interview by Yokota, 1 July 1997, transcript, p. 1.

100. Larry Kobota, "Yellow Power!" *Gidra*, April 1969, pp. 3–4; Amy Uyematsu, "The Emergence of Yellow Power in America," *Gidra*, October 1969, pp. 8–11.

101. Sumi, interview by Yokota, 1 July 1997, transcript, p. 10.

102. Pat Sumi, "A Mountain Was Moved," *Gidra*, June 1971, p. 14.

103. Sumi, interview by Yokota, 1 July 1997, transcript, p. 11.

104. "People of the World Unite," p. 11.

105. "Asian Americans for Peace Rally," *Gidra*, January 1970, p. 15; Yuji Ichioka, "Hiroshima-Nagasaki, Twenty-Five Years Ago," and Joanne Miyamoto and Foo Gwah, "People's Page: Hiroshima-Nagasaki and Hiroshima Revisited," both in *Gidra*, August 1970, pp. 6–9; and Patricia Sumi, "Hiroshima-Nagasaki Indochina," *Gidra*, August 1971, p. 15.

106. "Chinese Workers Support Afro-American Struggle," *Black Panther*, 27 April 1969, p. 12; "The Just Struggle of Afro-Americans Is Sure to Win," *Black Panther*, 11 May 1969, reprinted on 25 May 1969; Ho Chi Minh, "Lynching," *Black Panther*, 13 September 1969, p. 16, reprinted from *La Correspondence International*, no. 59 (1924); "The Association of Democratic Jurists of Korea, the Committee for Afro-Asian Solidarity of Korea, Telegram to Mr. Bobby Seale," *Black Panther*, 4 October 1969, p. 10; "Copy of Telegram from Korea," *Black Panther*, 20 December 1969, p. 16; Rochom Briu, "Letter to Black Americans," *Black Panther*, 11 April 1970, p. 15; "Telegram from Comrade Kim Il Sung, the Courageous Revolutionary Leader of the 40 Million Korean People," *Black Panther*, 29 August 1970, p. 16.

5. A Revolutionary Pilgrimage

1. "Cleaver in North Korea," *New York Times*, 15 July 1970, p. 11.

2. Sumi, interview by Yokota, 1 July 1997, transcript, p. 12.

3. Director, FBI, "Memo to SACs," 20 August 1970, p. 2, Section 18, Eldridge Cleaver FBI File, 100-HQ-447251.

4. "Cleaver and 10 Others Flying into North Korea," *Evening Star*, 13 July 1970. Clipping found in Section 18, Cleaver FBI File, 100-HQ-447251.

5. Alex Hing to Dear Comrades, *Gidra*, August 1970, p. 17.

6. Martin Wong, "Alex Hing: IWK," *Giant Robot* no. 10 (Spring 1998): 81.

7. Sumi, interview by Yokota, 19 June 1997.

8. Tranh Minh Quoc, interview with author, Hanoi, Vietnam, 10 August 2009.

9. "In North Korea, North Vietnam, Peking China, We Were Greeted as the Anti-Imperialist Delegation and Treated as Human Beings as Respected Members of the Human Race: An Interview with Elaine Brown, Deputy Minister of Information Black Panther Party, Los Angeles, California," *Black Panther*, 3 October 1970, p. B.

10. Eldridge Cleaver, "Gangster Cigarettes," in *Target Zero*, p. 225.

11. Gitlin, *The Sixties*, pp. 262–63. My thanks to Bob McMahon and Michael Flamm for reminding me of Gitlin's work.

12. Ibid., p. 264.

13. Venceremos Brigade, *The Venceremos Brigade: Four Years Building Solidarity with Cuba* (New York: Educational Commission, 1974); Lekus, "Queer Harvests."

14. Gitlin, *The Sixties*, p. 264.

15. Mary Louise Pratt, *Imperial Eyes: Travel Writing and Transculturation* (New York: Routledge, 1992), p. 7.

16. Bruce Cumings, *Korea's Place in the Sun: A Modern History*, updated ed. (New York: W. W. Norton, 2005), p. 270.

17. "In North Korea, North Vietnam," p. B.

18. Suzanne Kelly McCormack, " 'Good Politics Is Doing Something': Independent Diplomats and Anti-War Activists in the Vietnam-Era Peace Movement, a Collective Biography," PhD diss., Boston College, 2002, p. 205.

19. "This is the second in a series of programs . . . ," p. 1, box 5, folder 7, Eldridge Cleaver Papers.

20. Ibid., p. 4.

21. Cumings, *Korea's Place in the Sun*, p. 293.

22. Ibid., p. 295.

23. Ibid., p. 269.

24. Ibid., p. 271.

25. Green, *Black Yanks in the Pacific*, p. 114.

26. Ibid., pp. 115, 114.

27. Rappaport, interview.

28. "People of the World Unite," p. 11.

29. Ibid.

30. Pat Sumi, "Laos: A Nation in Struggle," *Gidra*, March 1971, p. 14.

31. Clyde H. Farnsworth, "Black Panthers Open Office in Algiers," *New York Times*, 14 September 1970, p. 2.

32. "People of the World Unite," p. 12.

33. Thai, "The World People's Front in Support of Viet Nam."

34. Maeda, *Chains of Babylon*; Maeda, *Rethinking the Asian American Movement*.

35. Farnsworth, "Black Panthers Open Office in Algiers"; also see McCormack, "'Good Politics Is Doing Something,'" p. 205.

36. Section 19, p. 102, Eldridge Cleaver FBI File, 100-HQ-447251.

37. "In North Korea, North Vietnam," p. D.

38. Eldridge Cleaver, "The Black Man's Stake in Vietnam," *Black Panther*, 23 March 1969, p. 16, which was reprinted in later issues as well; and Eldridge Cleaver, "To My Black Brothers in Viet Nam," *Black Panther*, 31 January 1970, p. B.

39. Director, FBI, "Memo," 26 September 1970, Section 18, Eldridge Cleaver FBI File, 100-HQ-447251.

40. Westheider, *Fighting on Two Fronts*, p. 109.

41. Ibid., pp. 154–56.

42. Ibid., p. 156.

43. Pham Khac Lam, interview.

44. "Cleaver and Black Panther Group Attend Hanoi Observance," *New York Times*, 19 August 1970, p. 13.

45. Kathleen Neal Cleaver, "Back to Africa," in *The Black Panther Party Reconsidered*, ed. Charles E. Jones (Baltimore, MD: Black Classic Press, 1998), p. 234.

46. Farnsworth, "Black Panthers Open Office in Algiers."

47. Cleaver, *Soul on Fire*, pp. 148–49.

48. "Pacifists and Panthers Get P.O.W. Letters from Hanoi," *New York Times*, 4 September 1970, p. 5.

49. Hing, interview.

50. Kristi Siegel, ed. *Issues in Travel Writing: Empire, Spectacle, and Displacement* (New York: Peter Lang, 2002), p. 4.

51. Elaine Brown, "Transcript of Speech," box 5, folder 6, Eldridge Cleaver Papers.

52. "In North Korea, North Vietnam," pp. B–C.

53. Ibid., p. C.

54. Brown, *A Taste of Power*, p. 226.

55. "In North Korea, North Vietnam," pp. B–C.

56. Cumings, *Korea's Place in the Sun*, p. 433.

57. Ibid.

58. The United States gave an estimated twelve billion dollars to South Korea from 1945 to 1965 (ibid., p. 307).

59. Ibid., p. 310.

60. Ibid., p. 309.

61. Ibid., p. 429.

62. Ibid., p. 435.

63. "In North Korea, North Vietnam," p. B.

64. "Life in New Asia," *Getting Together* 1, no. 6 (November–December 1970): 16.

65. Kyung Ae Park, "Women and Revolution in North Korea," *Pacific Affairs* 65, no. 4 (1992–1993), p. 532. My thanks to Suzy Kim for suggesting this source.

66. Ibid., p. 536.

67. Ibid.

68. Alex Hing, "Dear Comrades," *Gidra*, October 1970, p. 6.

69. Hing, interview.

70. "Pacifists and Panthers Get P.O.W. Letters from Hanoi," p. 5.

71. Hing, "Dear Comrades," p. 6.

72. Edward Wong, dir., *Comrades: A Documentary* (San Francisco: National Asian American Telecommunications Association, 1999).

73. "In North Korea, North Vietnam," p. E.

74. Cleaver, *Soul on Fire*, p. 147.

75. Chinese tend to use the measurement of *wan* or ten thousand for expressing large numbers. It is possible that the Chinese official misinterpreted Cleaver's claim of forty million as forty wan, the equivalent of four hundred thousand. My thanks to Gordon Chang for suggesting this interpretation.

76. "In North Korea, North Vietnam," p. E.

77. Ibid., pp. C–D.

78. Ibid., p. D.

79. Sumi, interview by Yokota, 1 July 1997, pp. 13–14.

80. Ibid., p. 14.

81. Ibid., p. 15.

82. Pratt, *Imperial Eyes*, p. 96. For analyses of the Madame Butterfly storyline, which surfaces in popular culture, see Lee, *Orientals*; Gina Marchetti, *Romance and the "Yellow Peril": Race, Sex, and Discursive Strategies in Hollywood Fiction* (Berkeley: University of California Press, 1993); and Yoshihara, *Embracing the East*.

83. McCormack, "Good Politics Is Doing Something," p. 204. McCormack studied the delegation from the perspective of Ann Froines. She interviewed Froines and also had access to her travel diaries.

84. Ibid., p. 205. Alex Hing's recollections of the tour suggest that this sense of cohesiveness might have been particularly strong among the five white women on the tour. Hing, interview.

85. June Culberson, "The Role of the A [*sic*] Revolutionary Woman," *Black Panther*, 4 May 1969, p. 9; "Sisters," *Black Panther*, 13 September 1969, pp. 12–13.

86. Brown, *A Taste of Power*, pp. 136–37.

87. Stur, *Beyond Combat*, p. 39.

88. In the DPRK, the Korean Democratic Women's Union was formed in 1946. In the PRC, the All-China Women's Democratic Foundation formed in 1949 and became the All-China Women's Federation in 1957.

89. Swerdlow, *Women Strike for Peace*.

90. "Life in New Asia," p. 16.

91. Ibid.

92. Ibid.

93. Ibid.

94. Ibid., p. 15.

95. Suzy Kim, "Revolutionary Mothers: Women in the North Korean Revolution, 1945–1950," *Contemporary Studies in Society and History* 52, no. 4 (2010): 742–67; Park, "Women and Revolution in North Korea"; and Sonia Ryang, "Gender in Oblivion: Women in the Democratic People's Republic of Korea (North Korea)," *Journal of Asian and African Studies* 35, no. 3 (2000): 325–49.

96. Ryang, "Gender in Oblivion," p. 332.

97. Park, "Women and Revolution in North Korea," p. 536.

98. Quoted in Ryang, "Gender in Oblivion," p. 335.

99. "Life in New Asia," p. 15.

100. Ibid.

101. "In North Korea, North Vietnam," p. E.

102. Emily Honig, "Maoist Mappings of Gender: Reassessing the Red Guards," in *Chinese Femininities, Chinese Masculinities: A Reader*, ed. Susan Brownell and Jeffrey N. Wasserstrom (Berkeley: University of California Press, 2002), p. 255.

103. Ibid.

104. Ibid., pp. 255–56.

105. Quoted in McCormack, "Good Politics Is Doing Something," p. 207. Originally from Ann Froines, 7 August 1970, Personal Journal #5.

106. Park, "Women and Revolution in North Korea," p. 540.

107. Ibid. Park is utilizing Gerhard Lenski's theory of social inequality, in which he "identifies three sources of power influencing inequality in society: the power of property (economic power), the power of position, and the power of force." Gerhard Lenski, *Power and Privilege: A Theory of Social Stratification* (New York: McGraw-Hill, 1966).

108. Park, "Women and Revolution in North Korea," p. 542. Park is also citing the work of Janet Salaff and Judith Merkle, "Women in Revolution: The Lessons of the Soviet Union and China," *Berkeley Journal of Sociology* 15 (1970): 182.

109. Swerdlow, *Women Strike for Peace*, p. 216.

110. "Life in New Asia," p. 15.

111. "In North Korea, North Vietnam," p. D.

112. This image appeared in the *Black Panther*, 20 September 1969, p. 3, and on the cover of *Gidra*, March 1970, with an accompanying article, "Vietnamese Sisters," reprinted from *Sisters United* no. 1 (January 1970): p. 10.

113. Sandra C. Taylor, *Vietnamese Women at War: Fighting for Ho Chi Minh and the Revolution* (Lawrence: University Press of Kansas, 1999), p. 12.

114. Ibid.

115. Ibid., p. 9.

116. Cynthia Enloe, "Women after Wars: Puzzles and Warnings," in Kathleen Barry, ed., *Vietnam's Women in Transition* (Houndsmill, UK: Macmillan, 1996), pp. 299–315. Also see Lisa Drummond and Helle Rydstrom, *Gender Practices in Contemporary Vietnam* (Singapore: Singapore University Press, 2004); and Arlene Eisen, *Women and Revolution in Viet Nam* (London: Zed Books, 1984).

117. Taylor, *Vietnamese Women at War*, p. 9.

118. Pham Khac Lam, interview.

119. Ibid.

120. Sumi, interview by Yokota, 19 June 1997.

121. Mullen, *Afro-Orientalism*.

6. The Belly of the Beast

1. Sumi, interview by Yokota, 19 June 1997.

2. I do not want to suggest that the private or later sources are somehow more "true." In fact, they need to be closely scrutinized and contextualized, because the writings also reveal the influence of political calculation and conflict.

3. For a wonderful analysis of how sexuality, race, and gender shaped the dynamics within Venceremos Brigades, see Lekus, "Queer Harvests."

4. Kathleen Neal Cleaver, "Back to Africa," in Jones, *The Black Panther Party Reconsidered*, p. 216.

5. For one account of the split, see ibid., pp. 211–54.

6. Churchill, "'To Disrupt, Discredit and Destroy,'" in Cleaver and Katsiaficas, *Liberation, Imagination and the Black Panther Party*, pp. 78–117; Eldridge Cleaver FBI Files.

7. Elaine Brown, "Hidden Traitor," p. 1, box 48, folder 16, Dr. Huey P. Newton Foundation Incorporation Collection, MS M0864, Special Collections and University Archives, Stanford University, Stanford, CA.

8. Brown, *A Taste of Power*, pp. 220–21.

9. Ibid.

10. Ibid., , pp. 227–28.

11. Brown, "Hidden Traitor," p. 17.

12. Elaine Brown, "Free Kathleen Cleaver: And All Political Prisoners," *Black Panther Party Intercommunal News Service*, 6 March 1971, pp. A–D.

13. Tracye Matthews, "'No One Ever Asks, What a Man's Role in the Revolution Is': Gender and the Politics of the Black Panther Party, 1966–1971," and Angela D. LeBlanc-Ernest, "'The Most Qualified Person to Handle the Job': Black Panther Party Women, 1966–1982," both in Jones, *The Black Panther Party Reconsidered*, pp. 267–334.

14. Susie Linfield, "The Education of Kathleen Neal Cleaver," *Transitions* 77 (1998), p. 195.

15. Ibid., p. 182.

16. Ibid., p. 191.

17. Kathleen Cleaver, interview.

18. Kathleen Cleaver, interview; Kathleen Cleaver, transcript of speech given at the University of California, Los Angeles, 22 October 1971, p. 120, Section 22, Eldridge Cleaver FBI Files, 100-HQ-447251.

19. Brown, "Hidden Traitor," p. 4.

20. Ibid., pp. 4–5.

21. Ibid., p. 5.

22. Ibid.

23. Ibid., p. 36.

24. Eldridge Cleaver, "On Becoming," in *Soul on Ice* (New York: Dell, 1968), p. 6.

25. Ibid., p. 10.

26. Ibid., p. 14.

27. Ibid.

28. Ibid., p. 15.

29. Eldridge Cleaver, "Enter the Devil," box 2, folder 31, Eldridge Cleaver Papers.

30. Eldridge Cleaver, "Slow Boat to Cuba," box 2, folder 31, Eldridge Cleaver Papers.

31. Alex Hing, e-mail correspondence, 26 February 2006.

32. Beth L. Bailey, *Sex in the Heartland* (Cambridge, MA: Harvard University Press, 2002).

33. Eldridge Cleaver, notebook, folder "U.S. Peoples' Anti-Imperialist Delegation, Korea Trip Notebooks, 1970," Eldridge Cleaver Papers.

34. Jeremy Varon, *Bringing the War Home: The Weather Underground, the Red Army Faction, and Revolutionary Violence in the Sixties and Seventies* (Berkeley: University of California Press, 2004).

35. Rappaport, interview.

36. Ibid.

37. Randy Rappaport, conversation with author, Amherst, MA, 11 June 2011.

38. Rappaport, interview.

39. Ibid.

40. Brown, "Hidden Traitor," p. 36.

41. Froines, telephone interview.

42. Rappaport, interview.

43. Rappaport, conversation.

44. Brown, "Hidden Traitor," p. 6.

45. Ibid., p. 39.

46. Ibid., p. 29.

47. Froines, telephone interview.

48. Rappaport, interview.

49. Ibid.

50. Cheryl Lynn Greenberg, *Troubling the Water: Black-Jewish Relations in the American Century* (Princeton, NJ: Princeton University Press, 2006).

51. Ibid., p. 9.

52. It appeared originally as James Baldwin, "Negroes Are Anti-Semitic because They're Anti-White," *New York Times Magazine*, 9 April 1967, www.nytimes.com/books/98/03/29/specials/baldwin-antisem.html.

53. Greenberg, *Troubling the Water*, p. 6.

54. Baldwin, "Negroes Are Anti-Semitic."

55. Earl Lewis, "The Need to Remember: Three Phases in Black and Jewish Educational Relations," in Salzman and West, *Struggles in the Promised Land*, p. 246. Also see Wendell Pritchett, *Brownsville, Brooklyn: Blacks, Jews, and the Changing Face of the Ghetto* (Chicago: University of Chicago Press, 2002).

56. Lewis, "The Need to Remember," p. 246.

57. Salzman and West, *Struggles in the Promised Land*.

58. Cleaver, "Slow Boat to Cuba," p. 11.

59. Ibid., p. 9. Some of the names are misspelled in this draft essay.

60. Cleaver, "Enter the Devil," p. 32.

61. Cleaver, "Slow Boat to Cuba," p. 12.

62. For discussions about the controversy regarding Palestine and black power leader Stokely Carmichael, see Clayborne Carson, "Black-Jewish Universalism in the Era of Identity Politics," and Waldo E. Martin Jr., " 'Nation Time!' Black Nationalism, the Third World, and Jews," both in Salzman and West, *Struggles in the Promised Land*, pp. 177–96, 341–55.

63. Cleaver, "Slow Boat to Cuba," p. 13.

64. Memo from San Francisco Office to the Director of the FBI, 9 February 1970, box 24, folder 1, Eldridge Cleaver Papers.

65. Anonymous, conversation with author, Berkeley, CA, 21 March 2007.

66. Brown, *A Taste of Power*, p. 220.

67. Hing, interview; and Sumi, interview by Yokota, 19 June 1997.

68. Cleaver, *Soul on Fire*, p. 122.

69. Ibid., p. 134.

70. Hing, interview.

71. Cleaver, *Soul on Fire*, p. 122.

72. Ibid.

73. Eldridge Cleaver, "Gangster Cigarettes," in *Target Zero*, p. 225.

74. Hing, interview.

75. Cleaver, "Gangster Cigarettes," p. 227.

76. Rappaport, interview.

77. Hing, e-mail correspondence.

78. Sumi, interview by Yokota, 19 June 1997.

79. Rappaport, interview.

80. Sumi, interview by Yokota, 1 July 1997, p. 9.

81. Rappaport, interview.

82. Ibid.

83. Ibid.

84. Ibid.

85. Cleaver, *Soul on Fire*, p. 149.

86. Brown, *A Taste of Power*, p. 229.

87. "Black Panthers Open Office in Algiers," *New York Times*, 14 September 1970, p. 2.

88. Kathleen Cleaver, interview.

89. Director, FBI to SAC, New York, 16 September 1970, Section 18, Cleaver FBI Files, 100-HQ-447251.

90. Brown, *A Taste of Power.*

91. Ibid., p. 313.

92. Sumi, interview by Yokota, 1 July 1997, p. 12.

93. "I Wor Kuen," *Gidra*, June 1971, pp. 12–13; also see *Getting Together*, the periodical published by I Wor Kuen.

94. Sumi, interview by Yokota, 19 June 1997.

95. Takemoto, "Pat Sumi"; anonymous, telephone interview with author, 23 January 2006; and Jeffrey Chan, telephone interview with author, San Rafael, CA, 17 January 2005.

96. Ann Froines, letter to Eldridge Cleaver, 20 November 1970, box 5, folder 36, Eldridge Cleaver Papers.

97. Quote from an interview conducted by Suzanne McCormack, which appears in McCormack, "'Good Politics Is Doing Something,'" p. 213.

98. Rappaport, interview.

99. Ibid.

100. Siegel, *Issues in Travel Writing*, p. 4.

7. "We Met the 'Enemy'—and They Are Our Sisters"

1. The title "We Met the 'Enemy'—and They Are Our Sisters" was a headline in *Memo* 2, no. 1 (Fall 1971): 14–15. *Memo* is a newsletter published by Women Strike for Peace.

2. Grewal, *Transnational America*; Mohanty, "Under Western Eyes"; Rupp, *Worlds of Women*; Wu, "Journeys for Peace and Liberation"; Wu, "Rethinking Global Sisterhood."

3. Scholars of 1960s radicalism are increasingly emphasizing the diversity of backgrounds and political perspectives of activists from this era. Stephanie Gilmore, ed., *Feminist Coalitions: Historical Perspectives on Second-Wave Feminism in the United States* (Urbana: University of Illinois Press, 2008); and Young, *Soul Power.*

4. Swerdlow, *Women Strike for Peace.*

5. Ibid., p. 15.

6. Andrea Estepa, "Taking the White Gloves Off: Women Strike for Peace and 'the Movement,' 1967–73," in Gilmore, *Feminist Coalitions*, p. 87.

7. Jill Vickers, "The Intellectual Origins of the Women's Movements in Canada," in *Challenging Times: The Women's Movement in Canada and the United States*, ed. Constance Backhouse and David H. Flaherty (Montreal: McGill-Queen's University Press, 1992), pp. 53–55; and Candace Loewen, "Making Ourselves Heard: 'Voice of Women' and the Peace Movement in the Early Sixties," in *Framing Our Past: Canadian Women's History in the Twentieth Century*, ed. Sharon Anne Cook, Lorna R. McLean, and Kate O'Rourke (Montreal: McGill-Queen's University Press, 2001), p. 248.

8. Quoted in Judy Rebick, *Ten Thousand Roses: The Making of a Feminist Revolution* (Toronto: Penguin Canada, 2005), p. 3.

9. Quoted in Harriet Hyman Alonso, *Peace as a Women's Issue: A History of the U.S. Movement for World Peace and Women's Rights* (Syracuse, NY: Syracuse University Press, 1993), p. 86. WILPF was officially founded in 1919, but the organization evolved from the U.S. Women's Peace Party, which was established in 1915.

10. Estepa, "Taking the White Gloves Off," p. 88.

11. "Paris," *Memo* 6, no. 4 (March 1968): 2.

12. "To Canadian Press Representatives, London," 15 May 1968, vol. 3, file Hanoi Trip, Voice of Women (VOW) Fonds, Library and Archives Canada.

13. Ethel Taylor, "Conference: Paris, April 23–26," *Memo* 6, no. 5 (May–June 1968): 6.

14. Kay MacPherson, "October 9th 1967, Cambridge," vol. 3, file Hanoi Trip, VOW Fonds.

15. Cora Weiss, "The Face of the Enemy," *Memo* (Fall 1969): 4–7.

16. Swerdlow, *Women Strike for Peace*, p. 222.

17. Hershberger, *Traveling to Vietnam*.

18. Cora Weiss, interviews, 7 and 8 April 2006 and 4 May 2006. Also see Swerdlow, *Women Strike for Peace*, and Clinton, "Cora Weiss."

19. Taylor, *Vietnamese Women at War*, p. 123.

20. Swerdlow, *Women Strike for Peace*, p. 216.

21. "Madame Nguyen Thi Binh Speaking to American Women," text of film, October 1970, p. 1, series A, 2, box B, 2, Women Strike for Peace (WSP) Records (DG 115), SCPC, Swarthmore, PA.

22. "Talks Began in 1965 . . ." *Memo* 6, no. 8 (November–December 1968): 2.

23. *Vietnamese Women*, Vietnam Studies No. 10 (Hanoi, DRV: Xunhasaba, 1966), p. 42.

24. Ibid., p. 33.

25. Mary Ann Tetreault, "Women and Revolution in Vietnam," in Barry, *Vietnam's Women in Transition*, p. 45. Tetreault cites Frances Fitzgerald, *Fire in the Lake: The Vietnamese and the Americans in Vietnam* (Boston: Little, Brown, 1972).

26. For an analysis of how WSP emphasized a maternalist construction of Vietnamese female identity to foster a common politics based on pacifism, see Jessica M. Frazier, "Collaborative Efforts: Women Strike for Peace's Interactions with Vietnamese Women during the Vietnam War, 1965–1968," paper presented at the Berkshires Conference on the History of Women, Amherst, MA, June 2011.

27. Nancy Hewitt, ed., *No Permanent Waves: Recasting Histories of U.S. Feminism* (New Brunswick, NJ: Rutgers University Press, 2010).

28. *Vietnamese Women*, p. 3.

29. Ibid.

30. Ibid., p. 307.

31. Agatha Beins's dissertation and forthcoming book will examine how women's movement periodicals created political meaning and fostered a sense of community among activists. She places a strong emphasis on the representations of Vietnamese women in American women's movement periodicals. Agatha Beins, "Free Our Sisters, Free Ourselves! Locating U.S. Feminism through Feminist Publishing" (PhD diss., Rutgers University, 2011); Agatha Beins, "Sisters Rise Up! Feminist Identities and Communities in the Women's Liberation Movement," paper presented at NEH Summer Institute, Sequel to the 60s, Schlesinger Library, Harvard University, Cambridge, MA, 2008; and Agatha Beins, "Radical Others: Women of Color and Revolutionary Feminism" (unpublished manuscript, 2011).

32. Taylor, *Vietnamese Women at War*.

33. Hershberger, *Traveling to Vietnam*, p. 139.

34. Vivian Rothstein, telephone interview with author, 9 March 2007.

35. Ibid.

36. Charlotte Bunch, interview with author, New York City, 30 November 2006. Also see Sara Evans, ed., *Journeys That Opened Up the World: Women, Student Christian Movements, and Social Justice, 1955–1975* (New Brunswick, NJ: Rutgers University Press, 2003).

37. Anne M. Valk, *Radical Sisters: Second-Wave Feminism and Black Liberation in Washington, D.C.* (Urbana: University of Illinois Press, 2010).

38. Charlotte Bunch-Weeks and Frank Joyce, "North Vietnam: A Photo Essay," *Motive* (February 1971), p. 18.

39. Ibid., p. 20.

40. Jan Fenty and Charlotte Bunch-Weeks, "Women and the Anti-War Movement," box 1, folder 33, Charlotte Bunch Papers, Schlesinger Library, Radcliffe Institute, Harvard University. Cambridge, MA.

41. Bunch, interview.

42. Nguyen Thi Ngoc Dung, interview with author, Ho Chi Minh City, Vietnam, 19 August 2009.

43. Phan Thi Minh, interview with author, Da Nang, Vietnam, 17 August 2009. I am uncertain as to the spelling of the names of the two non-Vietnamese women who helped Dung and Minh produce their newspaper.

44. Alice Wolfson to "Companeras," n.d., pp. 1–2, box 1, folder 34, Charlotte Bunch Papers.

45. Hershberger, *Traveling to Vietnam*; and Joyce Blackwell, *No Peace without Freedom: Race and the Women's International League for Peace and Freedom, 1915–1975* (Carbondale: Southern Illinois University Press, 2004).

46. "New President, Board Elected," *Peace and Freedom* 31, no. 7 (July 1971): 1.

47. Other religiously inspired social organizations and women's reform organizations, like the American Friends Service Committee and the Young Women's Christian Association, also provided similar services for Japanese American internees.

48. Wu, "Journeys for Peace and Liberation."

49. Frances Beale, "Double Jeopardy: To Be Black and Female," *Sisterhood Is Powerful: An Anthology of Writings from the Women's Liberation Movement*, ed. Robin Morgan (New York: Vintage Books, 1970), pp. 382–96; and Benita Roth, *Separate Roads to Feminism: Black, Chicana, and White Feminist Movements in America's Second Wave* (New York: Cambridge University Press, 2003).

50. Betita Martinez, telephone interview with author, 7 December 2006. Also see Oropeza, *¡Raza Sí! ¡Guerra No!*

51. Martinez, telephone interview.

52. Ibid.

53. Ibid.

54. Ibid.

55. Ibid.

56. Ibid.

57. Ibid.

58. Oropeza, *¡Raza Sí! ¡Guerra No!*, pp. 99–100.

59. Lorena Oropeza points out that by 1960, 80 percent of Mexican Americans were living in urban areas. However, the Chicano/a movement was heavily invested in the symbolic identity of being "agricultural people tied to the land." Ibid., p. 86.

60. "Viet Nam War—Why? Their People . . . Our People . . ." *El Grito del Norte*, 29 August 1970. Betita Martinez also reported on the treatment of ethnic minorities in Vietnam, who had the right to bilingual education.

61. Martinez, telephone interview.

62. Ibid.

63. Ibid.

64. Ibid.

65. Loreno Oropeza makes a similar argument about the significance of the Vietnam War for the Chicano/a movement. Oropeza, *¡Raza Sí! ¡Guerra No!*

66. Maylei Blackwell, *¡Chicana Power! Contested Histories of Feminism in the Chicano Movement* (Austin: University of Texas Press, 2011).

67. Martinez, telephone interview. For more information about La Alianza Federal de Pueblos Libres, see Oropeza, *¡Raza Sí! ¡Guerra No!*

68. Martinez, telephone interview.

69. "The Land: A Constant Struggle," *El Grito del Norte*, 7 December 1970.

70. Martinez, telephone interview. Lorena Oropeza also concurs with Betita Martinez's characterization of *El Grito del Norte* as being on the forefront of Third World politics in the Chicano/a movement. Oropeza, *¡Raza Sí! ¡Guerra No!*

71. Oropeza, *¡Raza Sí! ¡Guerra No!*

72. Ibid., p. 6.

73. Ibid.

74. Martinez, telephone interview.

75. "Chicanas Meet Indo-Chinese," *El Grito del Norte*, 5 June 1971, p. K.

76. Ibid.

77. Rothstein, telephone interview.

8. War at a Peace Conference

1. "Curses," *Georgia Straight*, 8–13 April 1971, p. 17.

2. Ibid.

3. Ibid.

4. Canada's support for the U.S. antiwar movement should not be overstated. Although the country was officially neutral, Canadian citizens volunteered to fight in the U.S.-led war in Southeast Asia. In addition, the Canadian government engaged in "secret missions, weapons testing and arms production." "Canada, Vietnam, and the Pentagon Papers," www.cbc.ca/archives/categories/war-conflict/vietnam-war/canadas-secret-war-vietnam/canada-and-the-pentagon-papers.html.

5. Vo Thi The, a professor of literature at Hanoi University and an executive of the Vietnam Women's Union, participated in the 1969 delegation and would return again in 1971. Le Thi Cao, a former teacher and an organizer for the National Liberation Front, came directly from South Vietnam, while Madame Nguyen Ngoc Dung, an executive of the Women's Union for the Liberation of South Vietnam as well as the Students' Liberation Movement, arrived from Paris where she had recently been appointed to the staff of the peace talks. They made public presentations and attended meetings in Vancouver, Nanimo, Regina, Winnipeg, Toronto, Niagara Falls, Ottawa, North Hatley, and Montreal. "Vietnamese Women Visit Canada," July 1969, vol. 18, folder "Vietnam Visits and Visas 1965–1971," VOW Fonds.

6. Muriel Duckworth, "VOW Visit Information (from Visit Committee)," vol. 45, folder 28, VOW Fonds.

7. Voice of Women/La Voix des Femmes, "Visit of the Indochinese Women to Canada, April 1971: An Assessment," September 1971, p. 2, vol. 3, file "Indochina Visit," VOW Fonds.

8. "Projected Conference in North America with Indochinese Women," pp. 1–2, subject files, folder "Indochinese Women Conference," Kathleen Hudson Women's Bookstore Collection Fonds, F-111, Archives and Records Management Department, Simon Fraser University.

9. Kristin Anderson-Bricker, "'Triple Jeopardy': Black Women and the Growth of Feminist Consciousness in SNCC, 1964–1975," in Kimberly Springer, ed., *Still Lifting, Still Climbing: African American Women's Contemporary Activism* (New York: New York University Press, 1999); Kimberly Springer, "Black Feminists Respond to Black Power Masculinism," and Stephen Ward, "The Third World Women's Alliance: Black Feminist Radicalism and Black Power Politics," in Peniel E. Joseph, ed., *The Black Power Movement* (New York: Routledge, 2006), pp. 105–44; and Kimberly Springer, *Living for the Revolution: Black Feminist Organizations, 1968–1980* (Durham, NC: Duke University Press, 2005).

10. "An Evaluation of the Canadian Conference Process," p. 11, box 1, folder 34, Charlotte Bunch Papers.

11. Ibid., p. 10.

12. "We as Third World Women . . . ," subject files, folder "Indochinese Women Conference," Kathleen Hudson Women's Bookstore Collection.

13. "Statement from a Number of the White Women in Los Angeles Who Are Working on the Indochinese Women's Conference," p. 2, subject files, folder "Indochinese Women Conference," Kathleen Hudson Women's Bookstore Collection.

14. "An Evaluation of the Canadian Conference Process," p. 11.

15. Naomi Weisstein, telephone interview with author, 5 February 2007.

16. "An Evaluation of the Canadian Conference Process," p. 13.

17. Ibid., p. 16.

18. Jeremy Varon points out that white activists in the United States tended not to face the same type of state-sponsored repression as activists of color. See Varon, *Bringing the War Home*. For an account of Canadian state surveillance of the IWC, see Steve Hewitt and Christabelle Sethna, "'Sweating and Uncombed': Canadian State Security, the Indochinese Conference and the Feminist Threat, 1968–1972," paper presented at the Canadian Historical Association, University of British Columbia, Vancouver, Canada, May–June 2008.

19. Letter to "Dear Sisters" from the Indochinese Conference Committee, pp. 1–2, folder "Indo-Chinese Women's Conference" no. 3, Anne Roberts Women's Movement Collection Fond, Archives and Records Management Department, Simon Fraser University.

20. "General Information for all Third World Delegates," folder "Indo-Chinese Women's Conference" no. 3, Anne Roberts Women's Movement Collection Fond.

21. Nina Genera and Maria Ramirez, interview with author, Hayward, CA, 27 February 2007.

22. "Indochinese Women's Conference," *Asian Women's Journal* (1971; 3rd printing, 1975), p. 79.

23. "An Evaluation of the Canadian Conference Process," p. 12.

24. Weisstein, telephone interview.

25. Anne Roberts and Barbara Todd, "Murmurings after the Indochinese Conference," *The Pedestal* (May 1971): 6.

26. In an assessment of the conference, VOW indicated that "109 women from 6 states and 5 provinces" attended the Vancouver conference. In Toronto, "388 women from 19 states, 3 provinces and Australia" participated. These numbers do not include WL and TWWA women, which the memo indicates "had the maximum numbers for the available accommodation—approximately 500." Voice of Women/La Voix des Femmes, "Visit of the Indochinese Women to Canada," p. 1.

27. Madeline Duckles, interview with author, Berkeley, CA, 21 October 2006.

28. "We as Third World Women . . . ."

29. For an analysis of how sexuality constituted a key source of conflict in other international gatherings, see Lekus, "Queer Harvests"; and Jocelyn Olcott, "Cold War Conflicts and Cheap Cabaret: Sexual Politics at the 1975 United Nations International Women's Year Conference," *Gender and History* 22, no. 3 (2010): 733–54.

30. Ruth Rosen, *The World Split Open: How the Modern Women's Movement Changed America* (New York: Viking, 2000).

31. "Hello Sisters! We Are Radicalesbians . . . ," p. 1, folder "Indo-Chinese Women's Conference" no. 3, Anne Roberts Women's Movement Collection Fond.

32. Rosen, *The World Split Open*, p. 166.

33. "Hello Sisters!," p. 1.

34. Ibid., p. 2.

35. Barbara Burris, Kathy Barry, Terry Moon, Joann DeLor, Joann Parent, and Cate Stadelman, "Fourth World Manifesto," folder "Indo-Chinese Women's Conference" no. 1, Anne Roberts Women's Movement Collection Fond.

36. Ibid., p. 1.

37. Genera and Ramirez, interview. Also see Lorena Oropeza's discussion about how gender shaped Chicana activists' reactions to white feminists and to Vietnamese women. Oropeza, *¡Raza Sí! ¡Guerra No!*, pp. 111–12.

38. Judy Drummond, interview with author, San Francisco, CA, 21 March 2007.

39. These debates resonate with Jasbir K. Puar's critique of homonationalism. See Jasbir K. Puar, *Terrorist Assemblages: Homonationalism in Queer Times* (Durham, NC: Duke University Press, 2007).

40. Rita Mae Brown, "Hanoi to Hoboken, a Round Trip Ticket," in *Out of the Closets: Voices of Gay Liberation*, ed. Karla Jay and Allen Young (New York: Douglas, 1972).

41. Bunch, interview.

42. Liz Breimberg, interview with author, Vancouver, BC, Canada, 2 November 2005. For related accounts of U.S.-Canadian tensions, see Hewitt and Sethna, "'Sweating and Uncombed.'"

43. Breimberg, interview.

44. The original publication was authored by the Vancouver "Corrective Collective" in 1971. The members were identified as Karen Cameron, Collette French, Pat Hoffer, Marge Hollibaugh, Andrea Lebowitz, Barbara Todd, Cathy Walker, and Dodie Weppler.

45. The Montreal International Collective, "Memorandum to the Interim Work Committee," 19 December 1970, folder "Indo-Chinese Women's Conference" no. 2, Anne Roberts Women's Movement Collection Fond. The signers of the memo were Anne Cools, Marlene Dixon, Estelle Dorais, Susan Dubrofsky, Vickie Tabachnik, and Eileen Nixon.

46. Vickers, "The Intellectual Origins of the Women's Movements in Canada," p. 43.

47. Letter, *CWLU (Chicago Women's Liberation Union) News*, late January 1971, pp. 2–3, box 19, folder "News 1971," Chicago Women's Liberation Union Records, Research Center, Chicago History Museum.

48. "Dear Sisters, Greetings of Solidarity," p. 2, Charlotte Bunch Papers, box 1, folder 34, "Indo-China Women's Conference"; and Front de liberation des femmes du Quebec, "Letter," 4 December 1970, *Quebecoises Deboutte!* 1 (Quebec: Les éditions du remue-ménage), pp. 79–80. My thanks to Katie Bausch for translating the materials.

49. Voice of Women/La Voix des Femmes, "Visit of the Indochinese Women to Canada," p. 1.

50. Gerry Ambers, telephone interview with author, Vancouver, BC, Canada, 4 April 2007.

51. Ibid.

52. Lydia Sayle, "A Subjective Postmortem of the Indochinese Conference—Held in Vancouver April 1971," vol. 3, folder "Indochina Visit," VOW Fonds.

53. Peter Lee, "Indo-Chinese Women's Conference," *New Bridge* 1, no. 3 (May 1971): 15.

54. Genera and Ramirez, interview.

55. Sayle, "A Subjective Postmortem," p. 1.

56. Voice of Women / La Voix des Femmes, "Visit of the Indochinese Women to Canada," p. 3.

57. Mary Bolton, "Sisterhood at the Conference," entry in a collection of reflections about the conference, titled "Vietnamese Conference," partially archived as part of VOW Fonds, vol. 3, folder "Indochina Visit," p. 22.

58. Holly Near, telephone interview with author, 12 February 2007.

9. Woman Warriors

1. "The Indochinese Women's Conference," *Goodbye to All That* ("The Newspaper by San Diego Women"). 13, 20 April–4 May 1971, p. 3.

2. Each group was accompanied by a male translator: Nguyen Tri, forty-six, from North Vietnam; Trinh Van Anh, thirty-three, from the South; and Soukanh Srithirath, thirty-four, from Laos (ibid.).

3. Kathleen Gough, "An Indochinese Conference in Vancouver," p. 2, folder "Indo-Chinese Women's Conference" no. 1, Anne Roberts Women's Movement Collection Fond.

4. "Dinh Thi Huong: A Prisoner of War," *Goodbye to All That*, no. 13, 20 April–4 May 1971, p. 4.

5. Ibid.

6. "Indochinese Women's Conference," *Asian Women's Journal* (1971; 3rd printing, 1975), p. 84.

7. Ibid.

8. Ibid.

9. Cynthia Frederick, "Women Play Key Role in Growing Saigon Peace Movement," *Memo* 1, no. 3 (January 1971): 13.

10. "Women's Liberation: Boston Solidarity Saigon," flyer, box 1, folder 35, Charlotte Bunch Papers.

11. DC WLM Anti-Imperialist Collective, "Thoughts about the Women's Proclamation," 28 November 1970, box 1, folder 35, Charlotte Bunch Papers.

12. "Dear Mr. Agnew . . . ," *Peace and Freedom*, November 1970, p. 2.

13. Ngo Ba Thanh, letter to Mr. Vice President Agnew, box 1, folder 35, Charlotte Bunch Papers. Also see *Memo Quarterly* 1, no. 3 (Winter 1971): 13; *Memo Quarterly* 1, no. 4 (Spring 1971): 11; and *Memo Quarterly* 2, no. 2 (Winter 1972): 27.

14. "Indochinese Women's Conference," *Goodbye to All That*, no. 13, 20 April–4 May 1971, p. 3.

15. "A Reaction," *Goodbye to All That*, no. 13, 20 April–4 May 1971, p. 2.

16. Quoted in Michal R. Belknap, *The Vietnam War on Trial: The My Lai Massacre and the Court-Martial of Lieutenant Calley* (Lawrence: University Press of Kansas, 2002), p. 65.

17. Ibid., pp. 69, 60.

18. Ibid., p. 72.

19. Ibid., p. 73.

20. Ibid.

21. Ibid., p. 75.

22. Ibid.

23. Ibid., p. 4.

24. Gough, "An Indochinese Conference in Vancouver," p. 10.

25. "U.S. Govt. Blamed for My Lai Deaths," *Winnipeg Free Press*, 31 March 1971, reproduced in *The Visit* (March–April 1971), Voice of Women/La Voix des Femmes Supplementaire/Supplement (July 1971).

26. Bradley, *Vietnam at War*, p. 160.

27. Ibid., p. 158.

28. *The Visit*, VOW supplement.

29. Chandra Mohanty, *Feminism without Borders: Decolonizing Theory, Practicing Solidarity* (Durham, NC: Duke University Press, 2003).

30. "Impressions from the Conference of Indochinese and North American Women, April 1971, Sponsored by Voice of Women, WILPF, WSP," *Memo* 2, no. 1 (Fall 1971): 16.

31. "A Reaction," *Goodbye to All That*, p. 2.

32. "Indochinese Women's Conference," *Asian Women's Journal*, p. 78.

33. Genera and Ramirez, interview.

34. Kiku Uno, "Open Letter to Sansei," *Asian Women's Journal* (1971; 3rd printing, 1975), p. 82.

35. Cindy Takemoto, "Pat Sumi: Off the Pedestal," *Asian Women's Journal* (1971; 3rd printing, 1975), p. 107. Sumi also was the likely source for an essay profiling a North Korean manager

of a large cooperative farm as well as a song by Korean women guerrillas about their struggles against Japanese colonialism. The contributor, who chose to remain anonymous, is described having "recently returned from North Korea." Anonymous, "Chairwoman of Chongsan-ri" and "Women's Guerrilla Song," *Asian Women's Journal* (1971; 3rd printing, 1975), pp. 72–73.

36. Donna Kotake, interview with author, San Francisco, CA, 31 May 2006.

37. Maeda, *Chains of Babylon.*

38. Kotake, interview.

39. Uno, "Open Letter to Sansei," p. 82.

40. Evelyn Yoshimura, "GI's and Racism," *Asian Women's Journal* (1971; 3rd printing, 1975), p. 74.

41. Ibid.

42. Enloe, *Bananas, Beaches, and Bases*; Moon, *Sex among Allies*; and Yuh, *Beyond the Shadow of Camptown.*

43. Yoshimura, "GI's and Racism," p. 74.

44. For a similar analysis of how racialized sexuality fostered male bonding within the U.S. military, see Stur, *Beyond Combat.* Stur includes quotes from an article that appears to replicate Yoshimura's essay. Titled "Asian Women and the Lifer Mind," it appeared in *Dare to Struggle*, a newsletter published by Movement for a Democratic Military in San Diego. Given Pat Sumi's connections to both MDM and the Asian American movement, she very likely facilitated the reproduction of Yoshimura's essay in *Dare to Struggle.* Stur, *Beyond Combat*, pp. 198–99.

45. Yoshimura, "GI's and Racism," p. 76.

46. Kim, *Ends of Empire*; Paul A. Kramer, *The Blood of Government: Race, Empire, the United States, and the Philippines* (Chapel Hill: University of North Carolina Press, 2006); Lee, *Orientals*; and David Roediger, "Gook: The Short History of an Americanism," *Monthly Review* 43 (March 1992): 50.

47. Yen Le Espiritu, *Asian American Women and Men: Labor, Laws and Love* (Sage, 1996).

48. "Learning How to Do It," *The Pedestal* (May 1971), p. 11.

49. Kathleen Aberle, "An Indochinese Conference in Vancouver," *Bulletin of Concerned Asian Scholars* 3, no. 3–4 (1971): 20.

50. Ibid., p. 21.

51. Ibid., p. 23.

52. Ibid., p. 19.

53. Ibid., pp. 19, 21.

54. Juanita Tamayo, "Tripping to Vancouver," *Asian Women's Journal* (1971; 3rd printing, 1975), p. 81. The poem was originally published in *Kalayaan*, a Filipino American activist publication. My thanks to Juanita Tamayo Lott for giving me permission to republish portions of this poem.

55. Ibid.

56. "Indochinese Women's Conference," *Asian Women's Journal*, p. 78.

57. Genera and Ramirez, interview.

58. For more about the antiwar activism of Maria Ramirez and Nina Genera and how they articulated an alternative understanding of masculinity, see Oropeza, *¡Raza Sí! ¡Guerra No!*

59. In fact, Maria attended the August 1970 Chicano Moratorium with her mother and sisters because it was "a family thing." When the police attacked with tear gas and helicopters, they sought refuge in "some old grandmother's house. Luckily, it was in East Los Angeles, you know. . . . She let us in . . . because it was like pandemonium outside."

60. Genera and Ramirez, interview.

61. Judy Drummond, interview.

62. Blackwell, *¡Chicana Power!*

63. *Georgia Straight*, 7–13 April 1971, cover.

64. M. Tongue, "Straight Responds to Women's Demands," *Georgia Straight*, 16–20 April 1971, p. 3.

65. Union of Vietnamese Women Cable to Women's International League for Peace and Freedom (WILPF), 1 January 1973, part II, H, 4, box 20, folder "Visit to Hanoi (Vietnam), Feb. 1973," Women's International League for Peace and Freedom Collection (WILPF) (DG 043), SCPC, Swarthmore, PA.

66. "Statement of Dorothy R. Steffens, National Director of Women's International League for Peace and Freedom, on her return from Hanoi," 7 February 1973, p. 1, series H, 4, box 20, folder "WILPF delegation to Hanoi (Vietnam), Jan. 1973," WILPF Collection.

Legacies

1. Genera and Ramirez, interview.

2. Ibid.

3. Ibid.

4. United Nations Viet Nam, "Survivors Need Social and Economic Support to Avoid Life of Poverty Says UN on International Mine Awareness Day," 4 April 2008, www.un.org.vn /en/feature-articles-press-centre-submenu-252/443-survivors-need-social-and-economic-sup port-to-avoid-life-of-poverty-says-un-on-international-mine-awareness-day.html.

5. Brown, *A Taste of Power*, p. 229.

6. Froines, telephone interview.

7. Nancy Stearns, interview with author, New York City, 3 May 2006.

8. Ibid.

9. Quoted in Takaki, *Strangers from a Different Shore*, p. 461.

10. Tom Wolfe, "The 'Me' Decade and the Third Great Awakening," *New York Magazine*, 23 August 1976, pp. 26–40.

11. Meriwether, *Proudly We Can Be Africans*, p. 5.

12. Ibid., p. 244.

13. Sumi, interview by Yokota, 1 July 1997, p. 9.

14. Maria Ramirez, e-mail correspondence with author, 29 January 2011.

15. Pham Van Chuong, interview.

16. Olcott, "Cold War Conflicts and Cheap Cabaret"; and Ara Wilson, "Lesbian Visibility and Sexual Rights at Beijing," *Signs* 22, no. 1 (1996): 214–18.

17. Pham Thi Hoai Giang and Nguyen Thi Tuyet, interview with author, Hanoi, Vietnam, 12 August 2009.

18. Memorandum from Linda Forrest to FOR Staff, 13 February 1968, G-6, B. 17, folder "U.S. 1967–1968," FOR Records.

19. For a critique of how humanitarian aid enabled U.S. military destruction, see Hershberger, *Traveling to Vietnam*.

20. Cora Weiss, interview, 9 April 2006.

21. Robert Browne, "Vietnam's New Economics," *New York Times*, 6 July 1978.

22. Ibid.

23. Ibid.

24. Robert S. Browne, "America's Overdue Debt to Indochina," *New York Times*, 17 August 1979.

25. Ibid.

26. *Church World Service Sailed a Ship of Wheat to Viet Nam* (New York: Church World Service, [1978]), p. 8.

27. Ibid., p. 11.

28. Ibid., p. 14.

Bibliography

Archival Material

Anne Roberts Women's Movement Collection Fond. Archives and Records Management Department. Simon Fraser University, Vancouver, BC.

Browne, Robert S. Collected Papers (CDG-A). Swarthmore College Peace Collection (SCPC). Swarthmore, PA.

———. Department of State. Washington, DC. Freedom of Information Documents.

———. Papers. Schomburg Center for Research in Black Culture. Manuscripts, Archives and Rare Books Division. New York Public Library.

———. United States International Cooperation Administration (ICA). National Personnel Records Center, St. Louis, MO.

Bunch, Charlotte. Papers. Schlesinger Library, Radcliffe Institute, Harvard University. Cambridge, MA.

Chicago Women's Liberation Union (CWLU) Records. Research Center, Chicago History Museum.

Cleaver, Eldridge. Federal Bureau of Investigation Files. Washington, DC. Freedom of Information Documents.

———. Papers. BANC MSS 91/213c. Bancroft Library. University of California, Berkeley.

Dr. Huey P. Newton Foundation Incorporation Collection. MS M0864. Special Collections and University Archives. Stanford University, Stanford, CA.

Fellowship of Reconciliation Records (FOR) (DG 013). Swarthmore College Peace Collection (SCPC), Swarthmore, PA.

Kathleen Hudson Women's Bookstore Collection. F-111. Archives and Records Management Department. Simon Fraser University, Vancouver, BC.

Record Group 84. Civilian Agency Records. National Archives Records Administration (NARA), College Park, MD.

Record Group 469. Records of the U.S. Foreign Assistance Agencies. National Archives Records Administration (NARA), College Park, MD.

Sumi, Pat. Department of State. Washington, DC. Freedom of Information Documents.

Voice of Women (VOW) Fonds. Library and Archives Canada, Ottawa, ON.

Willard, Arthur C. Files for President. Record Series Number 2/9/1. University of Illinois Archives, Urbana-Champaign, IL.

Women's International League for Peace and Freedom Collection (WILPF) (DG 043). Swarthmore College Peace Collection (SCPC), Swarthmore, PA.

Women Strike for Peace Records (WSP) (DG 115). Swarthmore College Peace Collection (SCPC), Swarthmore, PA.

Cited Oral Histories

Ambers, Gerry. Telephone interview with author. Vancouver, BC, Canada, 4 April 2007.

Breimberg, Liz. Interview with author. Vancouver, BC, Canada, 2 November 2005.

Browne, Hoa. Conversation with author. New York City, 3 May 2005.

Browne, Hoa, and Houi Browne. Conversation with author. Teaneck, NJ, 1 December 2006.

Browne, Wendelle. Interview with author. Chicago, 21 May 2006.

Bunch, Charlotte. Interview with author, New York City, 30 November 2006.

Chan, Jeffrey. Telephone interview with author. San Rafael, CA, 17 January 2005.

Cleaver, Kathleen. Interview with author. New Haven, CT, 22 February 2006.

Drummond, Judy. Interview with author. San Francisco, CA, 21 March 2007.

Duckles, Madeline. Interview with author. Berkeley, CA, 21 October 2006.

Easley-Cox, Barbara. Interview with Robin J. Haynes. Philadelphia, PA, 22 July 2005.

———. Telephone interview with author. Philadelphia, PA, 21 December 2006.

Esman, Milton. Telephone interview with author. Ithaca, NY, 26 October 2005.

Fournier, Frances. Conversation with author. Vancouver, BC, Canada, 31 October 2005.

Froines, Ann. Telephone interview with author. 21 December 2006.

Genera, Nina, and Maria Ramirez. Interview with author. Hayward, CA, 27 February 2007.

Haynes, Robin. Conversation with author. Chicago, 9 January 2006.

Hing, Alex. E-mail correspondence. 26 February 2006.

———. Interview with author. New York City, 19 March 2005.

Kotake, Donna. Interview with author. San Francisco, CA, 31 May 2006.

Martinez, Betita. Telephone interview with author. 7 December 2006.

Matthews, Tracye. Conversations with author. Chicago, Winter 2006.

Near, Holly. Telephone interview with author. 12 February 2007.

Nguyen Thi Ngoc Dung. Interview with author. Ho Chi Minh City, Vietnam, 19 August 2009.

Pham Khac Lam. Interview with author. Hanoi, Vietnam, 12 August 2009.

Pham Thi Hoai Giang and Nguyen Thi Tuyet. Interview with author. Hanoi, Vietnam, 12 August 2009.

Pham Van Chuong. Interview with author. Hanoi, Vietnam, 12 August 2009.

Ramirez, Maria. E-mail correspondence with author. 29 January 2011.

Rappaport, Randy. Conversation with author. Amherst, MA, 11 June 2011.

———. Interview with author. Columbus, OH, 7 July 2007.

Rothstein, Vivian. Telephone interview with author. 9 March 2007.

Smith, Ed. Interview with author. Honolulu, HI, 25 April 2009.

Stearns, Nancy. Interview with author. New York City, 3 May 2006.

Sumi, Pat. Interview by Ryan Yokota. Los Angeles, 19 June 1997 and 1 July 1997. Transcript from 1 July session.

Tranh Minh Quoc. Interview with author, Hanoi, Vietnam, 10 August 2009.

Weiss, Cora. Interview with author. Brooklyn, NY, 7 April 2006.

———. Interviews with author. New York City, 8 and 9 April 2006, and 4 May 2006.

Weiss, Cora, and Peter Weiss. Interview with author. New York City, 9 April 2006.

Weisstein, Naomi. Telephone interview with author. 5 February 2007.

Books, Articles, and Films

Aberle, Kathleen. "An Indochinese Conference in Vancouver." *Bulletin of Concerned Asian Scholars* 3, no. 3–4 (1971): 19–23.

Alonso, Harriet Hyman. *Peace as a Women's Issue: A History of the U.S. Movement for World Peace and Women's Rights.* Syracuse, NY: Syracuse University Press, 1993.

Alvah, Donna. *Unofficial Ambassadors: American Military Families Overseas and the Cold War.* New York: New York University Press, 2007.

Anderson, Benedict. *Imagined Communities: Reflections on the Origin and Spread of Nationalism,* rev. ed. London: Verso, 1991.

Anderson, Carol. *Eyes off the Prize: The United Nations and the African American Struggle for Human Rights, 1944–1955.* Cambridge: Cambridge University Press, 2003.

Anderson, Terry H. *The Movement and the Sixties: Protest in America from Greensboro to Wounded Knee.* New York: Oxford University Press, 1995.

Appy, Christian G. *Working-Class War: American Combat Soldiers and Vietnam.* Chapel Hill: University of North Carolina Press, 1993.

Asian Women's Journal (University of California, 1971; 3rd printing, Los Angeles: Asian American Studies Center, University of California, 1975).

Austin, Curtis J. *Up against the Wall: Violence in the Making and Unmaking of the Black Panther Party.* Fayetteville: University of Arkansas Press, 2006.

Bailey, Beth L. *Sex in the Heartland*. Cambridge, MA: Harvard University Press, 2002.

Baldwin, James. "Negroes Are Anti-Semitic because They're Anti-White." *New York Times Magazine*, 9 April 1967. http://www.nytimes.com/books/98/03/29/specials/baldwin-antisem.html.

Barry, Kathleen, ed. *Vietnam's Women in Transition*. Houndsmills, UK: Macmillan, 1996.

Bates, Beth Tompkins. *Pullman Porters and the Rise of Protest Politics in Black America, 1925–1945*. Chapel Hill: University of North Carolina Press, 2000.

Beins, Agatha. "Free Our Sisters, Free Ourselves! Locating U.S. Feminism through Feminist Publishing." PhD diss., Rutgers University, 2011.

———. "Radical Others: Women of Color and Revolutionary Feminism." Unpublished manuscript, 2011.

———. "Sisters Rise Up! Feminist Identities and Communities in the Women's Liberation Movement." Paper presented at NEH Summer Institute, Sequel to the 60s, Schlesinger Library, Harvard University, Cambridge, MA, 2008.

Belknap, Michal R. *The Vietnam War on Trial: The My Lai Massacre and the Court-Martial of Lieutenant Calley*. Lawrence: University Press of Kansas, 2002.

Blackwell, Joyce. *No Peace without Freedom: Race and the Women's International League for Peace and Freedom, 1915–1975*. Carbondale: Southern Illinois University Press, 2004.

Blackwell, Maylei. *¡Chicana Power! Contested Histories of Feminism in the Chicano Movement*. Austin: University of Texas Press, 2011.

Borstelmann, Thomas. *The Cold War and the Color Line: American Race Relations in the Global Arena*. Cambridge, MA: Harvard University Press, 2001.

Bradley, Mark Philip. *Vietnam at War*. New York: Oxford University Press, 2009.

Brigham, Robert K. *Guerrilla Diplomacy: The NLF's Foreign Relations and the Viet Nam War*. Ithaca, NY: Cornell University Press, 1999.

Brooks, Charlotte. "In the Twilight Zone between Black and White: Japanese American Resettlement and Community in Chicago, 1942–1945." *Journal of American History* 86, no. 4 (2000): 1655–87.

Brown, Elaine. *A Taste of Power: A Black Woman's Story*. New York: Anchor Books, 1994.

Brown, Rita Mae. "Hanoi to Hoboken, a Round Trip Ticket." In *Out of the Closets: Voices of Gay Liberation*, ed. Karla Jay and Allen Young. New York: Douglas, 1972.

Browne, Robert S. "The Black Man and the War in Vietnam." *Newsletter*, Coordinating Committee of Black Organizations against the Draft, no. 1 (April 1967): 5.

———. "Dance as if No One Is Watching: The Memoirs of Robert S. Browne." Unpublished manuscript, undated, Twentieth Century Foundation, New York, NY.

———. "FDU Prof. Visits Vietnam." *Tarrevir*, 25 October 1967, p. 3.

———. "The Freedom Movement and the War in Vietnam." In *Vietnam and Black America: An Anthology of Protest and Resistance*, ed. Clyde Taylor. Garden City, NY: Anchor Press, 1973. Originally published in *Freedomways* 5, no. 4 (1965).

———. *Race Relations in International Affairs.* Washington, DC: Public Affairs Press, 1961.

Bunch-Weeks, Charlotte, and Frank Joyce. "North Vietnam: A Photo Essay." *Motive* (February 1971).

Chan, Sucheng. *Asian Americans: An Interpretive History.* Boston: Twayne, 1991.

Chandler, David. *The Tragedy of Cambodian History: Politics, War, and Revolution since 1945.* New Haven, CT: Yale University Press, 1991.

Church World Service Sailed a Ship of Wheat to Viet Nam. New York: Church World Service, [1978].

Cleaver, Eldridge. "Address," *Ramparts* 7, no. 9 (14–28 December 1968): 6.

———. *Soul on Fire.* Waco, TX: Word Books, 1978.

———. *Soul on Ice.* New York: Dell, 1968.

———. *Target Zero: A Life in Writing*, ed. Kathleen Cleaver. New York: Palgrave Macmillan, 2006.

Cleaver, Kathleen, and George Katsiaficas, eds. *Liberation, Imagination, and the Black Panther Party: A New Look at the Panthers and Their Legacy.* New York: Routledge, 2001.

Clinton, James W. "Cora Weiss." In *The Loyal Opposition: Americans in North Vietnam, 1965–1972.* Niwot: University Press of Colorado, 1995.

Cohen, Lizabeth. *A Consumers' Republic: The Politics of Mass Consumption in Postwar America.* New York: Vintage, 2003.

Cooper, Frederick, and Randall Packard, eds. *International Development and the Social Sciences: Essays on the History and Politics of Knowledge.* Berkeley: University of California Press, 1999.

Cumings, Bruce. *Korea's Place in the Sun: A Modern History*, updated ed. New York: W. W. Norton, 2005.

———. *Parallax Visions: Making Sense of American–East Asian Relations at the End of the Century.* Chapel Hill: University of North Carolina Press, 1999.

Drake, St. Clair, and Horace C. Cayton. *Black Metropolis: A Study of Negro Life in a Northern City.* New York: Harcourt, 1945.

Drummond, Lisa, and Helle Rydstrom. *Gender Practices in Contemporary Vietnam.* Singapore: Singapore University Press, 2004.

Dudziak, Mary L. *Cold War Civil Rights: Race and the Image of American Democracy.* Princeton, NJ: Princeton University Press, 2000.

Duiker, William J. "The Foreign Policy of North Vietnam." In *Light at the End of the Tunnel: A Vietnam War Anthology*, 3rd ed., ed. Andrew J. Rotter, 172–90. Lanham, MD: Rowman and Littlefield, 2010.

———. *Ho Chi Minh.* New York: Hyperion, 2000.

Echols, Alice. *Daring to Be Bad: Radical Feminism in America 1967–1975.* Minneapolis: University of Minnesota Press, 1989.

Eisen, Arlene. *Women and Revolution in Viet Nam.* London: Zed Books, 1984.

Elbaum, Max. *Revolution in the Air: Sixties Radicals Turn to Lenin, Mao, and Che.* London: Verso, 2002.

Endy, Christopher. *Cold War Holidays: American Tourism in France.* Chapel Hill: University of North Carolina Press, 2004.

Enloe, Cynthia. *Bananas, Beaches, and Bases: Making Feminist Sense of International Politics*. London: Pandora, 1989.

———. *Maneuvers: The International Politics of Militarizing Women's Lives*. Berkeley: University of California Press, 2000.

Espiritu, Yen Le. *Asian American Panethnicity: Bridging Institutions and Identities*. Philadelphia: Temple University Press, 1992.

Evans, Sara, ed. *Journeys That Opened Up the World: Women, Student Christian Movements, and Social Justice, 1955–1975*. New Brunswick, NJ: Rutgers University Press, 2003.

———. *Personal Politics: The Roots of Women's Liberation in the Civil Rights Movement and the New Left*. New York: Vintage, 1980.

———. *Tidal Wave: How Women Changed America at Century's End*. New York: Free Press, 2004.

Fabre, Michel. *The Unfinished Quest of Richard Wright*, trans. Isabel Barzun. Urbana: University of Illinois Press, 1993.

Fitzgerald, Frances. *Fire in the Lake: The Vietnamese and the Americans in Vietnam*. Boston: Little, Brown, 1972.

Fox, Robert Elliot. "About Ishmael Reed's Life and Work." In *The Oxford Companion to African American Literature*, ed. William L. Andrews, Francis Smith Foster, and Trudier Harris New York: Oxford University Press, 1997. http://www.english .illinois.edu/maps/poets/m_r/reed/about.htm.

Frazier, Jessica M. "Collaborative Efforts to End the War in Viet Nam: The Interactions of Women Strike for Peace, the Vietnamese Women's Union, and the Women's Union of Liberation, 1965–1968." *Peace and Change* 37, no. 3 (July 2012): 339–365.

———. "Collaborative Efforts: Women Strike for Peace's Interactions with Vietnamese Women during the Vietnam War, 1965–1968." Paper presented at the Berkshires Conference on the History of Women, Amherst, MA, June 2011.

Froines, Ann. "Know Your Enemy." *Liberation* 15, no. 9 (1970): 20–21, 40.

Front de liberation des femmes du Quebec. "Letter," 4 December 1970. In *Quebecoises Deboutte!* Vol. 1, pp. 79–80 [in French, trans. Katie Bausch]. Quebec, Canada: Les éditions du remue-ménage, 1983.

Fujino, Diane. *Heartbeat of Struggle: The Revolutionary Life of Yuri Kochiyama*. Minneapolis: University of Minnesota Press, 2005.

———. *Samurai among Panthers: Richard Aoki on Race, Resistance, and a Paradoxical Life*. Minneapolis: University of Minnesota Press, 2012.

———. "Who Studies the Asian American Movement? A Historiographical Analysis." *Journal of Asian American Studies* 11, no. 2 (2008): 127–69.

Gallicchio, Marc. *The African American Encounter with Japan and China: Black Internationalism in Asia, 1895–1945*. Chapel Hill: University of North Carolina Press, 2000.

Gilmore, Stephanie, ed. *Feminist Coalitions: Historical Perspectives on Second-Wave Feminism in the United States*. Urbana: University of Illinois Press, 2008.

Gitlin, Todd. *The Sixties: Years of Hope, Days of Rage*. New York: Bantam, 1987.

Green, Michael Cullen. *Black Yanks in the Pacific: Race in the Making of American Military Empire after World War II*. Ithaca, NY: Cornell University Press, 2010.

Greenberg, Cheryl Lynn. *Troubling the Water: Black-Jewish Relations in the American Century.* Princeton, NJ: Princeton University Press, 2006.

Gregory, James N. *The Southern Diaspora: How the Great Migrations of Black and White Southerners Transformed America.* Chapel Hill: University of North Carolina Press, 2007.

Grewal, Inderpal. *Transnational America: Feminisms, Diasporas, Neoliberalisms.* Durham, NC: Duke University Press, 2005.

Habal, Estella. *San Francisco's International Hotel: Mobilizing the Filipino American Community in the Anti-Eviction Movement.* Philadelphia: Temple University Press, 2007.

Hall, Simon. *Peace and Freedom: The Civil Rights and Antiwar Movements in the 1960s.* Philadelphia: University of Pennsylvania Press, 2005.

———. *Rethinking the American Anti-War Movement.* New York: Routledge, 2012.

Hanh, Thich Nhat. *Vietnam: Lotus in a Sea of Fire.* New York: Hill and Wang, 1967.

Hansberry, Lorraine. *To Be Young, Gifted and Black: Lorraine Hansberry in Her Own Words,* adapted by Robert Nemiroff. Englewood Cliffs, NJ: Prentice-Hall, 1969.

Hassler, Alfred. *Diary of a Self-Made Convict.* London: Victor Gollancz, 1955.

Hayes, Robin J. "'A Free Black Mind Is a Concealed Weapon': Institutions and Social Movements in the African Diaspora." In *Transnational Blackness: Navigating the Global Color Line,* ed. Manning Marable and Vanessa Agard-Jones, 175–88. New York: Palgrave Macmillan, 2008.

Hershberger, Mary. *Traveling to Vietnam: American Peace Activists and the War.* Syracuse, NY: Syracuse University Press, 1998.

Hewitt, Nancy, ed. *No Permanent Waves: Recasting Histories of U.S. Feminism.* New Brunswick, NJ: Rutgers University Press, 2010.

Hewitt, Steve, and Christabelle Sethna. "'Sweating and Uncombed': Canadian State Security, the Indochinese Conference and the Feminist Threat, 1968–1972." Paper presented at the Canadian Historical Association, University of British Columbia, Vancouver, Canada, May–June 2008.

Higashida, Cheryl. *Black Internationalist Feminism: Women Writers of the Black Left, 1945–1995.* Urbana: University of Illinois Press, 2011.

Ho, Fred, with Carolyn Antonio, Diane Fujino, and Steve Yip, eds. *Legacy to Liberation: Politics and Culture of Revolutionary Asian Pacific America.* Brooklyn, NY: Big Red Media, 2000.

Hoganson, Kristin L. *Fighting for American Manhood: How Gender Politics Provoked the Spanish-American and Philippine-American Wars.* New Haven, CT: Yale University Press, 2000.

Höhn, Maria, and Seungsook Moon, eds. *Over There: Living with the U.S. Military Empire from World War Two to the Present.* Durham, NC: Duke University Press, 2010.

Honig, Emily. "Maoist Mappings of Gender: Reassessing the Red Guards." In *Chinese Femininities, Chinese Masculinities: A Reader,* ed. Susan Brownell and Jeffrey N. Wasserstrom. Berkeley: University of California Press, 2002.

Horne, Gerald. *Black and Red: W.E.B. DuBois and the Afro-American Response to the Cold War, 1944–1963.* Albany: State University of New York Press, 1986.

Hurst, Jim, and Sam Weaver, eds. *Barrister 1962: John Marshall High School*. Los Angeles, 1962.

Iwamura, Jane Naomi. *Virtual Orientalism*. Oxford: Oxford University Press, 2011.

Jacobs, Seth. *America's Miracle Man in Vietnam: Ngo Dinh Diem, Religion, Race, and U.S. Intervention in Southeast Asia*. Durham, NC: Duke University Press, 2004.

———. "'No Place to Fight a War': Laos and the Evolution of U.S. Policy toward Viet Nam, 1954–1963." In *Making Sense of the Vietnam Wars: Local, National, and Transnational Perspectives*, ed. Mark Philip Bradley and Marilyn B. Young. New York: Oxford University Press, 2008.

Jones, Charles E., ed. *The Black Panther Party Reconsidered*. Baltimore, MD: Black Classic Press, 1998.

Jones, Matthew. "A 'Segregated' Asia? Race, the Bandung Conference, and Pan-Asianist Fears in American Thought and Policy, 1954–1955." *Diplomatic History* 29, no. 5 (2005): 841–68.

Joseph, Peniel E., ed. *The Black Power Movement*. New York: Routledge, 2006.

Kapur, Sudarshan. *Rising Up a Prophet: The African American Encounter with Gandhi*. Boston: Beacon, 1992.

Karnow, Stanley. *Vietnam: A History*. New York: Penguin, 1983.

Katznelson, Ira. *When Affirmative Action Was White: An Untold History of Racial Inequality in Twentieth-Century America*. New York: W. W. Norton, 2005.

Kearney, Reginald. *African American Views of the Japanese: Solidarity or Sedition?* Albany: State University of New York Press, 1998.

Kelley, Robin D. G. *Freedom Dreams: The Black Radical Imagination*. Boston: Beacon, 2002.

Kelley, Robin D. G., and Betsy Esch. "Black Like Mao: Red China and Black Revolution." *Souls* (Fall 1999): 6–41.

Kerber, Linda K. *No Constitutional Right to Be Ladies: Women and the Obligations of Citizenship*. New York: Hill and Wang, 1998.

Kerr, Nora. "Vietnam's Closer to Their Hearth." *Sunday Record*, 8 February 1970.

Kim, Claire Jean. "The Racial Triangulation of Asian Americans." *Politics and Society* 27, no. 1 (1999): 105–38.

Kim, Jodi. *Ends of Empire: Asian American Critique and the Cold War*. Minneapolis: University of Minnesota Press, 2010.

Kim, Nadia Y. *Imperial Citizens: Koreans and Race from Seoul to L.A.* Stanford, CA: Stanford University Press, 2008.

Kim, Suzy. "Revolutionary Mothers: Women in the North Korean Revolution, 1945–1950." *Contemporary Studies in Society and History* 52, no. 4 (2010): 742–67.

Kimbrough, Natalie. *Equality or Discrimination? African Americans in the U.S. Military during the Vietnam War*. Lanham, MD: University Press of America, 2007.

King, Robert H. *Thomas Merton and Thich Nhat Hanh: Engaged Spirituality in an Age of Globalization*. New York: Continuum, 2001.

Klein, Christina. *Cold War Orientalism: Asia in the Middlebrow Imagination, 1945–1961*. Berkeley: University of California Press, 2003.

Kramer, Paul A. *The Blood of Government: Race, Empire, the United States, and the Philippines*. Chapel Hill: University of North Carolina Press, 2006.

Krenn, Michael L. *Black Diplomacy: African Americans and the State Department, 1945–1969.* Armonk, NY: M. E. Sharpe, 1999.

Kurashige, Lon. *Japanese American Celebration and Conflict: A History of Ethnic Identity and Festival in Los Angeles, 1934–1990.* Berkeley: University of California Press, 2002.

Kurashige, Scott. *The Shifting Grounds of Race: Black and Japanese Americans in the Making of Multiethnic Los Angeles.* Princeton, NJ: Princeton University Press, 2008.

Laderman, Scott. *Tours of Vietnam: War, Travel Guides, and Memory.* Durham, NC: Duke University Press, 2009.

Lai, Him Mark. *Chinese American Transnational Politics*, ed. Madeline Y. Hsu. Urbana: University of Illinois Press, 2010.

———. "The Kuomingtang in Chinese American Communities before World War I." In *Entry Denied: Exclusion and the Chinese Community in America, 1882–1943*, ed. Sucheng Chan. Philadelphia: Temple University Press, 1991.

Lawrence, Mark Atwood. *Assuming the Burden: Europe and the American Commitment to War in Vietnam.* Berkeley: University of California Press, 2005.

Layton, Azza Salama. *International Politics and Civil Rights Policies in the United States, 1941–1960.* New York: Cambridge University Press, 2000.

Lederer, William J., and Eugene Burdick. *The Ugly American.* New York: W. W. Norton, 1958.

Lee, Peter. "Indo-Chinese Women's Conference. " *New Bridge* 1, no. 3 (1971): 15.

Lee, Robert G. *Orientals: Asian Americans in Popular Culture.* Philadelphia: Temple University Press, 1999.

Lekus, Ian. "Queer and Present Dangers: Masculinity, Sexual Revolutions, and the New Left." PhD diss., Duke University, 2003.

———. "Queer Harvests: Homosexuality, the U.S. Left, and the Venceremos Brigades to Cuba." *Radical History Review* 89, no. 1 (2004): 57–91.

Lenski, Gerhard. *Power and Privilege: A Theory of Social Stratification.* New York: McGraw-Hill, 1966.

Leong, Karen J. *The China Mystique: Pearl S. Buck, Anna May Wong, Mayling Soong, and the Transformation of American Orientalism.* Berkeley: University of California Press, 2005.

Lerner, Mitchell B. *The Pueblo Incident: A Spy Ship and the Failure of American Foreign Policy.* Lawrence: University Press of Kansas, 2002.

Linfield, Susie. "The Education of Kathleen Neal Cleaver." *Transitions* 77 (1998): 172–195.

Loewen, Candace. "Making Ourselves Heard: 'Voice of Women' and the Peace Movement in the Early Sixties." In *Framing Our Past: Canadian Women's History in the Twentieth Century*, ed. Sharon Anne Cook, Lorna R. McLean, and Kate O'Rourke. Montreal: McGill-Queen's University Press, 2001.

Louie, Steve, and Glenn Omatsu, eds. *Asian Americans: The Movement and the Moment.* Los Angeles: UCLA Asian American Studies Center Press, 2001.

Maeda, Daryl J. "Black Panthers, Red Guards, and Chinamen: Constructing Asian American Identity through Performing Blackness, 1969–1972." *American Quarterly* 57 (2005): 1079–1103.

————. *Chains of Babylon: The Rise of Asian America*. Minneapolis: University of Minnesota Press, 2009.

————. *Rethinking the Asian American Movement*. New York: Routledge, 2012.

Makalani, Minkah. *In the Cause of Freedom: Radical Black Internationalism from Harlem to London, 1917–1939*. Chapel Hill: University of North Carolina Press, 2011.

Malloy, Sean. "Uptight in Babylon: Eldridge Cleaver's Cold War." *Diplomatic History* (forthcoming).

Marable, Manning. *Race, Reform and Rebellion: The Second Reconstruction in Black America*. Jackson: University Press of Mississippi, 1991.

Marchetti, Gina. *Romance and the "Yellow Peril": Race, Sex, and Discursive Strategies in Hollywood Fiction*. Berkeley: University of California Press, 1993.

Marr, David G. *Vietnam, 1945: A Quest for Power*. Berkeley: University of California Press, 2005.

McAlister, Melani. *Epic Encounters: Culture, Media, and U.S. Interests in the Middle East, 1945–2000*. Berkeley: University of California Press, 2001.

McCormack, Suzanne Kelly. "'Good Politics Is Doing Something': Independent Diplomats and Anti-War Activists in the Vietnam-Era Peace Movement, a Collective Biography." PhD diss., Boston College, 2002.

Meriwether, James H. *Proudly We Can Be Africans: Black Americans and Africa, 1935–1961*. Chapel Hill: University of North Carolina Press, 2002.

Miller, James. *Democracy Is in the Streets: From Port Huron to the Siege of Chicago*. New York: Touchstone, 1987.

Mohanty, Chandra. *Feminism without Borders: Decolonizing Theory, Practicing Solidarity*. Durham, NC: Duke University Press, 2003.

————. "Under Western Eyes: Feminist Scholarship and Colonial Discourses." *Feminist Review* 30 (Autumn 1988): 61–88.

Moon, Katharine H. S. *Sex among Allies: Military Prostitution in U.S.-Korea Relations*. New York: Columbia University Press, 1997.

Morgan, Robin, ed. *Sisterhood Is Powerful: An Anthology of Writings from the Women's Liberation Movement*. New York: Vintage, 1970.

Mullen, Bill V. *Afro-Orientalism*. Minneapolis: University of Minnesota Press, 2004.

Mullen, Bill V., and Cathryn Watson. *W.E.B. DuBois on Asia: Crossing the World Color Line*. Jackson: University Press of Mississippi, 2005.

Murch, Donna. *Living for the City: Migration, Education, and the Rise of the Black Panther Party in Oakland, California*. Chapel Hill: University of North Carolina Press, 2010.

Nagel, Joane. *Race, Ethnicity, and Sexuality: Intimate Intersections, Forbidden Frontiers*. New York: Oxford University Press, 2003.

Nakano, Satoshi. "South to South across the Pacific: Ernest E. Neal and Community Development Efforts in the American South and the Philippines." *Japanese Journal of American Studies* 16 (2005): 181–202.

Nee, Victor, and Brett de Bary Nee. *Longtime Californ': A Documentary Study of an American Chinatown*. Stanford, CA: Stanford University Press, 1972.

Ogbar, Jeffrey O. G. *Black Power: Radical Politics and African American Identity*. Baltimore, MD: Johns Hopkins University Press, 1994.

Okihiro, Gary. *Margins and Mainstreams: Asians in American History and Culture*. Seattle: University of Washington Press, 1994.

Olcott, Jocelyn. "Cold War Conflicts and Cheap Cabaret: Sexual Politics at the 1975 United Nations International Women's Year Conference." *Gender and History* 22, no. 3 (2010): 733–54.

Onishi, Yuichiro. *Moving in a Racial Groove: How Afro-Asian Solidarity Was Found in Black America, Japan, and Okinawa*. New York: New York University Press, 2013.

Oropeza, Lorena. *¡Raza Sí! ¡Guerra No! Chicano Protest and Patriotism during the Viet Nam War Era*. Berkeley: University of California Press, 2005.

Osgood, Kenneth. *Total Cold War: Eisenhower's Secret Propaganda Battle at Home and Abroad*. Lawrence: University Press of Kansas, 2006.

Park, Kyung Ae. "Women and Revolution in North Korea." *Pacific Affairs* 65, no. 4 (1992–93): 527–45.

Parker, Jason. "Cold War II: The Eisenhower Administration, the Bandung Conference, and the Reperiodization of the Postwar Era." *Diplomatic History* 30, no. 5 (2006): 867–92.

"People of the World Unite: An Interview with Alex Hing and Pat Sumi." *Getting Together* 1, no. 5 (September–October 1970): 11.

Plummer, Brenda Gayle. *Rising Wind: Black Americans and U.S. Foreign Affairs, 1935–1960*. Chapel Hill: University of North Carolina Press, 1996.

———, ed. *Window on Freedom: Race, Civil Rights, and Foreign Affairs, 1945–1988*. Chapel Hill: University of North Carolina Press, 2003.

Prashad, Vijay. *Everybody Was Kung Fu Fighting: Afro-Asian Connections and the Myth of Cultural Purity*. Boston: Beacon, 2001.

Pratt, Mary Louise. *Imperial Eyes: Travel Writing and Transculturation*. New York: Routledge, 1992.

Pritchett, Wendell. *Brownsville, Brooklyn: Blacks, Jews, and the Changing Face of the Ghetto*. Chicago: University of Chicago Press, 2002.

Puar, Jasbir K. *Terrorist Assemblages: Homonationalism in Queer Times*. Durham, NC: Duke University Press, 2007.

Pulido, Laura. *Black, Brown, Yellow and Left: Radical Activism in Los Angeles*. Berkeley: University of California Press, 2006.

Rebick, Judy. *Ten Thousand Roses: The Making of a Feminist Revolution*. Toronto: Penguin Canada, 2005.

Roediger, David. "Gook: The Short History of an Americanism." *Monthly Review* 43 (March 1992): 50.

Rosen, Ruth. *The World Split Open: How the Modern Women's Movement Changed America*. New York: Viking, 2000.

Roth, Benita. *Separate Roads to Feminism: Black, Chicana, and White Feminist Movements in America's Second Wave*. New York: Cambridge University Press, 2003.

Rupp, Leila J. *Worlds of Women: The Making of an International Women's Movement*. Princeton, NJ: Princeton University Press, 1997.

Ryang, Sonia. "Gender in Oblivion: Women in the Democratic People's Republic of Korea (North Korea)." *Journal of Asian and African Studies* 35, no. 3 (2000): 325–49.

Salaam, Kaluma ya. "Historical Overviews of the Black Arts Movement." In *The Oxford Companion to African American Literature*, ed. William L. Andrews, Francis Smith Foster, and Trudier Harris. New York: Oxford University Press, 1997. http://www.english.illinois.edu/maps/blackarts/historical.htm.

———. "In the Black: A Portrait of Economist Robert S. Browne." *Black Collegian* (September–October 1978).

Salaff, Janet, and Judith Merkle. "Women in Revolution: The Lessons of the Soviet Union and China." *Berkeley Journal of Sociology* 15 (1970): 182.

Salzman, Jack, and Cornel West, eds. *Struggles in the Promised Land: Toward a History of Black-Jewish Relations in the United States*. New York: Oxford University Press, 1997.

Schulzinger, Robert D. *A Time for War: The United States and Vietnam, 1941–1975*. New York: Oxford University Press, 1995.

Scott, Joan. "Gender: A Useful Category of Historical Analysis." *American Historical Review* 91, no. 5 (1986): 1053–75.

Shah, Nayan. *Contagious Divides: Epidemics and Race in San Francisco's Chinatown*. Berkeley: University of California Press, 2001.

Shibusawa, Naoko. *America's Geisha Ally: Reimagining the Japanese Enemy*. Cambridge, MA: Harvard University Press, 2010.

Shuman, Aaron. "A Sit-Down with Kathleen Cleaver." *Bad Subjects* 60 (April 2002).

Siegel, Kristi, ed. *Issues in Travel Writing: Empire, Spectacle, and Displacement*. New York: Peter Lang, 2002.

Simpson, Caroline Chung. *An Absent Presence: Japanese Americans in Postwar American Culture, 1945–1960*. Durham, NC: Duke University Press, 2001.

Singh, Nikhil Pal. *Black Is a Country: Race and the Unfinished Struggle for Democracy*. Cambridge, MA: Harvard University Press, 2004.

Slate, Nico. *Colored Cosmopolitanism: The Shared Struggle for Freedom in the United States and India*. Cambridge, MA: Harvard University Press, 2012.

Springer, Kimberly. *Living for the Revolution: Black Feminist Organizations, 1968–1980*. Durham, NC: Duke University Press, 2005.

———, ed. *Still Lifting, Still Climbing: African American Women's Contemporary Activism*. New York: New York University Press, 1999.

Strange, Maren. *Bronzeville: Black Chicago in Pictures 1941–1943*. New York: New Press, 2003.

Strickland, Arvarh E. *History of the Chicago Urban League*. Urbana: University of Illinois Press, 1966.

Stur, Heather Marie. *Beyond Combat: Women and Gender in the Vietnam War Era*. Cambridge: Cambridge University Press, 2011.

"Success Story of One Minority Group in U.S." *U.S. News and World Report*, 26 December 1966. Reprinted in *Roots: An Asian American Reader*, ed. Amy Tachiki, Eddie Wong, Franklin Odo, and Buck Wong. Los Angeles: UCLA Asian American Studies Center, 1971.

Swerdlow, Amy. *Women Strike for Peace: Traditional Motherhood and Radical Politics in the 1960s*. Chicago: University of Chicago Press, 1993.

Takaki, Ronald. *Strangers from a Different Shore: A History of Asian Americans*, rev. and updated ed. Boston: Little, Brown, 1998.

Taylor, Sandra C. *Vietnamese Women at War: Fighting for Ho Chi Minh and the Revolution*. Lawrence: University Press of Kansas, 1999.

Tchen, John. *New York before Chinatown: Orientalism and the Shaping of American Culture, 1776–1882*. Baltimore, MD: Johns Hopkins University Press, 1999.

"The Third Solution: A Neutral Coalition." *Vietnam: Matters for the Agenda* (Santa Barbara, CA: Center for the Study of Democratic Institutions) 1, no. 4 (1968).

Ting, Jennifer. "Bachelor Society: Deviant Heterosexuality and Asian American Historiography." In *Privileging Positions: The Sites of Asian American Studies*, ed. Gary Y. Okihiro, Marilyn Alquizola, Dorothy Fugita Rony, and K. Scott Wong, pp. 271–80. Pullman: Washington State University Press, 1995.

Topmiller, Robert J. *The Lotus Unleashed: The Buddhist Peace Movement in South Vietnam, 1964–1966*. Lexington: University Press of Kentucky, 2006.

Trinh Ngoc Thai. "The World People's Front in Support of Viet Nam: The Paris Agreement Negotiations Period." In *The Historical Negotiations* [in Vietnamese, trans. Quynh Phan]. Hanoi: Nha Xuat Ban Chinh Tri Quoc Gia, 2009.

Tyson, Timothy B. *Radio Free Dixie: Robert F. Williams and the Roots of Black Power*. Chapel Hill: University of North Carolina Press, 1999.

U.S. House. Committee on Internal Security. *Investigation of Attempts to Subvert the United States Armed Services Part 1, Hearings,* 20–22, 27–28, 1971. Washington, DC: U.S. Government Printing Office, 1972.

_____. Committee on Internal Security. *Investigation of Attempts to Subvert the United States Armed Services Part 3, Hearings,* 9–10 May and 1–20 June 1972. Washington, DC: U.S. Government Printing Office, 1972.

Valk, Anne M. *Radical Sisters: Second-Wave Feminism and Black Liberation in Washington, D.C.* Urbana: University of Illinois Press, 2010.

Varon, Jeremy. *Bringing the War Home: The Weather Underground, the Red Army Faction, and Revolutionary Violence in the Sixties and Seventies*. Berkeley: University of California Press, 2004.

Venceremos Brigade. *The Venceremos Brigade: Four Years Building Solidarity with Cuba*. New York: Educational Commission, 1974.

Vickers, Jill. "The Intellectual Origins of the Women's Movements in Canada." In *Challenging Times: The Women's Movement in Canada and the United States*, ed. Constance Backhouse and David H. Flaherty, pp. 39–60. Montreal: McGill-Queen's University Press, 1992.

Vietnamese Women. Vietnam Studies no. 10. Hanoi, Vietnam: Xunhasaba, 1966.

Võ, Linda Trinh. *Mobilizing an Asian American Community*. Philadelphia: Temple University Press, 2004.

Von Eschen, Penny M. *Race against Empire: Black Americans and Anticolonialism 1937–1957*. Ithaca, NY: Cornell University Press, 1997.

_____. *Satchmo Blows Up the World: Jazz Ambassadors Play the Cold War*. Cambridge, MA: Harvard University Press, 2004.

Wei, William. *The Asian American Movement.* Philadelphia: Temple University Press, 1993.

Wesley, Charles H. *The History of Alpha Phi Alpha: A Development in College Life, 1906–1969.* Chicago: Foundation, 1969.

Westad, Odd Arne. *The Global Cold War: Third World Interventions and the Making of Our Times.* New York: Cambridge University Press, 2005.

Westheider, James E. *The African American Experience in Vietnam: Brothers in Arms.* Lanham, MD: Rowman and Littlefield, 2008.

———. *Fighting on Two Fronts: African Americans and the Vietnam War.* New York: New York University Press, 1997.

Wilson, Ara. "Lesbian Visibility and Sexual Rights at Beijing." *Signs* 22, no. 1 (1996): 214–18.

Wolfe, Tom. "The 'Me' Decade and the Third Great Awakening." *New York Magazine* (23 August 1976): 26–40.

Wong, Edward, dir. *Comrades: A Documentary.* San Francisco: National Asian American Telecommunications Association, 1999.

Wong, Martin. "Alex Hing: IWK." *Giant Robot* no. 10 (Spring 1998): 79–81.

Wright, Richard. *The Color Curtain: A Report on the Bandung Conference.* Cleveland: World Publishing, 1956.

Wu, Judy Tzu-Chun. "An African-Vietnamese American: Robert S. Browne, the Anti-War Movement, and the Personal/Political Dimensions of Black Internationalism." *Journal of African American History* 92 (Fall 2007): 491–515.

———. "Journeys for Peace and Liberation: Third World Internationalism and Radical Orientalism during the U.S. War in Viet Nam." *Pacific Historical Review* 76, no. 4 (2007): 575–84.

———. "Rethinking Global Sisterhood: Peace Activism and Women's Orientalism." In *No Permanent Waves: Recasting Histories of U.S. Feminism*, ed. Nancy Hewitt, pp. 193–220. New Brunswick, NJ: Rutgers University Press, 2010.

Yokota, Ryan. "Interview with Pat Sumi." In *Asian Americans: The Movement and the Moment*, ed. Steve Louie and Glenn Omatsu, pp. 16–31. Los Angeles: UCLA Asian American Studies Center Press, 2001.

Yoshihara, Mari. *Embracing the East: White Women and American Orientalism.* New York: Oxford University Press, 2003.

Young, Cynthia A. *Soul Power: Culture, Radicalism, and the Making of a U.S. Third World Left.* Durham, NC: Duke University Press, 2006.

Yu, Henry. *Thinking Orientals: Migration, Contact, and Exoticism in Modern America.* New York: Oxford University Press, 2001.

Yu, Renqiu. *To Save China, to Save Ourselves: The Chinese Hand Laundry Alliance of New York.* Philadelphia: Temple University Press, 1992.

Yuh, Ji-Yeon. *Beyond the Shadow of Camptown: Korean Military Brides in America.* New York: New York University Press, 2002.

Zeiger, Susan. *Entangling Alliances: Foreign War Brides and American Soldiers in the Twentieth Century.* New York: New York University Press, 2010.

Index

Page numbers followed by *f* refer to figures.